Introduction to Digital Computer Technology

Introduction to Digital Computer Technology

Louis Nashelsky

Associate Professor
Department of Electrical Technology
Queensborough Community College
of the City University of New York

John Wiley & Sons, Inc.
New York • London • Sydney • Toronto

Copyright© 1972, by John Wiley & Sons, Inc.

All rights reserved. Published simultaneously in Canada.

No.part of this book may be reproduced by any means, nor transmitted, nor translated into a machine language without the written permission of the publisher.

Library of Congress Cataloging in Publication Data:

Nashelsky, Louis.

Introduction to digital computer technology.
1. Electronic digital computers. I. Title.

TK7888.3.N37   621.3819′58   72-3855
ISBN 0-471-63046-2

Printed in the United States of America

10 9 8 7 6 5 4 3 2 1

To Katrin, Kira, and Larren

Preface

Since *Digital Computer Theory* (on which this book is based) was published in 1966, the digital computer field has changed considerably. Integrated circuits (ICs), including the now widespread use of medium-scale integrated (MSI) and large-scale integrated (LSI) circuits, have changed the basic building blocks of digital circuitry. *Introduction to Digital Computer Technology* includes this up-to-date material. Several other topics have been revised, but the basic nature of the book remains unchanged.

Surprisingly, the basic material of the first text remained appropriate over the years and, in fact, is still appropriate today. The need for this new text comes from a number of different factors. First, the material is better organized and developed in this text, based on my experience and the experiences of other teachers with the first text. Second, many helpful suggestions of additional material in certain important areas — for instance, logic design and memory systems — have been considered. Third, the addition of material on integrated circuits was necessary.

I have retained the original organization with sections on fundamentals, computer circuits, and computer units. The fundamentals section covers basic number systems, machine language programming, basic computer codes, and Boolean algebra. The computer circuits section presents separate chapters on logic circuits and multivibrator circuits of both discrete and IC form. Logic circuits covered are AND, OR, NAND, and NOR gates. The computer multivibrator circuits include bistable (or flip-flop), monostable (or one-shot), and astable (or clock) circuits, as well as the Schmitt trigger circuit. A chapter on counter and data transfer registers emphasizes the use of IC circuits in this important area. The section on computer units covers computer timing and control, the memory unit, arithmetic unit, and computer input/output (I/O) units.

As in the first text, this book contains numerous examples that highlight the important aspects of the chapters to the student. Exercises are provided at appropriate places within the chapter and problems (keyed to the section of coverage) appear at the end of each chapter. This breakdown of exercise and problem presentation should allow the instructor suitable exercises to assign when he is covering the chapter material and then problems to assign relating to the full material of the chapter after it has been completed. Answers to selected problems are given at the end of the book. A solution manual is available to instructors for both exercises and problems.

The text is also accompanied by many photographs and illustrations that should help the student understand the theory and the instructor to present it.

There is sufficient material in the three sections for curricula in which specific sections of study are more important than others or in which some material has already been covered in a previous course. For example, when digital computer circuits are covered in another course, the sections on computer fundamentals and computer units contain sufficient material for a one-term course. If only a single course is provided as an introduction to the digital computer, then Chapters 1 to 5 of the fundamentals section, parts of Chapters 7 to 9 on computer circuits, and parts of Chapters 10 to 13 on computer units can be integrated into a single course. When a number of courses are provided, as in a computer technology curriculum, separate courses covering fundamentals, computer circuits, and computer units can be offered using the full text material.

In essence, the amount of material provided in the book, and its sequence of presentation, is appropriate for either a single course in a two-year college curriculum or more detailed courses in a computer technology curriculum. The text may also serve as a supplementary text in a four-year computer course (especially the fundamentals and IC material); or the fundamentals and circuits sections may be used in a technical high school course.

I express my appreciation to the many companies who supplied illustrative material used in the text. International Business Machines Corporation supplied many of the illustrations and photographs that are used in several chapters (mainly in Chapter 13). A number of fine photographs were also supplied by the Digital Equipment Corporation, Control Data Corporation, Hazeltine Corporation, DIGIAC Corporation, Honeywell Corporation, and Burroughs Corporation.

I especially thank Professor Joseph B. Aidala, Chairman of the Electrical Technology Department of Queensborough Community College for his continual encouragement and support. I also thank Mrs. Doris Topel for her excellent typing of the original manuscript as well as Mrs. Sylvia Neiman.

Great Neck, New York, 1972   *Louis Nashelsky*

Contents

Appendix — Logic Operation of Flip-Flops 566

Introduction to Digital Computer Technology

Section One

FUNDAMENTALS

0001

Introduction

1-1. General

Digital computers have become an important item of study in the technology area as well as in mathematics, science, and business. The profound effect of computers on society is just beginning to be noticed. It is therefore essential to have an understanding of how the computer is used and how it operates. Although calculating machine history can be traced back to the nineteenth century (if not earlier) the modern computer was first considered in the 1930s and actually developed only around 1950. In essence, the modern electronic digital computer has been around for about 25 years. It seems incredible that in so short a time it could have advanced so far and become so essential a tool in scientific and business operation. There is no doubt that a combination of growth in the technological field and the need for high-speed data processors and calculators have spurred development in this short period of time.

Because the word "computer" is a general term, it is necessary to describe the various types of computers and to specify which types will be considered here. Broadly speaking, there are *digital computers* and *analog computers*. These devices are operationally quite different. The digital computer operates in a world of binary ONEs, and ZEROs (the two digits of the binary number system), manipulating these digits at fantastically high rates. Addition time in many modern computers is less than one microsecond (one millionth of a second) for binary numbers with as many as forty digits. In other words, the computer could do millions of additions per second (if it did not have to perform other information handling operations). Being able to perform arithmetic operations so quickly, the digital computer can perform calculations on large amounts of data in a short length of time. The analog computer, on the other hand, operates in the "real world," handling electrical signals and mechanical positions that represent the physical problem being considered. Neither general nor special-purpose analog computers can provide solution rates of much more than a few hundred cycles per second. However, this slower rate does not necessarily mean that the analog computer is a poorer device. Were this so, the digital computer would have quickly replaced it. Actually, each is superior for specific applications. In fact, in a growing number of fields a combination of analog and digital computer features is used to perform the required operation. *Hybrid computers* (the term to describe the resulting functional computer unit) are of increasing importance in certain types of problems, such as air guidance and navigation. It is necessary to convert any analog input data into binary form and after computation to reconvert the data to analog form for use in most present special-purpose digital computers. A good distinction between analog and digital computers cannot be made until more is understood about at least one of them.

Digital computers fall into two general categories: general-purpose and special-purpose computers. A general-purpose machine is designed to be programmed to solve a large variety of problems. Within a few minutes it can study some medical problem, do financial bookkeeping, study an engineering design, or play checkers with the operator. A special-purpose machine is designed around a specific problem and is optimized to do only that type of problem. As such it is usually smaller, less expensive, and more efficient in performing that specific task. Two applications of special-purpose computers are production control of a refinery and guidance control of a missile or plane. Both types of digital computer are basically the same in structure. The distinctions are in specific units used to bring data into the computer and feed information out, and in the flexible steps of operation of the general-purpose as compared to the special-purpose machine.

1-2.   Background History

We could start our brief view of computer history with the calculating "bones" of Napier in 1642 or the mechanical "analytical engine" of Babbage in the first half of the 1800s. The modern electronic computer, however, started with the ENIAC (Electronic Numerical Integrator And Calculator) completed in 1946 by Eckert and Mauchly at the University of Pennsylvania. The ENIAC, which was used for ballistic calculations, had limited storage capacity, and required laborious setup or programming by numerous switches and plugboards. It was however, a considerable improvement on the electromechanical calculator, the Mark I built for IBM by Aiken of Howard University in 1944. Whereas the Mark I used relays, the ENIAC memory and operations were performed by vacuum-tube electronic circuits.

The first electronic computer used in a commercial field was the UNIVAC I built for Sperry Rand, for use by the Bureau of Census, by Eckert and Mauchly. This early UNIVAC Computer (UNIVersal Automatic Computer) opened the door to the basic computer structure that is still used today. Although the ENIAC, for example, had to be programmed by a fixed, plugged-in set of instructions, the UNIVAC employed an internal stored program concept in which any desired program could be easily entered into memory *and changed by the computer itself.* The excitement of this new concept can be seen in the following report written by John von Neumann in 1946 based on work being carried out at the Moore School of Engineering at the University of Pennsylvania:

> "Since the orders that exercise the entire control are in the memory, a higher degree of flexibility is achieved than in any previous mode of control. Indeed, the machine, under control of its orders, can extract numbers (or orders, from memory, process them (as numbers!), and return them to the memory (to the same or other locations); i.e., it can change the contents of the memory — indeed this is its normal *modus operandi.* Hence it can, in particular, change the orders (since they are in memory!) — the very orders that control its actions. Thus all sorts of sophisticated order-systems become possible, which keep successively modifying themselves and hence also the computational processes that are likewise under its control."

The ENIAC, the first fully electronic machine, was followed quickly by a variety of machines such as the EDVAC, SEAC, and Whirlwind I which were one of a kind machines. The UNIVAC I and IBM 650 were the first machines built for production. These were *first generation* computers using tubes and operating in machine language. After about 1950 the advent of the transistor considerably affected the size and reliability of computers built as *second-generation* machines. In the 1960s the computer structure became quite important and operating systems were developed as integral to the operation of these *third-generation* computers. *Fourth-generation* computers are entering the market in the 1970s with integrated circuits (ICs) organized in the mass structure design (large scale integration or LSI) and operating systems of great complexity.

Such concepts as multiprocessing, multiplexed operation, and overlay operation have allowed more work to be performed by the computer. They also allow time-shared operation in which a number of users, at remote points, use the computer via telephone line connections, all at the "same" time. Actually, the third- and fourth-generation computers are so fast internally that the slow entry from keyboard, for example, allows sufficient time to switch around among the users so that all *seem* to be operating the machine at the same time.

1-3.   Digital Computer System

The basic parts of any digital computer are the input unit, arithmetic unit, control unit, memory unit, and output unit. Figure 1-1 shows a

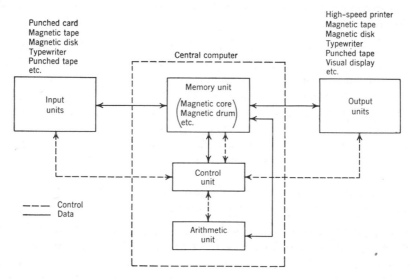

Figure 1-1.   Basic computer units, block diagram.

simplified block diagram indicating the many computer flow paths. Let us consider a general-purpose machine first; the input units may be paper tape, punched card, magnetic tape, typewriter (specially adapted), or magnetic disk, to list the most common. The input unit provides data and instructions to the computer. To change the type of problem being solved only requires feeding a new set of instructions and data to the computer. Each type of input device is suited to a particular use. Punched cards may contain individual instructions or data, any one of which can be easily changed. Each card can be used to represent a specific item or person, for example, the course card given to each student, the phone or electric bill of each customer, the item of purchase from a company, or the specific items held in stock by a company. Punched cards are one of the most useful input devices for such purposes. However, when large amounts of information are to be handled, punched cards become too slow. Magnetic tape can provide input data at a faster rate and allows data to be updated and stored back in the same place. Banking firms, for example, store their records on magnetic tape. So do insurance companies, which handle some of the largest amount of data in the business field. For processing customers' accounts, the computer calls for the input data from the magnetic tape, performs specified operations, and puts revised data back on the tape. Considering the large number of accounts handled, magnetic tape is an essential feature of the operation. Magnetic disk files are very similar to magnetic tape and may be considered the same for this discussion. Different details of each will be considered in the chapter on input–output devices (Chapter 13). Typewriter input provides an easy means of telling the computer to do an operation or asking it about its various parts. It is not used for large data input but mainly for "quick talk" with the computer. As such, it is very useful. The typewriter is also useful for small programs when little time is needed in communication with the computer (as in debugging or troubleshooting operations). Punched tape can be read inexpensively and requires less equipment and less space for data storage than punched cards. Whereas a magnetic tape can have millions of bits of data, a punched tape can be cut to a specific length (depending on the particular problem) and that piece of tape handled quite easily. A magnetic tape may store many different problems and must be handled carefully to avoid erasing the data. A paper tape may be a few inches or feet and is a permanent record. On the other hand, it cannot be updated (revised) as the magnetic tape can and is less useful in that respect.

In concluding this brief description, it should be clear that with the many types of problems to be solved and with so much data to be handled, many different input devices are needed. Each is best for a specific area of work. In fact, larger computer facilities can handle punched card as well as magnetic tape or disk and typewriter for more flexible and efficient operation.

Once data and instructions are fed into the computer, calculations may be carried out. Generally, the instructions (or program) and data are stored in the computer internal memory which is differentiated from the input device (also a memory) by its speed of operation. The internal memory is designed to handle small amounts of data but at very fast rates.

The most popular internal memory used at present is the magnetic core memory. It can operate at a rate of more than one million words (data or instruction) per second, which means that it can provide words for computation and accept the answers at the rate of over one million operations per second. The storage capacity, however, has been limited until recently to only a few hundred thousand words. Computers are now being designed for hundreds of thousands to millions of words of storage. Memory contents may be continually changing, as the computer takes in new data, updates the data, and then reads out the data to make space for more information. Fourth generation computers are turning to solid-state memories, which will allow much greater operational speeds than core memory.

Memory operation is controlled by a main computer unit called the "control unit." It provides control for all computer operations and the "heart-beat" of the system. It interprets the instructions in the memory and tells other units where to take data from, where to feed it to, and what operations to perform. The arithmetic unit performs the addition, subtraction, multiplication, and division operations. The results of arithmetic operations are fed back to the memory, for storage. It can be read out at a later time to an output unit, which may be a magnetic tape, punched card, typewriter, punched tape, magnetic disk, or high-speed printer. (Many output devices are also used for input operation.) The high-speed printer, the fastest permanent visible record of those just mentioned, is essential when large amounts of data are handled. Specific details of each type of unit are covered in Chapter 13.

The feature of a general-purpose digital computer that is most important in making it a versatile and useful device is its ability to be programmed. A program is a list of statements telling the computer what operations to perform, in what order, and on what data. Modern programming languages allow writing these commands in a simplified manner so that the programmer does not have to describe explicitly each step the computer is to perform. A few instructions may command the computer to perform hundreds of operations. An important point to remember is that if the computer cannot do repeated computations on a large amount of information, it will not be useful. A calculator can be used to solve a problem quickly *once* to many significant places. To do the same problem, varying the numbers used, for thousands of times may not be reasonable on the calculator, but is easy work for a computer.

In addition to programming languages, another important technical achievement that has improved the computer is the use of solid-state components. The first few computers used relays and then vacuum tubes. Relays operate much too slowly, require considerable power, take up large areas, and are not sufficiently reliable. The vacuum tube has too short a lifetime, uses considerable power (operating very hot), and takes up a large amount of space. If we consider that a modern computer requires millions of parts, and malfunctions if even one is bad, the need for reliable components is soon obvious.

The first vacuum-tube computers used thousands of tubes. Any one owning a television set will appreciate the fact that the unit would break down often from tube failure. Moreover, if all the tubes were not replaced after a period of time, the computer would continuously malfunction as one tube after another went bad. With solid-state components—bipolar transistors, field effect transistors, and micrologic circuits, for example— the occurrence of a malfunction because of a breakdown of these components is becoming virtually unknown in modern computers. At present, the auxiliary mechanical equipment—card punchers, card readers, magnetic tape drives, and so on—account for most of the small number of problems that do occur. Because of solid-state components, the computer design has been increased in complexity, allowing much more storage, control, and versatility, without undue taxing of the useful operating time of a computer. The IBM System/360 utilizes the improved reliability and smaller size of micrologic circuits to increase considerably the number of operations done. It has also increased memory size to allow for more computing facility. Figure 1-2 shows both large computer systems (IBM System 370/Model 135) and small computers (DIGIAC 3080 and Digital Equipment Corporation PDP-12).

A digital computer is designed to perform a specific group of operations. These may include addition of two numbers, subtraction, multiplication, and division. It has a large and fast electronic memory where the numbers (data) to be operated on, the results of the operations, and most essential of all, the instructions, are stored. In addition, the computer is designed to take these stored numbers, compare them to "see" whether they are positive or negative, and move data around within the memory. Finally, it can bring in new data and instructions and can feed out data from its memory to provide output of its calculations. Each step or operation of the computer is essentially very simple. It is the high speed at which it performs these operations that changes the simple nature of each step. The second aspect of the computer that moves the simple operations to a higher level of performance is the accuracy of the operations. The accuracy of any step is limited only by the amount of digits used for each number. In some machines the number length (number of binary digits) is fixed at as many as 64 bits (binary digits). The precision of such a number (2^{64}) is staggering. Of course, after many, many operations the final accuracy may be only satisfactory or possibly even poor because of number roundoff throughout the calculations. The performance can be improved,

Figure 1-2. Typical general-purpose digital computers: (a) IBM 370/135 computer system.

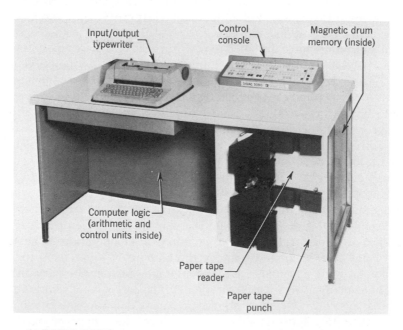

(b) DIGIAC 3080 computer.

10

however, by using a larger number of bits for a word. In this way the accuracy can always be made as good as desired. Analog computers are not able to be so manipulated. The last and most important aspect which gives the digital computer a dimension completely apart from its simple basic operations, is the program. The computer cannot solve a differential equation or do an integration as a basic mathematical operation. It can, though, perform both these calculations using only the few simple operations mentioned by virtue of a program. It is the program which specifies the order of these operations to enable the final outcome to be something other than a simple answer to a simple operation. It is the high rate of performing these operations that makes using them to solve large, complex problems possible.

One cannot point out too strongly that of all the things a computer does, and they grow more impressive each day, the real operations occurring are not something mysterious, nor does the machine really think and act by itself. Technology has not gotten that far yet. It may surprise some readers, but the computer is essentially very stupid. It takes each instruction provided it by the program and performs that operation. If the result were to put the machine into an endless loop of steps leading to no answer, it would never know the difference and would go on performing indefinitely. It does not use reason or thought other than that specifically programmed into it. However, the amount of information fed into the machine has increased so much that at times a computer may seem to be operating and acting as if it really did create what appears at its outputs. The people who write programs for the computer really do the thinking and deciding. The computer only carries out instructions as would a robot.

(c) DEC PDP 12 computer.

If you keep in mind that the machine can only do the simple steps mentioned, the operation of a computer will not seem mysterious at all and the technique of programming (covered in Chapter 3) will be more easily understood.

0010

Number systems

2-1. General

Those of you who have learned only the decimal number system are initially surprised and even uncertain when another system is introduced. In order to help you along in your reorientation, the base 10 (decimal) number system will be included in examples. Operations in the base 10 system may appear simple – they are. But as rules and operations in other base systems are explained, reference back to the "usual" number system (decimal) will reveal that there are some very basic ideas about numbers which have been learned or understood only intuitively and must now be logically examined. Only when these basic operations and laws of numbers are understood and accepted will the same rules and operations in other number systems appear simple. In fact it may be seen that for the particular uses discussed these other systems are even simpler to use and understand.

In examining a number in the decimal system we seldom consider the actual makeup of the number. For example, it should be clear that the number 576 really means 5 hundreds, 7 tens, and 6 units. The *digits* of the base 10 system go from 0 (a very important digit) to 9. Notice that the number of 10 which is called the base of the decimal system is not a basic digit in that system. It is the result of the digits 1 and 0, where 10 is specifically 1 ten and 0 units. Further examination of the number system reveals that the important concept of digit position can be formalized. The position referred to is the very important concept (growing out of the use of zero as a digit) which makes 061 mean 0 hundreds, 6 tens, and 1 unit; and 610 mean 6 hundreds, 1 ten, and 0 units. Thus, the position of the digits in the base 10 system determines the magnitude of the number read. This concept may seem simple, but the Romans used a numerical system which had to rely on new symbols for larger and larger numbers, thus losing out on the enormous benefits of the arithmetic manipulation possible in the positional number system.

When the number 623 is read, it of course means 6 hundreds, 2 tens, and 3 units. It also may be read as follows:

$$623 = 6 \times 10^2 + 2 \times 10^1 + 3 \times 10^0$$
$$= 6 \text{ hundreds} + 2 \text{ tens} + 3 \text{ units}$$

where, 10^2 is 10 squared or 100

10^1 is 10

10^0 is 1 (by definition)

From this examination of a decimal it can be seen how the idea of a base of 10 applies. The base of a number system is the number which, raised to the zero power, is the lowest position value; raised to the first power, it is the second position value; raised to the second power, it is the third position value, and so on.

A general description of any number system is

$$N = d_n R^n + \cdots + d_3 R^3 + d_2 R^2 + d_1 R^1 + d_0 R^0$$

where N is the number, d_n the digit in that position, and R the *radix* or *base* of the system, and the subscript or exponent gives the positional value.

For example, 1257 in the decimal system may be written

$$1257 = 1 \times 10^3 + 2 \times 10^2 + 5 \times 10^1 + 7 \times 10^0$$

$$N = d_3 R^3 + d_2 R^2 + d_1 R^1 + d_0 R^0$$

where, $R = 10, d_3 = 1, d_2 = 2, d_1 = 5,$ and $d_0 = 7$.

2-2.   Binary Number System

Were we to continue discussing only the decimal system, all this generalization would have little significance. Let us now apply the definition given to the lowest useful base system, which is quickly found to be the base of 2 (*binary*). Notice that the binary system has digits 0 and 1 only (again the radix is not a basic digit but is made of grouping digits). From this it is also seen that the base 0 system does not exist and base 1 system has only the digit 0 (not a very interesting system). This brings us again to base 2 as the lowest useful base. The following tabular comparison provides a start in the examination of base 2 numbers.

$$10^0 = 1 = \text{units} \qquad\qquad 2^0 = 1 = \text{units}$$
$$10^1 = 10 = \text{tens} \qquad\qquad 2^1 = 2 = \text{twos}$$
$$10^2 = 100 = \text{hundreds} \qquad 2^2 = 4 = \text{fours}$$
$$10^3 = 1000 = \text{thousands} \qquad 2^3 = 8 = \text{eights}$$
$$\text{etc.} \qquad\qquad\qquad\qquad \text{etc.}$$

A binary number is made up of only the basic digits 0 and 1 so that the general definition simplifies to

$$N = \cdots + 8d_3 + 4d_2 + 2d_1 + d_0$$

where d_3, d_2, d_1, d_0 are either 0 or 1. For example, binary 1101 is $1 \times 2^3 + 1 \times 2^2 + 0 \times 2^1 + 1 \times 2^0 = N = 8 + 4 + 0 + 1 = 13$, where 8, 4, 0, 1, and 13 are terms of the familiar decimal system. Table 2-1 lists the numbers 0 to 9 (decimal) in both base systems.

Table 2-1.

Decimal	Binary
0	0
1	1 (1×2^0)
2	10 $(1 \times 2^1 + 0 \times 2^0)$
3	11 $(1 \times 2^1 + 1 \times 2^0)$
4	100 $(1 \times 2^2 + 0 \times 2^1 + 0 \times 2^0)$
5	101 $(1 \times 2^2 + 0 \times 2^1 + 1 \times 2^0)$
6	110 $(1 \times 2^2 + 1 \times 2^1 + 0 \times 2^0)$
7	111 $(1 \times 2^2 + 1 \times 2^1 + 1 \times 2^0)$
8	1000 $(1 \times 2^3 + 0 \times 2^2 + 0 \times 2^1 + 0 \times 2^0)$
9	1001 $(1 \times 2^3 + 0 \times 2^2 + 0 \times 2^1 + 1 \times 2^0)$

It is obvious that the binary system is wasteful of space needing four digits to specify a number that only requires one digit in decimal. The large use of binary (mainly in computers) comes from the simplicity of the basic digits 0 and 1. Since there are only two they can be represented in a computer by a switch being ON (1) or OFF (0), an indicator light being ON (1) or OFF (0), a transistor ON (1) or OFF (0), a voltage being present (1) or zero volts (0), and so on. The use of binary by computers will be more fully discussed in later chapters. At present the binary system and arithmetic operations with it will be considered.

Converting Binary to Decimal. Conversion of binary to decimal only requires adding the value for each position of the number having a binary digit of 1.

Example 2-1.   Prepare a table of binary numbers for decimal 0 to 15.

Solution :

Decimal	Binary
0	0000
1	0001
2	0010
3	0011
4	0100
5	0101
6	0110
7	0111
8	1000
9	1001
10	1010
11	1011
12	1100
13	1101
14	1110
15	1111

Example 2-2.   Determine the decimal values of the following binary numbers:

$$(a) \ 10110 \qquad (b) \ 110111$$

Solution : (a) $N = 1 \times 2^4 + 0 \times 2^3 + 1 \times 2^2 + 1 \times 2^1 + 0 \times 2^0$
$$\qquad\qquad = 16 \quad +0 \quad\quad +4 \quad\quad +2 \quad\quad +0$$
$$\qquad\qquad = 22 \ (\text{decimal})$$

(b) $N = 1 \times 2^5 + 1 \times 2^4 + 0 \times 2^3 + 1 \times 2^2 + 1 \times 2^1 + 1 \times 2^0$
$$\qquad\qquad = 32 \quad +16 \quad +0 \quad\quad +4 \quad\quad +2 \quad\quad +1$$
$$\qquad\qquad = 55 \ (\text{decimal})$$

Exercise 2-1.   Convert the following numbers to decimal equivalents:

$$(a) \ 1101101 \qquad (b) \ 10111 \qquad (c) \ 11011$$

Converting Decimal to Binary.   Converting a binary number to decimal now seems simple enough. How about converting a decimal number to binary? What is the binary number for 2576 (decimal)? This problem is not as straightforward, is it? It can be, though, if the following method is used. Starting with a simple example the conversion of $(26)_{10}$ — which is read as 26 in base 10 — is as follows.

quotient   remainder

$$\frac{26}{2} = 13 + 0 \longrightarrow \text{LSD}$$

$$\frac{13}{2} = 6 + 1$$

$$\frac{6}{2} = 3 + 0$$

$$\frac{3}{2} = 1 + 1$$

$$\frac{1}{2} = 0 + 1 \longrightarrow \text{MSD} \longrightarrow 11010$$

Read the last remainder as most significant digit (MSD) and the first remainder as least significant digit (LSD). *Answer*: $(26)_{10} = (11010)_2$. To check our answer let us convert back to decimal:

$$N = 1 \times 2^4 + 1 \times 2^3 + 0 \times 2^2 + 1 \times 2^1 + 0 \times 2^0$$
$$= 16 + 8 + 2 = (26)_{10}$$

The continuous division by 2, keeping track of the remainder, allows a simple method of conversion. It will be seen later that conversion from the decimal system to any other number system requires division by the base of that number system, keeping track of the remainder, and reading the answer from the last remainder back. Conversion stops when the quotient is zero.

Example 2-3. Convert the decimal number $(35)_{10}$ to binary.

Solution :

quotient   remainder

$$\frac{35}{2} = 17 + 1$$

$$\frac{17}{2} = 8 + 1$$

$$\frac{8}{2} = 4 + 0$$

$$\frac{4}{2} = 2 + 0$$

$$\frac{2}{2} = 1 + 0$$

$$\frac{1}{2} = 0 + 1 \longrightarrow 100011$$

Answer : $(35)_{10} = (100011)_2$

Check : $N = 1 \times 2^5 + 0 \times 2^4 + 0 \times 2^3 + 0 \times 2^2 + 1 \times 2^1 + 1 \times 2^0$
$$= 32 + 2 + 1$$
$$= (35)_{10}$$

Example 2-4.   Convert $(353)_{10}$ to binary.

quotient   remainder

Solution : $\dfrac{353}{2} = 176 \;+\; 1$

$\dfrac{176}{2} = 88 \;+\; 0$

$\dfrac{88}{2} = 44 \;+\; 0$

$\dfrac{44}{2} = 22 \;+\; 0$

$\dfrac{22}{2} = 11 \;+\; 0$

$\dfrac{11}{2} = 5 \;+\; 1$

$\dfrac{5}{2} = 2 \;+\; 1$

$\dfrac{2}{2} = 1 \;+\; 0$

$\dfrac{1}{2} = 0 \;+\; 1 \longrightarrow 101100001$

Answer : $(353)_{10} = (101100001)_2$

Exercise 2-2.   Do the following decimal to binary conversions.

   (a) $(37)_{10} = (?)_2$ (b) $(49)_{10} = (?)_2$ (c) $(83)_{10} = (?)_2$

Fractional Binary Numbers.   Having considered the integer (whole) numbers of the binary system, we now turn our attention to fractional numbers. In decimal the number 0.5176 is read 5 tenths, 1 hundredth, 7 thousandths, and 6 ten thousandths. Notice that the first position was tenths. A fractional number may be written in general as

$$N = d_1 \times R^{-1} + d_2 \times R^{-2} + d_3 \times R^{-3} + \cdots + d_n \times R^{-n}$$

In decimal 0.725 is $N = 7 \times 10^{-1} + 2 \times 10^{-2} + 5 \times 10^{-3}$

$$N = d_1 \times R^{-1} + d_2 \times R^{-2} + d_3 \times R^{-3}$$

A binary fractional number 0.1011 is read as

$$1 \times 2^{-1} + 0 \times 2^{-2} + 1 \times 2^{-3} + 1 \times 2^{-4}$$

where $2^{-1} = \dfrac{1}{2^1} = 0.5$, $2^{-2} = \dfrac{1}{2^2} = 0.25$, $2^{-3} = \dfrac{1}{2^3} = 0.125$,

and, $2^{-4} = \dfrac{1}{2^4} = 0.0625$.

Therefore $(0.1011)_2 = (0.5 + 0.125 + 0.0625)_{10}$
$$= (0.6875)_{10}$$

Example 2-5.   Convert $(0.101101)_2$ to decimal.

Solution : $(0.101101)_2 = 1 \times 2^{-1} + 0 \times 2^{-2} + 1 \times 2^{-3} + 1 \times 2^{-4} + 0 \times 2^{-5}$
$$+ 1 \times 2^{-6}$$
$$= 0.5 + 0.125 + 0.0625 + 0.015625$$
$$= (0.703125)_{10}$$

Example 2-6.   Convert $(0.10001)_2$ to decimal.

Solution : $(0.10001)_2 = 1 \times 2^{-1} + 0 \times 2^{-2} + 0 \times 2^{-3} + 0 \times 2^{-4} + 1 \times 2^{-5}$
$$= 0.5 + 0.03125$$
$$= (0.53125)_{10}$$

Exercise 2-3.   Convert the given binary fractional numbers to decimal.

(a) 0.11011   (b) 0.01010   (c) 0.0010

Conversion of Fractional Decimal to Binary.   Converting fractional binary numbers to decimal seems straightforward enough. How about converting 0.57251_{10} to binary? It appears to be quite a formidable problem, but it is not. You merely use the following method.

0 . 57251	0 . 14502	0 . 29004	0 . 58008	0.16016
× 2	× 2	× 2	× 2	× 2 , etc.
①. 14502	⓪. 29004	⓪. 58008	①. 16016	⓪. 32032
1	0	0	1	0

The answer is read as $(0.10010 \ldots)_2$. As a check,

$$(0.10010)_2 = 1 \times 2^{-1} + 0 \times 2^{-2} + 0 \times 2^{-3} + 1 \times 2^{-4}$$
$$= 0.5 + 0.0625$$
$$= (0.5625)_{10}$$

It can be seen that these two numbers are not exactly the same. If the number of places of the binary number is carried out further to the right, the value approaches closer and closer to the given decimal number. Only if the decimal number is a fraction such as 1/2, 1/8, 1/16, or an exact combination of these will there be a finite length binary fraction. There is no difficulty if the binary equivalent of the decimal fraction is not finite, for we can always carry out the conversion to the desired accuracy (or number of significant places) required. Here are two examples, one of which ends and one that does not.

Example 2-7.   Convert $(0.65625)_{10}$ to binary.

Solution:

$$
\begin{array}{ccccc}
0.65625 & 0.31250 & 0.62500 & 0.25000 & 0.50000 \\
\underline{\times\ \ 2} & \underline{\times\ \ 2} & \underline{\times\ \ 2} & \underline{\times\ \ 2} & \underline{\times\ \ 2} \\
1.31250 & 0.65200 & 1.25000 & 0.50000 & 1.00000 \\
\downarrow & \downarrow & \downarrow & \downarrow & \downarrow \\
1 & 0 & 1 & 0 & 1
\end{array}
$$

Answer :   0.10101

Check : $(0.10101)_2 = 1 \times 2^{-1} + 0 \times 2^{-2} + 1 \times 2^{-3} + 0 \times 2^{-4} + 1 \times 2^{-5}$
$$= 0.5 + 0.125 + 0.03125$$
$$= (0.65625)_{10}$$

Example 2-8.   Convert $(0.8176)_{10}$ to binary.

Solution :

$$
\begin{array}{cccccc}
0.8176 & 0.6352 & 0.2704 & 0.5408 & 0.0816 & 0.1632 \\
\underline{\times\ 2} & \underline{\times\ 2} & \underline{\times\ 2} & \underline{\times\ 2} & \underline{\times\ 2} & \underline{\times\ 2}\ \text{etc.} \\
1.6352 & 1.2704 & 0.5408 & 1.0816 & 0.1632 & 0.3264 \\
\downarrow & \downarrow & \downarrow & \downarrow & \downarrow & \downarrow \\
1 & 1 & 0 & 1 & 0 & 0
\end{array}
$$

Answer : $(0.110100\ldots)_2$

Check : $(0.110100)_2 = 1 \times 2^{-1} + 1 \times 2^{-2} + 0 \times 2^{-3} + 1 \times 2^{-4} + 0 \times 2^{-5}$
$$+ 0 \times 2^{-6}$$
$$= 0.5 + 0.25 + 0.0625$$
$$= (0.8125)_{10}$$

This answer may not be accurate enough, requiring the conversion to be carried out to more places.

Exercise 2-4.   Convert the given decimal fractional numbers into binary.

(a) $(0.7257)_{10}$ (b) $(0.9765)_{10}$ (c) $(0.1975)_{10}$

Converting a Mixed (Integer and Fractional) Binary Number to Decimal.
Converting a number made up of an integer and a fractional part from
binary to decimal is straightforward. For example, $(11010.10110)_2$ gives

$$N = 1 \times 2^4 + 1 \times 2^3 + 0 \times 2^2 + 1 \times 2^1 + 0 \times 2^0 + 1 \times 2^{-1} + 0 \times 2^{-2} + 1 \times 2^{-3}$$
$$+ 1 \times 2^{-4} + 0 \times 2^{-5}$$
$$= 16 + 8 + 2 + 0.5 + 0.125 + 0.0625$$
$$= (26.6875)_{10}$$

Example 2-9.   Convert from binary to decimal: 10110.1101.

Solution : $(10110.1101)_2 = 1 \times 2^4 + 0 \times 2^3 + 1 \times 2^2 + 1 \times 2^1 + 0 \times 2^0 + 1$
$$\times 2^{-1} + 1 \times 2^{-2} + 0 \times 2^{-3} + 1 \times 2^{-4}$$
$$= 16 + 4 + 2 + 0.5 + 0.25 + 0.0625$$
$$= (22.8125)_{10}$$

Example 2-10. $(101101.110001)_2 = (?)_{10}$

Solution : $(101101.110001)_2 = 1 \times 2^5 + 0 \times 2^4 + 1 \times 2^3 + 1 \times 2^2 + 0 \times 2^1$
$$+ 1 \times 2^0 + 1 \times 2^{-1} + 1 \times 2^{-2} + 0 \times 2^{-3}$$
$$+ 0 \times 2^{-4} + 0 \times 2^{-5} + 1 \times 2^{-6}$$
$$= 32 + 8 + 4 + 1 + 0.5 + 0.25 + 0.015625$$
$$= (45.765625)_{10}$$

Exercise 2-5.   Convert from binary to decimal:

(a) $(10111.011)_2$ (b) $(1011.101)_2$ (c) $(11011.111)_2$

Converting a Mixed Decimal Number to Binary.   Now convert $(274.1875)_{10}$
to binary. This can be done piecemeal using the repeated division by 2,
reading the remainder for integer digits, and the repeated multiplication by
2, using the units integer as the binary value. The following example
demonstrates the procedure.

Example 2-11.   Convert $(274.1875)_{10}$ into binary.

Solution :

$$\frac{274}{2} = 137 + 0$$

$$\frac{137}{2} = 68 + 1$$

$$\frac{68}{2} = 34 + 0$$

$$\frac{34}{2} = 17 + 0$$

$$\frac{17}{2} = 8 + 1$$

$$\frac{8}{2} = 4 + 0$$

$$\frac{4}{2} = 2 + 0$$

$$\frac{2}{2} = 1 + 0$$

$$\frac{1}{2} = 0 + 1 \longrightarrow 100010010$$

Read as $(100010010)_2$.

$$
\begin{array}{cccc}
0.1875 & 0.3750 & 0.7500 & 0.5000 \\
\times\ 2 & \times\ 2 & \times\ 2 & \times\ 2 \\
\hline
0.3750 & 0.7500 & 1.5000 & 1.0000 \\
\downarrow & \downarrow & \downarrow & \downarrow \\
0 & 0 & 1 & 1
\end{array}
$$

Read as 0.0011.

Answer : $(274.1875)_{10} = (100010010.0011)_2$

Exercise 2-6.   Convert the following decimal numbers into binary.

$\quad$ (a) $(27.75)_{10}$ $\quad$ (b) $(37.875)_{10}$ $\quad$ (c) $(521.1875)_{10}$

2-3.   Octal Number System

The octal or base 8 number system is one that is presently popular in a number of computer systems. Digital computers such as the IBM 7090, and a number of the Digital Equipment Corporation machines — PDP-7,

PDP-8 use octal numbers for easy, direct input-output operation. For the octal number system the radix or base is 8 and the digits go from 0 to 7. *No digits 8 or 9 exist in octal.* Since octal is a number system it can be written as

$$N = d_n \times R^n + \cdots + d_2 \times R^2 + d_1 \times R^1 + d_0 \times R^0$$
$$= d_n \times 8^n + \cdots + d_2 \times 8^2 + d_1 \times 8^1 + d_0 \times 8^0$$

where the digits $d_n, \ldots, d_2, d_1, d_0$ are 0, 1, 2, 3, 4, 5, 6 or 7.

Conversion from Octal to Decimal.   An octal number such as $(37)_8$ – read *37 base 8* can also be written as

$$(37)_8 = 3 \times 8^1 + 7 \times 8^0$$
$$= 3 \times 8 + 7 \times 1$$
$$= 24 + 7 = (31)_{10}$$

To show the relation between small numbers in decimal and octal, Table 2-2 lists both number system values from octal 0 to octal 100.

Table 2-2.   *Decimal-Octal Numbers from $(0\text{-}100)_8$*

Decimal $10^1\,10^0$	Octal $8^1\,8^0$	Decimal $10^1\,10^0$	Octal $8^1\,8^0$	Decimal $10^1\,10^0$	Octal $8^1\,8^0$	Decimal $10^1\,10^0$	Octal $8^1\,8^0$
00	00	17	21	34	42	51	63
01	01	18	22	35	43	52	64
02	02	19	23	36	44	53	65
03	03	20	24	37	45	54	66
04	04	21	25	38	46	55	67
05	05	22	26	39	47	56	70
06	06	23	27	40	50	57	71
07	07	24	30	41	51	58	72
08	10	25	31	42	52	59	73
09	11	26	32	43	53	60	74
10	12	27	33	44	54	61	75
11	13	28	34	45	55	62	76
12	14	29	35	46	56	63	77
13	15	30	36	47	57	64	100
14	16	31	37	48	60		
15	17	32	40	49	61		
16	20	33	41	50	62		

As a check, converting $(63)_8$ into decimal gives

$$(63)_8 = 6 \times 8^1 + 3 \times 8^0$$
$$= 6 \times 8 + 3 \times 1$$
$$= 48 + 3 = (51)_{10} \qquad \text{(check with Table 2-2)}$$

Example 2-12.   Convert $(142)_8$ into decimal.

Solution: $(142)_8 = 1 \times 8^2 + 4 \times 8^1 + 2 \times 8^0$
$$= 1 \times 64 + 4 \times 8 + 2 \times 1$$
$$= 64 + 32 + 2$$
$$= (98)_{10}$$

Example 2-13.   Convert $(364)_8$ into decimal.

Solution: $(364)_8 = 3 \times 8^2 + 6 \times 8^1 + 4 \times 8^0$
$$= 3 \times 64 + 6 \times 8 + 4 \times 1$$
$$= 192 + 48 + 4$$
$$= (244)_{10}$$

Exercise 2-7.   Convert from octal to decimal:

(a) $(376)_8$ (b) $(256)_8$ (c) $(143)_8$

Converting fractional octal numbers to decimal requires adding the appropriate weights according to the octal fractional positions.

$$N = d_1 8^{-1} + d_2 8^{-2} + d_3 8^{-3} + \cdots$$

where

$$8^{-1} = \frac{1}{8} = 0.125, \; 8^{-2} = \frac{1}{8^2} = \frac{1}{64} = 0.015625, \text{ etc.}$$

For example, $(0.23)_8 = 2 \times 8^{-1} + 3 \times 8^{-2}$
$$= 2 \times 0.125 + 3 \times 0.015625$$
$$= 0.250 + 0.046875$$
$$= (0.296875)_{10}$$

Conversion from Decimal into Octal.   Conversion from decimal to octal is accomplished by using the repeated division for the integer part of a number and repeated multiplication for the fractional part. Some examples will demonstrate the method.

Example 2-14. $(127)_{10} = (?)_8$

Solution: $\dfrac{127}{8} = 15 + 7$

$\dfrac{15}{8} = 1 + 7$

$\dfrac{1}{8} = 0 + 1 \longrightarrow 177$

Read as $(177)_8$

Example 2-15. $(254)_{10} = (?)_8$

Solution: $\dfrac{254}{8} = 31 + 6$

$\dfrac{31}{8} = 3 + 7$

$\dfrac{3}{8} = 0 + 3 \longrightarrow 376$

Answer: $(254)_{10} = (376)_8$

Example 2-16. $(0.1875)_{10} = (?)_8$

Solution:

```
   0 . 1875        0 . 5000
     ×  8            ×  8
  ①. 5000        ④. 0000
     ↓               ↓
     1               4
```

$(0.1875)_{10} = (0.14)_8$

Example 2-17. $(49.21875)_{10} = (?)_8$

Solution: Integer part   Fractional Part

$\dfrac{49}{8} = 6 + 1$

$\dfrac{6}{8} = 0 + 6 \longrightarrow 61$

```
   0 . 21875       0 . 75
     ×   8           ×8
  ①. 75000       ⑥. 00
     ↓               ↓
     1               6
```

Answer: $(49.21875)_{10} = (61.16)_8$

Exercise 2-8.   Convert the following numbers from decimal to octal:

(a) $(139)_{10}$ (b) $(2137)_{10}$ (c) $(675.75)_{10}$

2-4.   Hexadecimal Number System

The *hexadecimal* or base 16 number system is presently used by such computers as the IBM System 360, IBM System 370, IBM 1130, Honeywell 200, RCA Spectra 70, and many others. At first the hexadecimal system appears quite strange because it requires additional number symbols to represent digits of 10, 11, 12, 13, 14 and 15, in addition to the digits 0 to 9. For a base 16 number system the digits go from 0 to 15. Using the commonly accepted IBM terminology these digits are represented as follows:

Decimal Value	Hexadecimal Digit
0	0
1	1
2	2
3	3
4	4
5	5
6	6
7	7
8	8
9	9
10	A
11	B
12	C
13	D
14	E
15	F

Integer Hexadecimal Numbers.   The positional values from right to left are 16^0, 16^1, 16^2, etc. For example, the hexadecimal number 23_{16} is the same as the decimal 35_{10} as follows:

$$(23)_{16} = 2 \times 16^1 + 3 \times 16^0$$
$$= 2 \times 16 + 3 \times 1 = 32 + 3 = (35)_{10}$$

As another example,

$$(3B)_{16} = 3 \times 16^1 + B \times 16^0$$
$$= 3 \times 16^1 + 11 \times 16^0$$
$$= 3 \times 16 + 11 \times 1 = 48 + 11 = (59)_{10}$$

Table 2-3 shows some of the equivalent decimal and hexadecimal numbers from $0\text{-}FFFF_{16}$. Note carefully the numbers in the hexadecimal columns which show the sequencing of some of the numbers. A few following examples will check the equivalence of decimal and hexadecimal values.

Example 2-18. Determine the decimal values of the following hexadecimal numbers:

(a) $(1F)_{16}$ (b) $(9E)_{16}$ (c) $(A2)_{16}$ (d) $(1FF)_{16}$

Solution:

(a) $(1F)_{16} = 1 \times 16^1 + F \times 16^0 = 1 \times 16 + 15 \times 1 = 16 + 15 = (31)_{10}$

(b) $(9E)_{16} = 9 \times 16^1 + E \times 16^0 = 9 \times 16 + 14 \times 1 = 144 + 14 = (158)_{10}$

(c) $(A2)_{16} = A \times 16^1 + 2 \times 16^0 = 10 \times 16 + 2 \times 1 = 160 + 2 = (162)_{10}$

(d) $(1FF)_{16} = 1 \times 16^2 + F \times 16^1 + F \times 16^0 = 1 \times 256 + 15 \times 16 + 15 \times 1$
$$= 256 + 240 + 15 = (511)_{10}.$$

Exercise 2-9. Determine the decimal values for

(a) $(2F)_{16}$ (b) $(A6)_{16}$ (c) $(F5)_{16}$

Fractional Hexadecimal Numbers. A fractional hexadecimal number such as 0.8_{16} is equal to 0.5_{10} as follows:

$$(0.8)_{16} = 8 \times 16^{-1} = \frac{8}{16} = (0.5)_{10}$$

A second example, 0.48_{16}, is:

$$(0.48)_{16} = 4 \times 16^{-1} + 8 \times 16^{-2} = 4 \times \frac{1}{16} + 8 \times \frac{1}{256}$$

$$= \frac{4}{16} + \frac{8}{256} = 0.2500 + 0.03125 = (0.28125)_{10}$$

Converting Integer Decimal to Hexadecimal. Conversion from decimal is carried by repeated division by 16 for integer and repeated multiplication by 16 for fractional parts of a number as the following examples demonstrate.

Table 2-3. *Decimal and Hexadecimal Numbers
from 0-FFFF$_{16}$*

Decimal	Hexadecimal	Decimal	Hexadecimal
0	0	155	9B
1	1	156	9C
2	2	157	9D
.	.	158	9E
.	.	159	9F
.	.	160	A0
9	9	161	A1
10	A	162	A2
11	B	.	.
12	C	.	.
13	D	.	.
14	E	248	F8
.	.	249	F9
15	F	250	FA
16	10	251	FB
17	11	252	FC
18	12	253	FD
19	13	254	FE
20	14	255	FF
21	15	256	100
22	16	257	101
23	17	258	102
24	18	.	.
25	19	.	.
26	1A	.	.
27	1B	511	1FF
28	1C	512	200
29	1D	.	.
30	1E	.	.
31	1F	.	.
32	20	4,095	FFF
.	.	4,096	1000
.	.	.	.
.	.	.	.
152	98	.	.
153	99	65,535	FFFF
154	9A		

Example 2-19.   Convert the following decimal numbers into hexadecimal:

(a) 152_{10} (b) 249_{10} (c) 567.1875_{10}

Solution: (a) $\dfrac{152}{16} = 9 + 8$

$\dfrac{9}{16} = 0 + 9 \longrightarrow 98$

$152_{10} = 98_{16}$

(b) $\dfrac{249}{16} = 15 + 9$

$\dfrac{15}{16} = 0 + 15 \, (= F) \longrightarrow F9$

$(249)_{10} = (F9)_{16}$

(c) $\dfrac{567}{16} = 35 + 7$

$\dfrac{35}{16} = 2 + 3$

$\dfrac{2}{16} = 0 + 2 \longrightarrow 237$

$$0.1875$$
$$\underline{\times 16}$$
$$1.1250$$
$$\underline{1.875}$$
$$3.0000$$

$(0.1876)_{10} = (0.3)_{16}$
$567.1875_{10} = 237.3_{16}$

Exercise 2-10.   Convert the following decimal numbers into hexadecimal:

(a) 28   (b) 192   (c) 825.75

2-5.   Binary-Octal-Hexadecimal Conversions

Binary-Octal Conversions.   Since octal numbers have practical importance in computers, conversion from octal to binary should be possible. In fact, the simplicity of this conversion (and back) is what makes octal numbers so useful. First try the conversion using the basic technique as before.

Example 2-20.   Convert $(275)_8$ into binary.

Solution:

$$\frac{275}{2} = 136 + 1$$

$$\frac{136}{2} = 57 + 1$$

$$\frac{57}{2} = 27 + 1$$

$$\frac{27}{2} = 13 + 1$$

$$\frac{13}{2} = 5 + 1$$

$$\frac{5}{2} = 2 + 1$$

$$\frac{2}{2} = 1 + 0$$

$$\frac{1}{2} = 0 + 1 \longrightarrow 10111101$$

Read as $(010111101)_2$.

By now you should be exclaiming that the example is all wrong, the divisions are incorrect, and even though the answer is correct (have you checked it?) the whole process looks phony. None of this is true and the method is entirely correct, as is the answer. What you have probably failed to consider is that the division was carried out using octal numbers. For example, 2 into 275 means 2 into 2 = 1, 2 into 7 = 3 with a remainder of 1 and 2 into 15 is really 2 base 8 into 15 base 8 [where $(15)_8$ is 13 base 10] and equals 6 base 8 with a remainder of 1. As was indicated before, there is a simple method of conversion — and this is obviously not it. See how simple the same conversion can be done.

$$(275)_8 = \quad \underline{010} \qquad \underline{111} \qquad \underline{101}$$

2 in binary   7 in binary   5 in binary

010 111 101 answer in binary

Look back to see that this is the same answer obtained by division. The procedure is to write a three-place binary number for *each* octal digit. Since base 8 has integers from 0 to 7 and a three-place binary number can handle numbers from 0 to 7, they match nicely. See how easily the following two conversions are done.

$$(3576)_8 = (011\ 101\ 111\ 110)_2$$
$$= (011101111110)_2$$
$$(2412)_8 = (010\ 100\ 001\ 010)_2$$
$$= (010100001010)_2$$

Can this conversion be done? $(3978)_8 = (?)_2$ No! This number is not an octal number — octal digits only go as high as 7.

Exercise 2-11.   Convert from octal to binary:

(a) $(261)_8$ (b) $(372)_8$ (c) $(1376)_8$

Converting from binary to octal is just as easy to do. Here are two examples and an exercise to try.

Example 2-21. $(101110110)_2 = (?)_8$

Solution: $(101\ \ 110\ \ 110)_2 = (566)_8$

Example 2-22. $(1011011110)_2 = (?)_8$

Solution: This problem requires an additional amount of care only in reading the number properly. Digits should be grouped in threes (number of places) starting from the *right*.

1 011 011 110   which is   001 011 011 110

This converts to $(1\ 3\ 3\ 6)_8$. Had you read the number 101 110 111 0, you would have been wrong. You must be careful not to make this mistake.

Exercise 2-12.   Convert from binary to octal:

(a) $(101110)_2$ (b) $(11101100)_2$ (c) $(11101)_2$

When a binary number is read its length tends to make it hard to recognize. For example, read 101111101110111. If this same number were read in octal, you would find it easier. It would read $(27567)_8$.

Some computers print the answers out in octal. Operations in the computer have been carried out in binary and when the answer is printed, the computer provides the result in octal, so that the human operator will find it easier to read. Of course it would be easier to print out the answer in the familiar decimal system. However, this requires that the computer "convert" from the internal binary "language" to the external decimal, which takes time and requires special circuits. Many computers do provide this facility, some use the quicker conversion to octal, and a few just read out in binary. The choice depends mainly on the user, and the conversion operation can usually be added on when desired as either a programmed conversion or additional circuitry.

Binary-Hexadecimal Conversion.   Extending the grouping of binary digits into groups of four provides simple conversion with hexadecimal numbers. The groupings are listed in Table 2-4 below.

Table 2-4.   *Binary-Hexadecimal Relations*

Binary	Hexadecimal
0000	0
0001	1
0010	2
0011	3
0100	4
0101	5
0110	6
0111	7
1000	8
1001	9
1010	A
1011	B
1100	C
1101	D
1110	E
1111	F

Conversion from binary to hexadecimal is then carried out by grouping each four binary digits (starting from the right) and replacing it by the hexadecimal equivalent as given in Table 2-4.

Example 2-23.   Convert the following binary numbers into hexadecimal:

(a) 011011110101   (b) 1011101010010010

Solution: (a) 0110 1111 0101
          6   F   5

$$(011011110101)_2 = (6F5)_{16}$$

(b) 1011 1010 1001 0010
     B   A   9   2

$$(1011101010010010)_2 = (BA92)_{16}$$

Conversion from hexadecimal to binary is carried out by expressing each hexadecimal digit by four (but exactly four in *all* cases) binary digits as in the next example.

Example 2-24.   Convert the given hexadecimal numbers into binary:

(a) 1A6   (b) F109   (c) A2C

Solution: (a) $(1A6)_{16} = 0001$ 1010   0110
$$= (000110100110)_2$$

(b) $(F109)_{16} = 1111$ 0001   0000   1001
$$= (1111000100001001)_2$$

(c) $(A2C)_{16} = 1010$ 0010   1100
$$= (101000101100)_2$$

Exercise 2-13.   Do the following conversions.

(a) $(10110101)_2 = (?)_{16}$ (b) $(1111001110100100)_2 = (?)_{16}$
(c) $(2C0)_{16} = (?)_2$ (d) $(A26F)_{16} = (?)_2$

2-6. Addition

Now that the binary, octal, and hexadecimal number systems and their relation to decimal numbers have been studied we can consider some arithmetic operations in these different base systems.

Binary Addition.   Binary addition can be learned from the following addition table (Table 2-5). It should be obvious that it is much simpler than the decimal addition table.

As the table shows, there are only four combinations to "memorize." In the decimal system you may recall that you had to "memorize" 100 combinations (many of which repeated). The addition of $0+0, 1+0, 0+1$ is obvious. The addition of $1+1$, which we know is 2, in binary must be written using two places. The largest digit possible in any position in

Table 2-5.   *Binary Addition Table*

		Addend		
	+	0	1	
Augend	0	0	1	Sum
	1	1	$0+c$	

Note: c means carry

binary is 1, just as the largest decimal digit in any position is 9. Thus $1+1$ is 0 and a carry. The carry, of course, is added into the next higher place.

Example 2-25.
$$
\begin{array}{r}
001101 \\
+\,100101 \\
\hline
110010
\end{array}
\qquad
\left(\begin{array}{r}
13 \\
+\,37 \\
\hline
50
\end{array}\right)_{10}
$$

Example 2-26.
$$
\begin{array}{r}
1011011 \\
+\,1011010 \\
\hline
10110101
\end{array}
\qquad
\left(\begin{array}{r}
91 \\
+\,90 \\
\hline
181
\end{array}\right)_{10}
$$

Example 2-27.
$$
\begin{array}{r}
110111011 \\
+\,100111011 \\
\hline
1011110110
\end{array}
\qquad
\left(\begin{array}{r}
443 \\
+\,315 \\
\hline
758
\end{array}\right)_{10}
$$

Exercise 2-14.   Do the following binary additions.

(a) $\begin{array}{r} 10101 \\ +\,01101 \\ \hline \end{array}$
(b) $\begin{array}{r} 101011 \\ +\,011010 \\ \hline \end{array}$
(c) $\begin{array}{r} 01011101 \\ +\,10001100 \\ \hline \end{array}$

Having dealt almost exclusively with decimal numbers most students find binary addition somewhat disconcerting at first. A little practice working in binary will cure this very quickly since binary operations are actually much simpler than decimal. Consider, for example, that the sum in any column will either be a 0 or a 1. It is even possible to determine which it will be *without* carrying out the addition. If the number of 1's in a column to be added is *odd* then the sum bit for that column will be a 1. If the number of 1's in a column is *even* then the sum bit is 0. In addition, for *every pair* of 1's in a column add a 1 — carry to the next higher position column of digits. Consider the following example adding four binary numbers.

Example 2-28. Add the following column of binary numbers:

```
  00011
  01010
  00011
+ 00110
```

Solution:

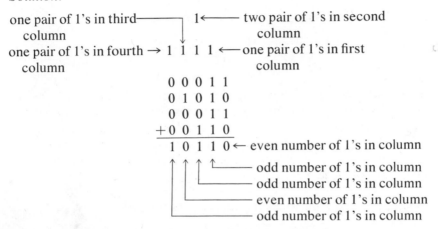

one pair of 1's in third───────┐ 1←──── two pair of 1's in second
   column   │   column

one pair of 1's in fourth → 1 1 1 1 ←── one pair of 1's in first
   column   column

```
    0 0 0 1 1
    0 1 0 1 0
    0 0 0 1 1
  + 0 0 1 1 0
    1 0 1 1 0 ← even number of 1's in column
```

─── odd number of 1's in column
─── odd number of 1's in column
─── even number of 1's in column
─── odd number of 1's in column

Octal Addition. Addition of octal numbers can be summarized in an addition table — Table 2-6 — which shows the result of adding all combinations of two octal digits. The carry indicated is always 1, and must be added to the next higher positional column when performing an addition:

Table 2-6. *Addition Table for Octal Numbers*

+	0	1	2	3	4	5	6	7
0	0	1	2	3	4	5	6	7
1	1	2	3	4	5	6	7	$0+c$
2	2	3	4	5	6	7	$0+c$	$1+c$
3	3	4	5	6	7	$0+c$	$1+c$	$2+c$
4	4	5	6	7	$0+c$	$1+c$	$2+c$	$3+c$
5	5	6	7	$0+c$	$1+c$	$2+c$	$3+c$	$4+c$
6	6	7	$0+c$	$1+c$	$2+c$	$3+c$	$4+c$	$5+c$
7	7	$0+c$	$1+c$	$2+c$	$3+c$	$4+c$	$5+c$	$6+c$

A few examples will demonstrate octal addition.

Example 2-29.   Perform the following octal additions:

$$\begin{array}{llll} \text{(a)} & 235 & \text{(b)} & 2017 & \text{(c) } 76 \\ & +126 & & +4674 & +23 \end{array}$$

Solution: (a)   235   (b)   2017   (c)   76
$$\begin{array}{l} +126 \\ \hline 363 \end{array} \qquad \begin{array}{l} +4674 \\ \hline 6713 \end{array} \qquad \begin{array}{l} +23 \\ \hline 121 \end{array}$$

Exercise 2-15.   Add the following octal numbers;

$$\begin{array}{llll} \text{(a)} & 625 & \text{(b)} & 1705 & \text{(c)} & 542 \\ & +113 & & +3076 & & +325 \end{array}$$

Hexadecimal Addition.   Unlike the simple choice in binary of having the sum bit either 0 or 1, the sum digit in hexadecimal could be any one of the 15 digits for the 256 combinations listed in the hexadecimal addition table, Table 2-7. It would be best to refer repeatedly to the addition table when first trying to add hexadecimal numbers. A few examples will demonstrate hexadecimal addition.

Example 2-30.   Add the following hexadecimal numbers:

$$\begin{array}{llll} \text{(a)} & 21A & \text{(b)} & 72C & \text{(c)} & 207A \\ & +352 & & +A3F & & +8194 \end{array}$$

Solution: (a)   21A   (b)   72C   (c)   207A
$$\begin{array}{l} +352 \\ \hline 56C \end{array} \qquad \begin{array}{l} +A3F \\ \hline 116B \end{array} \qquad \begin{array}{l} +8194 \\ \hline A21E \end{array}$$

Exercise 2-16.   Add the hexadecimal numbers:

$$\begin{array}{llll} \text{(a)} & 37C & \text{(b)} & 569A & \text{(c)} & 409 \\ & +A25 & & +108C & & +6F2 \end{array}$$

2-7.   Binary Subtraction and Complement Operation

Binary Subtraction.   Binary subtraction is again the same operation as in decimal. But you may find the operation more difficult than the addition. This will be either because you find subtraction itself harder (as most do) or because you cannot subtract well with decimal numbers and are even more confused with binary. This fact comes from first-hand classroom

Table 2-7.   *Hexadecimal Addition Table*

+	0	1	2	3	4	5	6	7	8	9	A	B	C	D	E	F
0	0	1	2	3	4	5	6	7	8	9	A	B	C	D	E	F
1	1	2	3	4	5	6	7	8	9	A	B	C	D	E	F	0+c
2	2	3	4	5	6	7	8	9	A	B	C	D	E	F	0+c	1+c
3	3	4	5	6	7	8	9	A	B	C	D	E	F	0+c	1+c	2+c
4	4	5	6	7	8	9	A	B	C	D	E	F	0+c	1+c	2+c	3+c
5	5	6	7	8	9	A	B	C	D	E	F	0+c	1+c	2+c	3+c	4+c
6	6	7	8	9	A	B	C	D	E	F	0+c	1+c	2+c	3+c	4+c	5+c
7	7	8	9	A	B	C	D	E	F	0+c	1+c	2+c	3+c	4+c	5+c	6+c
8	8	9	A	B	C	D	E	F	0+c	1+c	2+c	3+c	4+c	5+c	6+c	7+c
9	9	A	B	C	D	E	F	0+c	1+c	2+c	3+c	4+c	5+c	6+c	7+c	8+c
A	A	B	C	D	E	F	0+c	1+c	2+c	3+c	4+c	5+c	6+c	7+c	8+c	9+c
B	B	C	D	E	F	0+c	1+c	2+c	3+c	4+c	5+c	6+c	7+c	8+c	9+c	A+c
C	C	D	E	F	0+c	1+c	2+c	3+c	4+c	5+c	6+c	7+c	8+c	9+c	A+c	B+c
D	D	E	F	0+c	1+c	2+c	3+c	4+c	5+c	6+c	7+c	8+c	9+c	A+c	B+c	C+c
E	E	F	0+c	1+c	2+c	3+c	4+c	5+c	6+c	7+c	8+c	9+c	A+c	B+c	C+c	D+c
F	F	0+c	1+c	2+c	3+c	4+c	5+c	6+c	7+c	8+c	9+c	A+c	B+c	C+c	D+c	E+c

Note: Carry, c, is always 1 to the next higher position column.

experience, and it is suggested that you clear up subtraction in decimal so that binary operation (which should be simpler) is understood. A simple subtraction is indicated below in decimal.

$$
\begin{array}{rl}
1572 & \text{(minuend)} \\
-964 & \text{(subtrahend)} \\
\hline
608 & \text{(difference)}
\end{array}
$$

The terms in subtraction are defined as minuend (1572), subtrahend (964), and difference (608). Review the subtraction table (Table 2-8), the few examples, and the exercises using binary numbers.

Table 2-8.   *Binary Subtraction Table*

		Minuend		
	$-$	0	1	
Subtrahend	0	0	1	Difference
	1	$1+b$	0	

Note: b means borrow

Example 2-31.

$$
\begin{array}{r}
10110 \\
-01010 \\
\hline
01100
\end{array}
\qquad
\left(\begin{array}{r}
22 \\
-10 \\
\hline
12
\end{array}\right)_{10}
$$

Example 2-32.

$$
\begin{array}{r}
11011001 \\
-10101011 \\
\hline
00101110
\end{array}
\qquad
\left(\begin{array}{r}
217 \\
-171 \\
\hline
46
\end{array}\right)_{10}
$$

Try this example yourself (without looking at the answer). Is it so easy?

The way to become proficient at subtracting binary numbers is the same as with decimal — practice. Try the following as a start.

Exercise 2-17.   (a) $\begin{array}{r} 110101 \\ -101010 \\ \hline \end{array}$ (b) $\begin{array}{r} 1101101 \\ -0011110 \\ \hline \end{array}$ (c) $\begin{array}{r} 10110010 \\ -01101001 \\ \hline \end{array}$

One way to help simplify the subtraction is to read the numbers in groups. This is sometimes helpful. Here is one example in which it is an aid.

Example 2-33.

$$\begin{array}{r} 100110011101 \\ -010101110010 \end{array} \Rightarrow \begin{array}{ccc} 1001 & 1001 & 1101 \\ -0101 & 0111 & 0010 \end{array}$$

$$\Downarrow$$

$$\begin{array}{ccc} 1001 & 1001 & 1101 \\ 0101 & 0111 & 0010 \\ \hline 0100 & 0010 & 1011 \end{array}$$

Answer: 010000101011.

Binary Complement Operation.   Another technique that works well with subtraction is the use of complements. The use of complements in the decimal system could be shown, but because the main value comes in its use in the binary system, and to avoid any chance of confusion, only the binary system will be used. First, a few definitions. A TWO's complement of a number (N) of n binary places is defined as

$$\text{TWO's complement} \equiv 2^n - N$$

A ONE's complement of a number N of n binary places is defined as

$$\text{ONE's complement} \equiv (2^n - N) - 1$$

The ONE's complement is one less than the TWO's complement, or the TWO's complement is one greater than the ONE's complement. Here are a few examples.

Example 2-34.   Find the TWO's complement of $N = 101101$.

$$N = 45 \qquad n = 6 \text{ (6 places)}$$
$$2^n = 2^6 = 64$$
$$2^n - N = 64 - 45 = 19_{10} = 010011_2$$

The TWO's complement of 101101 is 010011.

In binary operation

$$N = 101101$$
$$2^n = 2^6 = 1000000$$
$$2^n - N = 1000000$$
$$\underline{ -101101}$$
$$ 0010011$$

The ONE's complement is then 010011

$$\underline{ -1}$$
$$010010$$

We started by saying that the use of complements would simplify subtraction, and so far all you have seen is that the procedure involved is as difficult as subtraction. Let us clear up the situation. Obtaining the ONE's complement of a number (binary of course) is really just rote operation. In Example 2-34 the number N was 101101 and its ONE's complement came out to be 010010. Looking at these two carefully we see that every bit in N is exactly opposite ($0 \to 1$, $1 \to 0$) in the ONE's complement. This is not just coincidence. It is always true, and it is this relation that makes the use of complements easy. Follow the next example of getting ONE's and TWO's complements of a number N.

Example 2-35. $N = 0110110101$

ONE's complement $= 1001001010$

TWO's complement $= 1001001011$ (ONE's complement $+ 1$)

Exercise 2-18.   Find the ONE's and TWO's complements for the following binary numbers.

(a) 0110101   (b) 011110111   (c) 110110111

Let us see how complements can be used to implement a subtraction and then how it is done practically. A subtraction may be obtained by adding the minuend to the TWO's complement of the subtrahend.

Example 2-36.

$$
\begin{array}{cc}
1011011 & N_1 \\
-0101110 & N_2 \\
\hline
0101101 &
\end{array}
\quad \Rightarrow \quad
\begin{array}{cc}
1011011 & N_1 \\
+1010010 & (2^n - N_2) \\
\hline
\text{disregard} \to (1)0101101 &
\end{array}
\quad
\left(\begin{array}{r} 91 \\ -46 \\ \hline 45 \end{array} \right)_{10}
$$

Notice that the two numbers to be subtracted each had the same number of places, the correct answer using complements was of this same length, and the extra ONE to the left is disregarded.

Example 2-37.

$$
\begin{array}{c}
11011011 \\
-10111 \\
\hline
11000100
\end{array}
\quad \Rightarrow \quad
\begin{array}{c}
11011011 \\
-00010111 \\
\hline
\end{array}
\quad \Rightarrow \quad
\begin{array}{c}
11011011 \\
+11101001 \\
\hline
1\ \ 11000100
\end{array}
\quad
\left(\begin{array}{r} 219 \\ -23 \\ \hline 196 \end{array} \right)_{10}
$$

Again the number had to be written using the same number of places for each (000 was added before the subtrahend) and the answer read with the same number of places, the extra ONE to the left being disregarded. Since the use of complements is easily shown using the ONE's complement, let us consider that next.

Obtaining the ONE's complement only requires changing all ONEs to ZEROs and all ZEROs to ONEs. This specific operation is called "complementing" a number, and the term "complement" refers here to the ONE's complement only. When the TWO's complement is discussed it will be called specifically the TWO's complement. As the correct answer is obtained mathematically from using the TWO's complement and the implementation is done here with the ONE's, all that is required is that the answer be increased by ONE. Since it is possible to subtract a smaller or larger number, the exact operation is best explained with the following examples.

Example 2-38.

$$
\begin{array}{cc}
1110111 \\
-0101101
\end{array}
\Rightarrow
\begin{array}{cc}
1110111 \\
+1010010 \\
\hline
(1)\,1001001
\end{array}
\quad
\left(
\begin{array}{r}
119 \\
-45 \\
\hline
74
\end{array}
\right)_{10}
$$

$\quad\quad\quad\quad\quad\quad\quad\quad\quad\quad \vdash\!\longrightarrow 1 \text{ add } 1$

$$\overline{1001010}$$

Since the extra ONE is present and a ONE must be added to obtain the answer, the procedure is mechanized with the addition of the extra ONE in the lowest-order position, called an *"end-around carry."* This is always done when using ONE's complement. If no extra ONE appears, no end-around carry is performed. Instead the answer is recognized as being a negative number (and in ONE's complement form). The number may be read by complementing and putting a minus sign in front when this condition occurs. Here is an example.

Example 2-39.
$$
\begin{array}{cc}
1011101 \\
-1101100
\end{array}
\Rightarrow
\begin{array}{cc}
1011101 \\
+0010011 \\
\hline
1110000
\end{array}
\quad
\left(
\begin{array}{r}
93 \\
-108 \\
\hline
-15
\end{array}
\right)_{10}
$$

Answer: -0001111.

There was no extra ONE, so no end-around carry was needed. The answer was read by complementing and putting a minus sign in front.

Try these next two examples and the following exercise.

Example 2-40.
$$
\begin{array}{cc}
10111011 \\
-01100110
\end{array}
\quad
\begin{array}{cc}
10111011 \\
+10011001 \\
\hline
(1)\,01010100
\end{array}
\quad
\left(
\begin{array}{r}
187 \\
-102 \\
\hline
85
\end{array}
\right)_{10}
$$

$\quad\quad\quad\quad\quad\quad\quad\quad\quad\quad \vdash\!\longrightarrow 1 \text{ end-around carry}$

$$\overline{01010101} \text{ Answer}$$

Example 2-41.   101110100111   101110100111 $\left(\begin{array}{r} 2983 \\ -3511 \\ \hline -528 \end{array}\right)_{10}$
             $-$ 110110110111 $+$ 001001001000
             _____   _____
                               110111101111

No extra one — answer is negative.

Answer: $-$ 001000010000.

Exercise 2-19.   Subtract using complements.

      (a)   110111   (b) 110101   (c)   1101101
         $-$ 101101   101101 $-$ 1110000

In review, subtraction of binary numbers may be implemented by adding the complement of the subtrahend (ONE's complement is understood).

Although the ONE's complement is easy to obtain, most computers perform subtraction using the TWO's complement. Whereas the use of the ONE's complement requires an additional step of adding the end-around carry, the TWO's complement operation is faster, since the TWO's complement itself is greater than the ONE's complement by ONE, thus requiring no additional end-around carry operation.

Example 2-42.   Subtract the following numbers using TWO's complement operation:

      (a)   10111011   (b)   101110100111
         $-$ 01100110 $-$ 110110110111

Solution: (a) TWO's complement of 01100110 is 10011010.

      10111011
    $+$ 10011010
    (1)01010101   *Answer:* 01010101
    disregard

    (b) TWO's complement of 110110110111 is 001001001001

      101110100111
    $+$ 001001001001
      110111110000   Answer in TWO's complement form
    no extra 1
    ∴ answer is negative and in TWO's complement form.

2-8. Binary Multiplication and Division

Binary Multiplication. Multiplication in the binary number system is probably easier than in any other number system. This should be apparent when you consider that a multiplier digit can only be a ZERO or a ONE. Thus the partial product formed is either zero or exactly the multiplicand. An example will show this very nicely.

Example 2-43.

$$
\begin{array}{l}
110101 \ \text{(multiplicand)} \\
\underline{\times \, 111 \ \text{(multiplier)}} \\
110101 \\
110101 \\
\underline{110101} \\
101110011 \ \text{(product)}
\end{array}
\qquad
\left(
\begin{array}{l}
53 \\
\underline{\times 7} \\
371
\end{array}
\right)_{10}
$$

In a computer the multiplication operation is formed by repeated additions, in much the same manner as the addition of all partial products to obtain the full product. Details of this procedure are covered when implementation of the operation is considered. The formation of partial products is quite easy. The addition of these may be more difficult, however, since each addition of two ONE's creates a carry. A little practice will help in learning to perform the operation properly. Example 2-44 is given with a large number of carries to impress the reader with how the carries must be handled, after which the exercise should be tried.

Example 2-44. Perform the following binary multiplication.

$$
\begin{array}{l}
110110111 \\
\underline{\times 1010111}
\end{array}
$$

Solution:

$$
\begin{array}{l}
110110111 \\
\underline{\times \, 1010111} \\
110110111 \\
110110111 \\
110110111 \\
000000000 \\
110110111 \\
000000000 \\
\underline{110110111} \\
1001010100110001
\end{array}
\qquad
\left(
\begin{array}{l}
439 \\
\underline{\times 87} \\
38193
\end{array}
\right)_{10}
$$

Recall that an easy way to add binary digits is to count the number of ONEs (and carries) in the column. If it is even, the sum is 0 and if odd, it is 1. Then count the pairs of ONEs to determine how many ONEs to carry to the next higher position. This procedure is more automatic and easier to follow (and should lead to fewer errors). Try the addition this way to see whether you find it easier.

Exercise 2-20.   Perform the indicated multiplications.

$$\text{(a)}\quad \begin{array}{r} 1011 \\ \times\,110 \\ \hline \end{array} \qquad \text{(b)}\quad \begin{array}{r} 1001 \\ \times\,1011 \\ \hline \end{array} \qquad \text{(c)}\quad \begin{array}{r} 111 \\ \times\,100 \\ \hline \end{array}$$

Binary Division.   As with multiplication, the reader will soon find that binary division is simple to perform. This, again, is because you can divide into a part of a number only once or not all. No quotient terms other than 1 or 0 are possible. Consider the following example.

Example 2-45.

$$\begin{array}{r} 1100\ \text{(quotient)} \\ \text{(divisor) } 110\,\overline{)\,1001000}\ \text{(dividend)} \\ -110 \\ \hline 00110 \\ -110 \\ \hline 0000000 \end{array} \qquad \left(6\,\overline{)\,\dfrac{12}{72}}\right)_{10}$$

Try to divide the dividend by the divisor using the same number of places as the divisor (110 into 100) in this example. If it does not divide in at all, try using a larger dividend (110 into 1001). If it does go in, it can only go in once, so the first quotient term is a ONE. The division procedure continues similar to decimal division.

Try the following exercise for practice.

Exercise 2-21.   Perform the following binary divisions:

$$\text{(a)}\quad 101\,\overline{)\,11001} \qquad \text{(b)}\quad 011\,\overline{)\,10010}$$
$$\text{(c)}\quad 1001\,\overline{)\,1010001}$$

Summary

The binary octal and hexadecimal systems were introduced, and conversion of both integer and fractional parts from binary octal and hexadecimal to decimal and decimal to binary octal and hexadecimal was covered. Proficiency using these number systems is essential when dealing with the basic operations in a digital computer.

The octal and hexadecimal number systems are important because they are used in machine operation in a large number of computers.

The use of complements to subtract binary numbers is important since that is the way it is carried out in most computers. Although the subtraction was shown mainly as an addition of the ONE's complement and the use of an end-around carry, TWO's complement may be obtained directly by using special computer circuits and then added to the minuend to effect the subtraction.

Binary multiplication and division are shown as done with pencil and paper. The computer actually performs these operations as repeated additions and repeated subtractions, respectively. These operations will be covered in Chapter 12 when the arithmetic unit is discussed.

PROBLEMS

§2-2   **1.** Convert the following integer binary numbers into decimal.

(a) 110111   (b) 111000   (c) 010101
(d) 101010   (e) 1111110

2. Convert the following decimal numbers into binary.

(a) 25   (b) 67   (c) 99   (d) 135   (e) 276

3. Convert the following fractional binary numbers into decimal.

(a) 0.1010   (b) 0.11   (c) 0.001
(d) 0.011   (e) 0.11001

4. Convert the following fractional decimal numbers into binary.

(a) 0.8750   (b) 0.375   (c) 0.53125

5. Convert the following decimal numbers into binary.

(a) 38.375   (b) 144.875   (c) 325.625

§2-3   **6.** Convert the following octal numbers into decimal.

(a) 45   (b) 125   (c) 476
(d) 231.25   (e) 75.6

7. Convert the following decimal numbers into octal.

(a) 63   (b) 119   (c) 625.5
(d) 389.25   (e) 4093

§2-4   **8.** Convert the following hexadecimal numbers into decimal.

(a) 3A   (b) 1F   (c) 32D

9. Convert the following decimal numbers into hexadecimal.

(a) 85   (b) 139   (c) 927.5

§2-5   **10.** Convert the following binary and octal numbers.

(a) $(1101101)_2 = (?)_8$ (b) $(372)_8 = (?)_2$
(c) $(101110.111)_2 = (?)_8$ (d) $(2753)_8 = (?)_2$
(e) $(25.57)_8 = (?)_2$

11. Convert the following binary and hexadecimal numbers.

(a) $(01101101)_2 = (?)_{16}$ (b) $(A2C)_{16} = (?)_2$
(c) $(4F)_{16} = (?)_2$ (d) $(0101111010100110)_2 = (?)_{16}$
(e) $(29D)_{16} = (?)_2$

§2-6   **12.** Perform the following additions in the indicated base system only.

(a) $\left(\dfrac{111011}{+\,110}\right)_2$ (b) $\left(\dfrac{111110111}{+\,111001}\right)_2$

(c) $\left(\dfrac{365}{+\,23}\right)_8$ (d) $\left(\dfrac{2732}{+\,1265}\right)_8$

(e) $\left(\dfrac{\begin{matrix}10111\\11011\\10111\end{matrix}}{}\right)_2$ (f) $\left(\dfrac{4A2}{+\,819}\right)_{16}$

§2-7   **13.** Perform the following binary subtractions.

(a) $\begin{matrix}11001\\-\,110\end{matrix}$ (b) $\begin{matrix}11001101\\-\,01001111\end{matrix}$

(c) $\begin{matrix}11011011110\\-\,10100111001\end{matrix}$

14. Obtain the ONE's and TWO's complements of the following numbers.

(a) 1001111   (b) 1010011   (c) 1110010

15. Perform the following subtraction by ONE's complement addition with *end-around carry*).

(a) $\begin{matrix}101011\\-\,011010\end{matrix}$ (b) $\begin{matrix}10110110\\-\,00110010\end{matrix}$ (c) $\begin{matrix}11011101\\-\,01110110\end{matrix}$

16. Perform the following subtraction using TWO's complement addition.

(a)   101011
  $-$ 011010

(b)   11101101
  $-$ 01001111

(c) 11001
  $-$ 110

§**2-8**   **17.** Perform the following binary multiplications or divisions.

(a) 1011
  $\times$ 11

(b)   110
  $\times$ 11011

(c) $1010\overline{)\,1100100}$

(d) $101\overline{)\,11110}$

0011

Machine language programming

3-1. General

After discussing the computer in general terms in Chapter 1 and number systems in Chapter 2, it would now be meaningful to consider how a problem is solved using a computer. The basic "language" for instructing a computer is called machine language. Here the machine is instructed using coded numbers to indicate the operation to be performed and where to take or place the data for that operation. Since the machine is operated by binary digits, the actual commands used are binary. For convenience to the programmer and operator, decimal or octal numbers may be used outside the computer, but these are converted into binary (or binary coded) numbers inside the machine. The control unit of the computer plays a basic part in interpreting the machine instruction and developing the necessary signals to carry out the operational step. It uses the memory and arithmetic units for a large number of operations.

A number of programming examples are shown and discussed to bring out the important features of how the computer is used to solve problems. The main value in considering machine language is that we are discussing computer operations at their basic level. This should help give perspective later on in the book when the different computer units are considered separately. Computer programmers who are more interested in solving problems than in discovering how the computer functions seldom use machine language. The value of higher-level computer languages is discussed after machine language coding.

3-2. Memory Words

Before going ahead with programming we should have some idea of the makeup of the main memory unit. Both the number of bits designated as a *word* of memory and the number of words of memory are important to the machine language structure. As an example for this chapter consider a 512_{10} word memory (small by modern computer standards — see Chapter 11) organized in octal words of five octal digits each. Recall from Chapter 2 that each octal digit can be considered a group of three bits so that the proposed memory holds fifteen bits per word (5 octal digits × 3 bits per octal digit). For convenience we will program in octal (although most modern computers are programmed in hexadecimal).

In our consideration a word of memory contains five octal digits, with all 512_{10} locations containing some octal numbers. Location values can range from 000_8 to 777_8 (512_{10} locations). It should be understood that when considering the memory each location stores an octal number (five octal digits) and that each location has some octal number, possibly that left by previous user(s). A memory word is thus made of five octal digits and is stored at a location specified by a three octal digit value. For example, location 013 could store the value 12345, while location 275 could store 01372, all values being octal.

3-3. Data Representations

The five octal digit number could store an integer value from 00000_8 to 77777_8. If, as usual, there is an additional sign bit, the numbers could be plus or minus. Thus, stored octal integer values could be $+00015$, -00027, $+32175$, and so on. The numbers stored could also contain integer and fractional parts but this is usually a matter of program setup. (Most modern computers provide extra hardware to handle what is referred to as floating point numbers, but we will not consider this detail here). The numbers stored could also be coded binary or octal to represent alphabetic characters (codes are covered in Chapter 4). In this case the number stored could represent alphabetic information. The computer is built so that the hardware could operate on the number stored as either octal numerical value or as alphabetic characters. Separate machine language instructions are necessary to specify either operation. It should be emphasized that it is the instruction that causes the machine to interpret a stored-number as either octal value or alphabetic data — the stored value being five octal digits in either case.

3-4.   Machine Instruction Words

Just as the five octal digit number stored could be either octal numeric value or alphabetic characters (in coded form), the instructions stored in machine language are only octal digits. Typical in computers, this octal instruction value contains at least two parts — an *operation code* (*op code*) and an *operand* or *address* value. In the present sample language we will consider the five-digit octal instruction to consist of a two octal digit op code and a three octal digit address. Table 3-1 lists the octal codes that we shall use in this chapter. Only a few of the two octal digit values are specified as particular operations, and those that are not specified as other possible operations will not be considered here.

An instruction such as 14300 is seen by the computer to contain an op code 14 and an address value 300. The computer control unit would understand this number to mean *add the value at address 300 to the arithmetic unit present value.* An instruction such as 30402 would similarily be interpreted as *store the arithmetic unit value at address 402 in memory.*

3-5.   Stored Program Concept

As stated in section 3-4 an instruction is a five-digit octal number. The instruction thus is a number that could be (and is) stored in the memory. As far as the memory is concerned it stores only five-digit octal numbers. These numbers may then be integer values, alphabetic data, or instructions. A program may then contain stored instructions and data all stored in memory. It is the programmer who decides where in memory he will store his program and where in memory he will store his data when programming in machine language.

With the program now in memory the computer is started operating at the first instruction and continues then at its own lightning fast pace doing all the operations specified in the program on the data provided or read in from computer input units.

The programmer, for example, may wish to start his program at location 100. If his first instruction is to reset the arithmetic unit accumulator to zero and add in the first value to be operated on from address 500 the program is written as

$$100 \qquad 10500$$

where, 100 is the location of the stored instruction 10500. It should be clear then that a program executed by the computer is first stored in memory where the computer can read it and perform at its own very fast rate.

Table 3-1.   *Machine Language Code*

Code Form	Operation	Description
00	Stop	Tells machine program is completed.
10	Reset and add	Resets accumulator to zero and adds number stored to operand address.
14	Add	Adds number at operand address to whatever is at present in the accumulator.
15	Subtract	Subtracts number at operand address from whatever is at present in the accumulator.
20	Multiply	Multiplies number at operand address by whatever is at present in the accumulator.
24	Divide	Divides number in accumulator by number at operand address.
30	Store	Stores number in accumulator in operand address.
44	Jump	Tells computer to take next instruction from operand address.
45	Branch if minus	Tells computer to take next instruction from operand address, if number now in accumulator is minus (negative); otherwise computer uses the instruction following sequentially as its next.
46	Branch if plus	Tells the computer to take next instruction from operand address if number now in accumulator is positive; otherwise the computer takes the instruction following sequentially as its next.
47	Branch if zero	Tells the computer to take next instruction from operand address if number now in accumulator is identically zero; otherwise the computer takes the instruction following sequentially as its next.
50	Print	Tells computer to print word stored at operand indicated.
60	Read	Tells computer to read in new word from input device to operand address.

3-6.   Machine Program Operation — Fetch/Execute Cycle

The program can be started after instructions and data have been stored in memory. The starting location is set into the control console and the run switch is pressed. The computer now goes through a repeated two-step basic cycle referred to as *fetch/execute*. During fetch the instruction is read out of memory by the control unit. Then during execute the control unit provides the necessary signals to perform or execute the instruction. The control unit also keeps track of *where* it should get the next instruction (typically, the location following where it read the present instruction). The control unit repeated fetches an instruction and executes it until a stop (or halt) instruction is received.

The above discussion should clarify how the computer differentiates between numbers (data) and numbers (instructions). An instruction is indicated by setting its location as the starting location and then placing subsequent instructions in following locations.

3-7.   Machine Language Programming

Basic Operation.   To introduce machine language programming, consider the simple program to solve the equation $Y = 2X + 6$ (Program 3-1).

Program 3-1.

Location	Instruction Operation-Address		Remarks
000	10	010	Reset and add 2
001	20	012	Multiply 2 by X
002	14	011	Add 6 to 2X (= Y)
003	30	013	Store Y
004	50	013	Print Y
005	00	—	Stop
010	00002		Stored value 2
011	00006		Stored value 6
012	(X)		Stored value X
013	(Y)		Computed value Y

The address on the left indicates which particular memory location we are considering. Each word in memory is assigned an address that can be used in looking for that word. This is very much the same as a postman knowing where to deliver mail by the address of the envelope. There is only one word residing at a particular address in memory to complete the analogy. The program indicates the sequential order of operations that are to be performed. This program is stored in memory and the computer, starting at the beginning, performs the operation specified in the first memory location. The instruction is made up of an operation command, which tells the machine what to do, and an address (operand), which tells the machine where to get the information to perform the operation on. In addition, it is understood that when the operation is completed, the result remains in an accumulator. An accumulator is the part of the computer arithmetic section where the results of an arithmetic operation are left at the end of the operation. In order to do another operation the word in the accumulator must be taken and stored in memory and new data (words) must be put into the accumulator for manipulation. Thus the machine steps specified are often just those of setting up an operation by loading the accumulator or those of taking data out of the accumulator to allow for further operations. The arithmetic section operates very quickly, information used in it being fed in from memory and results from it being fed back to memory. Input data goes first to memory and then to the arithmetic unit as needed. The answers produced are temporarily stored in memory and read out as required. Thus the arithmetic unit need not be slowed down by the slower speed of the input/output equipment.

Storage locations (addresses) 010 to 013 are used here to store data for this program. The data may be stored anywhere in the memory, since it usually takes as much time to reach one location as another. The program is stored in sequential order. However, the computer may also be directed by the program to jump around to nonsequential locations for the program. Jump commands will be considered in more detail in later examples. Finally, when data is read into the arithmetic unit it is still retained in memory (nondestructive readout). If a new word is written into a memory location, the old word is lost (or erased). This is the same as recording a new selection on a magnetic tape recorder. As the new selection is put on, the old one is erased and only the new one is present after recording.

Starting at location 000, the program tells the computer to reset the adder unit (specifically the accumulator) to zero in case any number was there at the start and then to add the number stored in address 010 to it. It should be made very clear that the number being placed in the accumulator is not 010. It is whatever number is at present stored in location 010 of the memory. Thus 2 (stored before the program begins) is added to zero resulting in the sum 2 in the accumulator. On the next instruction the number previously placed in location 012, X in this case, is multiplied by the number in the accumulator, 2 in this case, resulting in the product 2X in the accumulator. When we say 2X, we do not mean the algebraic expression as written but the number resulting when the number for X is multiplied by the number 2. Remember, the computer only performs operations on numbers, resulting in numbers. The expressions X and Y are just labels attached to these numbers. The third instruction causes the constant 6, stored in address 011, to be added to 2X, leaving the sum 2X+6 in the accumulator. Since this equals Y, it is stored in location 013 and on the next instruction the contents of address 013, Y in this case, is printed out. The final instruction, in location 005, tells the computer that the problem is completed, stopping any further operation of this program.

The operation code was indicated in the example just given by the two-digit number (10, 14, 20, etc.) which appears on the left of the instruction word. For the examples in this book the list of instructions and their coded form given in Table 3-1 will be used.

As a second example consider the program for solving $Y = X^2 + 8X + 12$ (Program 3-2).

Program 3-2.

Location	Instruction Operation-Address		Remarks
000	10	020	Reset and add X to accumulator
001	20	020	Multiply X by X
002	30	023	Store X^2
003	10	020	Reset and add X to accumulator
004	20	021	Multiply 8 by X
005	14	022	Add 12 to 8X
006	14	023	Add X^2 to $8X + 12$
007	30	023	Store $Y = X^2 + 8X + 12$
010	50	023	Print Y
011	00	—	Stop
020	(X)		Stored value of X
021	00010		Stored value of 8_{10}
022	00014		Stored value of 12_{10}
023	Temporary storage		Temporary storage location

Locations 020 to 023 are used to store the constants 8_{10} and 12_{10}, the value of X, and any temporary value computed. On the first step the computer looks at location 000 for the instruction and is directed to reset and add the number stored in address 020 to the accumulator. Step 2 (at location 001) tells the computer to multiply the value in 020 by the value in the accumulator. Since X is at present in the accumulator and X is the value in address 020, the result of this operation is the product X^2 in the accumulator. Since the accumulator will now be used for a different operation, the intermediate answer X^2 is stored in temporary storage location 023 on the next step. Then the value of X is again added into the accumulator, the accumulator first being reset to clear out X^2. The constant 8 is multiplied by X and 8X is now in the accumulator. The next instruction at location 005 tells the computer to add 12_{10} to the value in the accumulator resulting in $8X + 12$. Finally, the value X^2 previously calculated is added to $8X + 12$, resulting in Y. The computed value of Y is then stored in location 023 (erasing the value X^2 stored previously) and then printed. The last instruction tells the computer to stop scanning the memory for instructions. It is this step that keeps the computer from advancing to location 020 and mistaking the stored number X as an instruction. The computer is so stupid it would not know whether the value stored is a number or an instruction. The program leads the computer step by step and should not allow a situation to develop in which a stored number is read as an instruction. In this program the stop instruction is used to keep the computer from continuing to location 020 where data is stored.

Testing and Repeated Loops.   So far we have considered simple programs in which the solution required one cycle of operation and produced a single answer. Obviously, this would not prove to be of tremendous value because we could probably solve the problem faster than we could write the program. To even consider using a computer the problem must require a large number of calculations. In other words, the computer may do the same problem with many different sets of numbers producing hundreds to thousands of answers. For this case it is more efficient to write a program and have the computer do the tedious calculations. Problems that might take a person a lifetime to complete can be done in minutes by a computer.

Consider the simple example of a computer program (Program 3-3) directing the repeated solution of a problem. The object of the program is to calculate and print out the squares of the numbers from 1 to 100_8, inclusive. Even with a desk calculator the problem would take a fairly long time to execute. A computer will do it in seconds and, as we shall see, the program is short.

The key to the looped or repeated operation is the "branch if minus" statement. The jump or branch command may break the normal sequence of location examined for instructions. The next instruction is taken from

Program 3-3.

Location	Instruction Operation-Address		Remarks
000	10	020	Reset and add number in 020
001	14	021	Add 1 to the above
002	30	020	Store in 020
003	20	020	Multiply number by itself
004	30	023	Now store value squared in 023
005	50	023	Print value of square
006	10	020	Reset and add number to accumulator
007	15	022	Subtract 100 from number
010	45	000	Branch if minus to location 000
011	00	—	Stop
020	00000		Stored value (initially zero)
021	00001		Increment each cycle is 1
022	00100		Final value is 100_8
023	Temporary storage		

either a new place in memory or that following the branch instruction. The table of machine language codes indicates four different jump commands. The first is an unconditional jump (44) which directs the computer to take the next instruction from the address indicated. Thus, 44 216 will always cause the machine to go to location 216 for the next instruction to perform. Assuming this is an arithmetic instruction (or specifically not a branch instruction), the machine will perform that instruction and then take its next instruction from the next location in memory, 217 in this case.

The three conditional branch instructions operate in a similar manner, except that there is an alternate (conditional) operation. The computer looks at either the sign of the number presently in the accumulator or at its value to determine whether to perform the branch instruction or to ignore it. If, for example, the command is 45 216 and the number now in the accumulator is negative, the next instruction will be taken from location 216. If, however, the sign is positive, it will ignore the branch and continue to the next sequential instruction following 45 216. Two directions or two different actions are possible at the time of a branch instruction and only one is carried out. It is this choice or decision operation which gives the computer the appearance of a "thinking" device. With many programmed branches, the computer can follow a large variety of alternate procedures, thereby enabling it to solve complicated problems for a variety of conditions. Let us go back (44) to the program under consideration and see how the branch is used.

Locations 020, 021, and 022 control what value the computation is started at, by how much this value is incremented after each solution, and at what final value to do the last calculation. At the start of the computation the computer is instructed to reset and add 00000 to the accumulator and then add 00001 to that number. Although we could have started with one right away, we wanted to establish the pattern of incrementing the value in 020 by that in 021 before doing another cycle of computation. This value is also the number we want to form the square of on this cycle of the computation. On the first cycle (loop) the value is 00001 (or 1) and the square is formed by multiplying this value by itself (instructions in locations 002 and 003). The squared value is then stored and printed by instructions in locations 004 and 005, respectively. The next steps now consider whether to do another loop or to end the computation. After the accumulator is reset the present value is added into the accumulator. Then the final value is subtracted. If the final value is larger than the present value, at least one more loop must be executed, and the branch if minus directs that the next instruction is to be taken from address 000. This instruction, then, tells the computer to go back to the beginning and start again. Since the program sequence updates the value squared by an increment of 1 at the beginning of a loop, the next number to be squared will be one greater than on the previous loop. This repeated loop continues until the value in the accumulator is zero (or positive) on the branch if minus instruction. This "tells" the computer that it has done enough loops and the program now goes to the next step, which instructs it to stop.

This same program may now be used to calculate the squares of any simple set of numbers by changing the initial, final, and increment value stored in locations 020, 021, and 022. For example, if the initial value stored is 00020, the increment 00010, and the final value 02000, the computer will form the squares of 20, 30, 40, 50, etc., up to and including the square of 2000. Once programs are written it only requires changing specific values to obtain a variety of calculations. This then is a very powerful feature of a computer. For example, an insurance company may once program the calculations they must perform on a customer's account. To do the same calculations once, one hundred times, or a million times is easily controlled and, using a computer, it is quickly carried out.

Try the following problems to see whether you understand how the branch if minus is used in looped solutions.

Exercise 3-1.   Write a program to solve the equation $Y = 3X^2 + 2X + 6$ for values of X from 1 to 50_8, inclusive. Have the value Y printed out for each computation.

Exercise 3-2.   Write a program to compute and print out the cubes of the odd numbers from 1 to 61_8, inclusive.

Exercise 3-3.   Write a program to compute and print the values of $Y = 3X^3 + 2X$ for all even numbers less than 250_8.

Decision Making.   A relatively difficult problem, but one which will show the basic procedure of decision making is that of determining the largest of three numbers (Program 3-4). Although this program only goes through the operation for one set of three numbers, it could be additionally programmed to read new sets of three numbers and repeat the operation.

Program 3-4 does not easily show the method used to solve the

Program 3-4.

Location	Operation	Address	Remarks
	Instruction		
100	10	200	Reset and add X
101	15	201	Subtract Y from X; $(X - Y)$
102	45	110	If $Y > X$ branch to location 110
103	10	201	$X > Y$; reset and add X into accumulator
104	15	202	Subtract: $X - Z$
105	45	115	If $Z > X$ branch to 115
106	50	200	Print X as largest value
107	44	116	Jump to 116
110	10	201	Since $Y > X$ reset and add Y to accumulator
111	15	202	Subtract: $Y - Z$
112	45	115	If $Z > Y$ branch to 115
113	50	201	Print Y as largest number
114	44	116	Jump to 116
115	50	202	Print Z as largest number
116	00	—	Stop
200	(X)		
201	(Y)		
202	(Z)		

problem. Let us first consider how the problem is analyzed before discussing the way it is programmed. One of the valuable features of programming is the clear understanding that must be obtained before a program can be written. To facilitate this thought process a *flow chart* is often constructed. Let us only consider how the flow diagram shows the steps required to solve the problem. Referring to Figure 3-1, the first

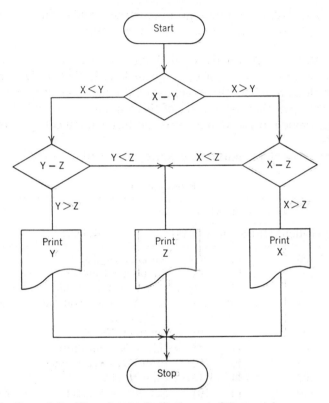

Figure 3-1.   Flow chart for finding largest of three numbers.

step is to place X in the accumulator. Next subtract Y from X and transfer the program in one of two directions (one for each possible outcome). If X is greater than Y, subtract Z from X to see whether X or Z is larger. Again there are two possible outcomes. If X is also larger than Z, then X is the largest – print X and stop. If Z is the largest, print out Z and stop. Had the outcome of the subtraction X – Y resulted in the answer X less than Y, the program would subtract Z from Y (which is larger than X). If Y is greater than Z, print Y and stop; if Z is greater than Y, print Z and stop. The flow chart shows how the problem is solved, as in the discussion just given. Once the method of solution is determined, the program can be written to accomplish this operation.

Returning to the given machine language program, we find the first instruction resets the accumulator and adds in X. Then Y is subtracted from X and the sign is used to determine where to branch. If Y is larger than X (sign in accumulator negative), the branch if minus command causes the program to look for its next instruction at location 110. If the sign is plus, the next instruction is taken in sequence. Since this would result if X is larger than Y, the next instruction (at location 103) resets the accumulator and adds in X. This was necessary because the accumulator contained the difference of X − Y. Now that it has been determined which of X or Y is larger, the next step is to subtract Z. Following the program in which X is larger and is set into the accumulator, the next instruction (at location 104) subtracts Z from X. The program branches to address location 115 if X is less than Z. If X is greater than Z, the next instruction (at 106) will print the number stored in 200 (X in this case). A jump instruction then directs the program to the stop command. Had X been largest the program would only have subtracted Y from X, then reset X and subtracted Z, printed X, and finally jumped to the stop instruction to end the operation. Since, in general, Y or Z could have been larger, the program contains the operations leading to the printing out of Y or Z as largest as well. To continue, if Y had been larger than X, the instruction at location 102 would cause the program steps stored in 103 to 107, inclusive, to be bypassed. The instruction at 110 causes the value Y to be set into the accumulator. The subtraction of Y − Z is done, and again a branch condition exists. If Y is larger than Z, the instruction at 112 allows the program to go on to 113 and Y is printed out as the largest number; instruction 114 unconditionally jumps the program to 116 where a stop instruction is present. Had Z been greater than Y, the result of instruction 112 would be to take the next instruction from location 115, so that Z is printed as the largest and step 116 then tells the computer to stop.

To go through all the trouble of developing the program just discussed in order to compare three numbers once would have been foolish. A quick look at the numbers would be enough to see which is greater. However, if a thousand sets of three numbers each had to be considered, the solution using a computer would then be practical. Then the written program would have to contain additional commands to cause the procedure to be repeated for each set of values. This might only require a few additional steps such as a few to read in the new set of X, Y, and Z values and an unconditional jump at the end to return the program to the start. Either the computer will stop if no more data is available or the program must contain additional steps to count the number of loops and

stop after a desired number have been carried out. The program considered did not handle the cases where any two of the numbers, or all
three, are equal. As an exercise draw some flow charts and write the
program for both additional cases.

Let us consider the same problem adding in the few extra steps which
will allow the computer to do the operation for many sets of values. Since
the basic procedure in finding the largest is still the same, we can use them
as shown in location 100 to 115. Rather than stop at step 116, however,
the values of X, Y, and Z will now be updated (a new set of numbers
placed in locations 200, 201, and 202, respectively). Since the program
reaches location 116 after the largest value has been computed (and
printed), it can then read in a new set of values before doing the program
again. A test is made to see whether there have been enough computations performed. For example, today there may be 1000 sets to be
operated on, whereas next week 2000 may be present. On some machines
the fact that no new data are present at the time of a new read command
will cause the machine to halt. This is true of punched cards, for example.
However, we often are doing this operation as one small part of a larger
program and therefore would want the machine to go on to another part
of the memory for new program instructions after these computations
are completed. A test is therefore necessary at this time. As in a previous
example, an initial value, increment, and final value must be stored somewhere in memory so that this test can be performed. A flow chart of the
modified problem is shown in Figure 3-2. The additional program steps
are given in Program 3-5.

The revised program starts in location 075. New values for X, Y, and
Z are placed in locations 200, 201, and 202, respectively. Then the main
part of the program is performed and the largest value printed out. The
instruction at 116 begins the test procedure. The initial count value stored
at 203 is placed in the accumulator. It is incremented (by one for this
example) and the new value is stored back at location 203. The next
instruction subtracts the final value from the count value. If the count is
less than the final value, the computer program instructs the next step to
be taken from 075, thereby repeating the loop with a new set of values for
X, Y, and Z. This will be repeated until the test on step 122 finds a
positive value in the accumulator. In this problem a positive value will
occur after 1000_8 computations. It should again be seen that the same
program can be run after a new final value is stored and the count can be
reset to zero for a different number of sets with very little effort. That is,
the program does not have to be rewritten; only a new final value must
be read in at the start.

When the program is completed and the branch if minus at step 122 is

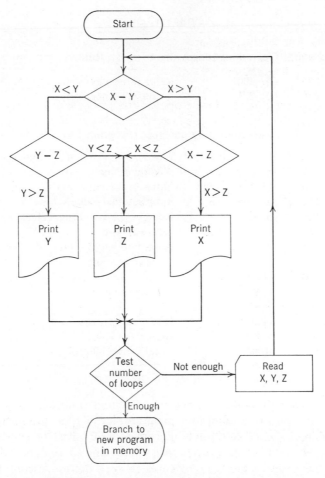

Figure 3-2.   Flow chart for finding largest of three numbers for repeated sets of X, Y, Z.

not carried out, the next instruction is performed which moves the calculations to a different program. In this way the computer need never stop operating, for part of the new program may be to read in more programs for later use. In fact, most large computers are kept operating continuously. Within a few minutes (or even seconds) it can perform a mathematical study, prepare a large table of data, perform a calculation on the recorded grades for all the students of a school, and so on. Each of these programs contains only a large number of steps like those just described and in terms of the computer are "all the same." The machine just keeps calculating and calculating with an amazing output of information.

Program 3-5.

Location	Instruction Operation-Address	Remark
075	60 200	Read three new values for X, Y,
076	60 201	and Z, respectively
077	60 202	
100⎫ 115⎭	see previous program steps (Program 3-4)	
116	10 203	Place initial value in accumulator
117	14 204	Add increment
120	30 203	Store as present count
121	15 205	Subtract final value
122	45 075	Read a new set of values and repeat loop
123	44 —	Branch to another program stored in the memory
200	(X)	Storage locations for the set of
201	(Y)	input numbers
202	(Z)	
203	00000	Initial value (and count)
204	00001	Increment value
205	01000	Final value (1000_8)

Repeated Solution Examples.   Since the repeated solution to a problem is so important a part of a computer program, let us look at a basic pattern for controlling a looped solution (Figure 3-3). The initialization steps reset counts to zero and set up proper test values and increment values. For example, the count value may be reset to zero before starting the computation. When the program is completed, the present count value is left as it is. Before the same procedure can be used again, the count must be reset to zero. It would therefore be best always to initialize to be sure that the program is set up as desired at the start. The computation is then carried out (equation solved or comparisons performed). Although this is the desired operation other steps must be performed for control. In the modifying steps new data may be read in, present values updated, and any count value incremented by a fixed amount. A test must now be performed to determine whether enough calculations have been performed. If there were enough, the test would instruct the computer to go on to a new program (or to halt). If not, the test would instruct the computer to go to the start of the computation (not initialization) to do another cycle or loop of steps. An example may help clarify this proce-

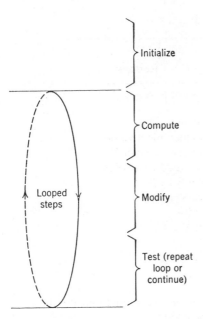

Figure 3-3. Form of program for repeated solution problems.

dure. Consider the solution of $Y = X^2$ for 100_8 values of X (Program 3-6).

The initialization steps reset the count to zero and read in the final value and increment value. These may be different each time the program is used. The program then calculates X^2 and prints X and Y ($= X^2$) for the compute operation. In the modify steps the increment value is added to the present count and stored as the new count value. If the new count value is less than the final value, the test instructs the program to repeat the loop. If the test for positive (46) is satisfied, the computer branches to a different program in the computer.

Another example is the solution of $Y = 20X^2 + 7X + 6$ for values of X from 0 to 10_8. A program to solve for Y is given in Program 3-7. The program is simple to follow and should require no detailed explanation. A few differences with the previous example should, however, be seen. The increment and final values are not read in but are always the same and are stored with the other program constants. This program is not as flexible and cannot be directly used for other final or increment values. A specific change in the constant of the program would be required instead of always having the program look for new values during initialization. Another difference is that the X value and count are the same. Thus when X is incremented it serves as both the new count value for the test and as the new X value on the next loop of the program. Finally, the end value was 11 rather than the indicated last value of 10. This value was

Program 3-6. $Y = X^2$.

Location	Instruction Operation-Address		Remark
200	10	600 ⎫	Set count to zero
201	30	300 ⎪ Initialize	
202	60	301 ⎪	Read final value
203	60	302 ⎭	Read increment value
204	60	250 ⎫	Read new value of X
205	10	250 ⎪	Clear – add value of X
206	20	250 ⎪ Compute	Multiply by X
207	30	251 ⎪	Store $X^2 (= Y)$
210	50	250 ⎪	Print X
211	50	251 ⎭	Print Y
212	10	300 ⎫	
213	14	302 ⎬ Modify	
214	30	300 ⎭	
215	15	301 ⎫	
216	46	— ⎬ Test	Exit to new program (if positive)
217	44	204 ⎭	Repeat loop
250	(X)		X storage
251	(Y)		Y storage
300	—		Count storage
301	—		Final value
302	—		Increment value
600	00000		Zero value

necessary because in this program X was updated before the test, and when it was equal to 10 the solution had been done on $X = 7$. To end after the solution with $X = 10$ requires using 11 as the final value, since X was incremented by 1 just before the test. Either of these two methods of setting up looped solutions may be used. It usually depends on the nature of the mathematical computation which is preferred.

Exercise 3-4.   Write a program for the following problem:

Compute $Y = X^3$ for values of X from 0 to 40_8. Print X and Y for each value of X.

Exercise 3-5.   Write a program to compute $Y = 3X + 17$ for values of X from 2 to 15_8, and print X and Y values for each value of X.

Program 3-7. $Y = 20X^2 + 7X + 6$

Location	Operation-Address			Remark
			Instruction	
000	10	115	Initialize	Reset count to zero
001	30	100		
002	10	100		
003	20	100		
004	20	110		
005	30	101		Store $20X^2$
006	10	100		Form 7X
007	20	111	Compute	
010	14	112		Add 6
011	14	101		Add $20X^2$
012	30	101		Store $Y (20X^2 + 7X + 6)$
013	50	100		Print X
014	50	101		Print Y
015	10	100		
016	14	113	Modify	Increment X by 1
017	30	100		
020	15	114		Subtract final value
021	47	—	Test	Exit to new program (if zero)
022	44	002		Repeat loop
100	(X)			X storage
101	(Y)			Y storage
110	00020			Constant 20_8
111	00007			Constant 7_8
112	00006			Constant 6_8
113	00001			Constant 1_8
114	00011			Final value (11_8)
115	00000			Constant 0_8

3-8.   Other Languages

Having considered machine language programming, it should be apparent that a long program will be tedious to write and will probably contain mistakes because of the large amount of numbers handled. Because of this, computer users in the middle 1950s developed problem-oriented languages to allow writing the instructions in a form of our every-day language. These languages (FORTRAN, ALGOL, etc.) must, however, be converted into machine language for use in the computer. The job of converting this "Source" program to an "Object" program (in machine language) is called *compilation* and is carried out using the computer. In other words, rather than writing out a machine language program, the program is written in FORTRAN and is compiled into machine language by the computer, thus providing a machine language program to be run. In all cases the program that actually operates the computer is in machine language.

Summary

This chapter covered the basic language of programming a digital computer. The instructions to the computer are numbers which are interpreted by the computer into two basic parts, operation code (op code), and instruction address (operand). The computer program directs the machine step by step, but branch command may be used to cause repeated use of steps. A number of examples were presented to show what programs are like and how they are used to solve problems.

An essential factor of this chapter is that the computer only performs simple operations and that the programmer "solves" the problem. The computer then follows the program stored in memory to effect the solution and put it on paper, display it, put it on tape or disk, and so on.

PROBLEMS

§3-7   1. Write a program to solve the equation $Z = 6X^2 - 7X - 12$ for values of X from 0 to 25_8 inclusive, and print X.

2. Write a program to solve the equation $X = 3Y^3 + 5Y^2 - 7Y + 125$ for values of Y from 10_8 to 45_8, inclusive, and print Y, X.

3. Write a program to compute and print the integer numbers from 1 to 100_8.

4. Write a program to compute and print the values of $N = 6M^3 + 3M + 2$ for odd integer values of M from 1 to 50_8.

5. Write a program to place the largest of two numbers stored in locations 100 and 101 in location 200 and the smallest in location 300. Start your program at location 000.

6. Write a program to determine whether any two of the numbers stored in locations 100 to 105 are the same. Print 0 if none are the same, print 1 if any two are the same.

7. Write a program to determine whether all the numbers stored in locations 200 to 210 are the same. Print 1 if all are the same, print 0 otherwise.

8. Write a program to read ten numbers into locations 100 to 111 and then ten more numbers into locations 250 to 261.

9. Write a program to print out the ten consecutive numbers stored in locations 100 to 111 and then the ten consecutive numbers in locations 250 to 261.

0100

Codes

Coding of information is a means of specifying characters (numeric or alphabetic, for example) using other symbols. Codes have been used for security reasons, so that others will not be able to read the message. In computers, however, codes provide a means of specifying these characters using only the 1 and 0 binary symbols available. In addition, the choice among the numerous binary codes depends on the function or use they are to serve. Some codes are suitable when arithmetic operations are being performed. Others are good because they are highly efficient— giving more information using fewer bits (a bit is a binary digit, 1 or 0). Of continuing importance are the codes that allow for error detection or correction—codes that enable the computer to determine whether a character which was coded and transmitted is received correctly and, if there is an error, to correct it. As coding itself is a detailed subject, only some of the more familiar codes are considered here.

4-1. Binary-Coded Decimal (BCD) — 8421 Code

A basic code to consider is called Binary-Coded Decimal, or BCD. It uses the binary number system to specify the decimal numbers 0 to 9. Since BCD numbers are written using 1's and 0's it is a code. Table 4-1 specifies the BCD code characters.

Notice that the code requires using a four-place (four-bit) binary character to specify the one-digit decimal character. Obviously this code is much less efficient than the decimal system, but it has the advantage that it is in the 1, 0 language of the computer and may thus be used

69

Table 4-1. *BCD Code*

Decimal	Binary-Coded Decimal
0	0000
1	0001
2	0010
3	0011
4	0100
5	0101
6	0110
7	0111
8	1000
9	1001

in a computer. A few examples of how numbers are written with this code are

Decimal	BCD
22	0010 0010
35	0011 0101
671	0110 0111 0001
2579	0010 0101 0111 1001

As you see, each decimal digit requires its 4-bit binary-coded equivalent. BCD code requires more positions to specify a number than the decimal system. However, it is in binary notation and therefore extremely useful. Another point to recognize is that the position within the four bits of a number is important (as in any number system). The weighting of a position can be specified and is sometimes used to describe this coded form. The weight of the first (right-most) position is 2^0, or 1, the second 2^1, or 2, the third 2^2, or 4, and the fourth 2^3, or 8. Reading from left to right the weighting is 8-4-2-1, and the code is also called an 8421 code.

To help you to see clearly that this code (8421) is not the same as binary numbers, consider the following. Ten in binary is 1010. Ten in binary-coded decimal is 0001 0000. Sixteen in binary is 10000. In 8421 (BCD) code it is 0001 0110. See the difference? Actually, any confusion between the two is that the first nine numbers in BCD and binary are exactly the same. After that they are completely different. Try the next exercise for practice.

Exercise 4-1.   Write the following decimal numbers in BCD code.

(a) 275   (b) 362   (c) 9256

The main value of BCD coding is that it can be recognized and read easily by people. For example, compare binary and BCD by reading numbers in each form.

Decimal	Binary	BCD
141	10001101	0001 0100 0001
2179	100010000011	0010 0001 0111 1001

When it comes to using this coded form in arithmetic operations, however, additional difficulties are involved. See what happens when adding 8 and 7 in both forms (binary and BCD).

Decimal	Binary	BCD	
8	1000	1000	
+7	+0111	+0111	
15	1111	1111	not an acceptable character in BCD (15 is 0001 0101)

Special adders are needed to operate with the BCD code.

4-2.   Octal and Hexadecimal Codes

Although it is nice to use a decimal-based code such as BCD, since our desired operations are to be carried out on decimal data in most cases, the required conversion from BCD code to decimal and extra circuitry are detriments. The operations of addition and subtraction are more involved for BCD than straight binary calculations. Most modern computers operate in the natural binary base system. For example, if a computer has a memory capacity of 16 bits per location, a stored binary number would be written as

0110111011101110   (16-bit number)

Looking at the number does not do much for us. It is hard to read; one might easily mistake the positional value of a particular bit and its value in decimal would be tedious to obtain. To provide some improved way of expressing a binary number so that it can be read and recognized easily the octal or hexadecimal coding — actually nothing more than the conversions covered in Chapter 2, are used. For example, the IBM System 360 uses hexadecimal coding to represent numbers in that computer. The IBM 7090 on the other hand uses octal coding to represent numbers in a more convenient form. Although these codings are nothing more than the grouping procedures covered already, they will presently be considered as coded representations of natural binary numbers.

Octal Coding.   The octal coding of natural binary numbers only involves grouping the bits in threes. Consider a 24-bit number stored in a computer. A binary number such as

$$101 \ 011 \ 010 \ 100 \ 010 \ 111 \ 000 \ 110$$

can be read in octal as the number

$$101 \ 011 \ 010 \ 100 \ 010 \ 111 \ 000 \ 110$$
$$\downarrow \quad \downarrow \quad \downarrow \quad \downarrow \quad \downarrow \quad \downarrow \quad \downarrow \quad \downarrow$$
$$5 \quad 3 \quad 2 \quad 4 \quad 2 \quad 7 \quad 0 \quad 6$$

The PDP-8, having a memory of 12-bit capacity, refers to stored numbers as four octal digits. For example, the binary number

$$011 \ 110 \ 101 \ 110$$

is referred to as the octal number

$$011 \ 110 \ 101 \ 110$$
$$\downarrow \quad \downarrow \quad \downarrow \quad \downarrow$$
$$3 \quad 6 \quad 5 \quad 6$$

When a number is given in octal it can easily be related to the binary value of the number as follows.

$$(1763)_8 = (001 \ 111 \ 110 \ 011)_2 = (00111110011)_2$$

One important feature of the octal code (other than the ease of recognition and conversion to binary) is that numbers expressed as octal code are really straight (natural) binary numbers and may be mathematically manipulated. For example, octal 26 expressed in the octal code is 010 110, which can be read as binary 010110. The resulting binary number used as one 6-bit number, in this example, is a natural binary value numerically equivalent to octal 26. As a check converting both to decimal gives:

$$(26)_8 = 2 \times 8^1 + 6 \times 8^0 = 16 + 6 = (22)_{10}$$
$$(010110)_2 = 1 \times 2^4 + 0 \times 2^3 + 1 \times 2^2 + 1 \times 2^1 + 0 \times 2^0$$
$$= 16 + 4 + 2 = (22)_{10}$$

Recall that when using the 8421 BCD code the resulting binary number still had to be considered a 4-bit grouping even to carry out addition operations and a special adder would be needed. In octal coding the 3-bit grouping may be used to more easily express a binary number in octal form *but* here the resulting binary number may be considered a single number of many bits and it is then in natural binary form. In other words, for the lesser convenience of dealing with octal instead of decimal numbers we gain the advantage of ending up with natural binary numbers rather than some special form (as the 8421 coding).

Exercise 4-2.   Express the following octal numbers in binary form.

(a) 1025   (b) 01234567 (c) 7620

Hexadecimal Coding.   The hexadecimal coding performs exactly the same function as the octal coding. The only advantage is that four bits are expressed by a single character, the disadvantage is that new symbols must be used to represent the values of 1010 to 1111 in binary. Refer back to section 2-4 for the relations between binary and hexadecimal characters.

The IBM System 360, for example, uses an 8-bit grouping (called a *byte*). Thus, each byte can be considered as two hexadecimal characters. For example, the binary number

$$1010 \quad 0010$$

can be expressed in hexadecimal as

$$\begin{array}{cc} 1010 & 0010 \\ \downarrow & \downarrow \\ A & 2 \end{array}$$

Similarly, the hexadecimal number C7 can be expressed as

$$\begin{array}{cc} C & 7 \\ \downarrow & \downarrow \\ 1100 & 0111 = (11000111)_2 \end{array}$$

An IBM 1130 has a 16-bit memory *word*[1] size. Thus, a binary number such as

$$1011101001011000$$

is interpreted as the four-digit hexadecimal number

$$\begin{array}{cccc} 1011 & 1010 & 0101 & 1000 \\ \downarrow & \downarrow & \downarrow & \downarrow \\ B & A & 5 & 8 \end{array}$$

[1]A word or memory word is the bits in a location in the memory — in this case it is fixed at 16 bits.

Similarly, a hexadecimal number such as 507A is stored as the binary number

$$5 \quad 0 \quad 7 \quad A$$
$$\downarrow \quad \downarrow \quad \downarrow \quad \downarrow$$
$$0101 \ 0000 \ 0111 \ 1010 = (0101000001111010)_2.$$

Exercise 4-3.   Express the following numbers as indicated.

   (a) $(37A9)_{16} = (?)_2$ (b) $(10110110)_2 = (?)_{16}$

To show that a resulting binary number is the same as the hexadecimal value consider the following example.

$$(3D)_{16} = 3 \times 16^1 + D \times 16^0 = 3 \times 16 + 14 \times 1 = (62)_{10}$$

$$3 \quad D$$
$$\downarrow \quad \downarrow$$
$$0011 \ 1110 \rightarrow (00111110)_2 = 1 \times 2^5 + 1 \times 2^4 + 1 \times 2^3 + 1 \times 2^2 + 1 \times 2^1 + 0 \times 2^0$$
$$= 32 + 16 + 8 + 4 + 2 + 0 = (62)_{10}$$

4-3.   Parity in Codes

Bit Parity.   Error detection and/or correction is a growing area of study and application in digital data transmission. A very popular means of detecting an error is the use of parity bits. Some magnetic tapes and disks, for example, have parity detection coding to improve the accuracy of reading from the tape or disk into a computer or vice versa. Parity can be either *odd* or *even*, and the addition of a parity bit (binary 1 or 0) will make the total number of 1's in a code character either an odd number or an even number, respectively. For illustrative purposes the 8421 BCD code will be modified by the addition of a parity bit. This bit will be added to the right of the 1 position.

In *even parity* the added parity bit will make the *total number* of 1s an *even* amount.

In *odd parity* the added parity bit will make the *total number* of 1s an *odd* amount.

When a code word is received it is checked for parity (even or odd being previously chosen) and is accepted as correct if it passes the test. Table 4-2 lists the BCD code, BCD with even parity and BCD with odd parity. Observe that the parity bit is opposite for the different parity types.

Table 4-2.   *BCD Code with Parity*

Decimal	BCD Code	BCD with Odd Parity	BCD with Even Parity
0	0000	0000 1 or 00001	0000 0 or 00000
1	0001	0001 0 or 00010	0001 1 or 00011
2	0010	0010 0 or 00100	0010 1 or 00101
3	0011	0011 1 or 00111	0011 0 or 00110
4	0100	0100 0 or 01000	0100 1 or 01001
5	0101	0101 1 or 01011	0101 0 or 01010
6	0110	0110 1 or 01101	0110 0 or 01100
7	0111	0111 0 or 01110	0111 1 or 01111
8	1000	1000 0 or 10000	1000 1 or 10001
9	1001	1001 1 or 10011	1001 0 or 10010

Example 4-1.   See whether you can determine an error (or not) in the following parity-coded BCD words.

	Word	Parity Bit	Parity Type
(a)	1001	0	odd parity
(b)	1000	0	odd parity
(c)	0001	0	even parity
(d)	1010	0	even parity
(e)	0110	1	odd parity

Examples (a) and (c) are incorrect and (b) and (e) are correct. Example (d) is incorrect only because it is not a BCD code character. The parity bit is, however, correct for even parity.

Parity bits are used elsewhere than in the BCD code. If a set of miscellaneous words are sent with a parity bit added, the parity bit is chosen as described above.

Example 4-2.   See if you can determine whether an error is present in the following.

	Word	Parity Bit	Parity Type
(a)	0110111101	1	even parity
(b)	1101110100	0	odd parity
(c)	1110111011	0	odd parity
(d)	1011011100	0	even parity
(e)	1010111010	1	odd parity

Examples (b) and (c) are incorrect; (a), (d), and (e) are correct. Getting back to BCD coding, here are a few more correct examples.

(f)   decimal 57 is   0101 1   0111 0   with odd parity bit per digit
(g)   decimal 79 is   0111 1   1001 0   with even parity bit per digit

Exercise 4-4.   Write the correct coded form using BCD with the indicated parity.

(a)   Decimal 95 with even parity bit per digit
(b)   Decimal 7986 with odd parity bit per digit
(c)   Decimal 605 with odd parity bit per digit.

Word Parity.   Using bit parity it is possible to determine or detect a single error occuring. It should be clear that more than one error occuring may not be detected by this method. When using bit parity it is possible that quite infrequently a single bit may be misread by the equipment and such an error will then be detected since the parity check of the number will fail. When the equipment is badly malfunctioning it will probably be quite noticeable in the misoperation resulting. If, however, only a single bit error occurs, it might go unnoticed if not for the inclusion of bit parity. Paper tape units often include a parity bit so that the numbers read into the computer can be checked to be sure that no punched hole was mis-read as could occasionally happen even in a well-operating unit.

Magnetic tape units also use parity to allow error detection. With magnetic tape, however, it is even more likely that a small section of the tape may not magnetize as well, or that a piece of dirt gets on the tape surface causing a reading error of a single bit. It would be quite helpful not only to *detect* the error but to be able to *correct* the error.

Up to now we have described the data and parity information representation when the data is correct. Let us now see how a single error is detected *and* corrected using bit and word parity. Some data words are listed below. The right-most bit of each word is the odd parity bit and the last word is an odd parity word, which makes each column of bits have odd parity.

Remember now, the computer cannot look back at the correct data to spot the error. It only has the received data to look at. It must first determine that an error does exist and then correct it using only the data received. The procedure used by the computer is to do a parity check of *each* word and of *each* column.

Word parity is a scheme which allows just that. It enables detecting *and* correcting the single-bit error. Figure 4-1 shows a representation of binary data stored on a magnetic tape. Dark spots are 1's and light spots are 0's. A block of words is shown, each of eight bits (one of which is the parity bit). There are seven words of data indicated and an additional

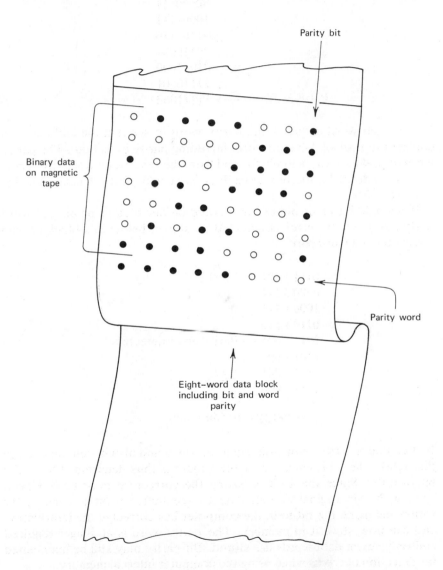

Figure 4-1.   Section of magnetic tape showing word parity operation.

parity word, which allows for the error correction. The same data is listed in binary form below.

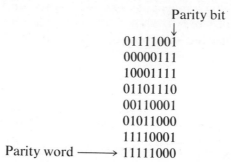

Parity bit
↓
01111001
00000111
10001111
01101110
00110001
01011000
11110001
Parity word ———→ 11111000

Check each word including the parity word to see that the odd parity is correct (number of 1-bits in word, including parity bit is odd). The parity word (last value) was actually formed from the seven data words by generating a bit to make the bits in each *column* odd parity. Check that this is also correct.

If a single bit error did occur it could be detected using bit and word parity. A single bit error is detected as shown below in a block of data having bit and word parity.

```
0111 1 001
0000 0 111
1000 1 111
0110 1 110
0011 1 001  ← Parity error detected
0101 1 000
1111 0 001
1111 1 000
          ↑
     Parity error detected
```

Notice that a parity error is detected in row 5 and also in column 4 (from the right). The 1-bit enclosed by the square is thus determined to be the bit in error. Since the 1-bit is wrong the correct bit must be 0. Check back with the original correct data to see that a 0 bit is correct. By simply changing the bit to 0, the computer has corrected the information and can now store it in memory. The parity word is no longer required and only seven data words are stored. Bit parity may still be maintained for detection of errors when using the computer internal memory.

Exercise 4-5.   Detect and correct any error in the following information which contains an odd parity bit and odd parity word.

$$10011$$
$$10111$$
$$01000$$
$$10000$$
$$10011 \leftarrow \text{Parity word}$$
$$\uparrow$$
Parity bit

4-4.   Excess-Three, Biquinary, and Other BCD Codes

Although the 8421 code is the most popular BCD code and is usually what is meant if one refers only to "BCD Code," there are many other codes using binary digits to represent the decimal digits 0 to 9. A number of 4-bit and 5-bit codes, a 7-bit (biquinary) code, and a 10-bit (ring counter) code will be presented.

Excess-Three Code.   Excess-three code, a modified form of BCD, is shown in Table 4-3 for the decimal numbers 0 to 9. If you compare BCD and excess-three carefully, it will become clear what the difference is and how excess-three is derived. As the name implies, each coded character in the excess-three code is three larger than in BCD. Thus six (or 0110) is written 1001, which is nine. It is only nine in BCD, though. In excess-three code 1001 is six! Do not make the mistake of forgetting the excess three.

Table 4-3.   *Excess-Three Code*

Decimal	BCD	Excess-Three
0	0000	0011
1	0001	0100
2	0010	0101
3	0011	0110
4	0100	0111
5	0101	1000
6	0110	1001
7	0111	1010
8	1000	1011
9	1001	1100

Here are a few examples of the code.

Decimal	Excess-Three
2	0101
25	0101 1000
629	1001 0101 1100
3271	0110 0101 1010 0100

The excess-three code provides a modification to the BCD code, enabling arithmetic operations to be implemented more easily. An example of how excess-three helps in the arithmetic operation is

$$
\begin{array}{rcl}
3 & & 0110 \\
+9 & & 1100 \\
\hline
12 & 1 & 0010 \\
& 0011 & 0011 \leftarrow \text{add 3 (to each digit position)} \\
\hline
& 0100 & 0101
\end{array}
$$

Read 0100 0101 or 12 (in excess-three).

There are a few special rules to follow in the addition (as the adding of 3 to each digit position in the example just given), but these steps are automatic in a computer and easy to implement, making excess-three more desirable for arithmetic operations. Recognition is poorer than BCD, but it is still easier than straight binary for large numbers. Try the following problem in writing excess-three code.

Exercise 4-6.   Write the following numbers in excess-three code.

(a) 279   (b) 301   (c) 2176

Recall that BCD is a weighted code; excess-three is not. A bit in the second position of BCD equals 2. In excess-three a bit present in any position does not indicate the addition of a numerical value to the number. For example, in BCD, 0100 is 4. Adding the 2-bit adds 2, making the number 0110 — two greater. In excess-three, 0111 is 4 and 1001 is 6 — no systematic numerical change.

Other 4-Bit Codes.   Although there are a number of 4-bit BCD codes presently popular, a few examples will be sufficient to show how they are used. The codes listed in Table 4-4 are all weighted codes — they have positional value as indicated by their name. The decimal value of any 4-bit binary number using a particular code can be easily obtained by adding the position values for those positions having binary 1 (or by

Table 4-4.   *Some Weighted 4-Bit BCD Codes*

Decimal	5421	2*421	7421	742$\overline{1}$
0	0000	0000	0000	0000
1	0001	0001	0001	0111
2	0010	0010	0010	0110
3	0011	0011	0011	0101
4	0100	0100	0100	0100
5	1000	1011	0101	1010
6	1001	1100	0110	1001
7	1010	1101	1000	1000
8	1011	1110	1001	1111
9	1100	1111	1010	1110

subtracting when a bar is present over the column designation). A few examples will show this clearly.

Example 4-3.   Convert the following 5421 code number into decimal:

$$0011 \quad 1000 \quad 1010$$

Solution: To show how the value has weighted significance the decimal value may be calculated as follows:

$$0011 = 0 \times 5 + 0 \times 4 + 1 \times 2 + 1 \times 1 = 3$$
$$1000 = 1 \times 5 + 0 \times 4 + 0 \times 2 + 0 \times 1 = 5$$
$$1010 = 1 \times 5 + 0 \times 4 + 1 \times 2 + 0 \times 1 = 7$$

Referring to Table 4-4 we can check that the answer is

$$(0011 \quad 1000 \quad 1010)_{5421} = (357)_{10}$$

Example 4-4.   Convert the following 2*421 code number into decimal:

$$1111 \quad 1101 \quad 0100$$

Solution: Using the weighted position values:

$$1111 = 1 \times 2 + 1 \times 4 + 1 \times 2 + 1 \times 1 = 9$$
$$1101 = 1 \times 2 + 1 \times 4 + 0 \times 2 + 1 \times 1 = 7$$
$$0100 = 0 \times 2 + 1 \times 4 + 0 \times 2 + 0 \times 1 = 4$$

(Check answer using Table 4-4.)

$$(1111 \, 1101 \quad 0100)_{2*421} = (974)_{10}$$

Note: 2* significance is to differentiate that position from the one marked 2 although, as the example shows, both have positional value of two.

Example 4-5. Convert the following 7421 code number into decimal:

$$1000 \quad 1001 \quad 1010$$

Solution: $1000 = 1 \times 7 + 0 \times 4 + 0 \times 2 + 0 \times 1 = 7$

$1001 = 1 \times 7 + 0 \times 4 + 0 \times 2 + 1 \times 1 = 8$

$1010 = 1 \times 7 + 0 \times 4 + 1 \times 2 + 0 \times 1 = 9$

$(1000 \quad 1001 \quad 1010)_{7421} = (789)_{10}$

Example 4-6. Convert the following $74\bar{2}\bar{1}$ code number into decimal:

$$0101 \quad 0110 \quad 1111$$

Solution: Since this is also a weighted code its positional values (corresponding to 1-bits in the code number) are summed to obtain the decimal value. The one difference here is that the columns $\bar{2}$ and $\bar{1}$ must be *subtracted* instead of added when a 1-bit occurs.

$$0101 = 0 \times 7 + 1 \times 4 - 0 \times 2 - 1 \times 1 = 3$$
$$0110 = 0 \times 7 + 1 \times 4 - 1 \times 2 - 0 \times 1 = 2$$
$$1111 = 1 \times 7 + 1 \times 4 - 1 \times 2 - 1 \times 1 = 8$$
$$(0101 \quad 0110 \quad 1111)_{74\bar{2}\bar{1}} = (328)_{10}$$

Exercise 4-7. Convert the following numbers in the indicated code forms into decimal.

(a)   5421 code: 1011 1100 0100
(b)   2*421 code: 0100 1101 1110
(c)   7421 code: 1010 0001 0110
(d) $74\bar{2}\bar{1}$ code: 1111 0100 1000

Self-Complementing Codes.   Two self-complementing codes representing the decimal digits 0 to 9 have already been presented – the unweighted excess-three code and the weighted 2*421 code. There are other self-complementing codes but these two will show the basic property of such a code form. Before going into the code properties we must consider what is meant by *NINE's complement*. Recall that in Chapter 2 the concept of ONE's complements was presented. Using the same idea for decimal numbers, a NINE's complement can be defined as follows:

A NINE's complement of a decimal digit d is the value computed by $9 - d$ (or in other words, the sum of a digit d and its NINE's complement adds up to the sum nine).

Example 4-7.   Calculate the NINE's complement of the numbers:

$$\text{(a) 6} \qquad \text{(b) 38} \qquad \text{(c) 725}$$

(a) $d = 6$
   NINE's complement $= 9 - d = 9 - 6 = 3$

(b) $d = 38$
   NINE's complement $= 99 - 38 = 61$

(c) $d = 725$
   NINE's complement $= 999 - 725 = 274$

In a self-complementing code if the 1's and 0's are interchanged in the code group representing the decimal digit d, the code group of $9 - d$ is obtained.

Referring to Table 4-4 the code group for decimal 0 is 000 and for the NINE's complement of 0, $9 - 0 = 9$, it is 1111. Some other comparisons are provided below.

d	2*421 Code	$9 - d$	2*421 Code
2	0010	7	1101
6	1100	3	0011
5	1011	4	0100

Notice in the corresponding 2*421 code values that the 1's and 0's are interchanged. This complementing property of the code digits makes it interesting for certain arithmetic operations such as the excess-three in simplifying addition-subtraction operations.

To see that the excess-three is also a self-complementing code consider a few examples.

d	Excess-Three	$9 - d$	Excess-Three
2	0101	7	1010
8	1011	1	0100
4	0111	5	1000

Exercise 4-8.   Prepare a complete table of the 2*421 code and excess-three code to show that for all digits the codes are self-complementing.

5-Bit Codes.   We have already encountered a 5-bit code when adding the parity bit to the BCD code word. In that case the extra bit allowed error detection of single errors. Although only four bits are needed to encode all digits from 0 to 9, the use of more bits usually allows some extra feature in the code, making it easier to operate with or providing code error detection and/or correction features. A few examples of 5-bit codes are listed in Table 4-5.

Table 4-5.   *5-Bit BCD Codes*

Decimal	2-Out-of-5	51111	Shift-Counter
0	00011	00000	00000
1	00101	00001	00001
2	00110	00011	00011
3	01001	00111	00111
4	01010	01111	01111
5	01100	10000	11111
6	10001	11000	11110
7	10010	11100	11100
8	10100	11110	11000
9	11000	11111	10000

The 2-out-of-5 code is unweighted and has the interesting property that there are two and only two 1's in each code group. This allows easy error detection and has been used in telephone and communications operation.

The 51111 code is a weighted code and additionally is self-complementing (check Table 4-5 to see that this is so). Notice the pattern of the code that from 1 to 4 a 1 is "pushed" in from the right on each successive count, and that from 5 to 9 a 1 is "pushed" in from the left. This pattern makes it easier for operation with electronic circuitry.

The shift-counter code (or Johnson code) is a nonweighted code that again is easily operated on with electronic circuitry because of its pattern. Notice that from 1 to 5 a 1 is "pushed or shifted" in from the right and from 6 to 9 that a 0 is shifted in from the right on each successive count.

Example 4-8.   Express the decimal number 285 in the following codes:

(a)   2-out-of-5 code
(b)   51111 code
(c)   Johnson code

Solution: Referring to Table 4-5:

(a) $(285)_{10} = 00110\ 10100\ 01100$
(b) $(285)_{10} = 00011\ 11110\ 10000$
(c) $(285)_{10} = 00011\ 11000\ 11111$

Exercise 4-9.   Convert the following code groups into decimal:

(a)   2-out-of-5:   01001 10010
(b)   51111   :   01111 11110
(c)   Johnson   :   11100 00111

More Than 5-Bit Codes.   Adding still more than the required four bits to encode the decimal digits 0 to 9 allows code features providing easily detected errors or ease of operation with the code groups. Two such codes are the 7-bit biquinary code and the ring-counter code. These are isted in Table 4-6.

Table 4-6.   *Biquinary and Ring-Counter Codes*

Decimal	Biquinary 50 43210	Ring-Counter 9876543210
0	01 00001	0000000001
1	01 00010	0000000010
2	01 00100	0000000100
3	01 01000	0000001000
4	01 10000	0000010000
5	10 00001	0000100000
6	10 00010	0001000000
7	10 00100	0010000000
8	10 01000	0100000000
9	10 10000	1000000000

The biquinary code is quite interesting. *Bi* meaning *two* and *quinary* meaning *five*, the code is seen to contain seven bits with only two bits being 1 in each code group. The code is weighted as indicated by the positional values, which is also why the code is called a 50 43210 code. The biquinary code has a number of interesting features. Error detection is possible since there are exactly two 1-bits in each code group. Any more or less indicates an error. The code group for zero contains 1-bits so that the case of bits being lost resulting in the more usual code group of all zeros is not interpreted as the decimal value zero. When a decimal zero is transmitted, there still are two 1-bits that must be present in the code group. Notice additionally, that not only must there be only two 1-bits, but that one of these must be in the two left positions and the other in the five right-most positions of the number. Thus, some double errors may also be detected.

Example 4-9.   See whether you can detect any errors in the following set of biquinary code words.

	Biquinary		Decimal
(a)		01 10001	4
(b)		01 10010	5
(c)		10 10101	6
(d)		11 00010	6
(e)	01 01000	01 00010	31
(f)	10 10000	10 10000	99
(g)		01 00001	0

Examples (a) to (d) are incorrect; (e) to (g) are correct.

Exercise 4-10.   Write the following numbers in biquinary code:

(a) 56   (b) 731   (c) 68.

Ring-Counter Code.   The ring-counter code is quite simple to recognize and most easy to decode using electronic circuits. Referring to Table 4-5 there is only one 1-bit in each code group of ten bits. The decimal value is simply obtained by counting over from the right to the 1-bit, starting with the right-most position as zero. As will be shown later in the text, a ring-counter circuit electronically provides for moving a 1-bit around in a closed ringlike connection so that after the 1-bit gets to the left-most position, the next count brings the 1-bit around to the zero position to repeat the count from 0 to 9. Although the code requires as many as ten positions, the ease of detecting errors with the code and of operating electronic circuits to implement the code makes it quite attractive.

4-5. Gray Code

Gray code is used largely with optical or mechanical shaft position encoders. It is a nonweighted code and only a single bit changes between each successive word. It is used on a type of code wheel that has successive positions which changes the binary data by only one bit (the Gray code allows ambiguity of only one place). This feature will be expanded in the discussion of input/output equipment (Chapter 13). For the present, the code itself is our main consideration.

Because there are a large number of codes of, say, ten bits per word that can be formed where only one bit at a time changes, the selection of one particular code—called "Gray"—is of interest. The code form on the input piece of equipment is important in improving reading accuracy and in simplifying construction problems. Its use in the computer, however, presents great difficulties because of its nonweighted feature. Thus, the code would best be used if it were converted to a weighted code in the computer—the best one being straight binary. Gray code is particularly useful because of its one-bit-change external feature and the simplicity of converting it to binary form.

A listing of straight binary and the Gray code equivalent is given for decimal numbers 0 to 12 in Table 4-7. There is a Gray code for every possible binary number, so that the listing is only illustrative.

Table 4-7. *Gray Code for Decimals 0 to 12*

Decimal	Binary	Gray Code
0	0000	0000
1	0001	0001
2	0010	0011
3	0011	0010
4	0100	0110
5	0101	0111
6	0110	0101
7	0111	0100
8	1000	1100
9	1001	1101
10	1010	1111
11	1011	1110
12	1100	1010

Notice how only one bit changes between any two successive words in Gray code. This is not true in binary. In going from decimal 7 to 8, the binary changes all four bits, whereas the Gray code only changes one. In going from decimal 9 to 10, the binary changes from 1001 to 1010, where the 2^0 bit goes from a 1 to a 0 and the 2^1 goes from a 0 to a 1—two changes. In Gray the change of 1101 to 1111 has the 2^1 bit changing from 0 to 1—one change only. Since there are clearly defined rules for converting from Gray to binary or from binary to Gray, a description of these, with examples, will be considered next.

Gray to Binary Conversion.   In converting a Gray-coded word into binary code, the conversion must begin with the most significant bit (MSB) first. In binary the least significant bit (LSB) is the 2^0 bit and the MSB is the one of highest weight position (with four bits the 2^3). A binary number and its Gray-code equivalent is

$$\text{MSB}$$
$$\downarrow$$

Gray	1011010111001
Binary	1101100101110

where the MSB is on the left.

To convert from Gray code to binary the rules are as follows:

1. Start with the most significant bit (MSB) of Gray code word. Binary bit is the same as Gray bit up to and including the first 1.

2. Now use the Gray code bit as a control:
If 1, change the preceding binary digit to obtain present binary digit.
If 0, repeat the same binary digit.
Use rule (2) repeatedly for each Gray code bit to be converted.

Note: The bit being changed or repeated is *only in the binary word*, the Gray code bit acting as control.

To help impress these rules note the arrows in the following examples. Whenever a Gray code 1 appears the arrow signifies changing the preceding binary digit to obtain the present binary digit. Otherwise the binary digits are repeated.

Example 4-10. Convert the Gray code number 01011101 into binary.

Solution: Using rule (1):

Gray	0	1
	↓	↓
Binary	0	1

Binary same as Gray until and including first 1.

Using rule (2):

┌─Control bit indicates preceding binary digit of 1
should be repeated *in binary number.*

Gray	0	1	0
Binary	0	1	1

Using rule (2):

┌─Control bit indicates preceding binary digit of 1
should be changed (to 0).

Gray	0	1	0	1
Binary	0	1	1	0

Using rule (2):

Control bit indicates preceding binary digit of 0 should be changed (to 1).

Gray   0 1 0 1 1

Binary   0 1 1 0 1

Using rule (2):

Control bit indicates preceding binary digit of 1 should be changed (to 0).

Gray   0 1 0 1 1 1

Binary   0 1 1 0 1 0

Using rule (2):

Control bit indicates preceding binary digit of 0 should be repeated *in binary number*.

Gray   0 1 0 1 1 1 0
Binary   0 1 1 0 1 0 0

Using rule (2):

Control bit indicates preceding binary digit of 0 should be changed (to 1).

Gray   0 1 0 1 1 1 0 1

Binary   0 1 1 0 1 0 0 1

The complete conversion can be shown as follows
Gray   0 1 0 1 1 1 0 1

Binary   0 1 1 0 1 0 0 1

(In fact, rule 1 could be considered the same as rule 2 if we assume that the first Gray bit of 1 means to change the binary digit from a starting value of 0 to 1).

Example 4-11.   Convert the Gray code number 10101100111 into binary.

Solution: *Gray*   1 0 1 0 1 1 0 0 1 1 1

              Binary   1 1 0 0 1 0 0 0 1 0 1

Example 4-12.   Convert the Gray code number 1111000101011 into binary.

Solution: Gray   1 1 1 1 0 0 0 1 0 1 0 1 1

              Binary   1 0 1 0 0 0 0 1 1 0 0 1 0

Exercise 4-11.   Convert the following Gray code words into binary:

(a)   1001110101101
(b)   10101010101
(c)   01110111011110
(d)   11111111

Binary to Gray Conversion.   The procedure for converting a binary word into Gray code form is somewhat easier to state.

Starting with the MSB of the binary number compare each pair of succeeding bits:

If they are the same place a 0 in the Gray code word.

If they are different place a 1 in the Gray code word. (Compare the first binary digit to 0 to start.)

This action is also the same as adding the pair of bits by modulo-2 addition.[2]

In the examples below the arrows are used to show which two binary digits are being compared (or added, modulo-2) and the resulting bit in the Gray code word.

Example 4-13.   Convert the following binary numbers into Gray code:

(a)   011010111101
(b)   111010101110

Solution:

(a)   Binary   0 1 1 0 1 0 1 1 1 1 0 1

Gray   0 1 0 1 1 1 1 0 0 0 1 1

(b)   Binary   1 1 1 0 1 0 1 0 1 1 1 0

Gray   1 0 0 1 1 1 1 1 1 0 0 1

Exercise 4-12.   Convert the following binary numbers into Gray code:

(a)   011010111101
(b)   100011110110
(c)   010011011100

---

[2]Modulo-2 addition is defined by $0+0=0$
$0+1=1$
$1+0=1$
$1+1=0$

Notice that if the bits added are the same, the result is 0 and if different, it is 1 as required by the rule stated above.

4-6.   Alphanumeric Codes

In addition to those binary codes covered up to now which represent the decimal digits 0 to 9, there are a large number of binary codes used to represent both alphabetic and numeric characters. These codes are called *alphanumeric* or sometimes *alphameric*. Different codes may be used to represent alphanumeric data stored on paper tape, punched card, or magnetic tape for use by a line printer or typewriter or just for internal storage in the computer memory. Of growing importance is the ASCII (American Standard Code for Information Interchange) which has become a standard code for use by input/output (I/O) equipment. Another I/O oriented code is EBCDIC (Extended Binary Coded Decimal Interchange Code). These and other alphanumeric codes will be presented in this section.

Octal Code.   As an example of a code used to represent alphanumeric characters consider the octal code listed in Table 4-8. A two-digit octal number is used to represent each alphameric character. Using octal digits from 00 to 77_8 allows 64_{10} different characters to be represented. The particular example is an alphameric code representing the characters used on an electric typewriter connected to the computer. Since each octal digit is the same as three binary digits, the code is either considered as two octal digits or six binary digits.

If a typewriter is used to provide alphameric data as input to the computer, each time a key is pressed a two-digit octal number (or six-digit binary number) is transmitted electrically into the computer. As an example the message

BEGIN TEST.

would appear as the following octal data to the computer

B	E	G	I	N		T	E	S	T	.
22	25	27	31	36	20	46	25	45	46	56

In this way the computer stores binary digits (represented above in octal form) to represent alphanumeric data in the computer.

Exercise 4-13.   Using the octal code of Table 4-8 encode the following message: DIGITAL COMPUTER 1234.

It should be clear that different computers may assign different alphanumeric characters to the two-digit octal code. Some machines use a two-digit hexadecimal code to represent alphanumeric data. As an attempt to

Table 4-8.   *Octal Alphanumeric Code*

Character	6-Bit Code (in octal)	Character	6-Bit Code (in octal)
0	00	tab	40
1	01	N	41
2	02	O	42
3	03	P	43
4	04	Q	44
5	05	R	45
6	06	S	46
7	07	T	47
8	10	U	50
9	11	V	51
-	12	W	52
;	13	X	53
/	14	Y	54
!	15	Z	55
'	16	.	56
=	17	skip line	57
space	20	)	60
A	21	±	61
B	22	@	62
C	23	#	63
D	24	$	64
E	25	%	65
F	26	¢	66
G	27	&	67
H	30	*	70
I	31	(	71
J	32	—	72
K	33	:	73
L	34	?	74
M	35	°	75
,	36	,,	76
carriage return	37	+	77

standardize the binary coding used, the ASCII and EBCDIC codes to be discussed have been widely accepted.

ASCII Input/Output Code.   A standardized code which has been widely accepted by industry is the ASCII code — American Standards Code for Information Interchange. The code is an 8-bit code and allows representation of both lower-case and upper-case alphabetic characters, special characters (e.g., $*$, $+$, $=$) and over 30 command or control operations (e.g., start of message, end of message, carriage return, line feed).

Table 4-9 lists the ASCII code for the decimal digits, alphabetic characters, and a few special characters. The ASCII numbering convention calls for a sequence from left to right, so that bit position 7 is the high-order position. The same code representation may be used with punched paper tape, magnetic tape, magnetic disk, high-speed printers, some tele-

Table 4-9.   *ASCII Code (partial listing)*

Character	7	6	5	X	4	3	2	1	Hex.	Character	7	6	5	X	4	3	2	1	Hex.
0	0	1	0	1	0	0	0	0	50	@	1	0	1	0	0	0	0	0	A0
1	0	1	0	1	0	0	0	1	51	A	1	0	1	0	0	0	0	1	A1
2	0	1	0	1	0	0	1	0	52	B	1	0	1	0	0	0	1	0	A2
3	0	1	0	1	0	0	1	1	53	C	1	0	1	0	0	0	1	1	A3
4	0	1	0	1	0	1	0	0	54	D	1	0	1	0	0	1	0	0	A4
5	0	1	0	1	0	1	0	1	55	E	1	0	1	0	0	1	0	1	A5
6	0	1	0	1	0	1	1	0	56	F	1	0	1	0	0	1	1	0	A6
7	0	1	0	1	0	1	1	1	57	G	1	0	1	0	0	1	1	1	A7
8	0	1	0	1	1	0	0	0	58	H	1	0	1	0	1	0	0	0	A8
9	0	1	0	1	1	0	0	1	59	I	1	0	1	0	1	0	0	1	A9
:	0	1	0	1	1	0	1	0	5A	J	1	0	1	0	1	0	1	0	AA
;	0	1	0	1	1	0	1	1	5B	K	1	0	1	0	1	0	1	1	AB
<	0	1	0	1	1	1	0	0	5C	L	1	0	1	0	1	1	0	0	AC
=	0	1	0	1	1	1	0	1	5D	M	1	0	1	0	1	1	0	1	AD
>	0	1	0	1	1	1	1	0	5E	N	1	0	1	0	1	1	1	0	AE
?	0	1	0	1	1	1	1	1	5F	O	1	0	1	0	1	1	1	1	AF
blank	0	1	0	0	0	0	0	0	40	P	1	0	1	1	0	0	0	0	B0
!	0	1	0	0	0	0	0	1	41	Q	1	0	1	1	0	0	0	1	B1
"	0	1	0	0	0	0	1	0	42	R	1	0	1	1	0	0	1	0	B2
#	0	1	0	0	0	0	1	1	43	S	1	0	1	1	0	0	1	1	B3
$	0	1	0	0	0	1	0	0	44	T	1	0	1	1	0	1	0	0	B4
%	0	1	0	0	0	1	0	1	45	U	1	0	1	1	0	1	0	1	B5
&	0	1	0	0	0	1	1	0	46	V	1	0	1	1	0	1	1	0	B6
'	0	1	0	0	0	1	1	1	47	W	1	0	1	1	0	1	1	1	B7
(	0	1	0	0	1	0	0	0	48	X	1	0	1	1	1	0	0	0	B8
)	0	1	0	0	1	0	0	1	49	Y	1	0	1	1	1	0	0	1	B9
*	0	1	0	0	1	0	1	0	4A	Z	1	0	1	1	1	0	1	0	BA
+	0	1	0	0	1	0	1	1	4B	[	1	0	1	1	1	0	1	1	BB
,	0	1	0	0	1	1	0	0	4C	\	1	0	1	1	1	1	0	0	BC
−	0	1	0	0	1	1	0	1	4D	]	1	0	1	1	1	1	0	1	BD
.	0	1	0	0	1	1	1	0	4E	↑	1	0	1	1	1	1	1	0	BE
/	0	1	0	0	1	1	1	1	4F	←	1	0	1	1	1	1	1	1	BF

type equipment, and so on. Examples of these are provided in the section on input/output units (Chapter 13).

Using eight bits allows as many as 2^8 or 256 code combinations, which is more than enough to provide for the lower-case alphabetic letters, upper-case alphabetic letters, numerals, special characters, and a number of control signals. If the alphanumeric data is read from a magnetic tape, for example, each character enters the computer as the eight-bit ASCII code so that the message

START 1.

would be received as the binary

S	T	A	R	T	1	.
10110011	10110100	10100001	10110010	10110100	01010001	01001110

Instead of writing 8 binary digits for each character it would be easier to use the hexadecimal form—expressing the 8-bit code by two hexadecimal digits. Thus the message above could also be considered as the following hexadecimal data

S	T	A	R	T	1	.
B3	B4	A1	B2	B4	51	4E

which is received as 14 hexadecimal digits rather than 56 binary digits.

In other words, alphanumeric data may be stored as an eight-binary digit word (or byte) which is the same as a two-digit hexadecimal word. Each alphanumeric character held in the computer memory then requires a two-hexadecimal digit location (or one byte).

The 4321 bits were purposely chosen as the BCD code form for the digits 0 to 9. By stripping off the 765X bits the computer need save only four bits in BCD form to represent decimal digits. If the standard word length is eight bits as indicated, the computer can handle decimal digits internally by grouping two four-bit BCD digits in a single word. This action is called "packing," since each word holds more than the usual single value. Consider Example 4-14.

Example 4-14.   Packing of two ASCII digits into one eight-bit word.

The number 29 represented as 0 1 0 1 0 0 1 0 0 1 0 1 1 0 0 1 in the input/output units can be regrouped in the computer as follows

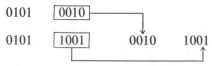

which is an eight-bit word of two decimal digits.

Since data is handled by byte instead of by bit within the computer the eight-bit byte could be used to represent either a single ASCII character as it comes into the computer memory (after packing has been carried out).

Exercise 4-14. Express the messages below in ASCII code as both eight-bit binary and two-digit hexadecimal.

(a) DIGITAL

(b) DIGIT329

EBCDIC Code. A second eight-bit code that has also been used to represent alphanumeric data is the Extended Binary Coded Decimal Information Code or EBCDIC. It is a different code form from ASCII only in the code grouping for the different alphanumeric characters. Table 4-10 lists the EBCDIC code in both binary and hexadecimal form. Using

Table 4-10. *EBCDIC Code (partial listing)*

Binary 0123	4567	Hex.	Alphanumeric Character	Binary 0123	4567	Hex.	Alphanumeric Character
·	·	·	·		1011	8B	
·	·	·	·		1100	8C	
·	·	·	·		1101	8D	
0100	1010	4A	¢		1110	8E	
0100	1011	4B	. (period)		1111	8F	
0100	1100	4C	<	1001	0000	90	
0100	1101	4D	(		0001	91	j
0100	1110	4E	+		0010	92	k
0100	1111	4F	| (logical or)		0011	93	l
0101	0000	50	&		0100	94	m
·	·	·	·		0101	95	n
·	·	·	·		0110	96	o
·	·	·	·		0111	97	p
1000	0000	80			1000	98	q
	0001	81	a		1001	99	r
	0010	82	b	·	·	·	·
	0011	83	c	·	·	·	·
	0100	84	d	·	·	·	·
	0101	85	e	1010	0000	A0	
	0110	86	f		0001	A1	
	0111	87	g		0010	A2	s
	1000	88	h		0011	A3	t
	1001	89	i		0100	A4	u
	1010	8A			0101	A5	v

Table 4-10 (*cont.*)

Binary 0123	4567	Hex.	Alphanumeric Character	Binary 0123	4567	Hex.	Alphanumeric Character
1010	0110	A6	w	1101	1001	D9	R
	0111	A7	x	.	.	.	.
	1000	A8	y	.	.	.	.
	1001	A9	z	.	.	.	.
	1010	AA		1110	0000	E0	
	.	.	.		0001	E1	
	.	.	.		0010	E2	S
	.	.	.		0011	E3	T
1100	0000	C0			0100	E4	U
	0001	C1	A		0101	E5	V
	0010	C2	B		0110	E6	W
	0011	C3	C		0111	E7	X
	0100	C4	D		1000	E8	Y
	0101	C5	E		1001	E9	Z
	0110	C6	F	.	.	.	.
	0111	C7	G	.	.	.	.
	1000	C8	H	.	.	.	.
	1001	C9	I	1111	0000	F0	0
	.	.	.		0001	F1	1
	.	.	.		0010	F2	2
	.	.	.		0011	F3	3
1101	0000	D0			0100	F4	4
	0001	D1	J		0101	F5	5
	0010	D2	K		0110	F6	6
	0011	D3	L		0111	F7	7
	0100	D4	M		1000	F8	8
	0101	D5	N		1001	F9	9
	0110	D6	O	.	.	.	.
	0111	D7	P	.	.	.	.
	1000	D8	Q	.	.	.	.

this code the message

START 1.

would be received in binary as

S	T	A	R	T	1	.
↓	↓	↓	↓	↓	↓	
11100010	11100011	11000001	11011001	11100011	11110001	01001011

or in hexadecimal as

S	T	A	R	T	1	.
↓	↓	↓	↓	↓	↓	↓
E2	E3	C1	D9	E3	F1	4B

Exercise 4-15. Write the messages below in binary and in hexadecimal using EBCDIC code.

(a) DIGIT   (b) 123GO

Summary

A number of popular binary codes was presented in this chapter. One group was binary coded decimal codes used to represent the decimal digits 0 to 9. Another group represents alphanumeric data to store alphabetic, numeric, special characters, and control signals in binary word form.

Of the BCD codes the 8421 code (generally referred to simply as BCD code) is the most common since it represents the decimal digits 0 to 9 by the binary values of 0000 to 1001 using four bits for each digit. However, BCD code characters require special adders or special conversion circuitry to change the form to straight (natural) binary form. Use of grouping in three bits provides octal and four bits provides hexadecimal coding to represent data. These forms of coding provide binary values which are in natural binary form so that arithmetic may be easily carried out.

Parity bits may be added to data in BCD or other code forms to provide error detection capability. Also, word parity may be used to add error correction capability.

Although the 8421 BCD code is most popular, a number of other BCD codes have been used because of some special feature allowing simpler operation in the equipment. Only a representative selection of these codes is presented.

Gray code used primarily to store data on code disks (see Chapter 13) may be converted to binary form for arithmetic operations within the computer. Also, binary data may be converted into Gray code form. These conversion techniques are presented in this chapter and electronic implementation of these conversions will be discussed in Chapter 13.

Finally, a number of alphanumeric codes are presented—an octal code and the ASCII and EBCDIC codes. The latter two are popular for representing the many characters and control signals of input/output (I/O) equipment. Some examples of the equipment using these codes will be shown in Chapter 13.

PROBLEMS

§4-1   **1.** Write the following decimal numbers in BCD code.

(a) 2573   (b) 9287

2. Write a listing of the BCD numbers 0 to 16.

§4-2   **3.** Express the following binary numbers in octal form.

(a) 110100111   (b) 010101001

4. Express the following binary numbers in hexadecimal form.

(a) 101101100011   (b) 1100101010010100

§4-3   **5.** Express the following decimal number in BCD form with an odd parity bit per decimal digit.

(a) 2573   (b) 9287

6. Write the following decimal digits in BCD form with odd parity and determine the parity word for error correction operation. List these in binary form.

2, 9, 6, 8, 7, 4.

7. Determine the bit in error in the following binary data containing even bit parity. The right-most bit is the parity bit and the last binary number 0 the parity word.

┌— parity bit
│
↓
101110
010111
100110
101101
010111
110101 ← parity word.

§4-4   **8.** Write the following numbers in excess-three code

(a) 279   (b) 381

9. Write decimal number 487 in the indicated code forms.

(a)   5421 code
(b)   2*421 code
(c)   7421 code
(d)   742$\bar{1}$ code

10. Write decimal number 549 in the indicated code forms.

(a)   2-out-of-5 code
(b)   51111 code
(c)   Johnson code

11. Write decimal number 83 in the following code forms.

(a) Biquinary
(b) Ring counter

§4-5 **12.** Convert the binary number 1101101101 into Gray code form.

13. Convert the Gray code number 110110101 into binary form.

§4-6 **14.** Write the decimal characters 29 using ASCII code (hexadecimal form).

15. Write the following character expression using ASCII code (hexa-decimal form):

$$A + B = C$$

16. Write the following alphanumeric expression using the EBCDIC code (expressed in hexadecimal form):

CHAPTER 4 IS OVER.

0101

Fundamentals of Boolean algebra

5-1. Boolean Algebra Fundamentals

Boolean algebra is the mathematical technique used when considering problems of a logical nature. In 1847, an English mathematician, George Boole, developed the basic laws and rules for a mathematics which could be applied to problems of deductive logic. Until 1938 these techniques remained in use in the mathematical field. At this time a very good scientist, Claude Shannon, seeing the useful features of such an algebra, adapted it for analyzing multicontact networks such as those considered in telephone work. (He worked for Bell Laboratories.) With the development of computers, the use of Boolean algebra in the electronics field increased to where it is now mainly used by engineers to aid them in logic design.

Originally, Boolean algebra described propositions whose outcome would be either true or false. Shannon used it to define a network of contacts that could be opened or closed. In computer work it is used in addition to describe circuits whose state can be either 1 or 0. The logical 1 or 0 can be those of the binary number system. They can also be identified with an open or closed condition or a true or false condition — these being binary in nature. Since the mathematics involves only two-valued variables and since the possible condition of any unknown in a problem can be specified as either 0 or 1, Boolean algebra will turn out to be quite simplified compared to regular algebra where the variables are continuous.

Basic Definitions. In presenting the basic rules of this algebra it will be quite helpful to refer to switch circuit examples to demonstrate the concepts. In that regard a few basic definitions are now presented.

101

Logical-1. We will associate a closed-switch contact or circuit path with the symbol "1." The contact or circuit path then has a transmission of 1.

Logical-0. We will associate an open-switch contact or circuit path with the symbol "0." The contact or circuit path then has a transmission of 0.

Variables. If the condition of a switch contact may be either open or closed during the operation of the circuit, we refer to the state of the contact by a letter symbol such as A, B, X, Y, ... These symbols or logical variables have value 1 if the contact is closed and 0 if the contact is open.

Figure 5-1 shows examples of the above definitions. Two symbols of a switch contact are provided; that of part (d) is the more popular in practice. If the switch in parts (c) or (d) are closed then X = 1, and if open then X = 0.

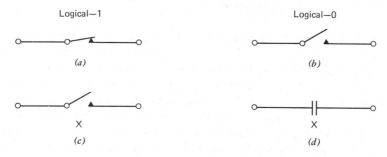

Figure 5-1.   Switch contact representations. (*a*) Closed switch contacts. (*b*) Open switch contacts. (*c*) Variable switch contact. (*d*) Variable switch contact.

In addition to the simple single contact switch of Figure 5-1, a number of other switch and relay types are now presented. Figure 5-2 shows some common contact configurations. Figure 5-2*a* shows *front or make contacts* of a relay. The contacts are normally open (N.O.) and close when the relay is energized. Figure 5-2*b* shows *back or break contacts* of a relay. The contacts are normally closed (N.C.) and open when the relay is energized. As a matter of definition when the front contacts are open X = 0 and when the front contacts are closed X = 1. With the back contacts energizing the relay gives the opposite effect. Figures 5-2*c* and *d* show multiple contacts for a single relay. When the relay coil is not energized, the normally open contact is in the 0 condition and the normally closed contact is in the 1 condition of operation. We assume that the relay contacts operate simultaneously and that when the relay is energized the N.O. contacts close and N.C. contacts open. Since these contacts are

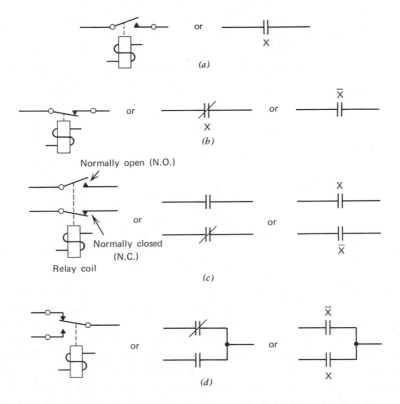

Figure 5-2. Symbols for various common contact configurations. (*a*) Front or make contacts (Normally Open). (*b*) Back or break contacts (Normally Closed). (*c*) Relay contacts. (*d*) Transfer contacts.

always exactly opposite in operating state, we indicate this condition by referring to the N.O. contact as the variable X and the N.C. contact by the variable $\overline{X}$ (X-bar or X-not). The use of the bar above the X then indicates that it is the *opposite-X* or *not-X* condition meaning that if X = 1, then $\overline{X}$ = 0 and if X = 0, then $\overline{X}$ = 1.

Inverse Operation. The logical inverse operation changes a logical-1 to logical-0 or vice versa. If a variable is called X, then its logical inverse is called $\overline{X}$ (read X-not or X-inverse or X-bar). In addition to the inverse operation there are two other basic logical operations to consider. These are the logical AND and logical OR operations.

Logical AND. Figure 5-3 shows a connection of two switches in *series* representing the AND operation. The series connection of switches or

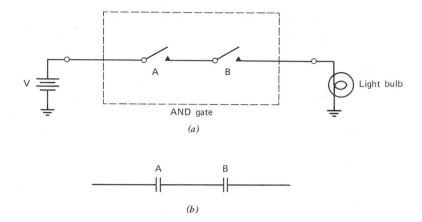

Figure 5-3. AND gate. (*a*) AND circuit using switches. (*b*) AND connection using contacts.

contacts is called an AND circuit or AND gate. Stated simply, the light bulb will go *on* when *both* switch A AND switch B are closed (both logical-1). The AND operation may be represented in circuits as the series connection of switches or contacts. The logical AND operation may be represented in Boolean (logical) algebra by the dot symbol (i.e., A AND B is written A·B, or even AB). The dot or AND operation may be compared to a multiplication operation by considering the possible cases of the values of A and B being 0 or 1. Since A could be either 0 or 1 and B could also be either 0 or 1 there are four possible conditions. The AND function or operation resulting from these four conditions are tabulated below to define the AND operation.

AND Operation. The logical AND operation between two Boolean variables, A and B, is written A·B and defined by Table 5-1.
Table 5-1 shows that the result of logically ANDing the variables A,B is logical-0 for all cases except when *both* A AND B are logical-1.

Table 5-1. *Logical AND Operation*

A	B	A·B
0	0	0
0	1	0
1	0	0
1	1	1

Logical OR. Figure 5-4 shows a connection of two switches in *parallel* representing the OR operation. The parallel connection of switches is called an OR circuit or OR gate. The light bulb will go *on* whenever *either* switch A OR switch B (or both) are closed. The OR operation may be represented in circuits as the parallel connection of switches. The logical

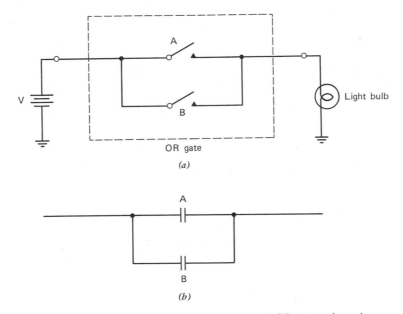

Figure 5-4.   OR gate. (*a*) OR gate circuit using switches. (*b*) OR connection using contacts.

OR operation may be represented in Boolean algebra by the plus (+) symbol (i.e., A OR B is written A + B). The plus or OR operation is *not* the same as addition in binary, as will be shown in the following definition.

OR operation. The logical OR operation between two Boolean variables A,B is written A + B and is defined by Table 5-2.

Table 5-2.   *Logical OR Operation*

A	B	A + B
0	0	0
0	1	1
1	0	1
1	1	1

Table 5.2 shows that the result of logically ORing the variables A,B is logical-1 when A OR B (or both) are logical-1. As example, $1 + 1$ (read one OR one) is 1. In terms of switches in parallel this means that if either switch A OR B is closed, or if both are closed, a transmission path exists.

Boolean Postulates.   Using the concepts presented so far, a number of postulates (a proposition which is taken for granted) are stated in Table 5-3.

Table 5-3.   *Table of Boolean Postulates*

Postulate	Remark	Circuit
P1: $X = 0$ or $X = 1$	A switch is either open or it is closed.	
P2: $0 \cdot 0 = 0$	An open circuit in series with an open circuit is an open circuit.	
P3: $1 + 1 = 1$	A closed switch in parallel with a closed switch is a closed switch.	
P4: $0 + 0 = 0$	An open circuit in parallel with an open circuit is an open circuit.	
P5: $1 \cdot 1 = 1$	A closed switch in series with a closed switch is a closed switch.	
P6: $1 \cdot 0 = 0 \cdot 1 = 0$	A closed circuit in series with an open circuit is an open circuit.	
P7: $1 + 0 = 0 + 1 = 1$	A closed circuit in parallel with an open circuit is a closed circuit.	

Although the postulates may seem self-evident and are, in fact, quite simple it is necessary to formally state them since we now build the rules of Boolean algebra on them. A number of Boolean theorems can now be presented. A theorem in Boolean algebra is a rule concerning a fundamental relation between the Boolean variables. Using the theorems will allow simplifications and manipulation of logical circuits into a variety of forms. Whereas in numerical algebra the variables may take on continuous values over a very wide range, in Boolean algebra the variables quite simply can only be one of the two values 0 or 1. Table 5-4 provides the basic Boolean theorems and a relay circuit example to demonstrate each theorem. Each theorem is described by two parts that are duals of each

Table 5-4.   *Theorems of Boolean Algebra*

Theorem	Circuit
T1: Commutative Law (a) $A + B = B + A$ (b) $A \cdot B = B \cdot A$	
T2: Associative Law (a) $(A + B) + C = A + (B + C)$ (b) $(A \cdot B) \cdot C = A \cdot (B \cdot C)$	
T3: Distributive Law (a) $A \cdot (B + C) = A \cdot B + A \cdot C$ (b) $A + (B \cdot C) = (A + B) \cdot (A + C)$	
T4: Identity Law (a) $A + A = A$ (b) $A \cdot A = A$	
T5: Negation Law (A) $(\overline{A}) = \overline{A}$ (b) $(\overline{A}) = A$	
T6: Redundance Law (a) $A + A \cdot B = A$ (b) $A \cdot (A + B) = A$	
T7: (a) $0 + A = A$ (b) $1 \cdot A = A$ (c) $1 + A = 1$ (d) $0 \cdot A = 0$	

Table 5-4 (*cont.*)

Theorem	Circuit

T8:

   (a) $\overline{A} + A = 1$

   (b) $\overline{A} \cdot A = 0$

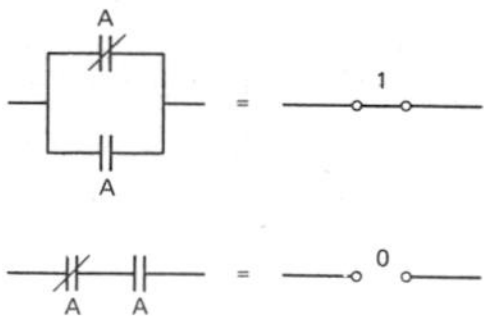

T9:

   (a) $A + \overline{A} \cdot B = A + B$

   (b) $A \cdot (\overline{A} + B) = A \cdot B$

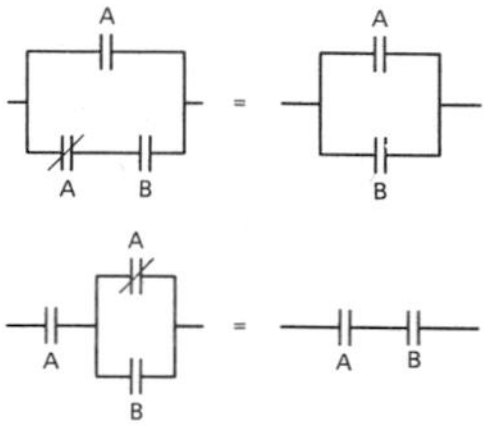

T10: De Morgan's Theorem

    (a) $\overline{(A + B)} = \overline{A} \cdot \overline{B}$

    (b) $\overline{(A \cdot B)} = \overline{A} + \overline{B}$

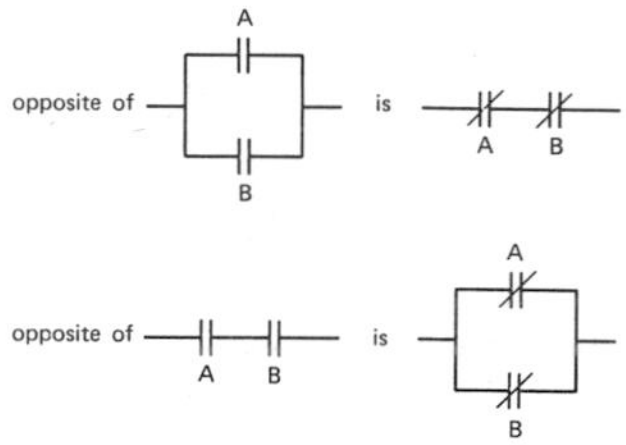

other. A dual here means that the OR and AND operations are inter-changed.

The first three theorems show that the familiar laws of commutation, association, and distribution of ordinary algebra are also true for Boolean algebra. The negation law is new and is only applicable to a two-valued logic. The redundance law comes from the simple nature of logical combination. In T6(a), for example, if switch A is closed the path is complete and if A is open the path is not complete, *regardless of switch B.* T7 and T8 show a few rules that should seem obvious. T9 requires some thought as does T10 before it is seen to be true.

Truth Table.   One means of proving that the theorems stated are correct, or in fact, that any logical expression is identical to another is the use of a *truth table.* Essentially, a truth table provides a listing of *every possible combination of the inputs* and lists the output resulting for each combination of inputs.

For example, consider checking part (a) of the redundance law (T6)

$$A + A \cdot B = A$$

using a truth table. Table 5-5 shows the truth table with the four possible combinations of the two variables A,B. Separate columns are provided for the expressions $A \cdot B$, and $A + A \cdot B$.

Table 5-5. *Truth Table for* $A + A \cdot B = A$

A	B	A·B	A + A·B
0	0	0	0
0	0	0	0
1	0	0	1
1	1	1	1

The column $A \cdot B$ is obtained by logically ANDing the values in columns A and B for each combination listed. Column $A + A \cdot B$ is obtained ORing the values in column $A \cdot B$ with those in column A on a line by line procedure. Notice that the results show that for all combinations of the table the values in column A and $A + A \cdot B$ are exactly the same. This shows that the expression $A + A \cdot B$ is the same as the simpler expression A. If even one line of values did not agree, then these two expressions would not be the same.

As a second example, T9(a) will be verified. Table 5-6, shows the resulting truth table, which has four possible combinations listed for the two variables. Notice that for convenience the logical values of A and B are listed in binary progression from zero to three. As a rule, listing the 0 and 1 values in binary progression assures that all combinations will be easily determined.

The $\overline{A} \cdot B$ column is obtained by ANDing the value of A-inverse ($\overline{A}$), obtained by logically inverting each A value listed, with the logical value

Table 5-6. *Truth Table for* $A + \overline{A}B = A + B$

A	B	$\overline{A} \cdot B$	$A + \overline{A}B$	$A + B$
0	0	0	0	0
0	1	1	1	1
1	0	0	1	1
1	1	0	1	1

of B. For example, with $A = 0$, $B = 0$, we have $\overline{A} = 1$, $B = 0$, which ANDed is 0. Similarly, for $A = 0$, $B = 1$, we have $\overline{A} = 1$, $B = 1$, which ANDed is 1, as on line two. The column headed $A + \overline{A} \cdot B$ is obtained by ORing the values in columns $\overline{A} \cdot B$, A on a line-by-line basis. The truth table shows (by *perfect induction*) that the columns for $A + \overline{A} \cdot B$ are the same as for $A + B$ for all cases, so that we have proven that $A + \overline{A} \cdot B = A + B$ is true.

Part (a) of the distributive law (T3) can be proven using a truth table. In this case there are three Boolean variables and thus eight (2^3) combinations. More generally, for n variables there would be 2^n combinations in the truth table. Table 5-7. shows the truth table which proves that

$$A \cdot (B + C) = A \cdot B + A \cdot C$$

Table 5-7.   *Truth Table for $A \cdot (B + C) = A \cdot B + A \cdot C$*

A	B	C	$(B + C)$	$A \cdot (B + C)$	$A \cdot B$	$A \cdot C$	$A \cdot B + A \cdot C$
0	0	0	0	0	0	0	0
0	0	1	1	0	0	0	0
0	1	0	1	0	0	0	0
0	1	1	1	0	0	0	0
1	0	0	0	0	0	0	0
1	0	1	1	1	0	1	1
1	1	0	1	1	1	0	1
1	1	1	1	1	1	1	1

Table 5-7 is obtained by forming the partial expression columns and then the columns for $A \cdot (B + C)$ and $A \cdot B + A \cdot C$, which are the same for all values of inputs. For more than three or four variables the truth by perfect induction (using the truth table) becomes quite tedious and other methods of proof might be better.

As a final example of the theorems, consider part (b) of De Morgan's Theorem (T10). Table 5-8 shows that $\overline{(A \cdot B)} = \overline{A} + \overline{B}$

Table 5-8.   *Truth Table for $\overline{(A \cdot B)} = \overline{A} + \overline{B}$*

A	B	$A \cdot B$	$\overline{(A \cdot B)}$	$\overline{A} + \overline{B}$
0	0	0	1	1
0	1	0	1	1
1	0	0	1	1
1	1	1	0	0

Exercise 5-1.   Use a truth table to determine whether the following expressions are identical:

(a) $X \cdot Y + \overline{X} \cdot Y + \overline{X} \cdot \overline{Y} = \overline{X} + Y$
(b) $\underline{A \cdot B \cdot C + A \cdot C + B \cdot C} = \underline{A + B} + C$
(c) $(\overline{X} \cdot Y + \overline{Y} \cdot X) + X \cdot \overline{Y} = \overline{(X \cdot \overline{Y})}$
(d) $A \cdot B \cdot D + \overline{A} \cdot \overline{B} \cdot D + A \cdot \overline{B} \cdot \overline{D} = A \cdot (\overline{B} \cdot \overline{D} + B \cdot D)$

Algebraic Simplifications and Manipulations.   In addition to using a truth table to prove that two expressions are identical it is possible to use algebraic simplifications or manipulations. The theorems of Table 5-4 provide the means of manipulating and, hopefully, simplifying Boolean algebraic expressions. A number of examples are provided to demonstrate how this algebraic manipulation is carried out.

Example 5-1.   Simplify $A \cdot (A \cdot B + C)$

Solution: $A \cdot (A \cdot B + C) = A \cdot A \cdot B + A \cdot C$ (T3a)
$\qquad\qquad\qquad = A \cdot B + A \cdot C$ (T4b)
$\qquad\qquad\qquad = A \cdot (B + C)$ (T3a)

Example 5-2.   Simplify $\overline{A} \cdot B + A \cdot B + \overline{A} \cdot \overline{B}$

Solution: $\overline{A} \cdot B + A \cdot B + \overline{A} \cdot \overline{B} = (\overline{A} + A) \cdot B + \overline{A} \cdot \overline{B}$ (T3a)
$\qquad\qquad\qquad\qquad = 1 \cdot B + \overline{A} \cdot \overline{B}$ (T8a)
$\qquad\qquad\qquad\qquad = B + \overline{A} \cdot \overline{B}$ (T7b)
$\qquad\qquad\qquad\qquad = B + \overline{A}$ (T9a)

Example 5-3.   Simplify $A + A \cdot \overline{B} + \overline{A} \cdot B$

Solution: $A + A \cdot \overline{B} + \overline{A} \cdot B = (A + A \cdot \overline{B}) + \overline{A} \cdot B$
$\qquad\qquad\qquad\qquad = A + \overline{A} \cdot B$ (T6a)
$\qquad\qquad\qquad\qquad = A + B$ (T9a)

If, as in the above examples, simplification is possible, then the same circuit operation can be obtained using less switches or contacts. The theorems used in each step of simplification were indicated although the symbols of the theorem are not exactly the same (i.e., theorem 9a states $A + \overline{A} \cdot B = A + B$ whereas in Example 5-2 it was $B + \overline{A} \cdot \overline{B} = B + \overline{A}$). The use of the Boolean theorems provides a manipulation of the Boolean expression without necessarily resulting in a simplified expression. This manipulative operation is probably most useful in logic design operation especially if in addition some simplification results. A few examples will demonstrate some Boolean expression manipulations.

Example 5-4.   Manipulate $\overline{(A+B \cdot C)}$

Solution: $\overline{(A+B \cdot C)} = \overline{A} \cdot (\overline{B} + \overline{C})$ (T10)

The application of De Morgan's theorem could have been done in two steps as follows:

$$\overline{(A+B \cdot C)} = \overline{[A+(B \cdot C)]}$$
$$= \overline{A} \cdot \overline{(B \cdot C)} \tag{T10a}$$
$$= \overline{A} \cdot (\overline{B} + \overline{C}) \tag{T10b}$$

In the second case the expression $B \cdot C$ was considered a single term when applying theorem 10a. Then theorem 10b was used on $\overline{(B \cdot C)}$ to obtain the final form.

Example 5-5.   Negate $\overline{A} \cdot B + A \cdot \overline{B}$

Solution: $\overline{(\overline{A} \cdot B + A \cdot \overline{B})} = \overline{(\overline{A} \cdot B)} \cdot \overline{(A \cdot \overline{B})}$ (T9a)

$$= (A + \overline{B}) \cdot (\overline{A} + B) \tag{T9b}$$
$$= A \cdot \overline{A} + A \cdot B + \overline{B} \cdot \overline{A} + \overline{B} \cdot B \tag{T3a}$$
$$= 0 + A \cdot B + \overline{A} \cdot \overline{B} + 0 \tag{T8b}$$
$$= A \cdot B + \overline{A} \cdot \overline{B} \tag{T7a}$$

Example 5-6.   Negate $(X \cdot \overline{Y} + \overline{X} + Y)$

Solution: $\overline{(X \cdot \overline{Y} + \overline{X} + Y)} = \overline{(X \cdot \overline{Y})} \cdot X \cdot \overline{Y}$ (T10a)

$$= (\overline{X} + Y) \cdot X \cdot \overline{Y} \tag{T10b}$$
$$= \overline{X} \cdot X \cdot \overline{Y} + Y \cdot X \cdot \overline{Y} \tag{T3a}$$
$$= (X \cdot \overline{X}) \cdot \overline{Y} + X \cdot (Y \cdot \overline{Y}) \tag{T2b}$$
$$= 0 \cdot \overline{Y} + X \cdot 0 \tag{T8a}$$
$$= 0 + 0 \tag{T7d}$$
$$= 0 \tag{P4}$$

In other words, the circuit corresponding to the Boolean expression $(X \cdot \overline{Y} + \overline{X} + Y)$ is always an open circuit. Check this by drawing the switch circuit connection of $(X \cdot \overline{Y} + \overline{X} + Y)$ and noting that this connection is always a closed transmission path (and its negation always an open transmission path).

Exercise 5-2.   Simplify the following expressions.

(a) $A \cdot \overline{B} + B \cdot C$

(b) $A \cdot \overline{B} + B \cdot C + \overline{C} \cdot A$

(c) $\overline{A} \cdot (B \cdot C + A \cdot B + B \cdot \overline{A})$

(d) $A \cdot B \cdot C + C \cdot A \cdot B + A \cdot B + A$

(e) $(\overline{A} + A \cdot B) \cdot (\overline{A} \cdot B)$

(f) $X \cdot Y + Y \cdot Z + \overline{Z} \cdot Y$
(g) $[(X + Y) + (X + Z)] \cdot Z$
(h) $\overline{(X \cdot Y \cdot Z + W \cdot \overline{X})}$
(i) $U \cdot V \cdot W + X \cdot V \cdot W + Y \cdot V \cdot W$.
(j) $B \cdot C + A \cdot D + A \cdot B \cdot C \cdot D + C \cdot D \cdot A + \overline{A}$

5-2. Relay Logic

When the OR function was introduced, a parallel arrangement of switches was used to illustrate the practical OR circuit. A series arrangement of switches illustrated a practical AND circuit. Complex circuits made of series, parallel, and series-parallel switch connections found largely in telephone operation are also used in other practical forms in computers. Considering first the switch as a gating element, we can see how Boolean operations can be used to simplify circuits. In this section we will use the Boolean operations of Section 5-1 to simplify and manipulate relay (contact) logic circuits.

Example 5-7. Write the Boolean expression for the circuit given in Figure 5-5.

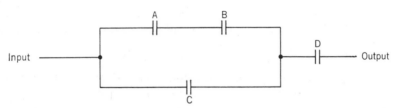

Figure 5-5. Relay circuit for Example 5-7.

Solution: Output $= (AB + C)D$

Example 5-8. Write and simplify the Boolean equation of the circuit given in Figure 5-6.

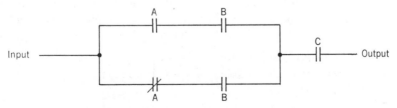

Figure 5-6. Relay circuit for Example 5-8.

Solution: Output $= (AB + \overline{A}B)C$
$$= (A + \overline{A})BC$$
$$= (1)BC$$
$$= BC$$

Notice that the letter B is used to represent more than one contact pair. This indicates that both switches are operated identically as are, for example, multiple contacts on a relay. When the relay is energized all switches of the relay are operated, even though they may be used to interconnect many different circuits or parts of circuits. Simplified, the circuit could be replaced by only two switches B,C. Referring to the circuit diagram, it should now be clear that when A is open, $\overline{A}$ is closed and the path is completed through B and C. If A is closed, $\overline{A}$ is open and there is also a path through B and C. In other words, it does not matter what state A is in; only the states of B and C matter. The simplified expression indicates this operation.

Although you may be skeptical about so simple a case requiring Boolean techniques to improve the circuit, you must appreciate the complex operation of switches in both telephone switching operation and logic circuit use and the large number of connections in a system. Boolean algebra has proved not only useful but essential in designing and simplifying computer logic circuits.

Exercise 5-3.   Write and simplify the output expression for the circuits of Figure 5-7.

Exercise 5-4.   Using relay logic, draw the circuit diagram of the following Boolean expressions (do not simplify the expressions). Then simplify, if possible, and redraw contact circuit.

(a) $WX + WZ + XY + \overline{X}\overline{Y}$
(b) $XUV + WX + \overline{U}V + \overline{X}$
(c) $AB + CD + (AB)(C + D)$
(d) $(AM + FM)(DC + AC)$

Control Circuits.   As an example of an application of relay logic, consider a few simple control circuits. For the first example a warning light operated from three locations is to go on under the following conditions:

(a)   Switches B and C both close.
(b)   Switch B is open and switches A and C both close.
(c)   Switch A closes.

A truth table can be used as a means of going from the verbal descrip-

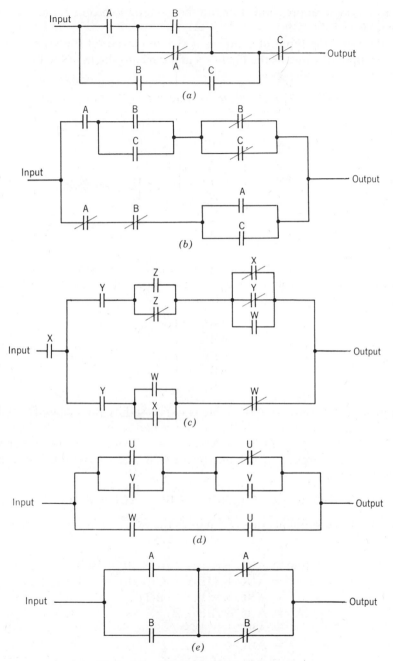

Figure 5-7. Relay circuits for Exercise 5-3.

tion to the logic expression. For the three-variable problem the resulting truth table is Table 5-9.

In the table the input of 1 means a switch closed, of 0 a switch open, and an output of 1 means the light ON and 0 means the light OFF.

Table 5.9.   *Truth Table for Warning Light Control Example*

A	B	C	Output
0	0	0	0
0	0	1	0
0	1	0	0
0	1	1	1
1	0	0	1
1	0	1	1
1	1	0	1
1	1	1	1

A logical expression for the output can be obtained by reading the conditions for the output of 1 occurring. A three-variable term is obtained for each output 1 in the table as follows:

$$\overline{A}BC = 1$$
$$A\overline{B}\,\overline{C} = 1$$
$$A\overline{B}C = 1$$
$$AB\overline{C} = 1$$
$$ABC = 1$$

Notice that an input 0 in the table is expressed by the negated variable since, for example, when A is 0 then $\overline{A}$ is a 1 and the expression $\overline{A}BC$ is a 1 only when $A = 0$ AND $B = 1$ AND $C = 1$. Writing the output expression as the occurrence of a 1 due to the first, second, or third term and so on, we obtain

$$\text{Output} = \overline{A}BC + A\overline{B}\,\overline{C} + A\overline{B}C + AB\overline{C} + ABC$$

Using algebraic simplification techniques the expression could be reduced to

$$
\begin{aligned}
\text{Output} &= \overline{A}BC + A(\overline{B}\,\overline{C} + \overline{B}C + B\overline{C} + BC)\\
&= \overline{A}BC + A[\overline{B}(C + \overline{C}) + B(\overline{C} + C)]\\
&= \overline{A}BC + A[\overline{B}(1) + B(1)]\\
&= \overline{A}BC + A(\overline{B} + B)\\
&= \overline{A}BC + A(1)\\
&= \overline{A}BC + A\\
&= A + \overline{A}(BC)\\
&= A + BC
\end{aligned}
$$

The resulting circuit for the simplified expression is given in Figure 5-8.

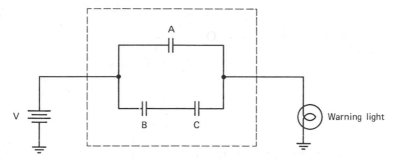

Figure 5-8.   Circuit connection for warning light control circuit.

The procedure used in working out the above problem can be stated more explicitly since it will apply to other control problems and many other electronic logic circuit problems to come.

1. Obtain verbal description of the problem (as clear as possible).
2. Construct a truth table from the verbal description defining the meaning of input 1 and 0 and output 1 and 0 logic signals.
3. Write logical expression from truth table.
4. Simplify logical expression or manipulate into more desirable form (experience here is quite important).
5. Draw resulting logic circuit for simplified logical expression.

These five steps will provide a useful procedure for obtaining a logic circuit that performs the desired logic operation in a fairly simple form.

Example 5-9. Obtain the relay logic circuit to provide a check on the operation of three doors by turning an indicator light ON if two but only two doors are closed at the same time.

Solution: With the verbal description stated above the truth table is obtained below (Table 5-10).

Table 5-10.   *Truth Table for Example 5-9*

A	B	C	Output
0	0	0	0
0	0	1	0
0	1	0	0
0	1	1	1
1	0	0	0
1	0	1	1
1	1	0	1
1	1	1	0

Writing the logical expression for the output

$$\text{Output} = \overline{A}BC + A\overline{B}C + AB\overline{C}$$

which can be written in the form

$$\text{Output} = \overline{A}(BC) + A(\overline{B}C + B\overline{C})$$

The logic circuit for the above expression is that of Figure 5-9.

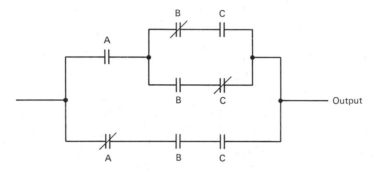

Figure 5-9.   Relay logic circuit for Example 5-9. (*Note*: contacts of same variable name are operated simultaneously by relay.)

Example 5-10.   A relay logic circuit is desired to determine when more than one of three elevators is operating.

Solution: A truth table (Table 5-11) can be generated for the stated problem with input 1 (contacts closed) meaning that an elevator is in operation and output 1 meaning that more than one elevator is operating.

Table 5-11.   *Truth Table for Example 5-10*

A	B	C	Output
0	0	0	0
0	0	1	0
0	1	0	0
0	1	1	1
1	0	0	0
1	0	1	1
1	1	0	1
1	1	1	1

The logic expression for the output is

$$\text{Output} = \overline{A}BC + A\overline{B}C + AB\overline{C} + ABC$$

which can be simplified to

$$
\begin{aligned}
\text{Output} &= \overline{A}BC + A(\overline{B}C + B\overline{C} + BC) \\
&= \overline{A}BC + A[\overline{B}C + B(C + \overline{C})] \\
&= \overline{A}BC + A[\overline{B}C + B(1)] \\
&= \overline{A}BC + A[\overline{B}C + B] \\
&= \overline{A}BC + A(B + C) \\
&= \overline{A}BC + AB + AC \\
&= B(\overline{A}C + A) + AC \\
&= B(A + C) + AC \\
&= AB + BC + AC \\
&= A(B + C) + BC
\end{aligned}
$$

The resulting logic circuit is shown in Figure 5-10. (Other slight variations using five switch contacts are possible by factoring out the B or C variable in the last step).

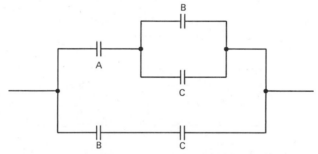

Figure 5-10.   Relay logic circuit for Example 5-10.

Exercise 5-5.   Carry out the design for the following problems specifying the truth table, logic expression reduced to simplest form, and logic circuit diagram.

(a) Design a logic circuit to drive an indicator light on when any two, *but only two*, of three control switches are closed.
(b) Design a logic circuit to operate a warning light when two or more of four safety switches are operated.
(c) Design a logic circuit to drive an alarm when, for three switches, A, B, C, switches A and C are both closed, B is open and A is closed, or B is closed and C is closed.

5-3.   Electronic Logic Gates

The previous section showed how relay logic connections are used to carry out logical operations. Although relay logic is sometimes appropriate for small mechanical control systems (fluidic logic components are taking over in the mechanical controls area), the most popular type of logic component, by far, are the solid-state electronic circuitry. Used primarily in digital computers, the electronic logic gates are manufactured mainly as integrated circuit (IC) units employing transistors, diodes, and other solid-state components. Logic gates are available to perform the AND, OR, and inversion operations defined previously as well as two popular combinations of these functions. An inverter following an AND gate is called a *Not-AND* gate or NAND gate and an inverter following an OR gate is called a *Not-OR* gate or NOR gate. We can formally define these two newer gates as follows.

NAND Gate. A NAND gate provides an output of logical-0 only when all inputs are logical-1. A truth table of the NAND function is given in Table 5-12 corresponding to the logical expression, Output $= \overline{(AB)}$.

Table 5-12.   *Truth Table for NAND Function (Output $= \overline{AB}$)*

A	B	Output
0	0	1
0	1	1
1	0	1
1	1	0

NOR Gate. A NOR gate provides an output of logical-0 when any one or more inputs is logical-1. A truth table of the NOR function is given in Table 5-13 corresponding to the logical expression, Output $= \overline{(A+B)}$.

Table 5-13.   *Truth Table for NOR Function (Output $= \overline{A+B}$)*

A	B	Output
0	0	1
0	1	0
1	0	0
1	1	0

The ASA (American Standard Association) symbols for electronic logic gates will be used in this text, as shown in Figure 5-11. A variety of other gate symbols exist and are preferred by one user or another, but the ASA symbols are generally the most widely accepted. Notice in Figure 5-11 that a circle at the output of the NAND, NOR, and inverter symbols

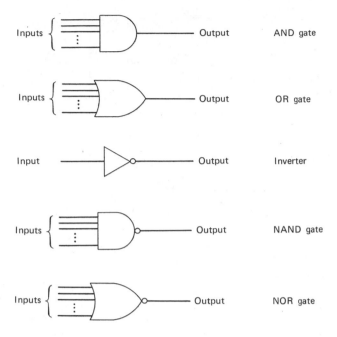

Figure 5-11.   ASA standard electronic logic gate symbols.

designates the inversion operation. For convenience, signal flow on diagrams will be from top to bottom or left to right, unless otherwise specified.

Preparing Logic Diagrams.   As a start using the electronic logic gates consider the next few examples showing how a logic diagram may be drawn to implement a given logical expression or function.

Example 5-11.   Draw the logic diagram to implement the following logic expressions (don't simplify).

$$\text{(a)} \quad D = \overline{A}\overline{B}C + \overline{A}B\overline{C} + A\overline{B}$$
$$\text{(b)} \quad W = X\overline{Y}(Z + \overline{Y}) + \overline{X}Z$$
$$\text{(c)} \quad D = [A(B + \overline{C}) + \overline{A}B]C$$

Solution: The logic circuits are drawn in Figure 5-12.

In Figure 5-12(*a*) the inverters used to obtain the inverted signals $\overline{A}$, $\overline{B}$, and $\overline{C}$ are included on the logic diagram. In Figures 5-12(*b*) and 5-12(*c*) the inverted inputs are assumed available. If they were not, then additional inverters would have to be included.

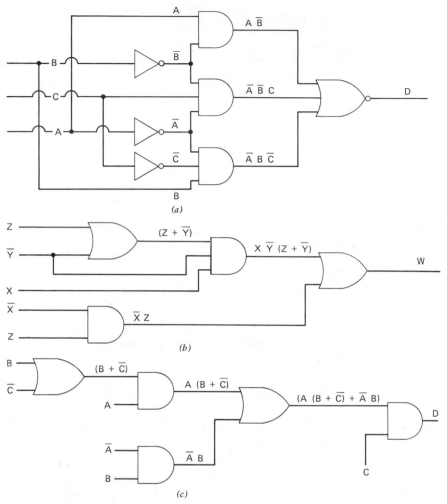

Figure 5-12. Logic diagrams for Example 5-11. (*a*) $D = \bar{A}\bar{B}C + \bar{A}B\bar{C} + A\bar{B}$ (*b*) $W = X\bar{Y}(Z+\bar{Y}) + \bar{X}Z$ (*c*) $D = [A(B+\bar{C}) + \bar{A}B]C$.

Exercise 5-6.   Draw the logical diagrams for the given equations. Do not simplify.

(a) $(AB+CD)\bar{C}$

(b) $(AB+CD)(AB+C)$

(c) $(\overline{XY+Z})(\overline{XYZ})$

(d) $WUV + \overline{WU}\bar{V} + (UV+WX)$

(e) $(\overline{X+Y}) + (X+Z)(UY)(X+Z)$

Obtaining Logic Expression. When a logic circuit is provided, the logic expression is easily obtained. A few examples should show the straight-forward procedure.

Example 5-12. Obtain the logic expression for the logic diagrams of Figure 5-13. Do not simplify the resulting logic expression at this time.

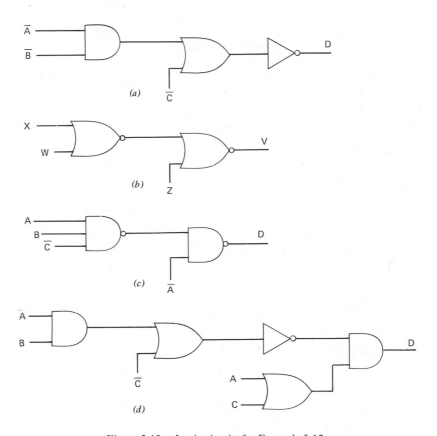

Figure 5-13.   Logic circuits for Example 5-12.

Solution: (a) $D = \overline{(\overline{A}\,\overline{B} + \overline{C})}$
       (b) $V = \overline{(\overline{X + W}) + Z}$
       (c) $D = \overline{(\overline{ABC})\overline{A}}$
       (d) $D = (\overline{A}B + C)(A + C)$

Exercise 5-7. Write the Boolean (logical) expressions for the block diagrams of Figure 5-14.

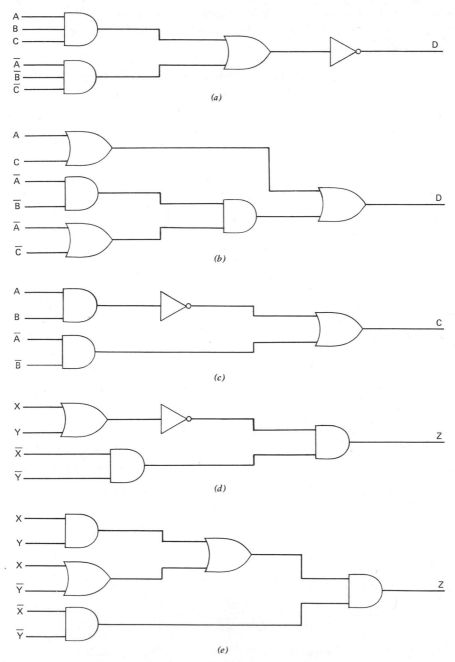

Figure 5-14. Logic diagram for Exercise 5-7.

124

Logic Simplification and Manipulation.   Using the theorems of Table 5-4 it is possible to either simplify or manipulate a logical expression to obtain a desirable form. A few examples should show what can be done.

Example 5-13.   Simplify the following Boolean expressions and draw a logic diagram for the simplified expression.

$$\text{(a)}\quad D = \overline{A}BC + A\overline{B}C + ABC + B\overline{C}$$
$$\text{(b)}\quad W = X\overline{Y} + \overline{X}(Z + Y) + X\overline{Z}$$

Solution: (a) $D = \overline{A}BC + A\overline{B}C + ABC + B\overline{C}$
$$= (\overline{A} + A)(BC) + (AC)(\overline{B} + B) + B\overline{C}$$
$$= BC + AC + B\overline{C}$$
$$= B(C + \overline{C}) + AC$$
$$= AC + B$$

The simplified circuit is shown in Figure 5-15a. Notice that in the second line the term ABC was used twice, since this does not change the expression.

$$\text{(b)}\quad W = X\overline{Y} + \overline{X}(Z + Y) + X\overline{Z}$$
$$= X\overline{Y} + \overline{X}Z + \overline{X}Y + X\overline{Z}$$
$$= X(\overline{Y} + \overline{Z}) + \overline{X}(Z + Y)$$

The logic diagram for this simplified expression is shown in Figure 5-15(*b*).

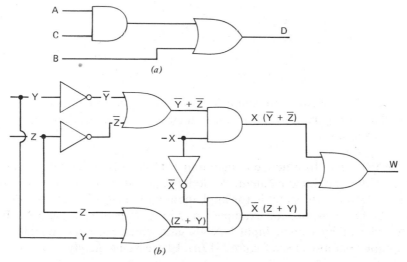

(a)

(b)

Figure 5-15.   Logic circuits for Example 5-13. (*a*) $D = AC + B$. (*b*) $W = X(\overline{Y} + \overline{Z}) + \overline{X}(Y + Z)$.

Example 5-14. Write and simplify the Boolean expression obtained from the logic diagrams of Figure 5-16.

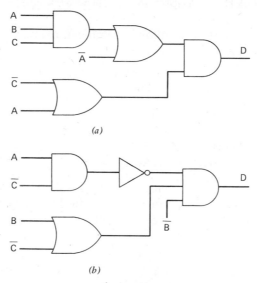

(a)

(b)

Figure 5-16.   Logic circuits for Example 5-14.

Solution: (a) $D = (ABC + \overline{A})(A + \overline{C})$
$$= AABC + ABC\overline{C} + \overline{A}A + \overline{A}\overline{C}$$
$$= ABC + 0 + 0 + \overline{A}\overline{C}$$
$$= ABC + \overline{A}\overline{C}$$

(b) $D = (\overline{AC})(B + C)\overline{B}$
$$= (\overline{A} + \overline{C})(B + \overline{C})\overline{B} = (\overline{A} + \overline{C})(B\overline{B} + \overline{B}\overline{C})$$
$$= (\overline{A} + \overline{C})\overline{B}\overline{C} = \overline{A}\overline{B}\overline{C} + \overline{B}\overline{C}\overline{C} = \overline{A}\overline{B}\overline{C}$$

Exercise 5-8. Write and simplify the logic expressions for the logic diagrams of Figure 5-14. Draw logic diagrams for the resulting simplified logic expressions.

NAND logic. In practice a logic unit such as a NAND gate might be used as the only logic element. All logic expressions must then be manipulated into a form suitable for implementation using only NAND logic. The AND operation, for example, may be obtained by using a NAND gate followed by a single input NAND gate which provides an additional inversion operation. (See Figure 5-17a). Expressed logically

$$\overline{(\overline{ABC})} = ABC$$

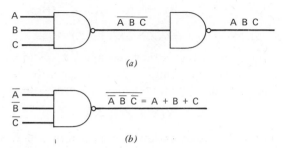

(a)

(b)

Figure 5-17.   Obtaining AND and OR operations using NAND gates. (*a*) AND operation using NAND gates. (*b*) OR operation using NAND gates.

The OR operation may be obtained by using inverted inputs as shown in Figure 5-17*b*. Using De Morgan's theorem the logical relation is

$$\overline{\overline{A}\,\overline{B}\,\overline{C}} = A + B + C$$

De Morgan's theorem will be helpful for manipulating logical expressions into a suitable form for NAND gate implementation.

To see how more involved logical expressions are implemented using only NAND gates, consider the next example.

Example 5-15.   Develop the logic expressions given below into a form suitable for NAND gate implementation and draw the logic diagram.

$$\text{(a)} \quad D = A + \overline{B}C$$
$$\text{(b)} \quad W = X\overline{Y} + \overline{X}Z$$

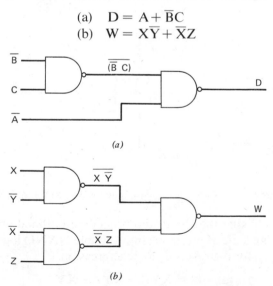

(a)

(b)

Figure 5-18.   Logic diagrams for Example 5-15. (*a*) $D = A + \overline{B}C$ (*b*) $W = X\overline{Y} + \overline{X}Z$.

Solution: (a) $D = A + \overline{B}C = \overline{\overline{(A + \overline{B}C)}} = \overline{\overline{A}(\overline{\overline{B}C})}$

  b) $W = X\overline{Y} + \overline{X}Z + \overline{(X\overline{Y})(\overline{X}Z)}$

When the logic expression gets more complex a systematic procedure is often helpful. One such technique for working with NAND logic is the following. Consider manipulating the logic expression

$$W = X(\overline{Y} + Z) + \overline{X}Y$$

1. Manipulate the logic expression into a form in which the terms are ORed.

$$W = X(\overline{Y} + Z) + \overline{X}Y = X\overline{Y} + XZ + \overline{X}Y$$

2. Double negate the logical expression (recall that $\overline{(\overline{A})} = A$, so that the double negation does not change the expression).

$$W = \overline{[\overline{(X\overline{Y} + XZ + \overline{X}Y)}]}$$

3. Apply De Morgan's theorem, $\overline{A + B} = \overline{A}\,\overline{B}$, to the *inner* negation sign, leaving each term as is.

$$W = \overline{[(\overline{X\overline{Y}})(\overline{XZ})(\overline{\overline{X}Y})]}$$

The result is in NAND form for logic implementation. Figure 5-19 shows the resulting logic diagram for the expression in step 3.

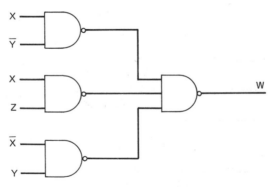

Figure 5-19.   NAND gate logic circuit for $W = X(Y + Z) + \overline{X}Y$.

Example 5-16.   Using the three-step procedure outlined above, manipulate the following logic expressions into suitable NAND logic form. Draw the logic diagram for the resulting logic expression.

  (a) $W = XYZ + X\overline{Y}Z + \overline{X}\,\overline{Y}$
  (b) $D = A(B + \overline{C}) + \overline{B}\overline{C} + \overline{A}B$

Solution: (a)   1. $W = XYZ + X\overline{Y}Z + \overline{X}\,\overline{Y}$

2. $W = \overline{\overline{(XYZ + X\overline{Y}Z + \overline{X}\,\overline{Y})}}$

3. $W = \overline{[(\overline{XYZ})(\overline{X\overline{Y}Z})(\overline{\overline{X}\,\overline{Y}})]}$

The logic diagram is shown in Figure 5-20a.

(b)   1. $D = A(B + \overline{C}) + \overline{B}\,\overline{C} + \overline{A}B = AB + A\overline{C} + B\overline{C} + \overline{A}B$

2. $D = \overline{\overline{(AB + A\overline{C} + B\overline{C} + \overline{A}B)}}$

3. $D = \overline{[(\overline{AB})(\overline{A\overline{C}})(\overline{B\overline{C}})(\overline{\overline{A}B})]}$

The logic diagram is in Figure 5-20b.

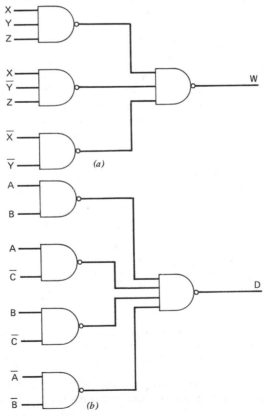

Figure 5-20.   NAND gate logic diagrams for Example 5-16. (a) $W = XYZ + X\overline{Y}Z + \overline{X}\,\overline{Y}$.
(b) $D = A(B + \overline{C}) + \overline{B}\,\overline{C} + \overline{A}B$.

Exercise 5-9. Develop the simplest logic circuit to implement the logic expressions given below using *only* NAND gates. Draw the logic circuit diagram.

(a) $\overline{X} + Y + \overline{Z}$

(b) $XY + \overline{X}Z + Y\overline{Z}$

(c) $AC + BD + \overline{B}C + \overline{A}B$

(d) $(XYZ)(XW) + (YW)$

(e) $(A\overline{B} + C)(\overline{DE} + F)$

NOR Logic. If NOR gate logic units were used as the only logic element, it would be possible to still implement any logic expression. The OR function could be obtained using a NOR gate followed by a single input NOR gate which provides the inversion operation (see Figure 5-21*a*). Expressed logically

$$\overline{\overline{(A + B + C)}} = A + B + C$$

The AND operation could also be obtained using inverted inputs as shown in Figure 5-21*b*. Using De Morgan's theorem the logical relation is

$$\overline{\overline{A} + \overline{B} + \overline{C}} = ABC$$

A few examples should show how NOR gates may be used to implement a logical expression.

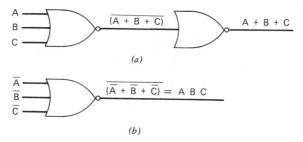

(a)

(b)

Figure 5-21.   OR and AND operations using NOR gates. (*a*) OR operation using NOR gates. (*b*) AND operation using NOR gates.

Example 5-17. Develop the logic expressions given below into a form suitable for NOR gate implementation and draw the logic diagram.

(a) $X\overline{Y} + Z$

(b) $(U + V)(X + \overline{Y} + \overline{Z})$

Solution: (a)   The term $X\overline{Y}$ may be replaced from

$$\overline{X+Y} = X\overline{Y}$$

and the full expression may be written as

$$\overline{[(\overline{X+Y})+Z]}$$

To obtain the ORing of Z with $\overline{X+Y}$ we need a NOR gate resulting in $(\overline{\overline{X+Y}+Z})$, the negation of the desired output. We thus need one more NOR gate as an inverter to finally obtain

$$\overline{(\overline{\overline{X+Y}+Z})} = X\overline{Y}+Z$$

The logic diagram is shown in Figure 5-22*a*.

(b) The logic expression may be manipulated as follows.

$$\overline{[(U+V)+\overline{(X+\overline{Y}+\overline{Z})}]} = (U+V)(X+\overline{Y}+\overline{Z})$$

Figure 5-22*b* shows the resulting logic diagram.

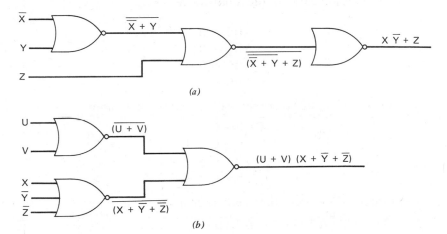

(a)

(b)

Figure 5-22.   Logic diagrams for Example 5-17. (*a*) NOR gate circuit for $X\overline{Y}+Z$. (*b*) NOR gate circuit for $(U+V)(X+\overline{Y}+\overline{Z})$.

A technique similar to that used to manipulate logic expressions into suitable NAND logic form could be stated for NOR logic operation. Basically, this would require manipulating the logic expression first into a form of a number of terms of ORed variables all ANDed to gether for example, $(U+V)(X+\overline{Y}+\overline{Z})$. Manipulation into this form requires writing the logic expression using the logical-0 values of the truth table.

This procedure is demonstrated in the next example.

Example 5-18. Obtain a suitable starting form of the logic expression $A\overline{B}C + \overline{A}B\overline{C} + AB$ for **NOR** gate implementation.

Solution: The truth table for this logic expression is Table 5-14.

Table 5-14.   *Truth Table for* $D = A\overline{B}C + \overline{A}B\overline{C} + AB$

A	B	C	D
0	0	0	0
0	0	1	0
0	1	0	1
0	1	1	0
1	0	0	0
1	0	1	1
1	1	0	1
1	1	1	1

The value of D is logical-0 for the following terms

$$\overline{A}\,\overline{B}\,\overline{C} = 0$$
$$\overline{A}\,\overline{B}C = 0$$
$$\overline{A}B C = 0$$
$$A\overline{B}\,\overline{C} = 0$$

Applying De Morgan's theorem to each term we can write

$$A + B + C = 1$$
$$A + B + \overline{C} = 1$$
$$A + \overline{B} + \overline{C} = 1$$
$$\overline{A} + B + C = 1$$

The expression for D can then be written in the form

$$D = (A + B + C) \cdot (A + B + \overline{C}) \cdot (A + \overline{B} + \overline{C}) \cdot (\overline{A} + B + C)$$

This form is suitable for **NOR** gate logic implementation using a technique similar to the three-step procedure outlined for **NAND** gates.

From experience the above expression could be written slightly simpler as

$$D = (A + B) \cdot (A + \overline{B} + \overline{C}) \cdot (\overline{A} + B + C)$$

The resulting form is suitable as a starting point for **NOR** gate implementation as the following procedure will show. The logical expression of Example 5-18 will be used to demonstrate the procedure.

1. Manipulate the logic expression into a form in which the terms are ANDed. Use the procedure of Example 5-18 to obtain this desired form from the logic truth table 0's.

$$D = A\overline{B}C + \overline{A}B\overline{C} + AB$$
$$= (A + B)(A + \overline{B} + \overline{C})(\overline{A} + B + C)$$

2. Double negate the logical expression.

$$D = \overline{\overline{[(A + B)(A + \overline{B} + \overline{C})(\overline{A} + B + C)]}}$$

3. Apply De Morgan's theorem, $\overline{AB} = \overline{A} + \overline{B}$, to the *inner* negation sign, leaving each term as is.

$$D = \overline{[\overline{(A + B)} + \overline{(A + \overline{B} + \overline{C})} + \overline{(\overline{A} + B + C)}]}$$

The result is in NOR form for logic implementation. Figure 5-23 shows the resulting logic diagram for the expression in step 3.

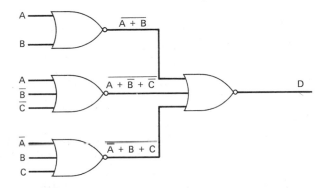

Figure 5-23.   Logic diagram of $A\overline{B}C + \overline{A}B\overline{C} + AB$ using NOR gates only.

Example 5-19.   Implement the logic expression $\overline{X}Y\overline{Z} + XZ + \overline{Y}$ using only NOR gates. Follow the three-step procedure outlined above.

Solution: 1. First, a truth table of logic expression is obtained (Table 5-15).
Second, the logical-0 terms are read off the table to obtain

$$W = (X + \overline{Y} + \overline{Z})(\overline{X} + \overline{Y} + Z)$$

2. Using the double negation:

$$W = \overline{\overline{[(X + \overline{Y} + \overline{Z})(\overline{X} + \overline{Y} + Z)]}}$$

Table 5-15.   *Truth Table for* $W = \overline{X}Y\overline{Z} + XZ + \overline{Y}$

X	Y	Z	W
0	0	0	1
0	0	1	1
0	1	0	1
0	1	1	0
1	0	0	1
1	0	1	1
1	1	0	0
1	1	1	1

3. Applying De Morgan's theorem to the inner negation sign:

$$W = \overline{[(X + \overline{Y} + \overline{Z}) + (\overline{X} + \overline{Y} + Z)]}$$

The resulting NOR gate logic circuit is shown in Figure 5-24.

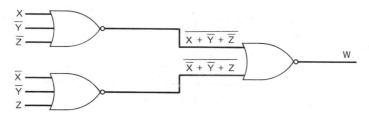

Figure 5-24.   Logic circuit for Example 5-19 using only NOR gates to implement $W = \overline{X}Y\overline{Z} + XZ + \overline{Y}$.

Exercise 5-10.   Develop the simplest logic diagrams to implement the logic expressions given using *only* NOR gates.

$$\begin{aligned}
&\text{(a)} \quad \overline{X}Y\overline{Z} \\
&\text{(b)} \quad (X + Y)(\overline{X} + Y) \\
&\text{(c)} \quad \overline{X}Y\overline{Z} + XYZ + \overline{Y}\overline{Z} \\
&\text{(d)} \quad (XY + Z) + (\overline{X} + YZ)
\end{aligned}$$

5-4.   Logic Design Examples

A few design problems will serve to tie some of the basic logic concepts together. The step-by-step procedure in obtaining a logic circuit was used in relay logic examples in Section 5-2. To restate the method:

1. Clearly state problem and define input and output logic levels when necessary.
2. Prepare a logic truth table from the problem description.
3. Obtain a logic expression from the truth table.
4. Manipulate and simplify the logic expression to a desired form.
5. Draw the logic circuit diagram.

A number of examples follow to show how a logic circuit can be obtained to satisfy a specified problem. Some of these circuits will be designed using only **NAND** or **NOR** logic to allow some comparison.

Example 5-20.   Design a two-bit comparator logic circuit that will provide a logical-1 output if the two input signals are identical. Figure 5-25*a* shows a block version of the overall circuit operation.

Solution: (a)   The verbal statement of the problem is given above.

(b)   A truth table for the comparator is given in Table 5-16.

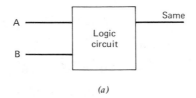

(a)

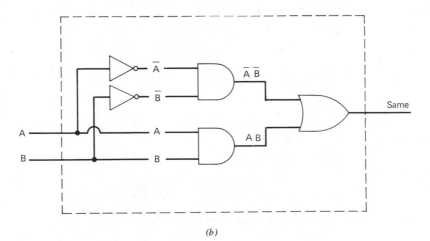

(b)

Figure 5-25.   Logic block and circuit for two-bit comparator. (*a*) Block form two-bit comparator unit. (*b*) Logic circuit of two-bit comparator.

Table 5-16.   *Logic Truth Table for Two-Bit Comparator*

A	B	SAME
0	0	1
0	1	0
1	0	0
1	1	1

(c)   From Table 5-16

$$SAME = \overline{A}\overline{B} + AB$$

(d)   Using the logic expression above a logic circuit diagram is shown in Figure 15-25(*b*).

Example 5-21.   Design a NAND and a NOR form of the two-bit logic comparator circuit of Example 5-20.

Solution:

NAND form
Using the logic expression

$$SAME = \overline{A}\overline{B} + AB$$

The NAND logic form can be obtained as follows:

$$SAME = \overline{[(\overline{\overline{A}\overline{B} + AB})]}$$

$$SAME = \overline{[(\overline{\overline{A}\overline{B}})(\overline{AB})]}$$

which is drawn as the logic circuit of Figure 15-26*a*.

NOR form
Using the truth table (Table 5-16) for the comparator, the following logic expression is obtained:

$$SAME = (\overline{A} + B)(A + \overline{B})$$

$$= \overline{[(\overline{A} + B)(A + \overline{B})]} = \overline{[(\overline{\overline{A} + B}) + (\overline{A + \overline{B}})]}$$

A NOR gate logic circuit is given in Figure 5-26*b*.

Example 5-22.   Design a logic circuit to provide an odd parity bit for a three-bit octal code. The logic circuit will thus generate the odd parity

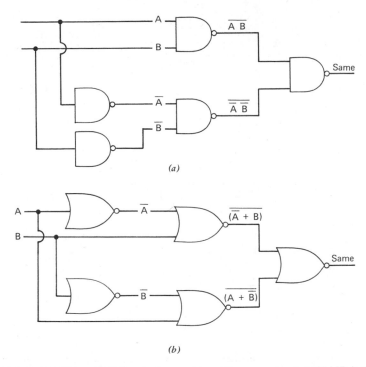

Figure 5-26.   NAND and NOR gate forms of two-bit comparator. (*a*) NAND logic form. (*b*) NOR logic form.

bit for any combination of the three-bit octal code. A block diagram of this operation is shown in Figure 5-27*a*.

Solution: (a)   The verbal description of the problem is stated above.
            (b)   Table 5-17 provides the logic truth table.

Table 5-17.   *Logic Truth Table for Odd Parity Bit with Three-Bit Octal Code*

A	B	C	P (Odd parity bit)
0	0	0	1
0	0	1	0
0	1	0	0
0	1	1	1
1	0	0	0
1	0	1	1
1	1	0	1
1	1	1	0

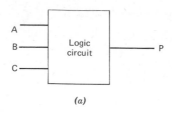

(a)

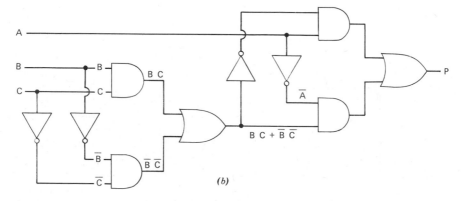

(b)

Figure 5-27.   Odd parity bit generator for octal code. (*a*) Block diagram. (*b*) Logic circuit.

(c)   From the logic truth table:

$$P = \overline{A}\overline{B}\overline{C} + \overline{A}BC + A\overline{B}C + AB\overline{C}$$

(d) $P = \overline{A}(\overline{B}\overline{C} + BC) + A(\overline{B}C + B\overline{C})$

(e)   Figure 5-27*b* shows the resulting logic circuit.

Example 5-23.   Design a half-adder logic circuit to provide sum and carry-out bits as shown in the block diagram of Figure 5-28*a*.

Solution: A logic truth table for a half-adder is shown in Table 5-18.

Table 5-18.   *Truth Table for Half-Adder*

A B	Sum	Carry
0 0	0	0
0 0	1	0
1 0	1	0
1 1	0	1

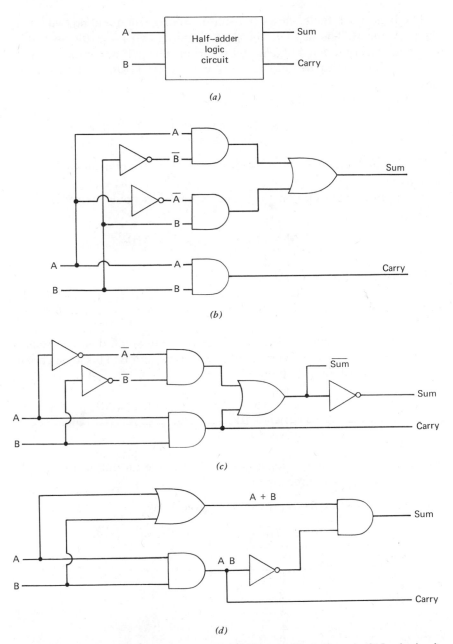

Figure 5-28. Logic operation and circuit of half-adder. (*a*) Block diagram. (*b*) Logic circuit. (*c*) Alternate logic circuit for half-adder. (*d*) Logic version of half-adder requiring no inversion of inputs.

139

The logic truth table shows the sum resulting when adding two binary digits A and B. The last line shows that adding two 1's results in a SUM of 0 and a carry to a next higher bit position. The half-adder thus is useful as the adder circuit for adding the lowest-order position of two binary numbers.

A resulting set of logic expressions are

$$SUM = \overline{A}B + A\overline{B}$$
$$CARRY = AB$$

These can be implemented directly by the logic circuit shown in Figure 5-28b.

As an alternate solution the logic expressions could be reworked as follows:

$$SUM = \overline{A}B + A\overline{B} = \overline{(\overline{A}B + AB)}$$
$$CARRY = AB$$

which provides the logic circuit of Figure 5-28c.

The second version of the circuit replaces an AND gate by an inverter and provides the SUM output from an inverter (as well as having available the $\overline{SUM}$ signal).

A third logic circuit version can be developed which does not require inverters to develop the inverted input signals, $\overline{A}$ and $\overline{B}$. This logic version is obtained as follows (see Figure 5-28d):

$$SUM = \overline{A}B + A\overline{B} = \overline{(AB + \overline{A}\,\overline{B})} = \overline{(AB)}\,\overline{(\overline{A}\,\overline{B})}$$
$$SUM = \overline{(AB)}(A + B)$$
$$CARRY = AB$$

Example 5-24.   Design a logic circuit to provide an output of logical-1 whenever any two of three inputs are logical-1.

Solution: A truth table is provided in Table 5-19.

Table 5-19. *Truth Table for Example 5-24.*

X	Y	Z	W
0	0	0	0
0	0	1	0
0	1	0	0
0	1	1	1
1	0	0	0
1	0	1	1
1	1	0	1
1	1	1	1

A logic expression for the output, W, is

$$W = \overline{X}YZ + X\overline{Y}Z + XY\overline{Z} + XYZ$$
$$= \overline{X}YZ + X(\overline{Y}Z + Y\overline{Z} + YZ)$$
$$= \overline{X}YZ + X[\overline{Y}Z + Y(\overline{Z} + Z)]$$
$$= \overline{X}YZ + X[\overline{Y}Z + Y]$$
$$= \overline{X}YZ + X(Z + Y)$$
$$= \overline{X}YZ + XZ + XY$$
$$= XZ + Y(\overline{X}Z + X)$$
$$= XZ + Y(Z + X)$$
$$= XY + XZ + YZ$$

A logic circuit for the resulting logic expression is shown in Figure 5-29.

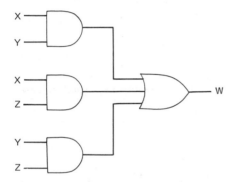

Figure 5-29.   Logic circuit for Example 5-24.

Exercise 5-11.   Design logic circuits as described below.

(a)   Design a logic circuit for two inputs to provide a logical-1 output when the two inputs are different.

(b)   Design an odd parity bit logic circuit for the octal code using only NAND logic circuits.

(c)   Design the half-adder circuit using only NOR logic circuits.

(d)   Design a logic circuit to provide an output when two, but only two of three inputs are present (logical-1).

(e)   Design a logic circuit to provide an output when of three inputs, either one or two inputs are simultaneously present (logical-1), but not all three.

Summary

Boolean algebra is introduced and then applied to practical problems. The AND, OR, INVERTER, NOR, and NAND functions are used. It is important to be able to "read" logic diagrams or prepare them from a Boolean equation. Using rules of operation logic equations can be re-worked into either a more suitable form or a simplified form. One very important theorem used in Boolean algebra is De Morgan's theorem which states that

$$\overline{(X + Y)} = \overline{X} \cdot \overline{Y}$$

or that

$$\overline{(X \cdot Y)} = (\overline{X} + \overline{Y})$$

PROBLEMS

§5-1 **1.** Use a truth table to determine whether the following expressions are identical

(a) $\overline{X}Y + X\overline{Y} = \overline{(XY + \overline{X}\overline{Y})}$

(b) $\overline{X + Y} = \overline{X} + \overline{Y}$

(c) $A(B + \overline{C}) = ABC + AB\overline{C}$

2. Simplify the following logic expressions.

(a) $C = (A + \overline{A}B)(A + \overline{B})$

(b) $X + UV + VW + UW + V\overline{W}$

(c) $D = \overline{A}BC + AB\overline{C} + ABC + \overline{A}B$

(d) $C = (A\overline{B} + AB)(A + B)$

§5-2 **3.** Draw the circuit diagrams of the Boolean expressions of Problem 2 (don't simplify) using relay logic.

4. Design a logic circuit to drive an indicator light on whenever either only one or all of three control switches are closed, using relay logic.

§5-3 **5.** Draw the logic diagram of the Boolean expressions of Problem 2 (don't simplify) using electronic logic gates.

6. Write the Boolean expression for the following logic circuits (Figure 5-30); simplify where possible.

7. Manipulate the following logical expressions into a form suitable for NAND logic operation.

(a) $AB + \overline{A}C + A\overline{C}$

(b) $(AC + \overline{B})(\overline{B} + C)$

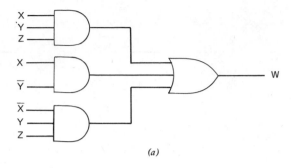

(a)

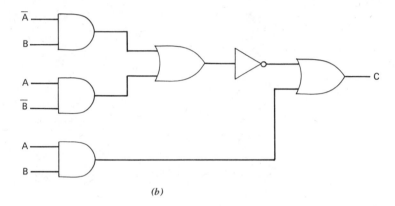

(b)

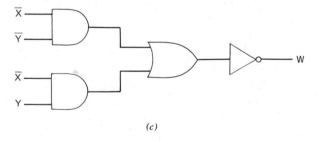

(c)

Figure 5-30.   Logic circuits for Problem 6.

8. Manipulate the logical expressions of Problem 7 into a form suitable for **NOR** logic operation.

§5-4   **9.** Design a logic circuit to provide an output when no inputs or all inputs of three input signals are present.

10. Design a logic circuit to provide an even parity bit for octal code using only **NOR** logic.

0110

Advanced logic techniques and problems

6-1. Introduction to Karnaugh Maps

The little exposure to logic simplication and manipulation covered in Chapter 5 should point out some limitation. It should be obvious that it is often quite difficult to be sure that a logical expression can be simplified, and also how much it can be simplified. A *Karnaugh map* technique, to be described presently, provides a systematic method for simplifying and manipulating Boolean expressions. Although the technique may be used for any number of variables, it is seldom used for more than six, and four variables will be the maximum number presented here.

Two-Variable Karnaugh Map. A Karnaugh map provides a group of boxes or areas labeled in a particular way. Figure 6-1a shows a two variable Karnaugh map with the four boxes each representing a unique combination of the variables.

The boxes represent the four possible conditions with two variables as shown in Figure 6-1b. Thus, the upper-right box corresponds to the condi-

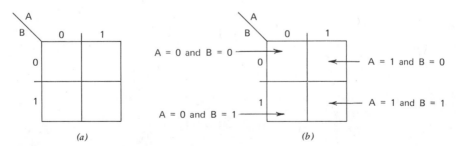

Figure 6-1. Two-variable Karnaugh map. (*a*) Two-variable Karnaugh map. (*b*) Unique specification of each box.

tion of A being logical-1 AND B being logical-0. Notice that the two conditions for the variable A are listed along the top of the map, and for the variable B they are listed along the left side. The boxes represent the unique combinations of the two variables A, B.

$$\overline{A}\overline{B} \qquad (A = 0 \text{ AND } B = 0)$$
$$\overline{A}B \qquad (A = 0 \text{ AND } B = 1)$$
$$A\overline{B} \qquad (A = 1 \text{ AND } B = 0)$$
$$AB \qquad (A = 1 \text{ AND } B = 1)$$

The maps of Figure 6-2 show how a Boolean expression may be obtained from the map. Figure 6-2*a* shows a Karnaugh map having two

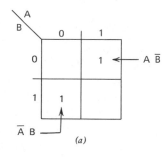

(a)

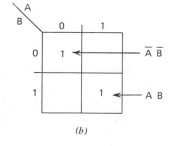

(b)

Figure 6-2.   Obtaining the Boolean expression from a Karnaugh map. (*a*) Map of $A\overline{B} + \overline{A}B$. (*b*) Map of $AB + \overline{A}\overline{B}$.

1's plotted on the map. These 1's indicate the logical conditions for which the Boolean expression is logical-1. Expressed logically

$$\text{Map expression} = A\overline{B} + \overline{A}B$$

Figure 6-2*b* shows a Karnaugh map of the expression

$$M = AB + \overline{A}\overline{B}$$

In some ways the Karnaugh map is like a truth table. It does provide a listing or picture of the conditions for which the function is logical-1.

In a Karnaugh map it is usual to indicate only the logical-1 conditions, all other empty boxes being understood to correspond to the Boolean function being logical-0. The Karnaugh map differs from the truth table in the groupings of the map 1's and results in a simplified expression. For example, consider the Karnaugh maps of Figure 6-3.

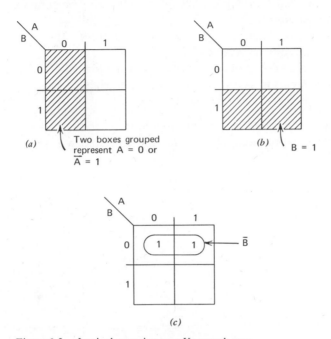

Figure 6-3.   Logical grouping on a Karnaugh map.

Figure 6-3a shows that a grouping of the two boxes below the $A = 0$ heading represents the logical condition of $A = 0$ or of $\overline{A} = 1$. Figure 6-3b shows the Karnaugh map grouping for the logical condition $B = 1$. The Karnaugh map of Figure 6-3c shows two 1's plotted on the map. Since these are *adjacent* they can be grouped together and expressed simply as the logical expression

$$\text{Map expression} = \overline{B}$$

It should be made clear that although the logical-1's on the map may be read as individual terms, which for Figure 6-3c would be

$$\overline{A}\,\overline{B} + A\overline{B}$$

two adjacent's may be read off as a simpler expression, in this case $\overline{B}$.

As verification, notice that

$$\overline{A}\overline{B} + A\overline{B} = \overline{B}(\overline{A} + A) = \overline{B}(1) = \overline{B}$$

For a two-variable Karnaugh map the rules are as follows:

1. Any *two adjacent logical-1's* on the map may be combined to represent a *single* variable.
2. Any single logical-1 on the map represents the AND function (product) of two variables.
3. The total expression corresponding to the logical-1's of a map are the ORed function (sum) of the various variable terms, which covers *all* the logical-1's in the map.

(Notice that a logical-1 may be combined in more than one term to obtain the simplest expression.) The following example will show how these rules apply.

Example 6-1.   Obtain a logical expression from the following Karnaugh map (Figure 6-4a).

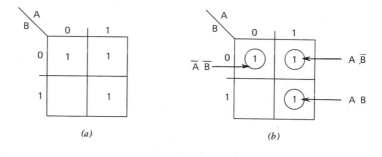

(a)   (b)

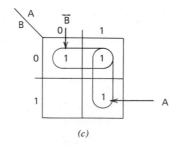

(c)

Figure 6-4.   Karnaugh maps for Example 6-1. (*a*) Map for Example 6-1. (*b*) Using single 1's from map. (*c*) Combining two adjacent 1's.

Solution:

(a) The individual 1's may be read off the map as indicated in Figure 6-4*b* to provide the resulting logical expression

$$M = \overline{A}\overline{B} + A\overline{B} + AB$$

(b) If the adjacent's are combined, the map function may be read off as the expression (see Figure 6-4*c*)

$$M = A + \overline{B}$$

which is simpler than that of part (a) above.

As a rule, then, the simplest expression is obtained directly from the map by combining 1's in the largest grouping possible (two adjacent 1's for a two-variable map).

Exercise 6-1. Write the simplest logical expression for the following Karnaugh maps (see Figure 6-5).

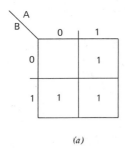

(a)

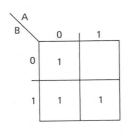

(b)   Figure 6-5.   Karnaugh maps for Exercise 6-1.

Three-Variable Karnaugh Map.   For three variables there are eight (2^3) possible combinations. A Karnaugh map for three variables is shown in Figure 6-6*a*.

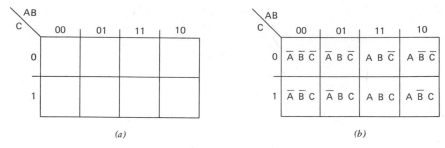

Figure 6-6.   (*a*) Three variable Karnaugh map. (*b*) Individual box designation.

For a three-variable map each box represents the logical product of three variables. Figure 6-6*b* shows the box designation for each box of the map. Notice the order of the binary designation for the combinations of the variables A, B. The order shown − 00, 01, 11, 10 − should always be used for a Karnaugh map to allow the simplifications possible by grouping adjacent 1's, as will be described.

The rules for simplification using a three-variable Karnaugh map are the following:

1. A group of four adjacent boxes can be combined to represent a *single* variable.
2. A group of two adjacent boxes can be combined to represent a two-variable term.
3. A single box represents a three-variable term. (Notice that no grouping of 3, 5, 6, 7 boxes is represented by one term).

As an example of grouping four adjacent boxes, Figure 6-7*a* shows adjacent 1's which can be grouped to represent the single variable term A. Referring to the Karnaugh map note that the adjacent 1's are not affected by the B or C variables, since they cover boxes where B or C are 0 and 1. Only the A variable is always 1 for all four boxes. Figure 6-7*b* shows an adjacency of four boxes which presents a new feature. That is, the map can be considered to be *closed* in that the outside boxes are adjacent. In the present case the B variable is 0 for all four boxes, whereas the A or C variables are 0 or 1, so that the four boxes represent the single variable term $\bar{B}$.

Examples of grouping two adjacent boxes are provided in Figure 6-8. The first map shows that two adjacent boxes represent the term $A\bar{C}$ with the B variable being 1 or 0 for the two boxes. Similarly, the second term BC results from grouping two adjacent boxes. Figure 6-8*b* shows how two end boxes are also considered adjacent. In this case, the A variable is 1 or 0 for the two boxes and the B variable is always 0, with C always 1 resulting in the term $\bar{B}C$.

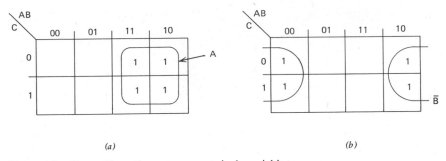

Figure 6-7.   Four adjacent boxes represent single variable term.

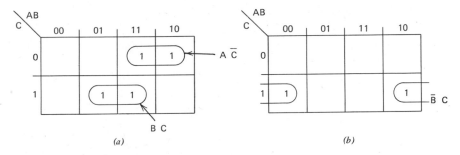

Figure 6-8.   Two adjacent boxes represent two-variable term.

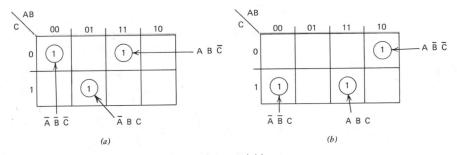

Figure 6-9.   Individual boxes represent three-variable term.

Figure 6-9 shows how single boxes may be read off the map as three variable terms. Notice that the variable designation can be directly interpreted from the binary value headings coincident with a particular box (that is, for the AB heading 11 and C heading 0, the box is represented by the three variable term $AB\overline{C}$.)

Example 6-2.   Write the simplest Boolean expressions represented on the following Karnaugh map (Figure 6-10*a*).

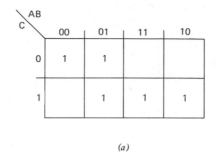

(a)

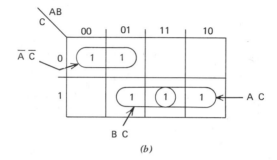

(b)

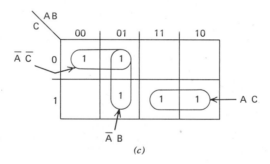

(c)

Figure 6-10.   Karnaugh maps for Example 6-2.

Solution: Figure 6-10*b* shows one grouping of two adjacent boxes. Notice that all the 1's have been included but that, in this case, a particular 1 was used more than once to allow a simpler variable term. The resulting expression is

$$M = \overline{A}\overline{C} + AC + BC$$

In this example the map can be grouped slightly differently, as shown in Figure 6-10*c*, resulting in the logical expression

$$M = \overline{A}\overline{C} + AC + \overline{A}B$$

One might use a truth table to verify that the two expressions are truly identical; however, they result in the exact same map and can thus also be seen to be the same.

Example 6-3. Write the simplest logical expression for the Karnaugh map of Figure 6-11a.

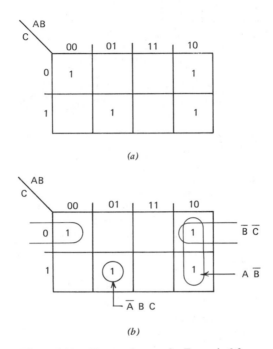

(a)

(b)

Figure 6-11.   Karnaugh maps for Example 6-3.

Solution: The map may be covered (all 1's included) using two pairs of adjacent boxes and a single box. The resulting logical expression (see Figure 6-11b) is

$$M = \overline{A}BC + A\overline{B} + \overline{B}\,\overline{C}$$

Exercise 6-2. Write the simplest logical expression for the following Karnaugh maps (see Figure 6-12).

Preparing a Karnaugh map. Usually, a Boolean expression is first obtained and then the expression is simplified. Previously, we had to resort to algebraic manipulation to obtain a simplified expression. It should be obvious, having tried some algebraic simplifications in Chapter

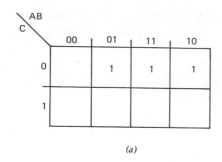

(a)

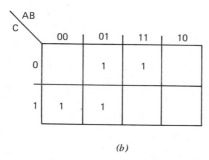

(b)

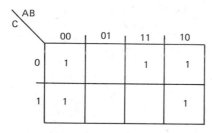

(c)   Figure 6-12.   Karnaugh maps for Exercise 6-2.

5, that it is often difficult to be sure how to proceed, and to be sure that the expression cannot be further simplified. Using a Karnaugh map, a given Boolean expression can be "pictured" in a way that shows, by adjacency of 1's, that some simplification is possible. Consider the following examples.

Example 6-4.   Use a Karnaugh map to help simplify the Boolean expression

$$D = ABC + A\bar{B}\bar{C} + AB\bar{C} + A\bar{B}C + \bar{A}BC$$

Solution: The Karnaugh map of the Boolean expression given is obtained by plotting the 1's corresponding to each term of the given expression (see Figure 6-13a).

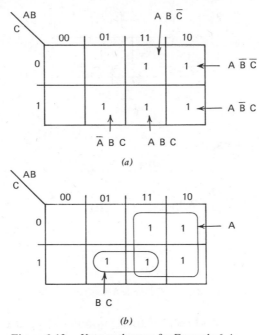

(a)

(b)

Figure 6-13.   Karnaugh maps for Example 6-4.

Grouping the 1's of the resulting map we can "read off" a simpler Boolean expression from Figure 6-13b.

$$D = A + BC$$

Example 6-5.   Prepare Karnaugh maps for the following Boolean expressions.

$$\text{(a)}\quad XY + \overline{X}Z$$
$$\text{(b)}\quad B + AC + \overline{A}\overline{C}$$

Solution: The Karnaugh maps are shown in Figure 6-14.

Exercise 6-3.   Draw a Karnaugh map for each of the following logical expressions. Obtain a simplified expression from the map where possible.

$$\text{(a)}\quad AB + \overline{B}C + \overline{A}\overline{B}$$
$$\text{(b)}\quad AC + A\overline{C}B + BC + \overline{B}\overline{C}$$
$$\text{(c)}\quad XY + \overline{X}Z + \overline{Y}\overline{Z}$$
$$\text{(d)}\quad XY + YZ + XZ + \overline{X}\overline{Y}$$

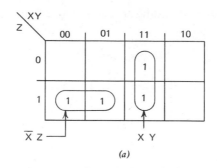

(a)

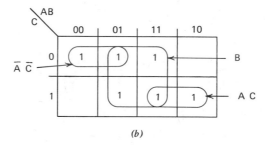

(b)

Figure 6-14.   Karnaugh maps for Example 6-5. (a) $XY + \overline{X}Z$. (b) $B + AC + \overline{A}\overline{C}$.

Four-Variable Karnaugh Maps.   A four-variable Boolean expression may be plotted on a Karnaugh map having 2^4 or 16 boxes, as shown in Figure 6-15.

Notice carefully the ordering of the binary designations both horizontally and vertically. The ordering shown for a Karnaugh map allows adjacent 1's to be grouped to obtain simplest Boolean expressions from

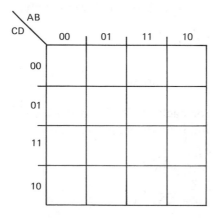

Figure 6-15.   Karnaugh map for four-variable Boolean expressions.

a map. The rules for operating with a four-variable Karnaugh map are the following:

1. A grouping of *eight adjacent boxes* represents a single variable term.
2. A grouping of *four adjacent boxes* represents a two-variable term.
3. A grouping of *two adjacent boxes* represents a three-variable term.
4. *Individual boxes* represent a four-variable term.

Figure 6-16 shows a few examples of groupings as described in the rules above. Using the prescribed Karnaugh map it might be helpful to additionally label the map as shown in Figure 6-17.

The additional labeling reinforces the knowledge of which logical variables are covered by particular areas of the map. For example,

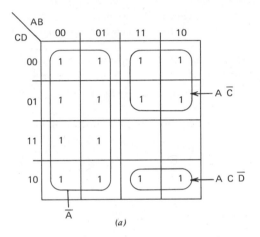

(a)

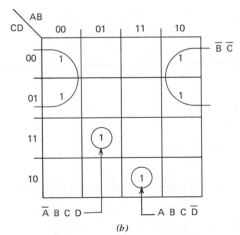

(b)

Figure 6-16.   Four-variable Karnaugh map examples.

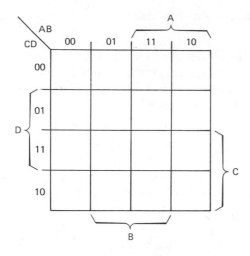

Figure 6-17.   Additional designation of four-variable Karnaugh map.

Figure 6-17 shows that any 1 in the right two columns represents the variable A, with the understanding that the left two columns represent the variable $\overline{A}$. Similarly, the bottom two rows represent the variable C, the middle two rows the variable D, and so on.

However, if the binary headings are used, then the interpretation is, for example, that

A	B	C	D
0	0	1	1

is the four-variable term.

$$\overline{A}\overline{B}CD$$

As always, the largest adjacent box grouping (either eight, four, or two) provides the least variable terms. A number of examples should be helpful.

Example 6-6.   Write the Boolean expression of the following Karnaugh map (Figure 6-18a).

Solution: Figure 6-18b shows a grouping to cover all the 1's resulting in the following logical expression:

$$M = \overline{A}C + \overline{A}\overline{B}D + AB\overline{C}\overline{D}$$

Example 6-7.   Write the Boolean expression of the Karnaugh map in Figure 6-19a.

Solution: Figure 6-19b shows one possible grouping resulting in the

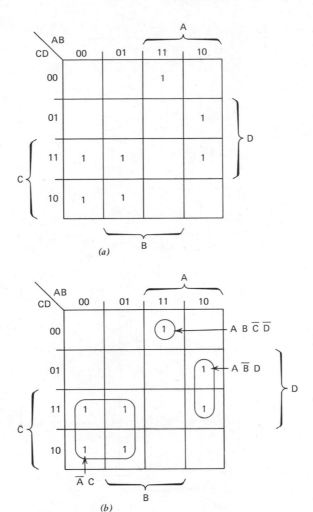

Figure 6-18.   Karnaugh maps for Example 6-6.

logical expression

$$M = W\overline{X}Z + YZ + WX\overline{Z} + \overline{W}\,\overline{X}\,\overline{Y}\,\overline{Z}$$

Example 6-8.   Plot the logical expression

$$WXYZ + \overline{W}\,\overline{X}Y\overline{Z} + WY\overline{Z} + YZ$$

on a four-variable Karnaugh map and obtain a simpler expression from the map, if possible.

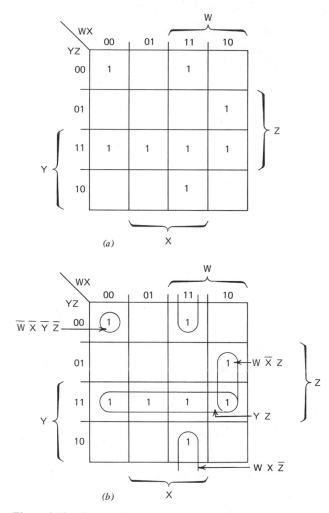

Figure 6-19.   Karnaugh maps for Example 6-7.

Solution: See Figure 6-20.

From the map, one logical expression is

$$YZ + WY\overline{Z} + \overline{W}\overline{X}Y$$

Example 6-9.   Plot the logical expression

$$\overline{A}\overline{B}CD + ABCD + \overline{A}C\overline{D} + \overline{A}CD + A\overline{B}D$$

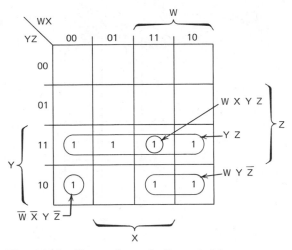

Figure 6-20.   Karnaugh map for Example 6-8.

on a four-variable Karnaugh map and obtain a simpler expression from the map, if possible.

Solution: See Figure 6-21.

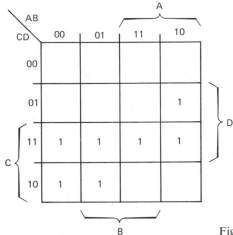

Figure 6-21.   Karnaugh map for Example 6-9.

From the map the expression can be read as

$$\overline{A}C + A\overline{B}D + CD$$

Exercise 6-4.   Write the simplest logical expression from the following Karnaugh maps in Figure 6-22.

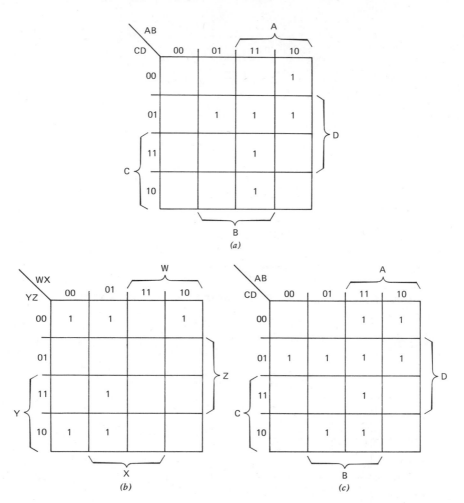

Figure 6-22.   Karnaugh maps for Exercise 6-4.

6-2.   Truth Table to Karnaugh Map

Truth Table and Karnaugh Map.   We previously considered a problem-solving procedure in which a truth table was developed corresponding to the given verbal problem. Having obtained a truth table the next step is to write the function in a logical expression and then simplify, if possible. One technique for simplifying would be to go from the truth table directly to a Karnaugh map and then obtain a simple expression from the map. Going from a truth table to a Karnaugh map is quite easy.

Table 6-1 is a truth table for obtaining the odd parity bit for octal code.

Table 6-1. *Odd Parity for Octal Code*

A	B	C	P
0	0	0	1
0	0	1	0
0	1	0	0
0	1	1	1
1	0	0	0
1	0	1	1
1	1	0	1
1	1	1	0

To plot the terms for which P is 1, the binary values of the table are used directly as follows:

$$P = 1 \text{ for } A = 0, B = 0, C = 0$$

This is plotted by a 1 in the upper left box of Figure 6-23. Similarly, for

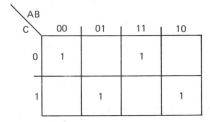

Figure 6-23.   Karnaugh map from Table 6-1.

the other terms for P = 1,

$$
\begin{array}{cccccccc}
 & & & & & A & B & C \\
A = 0, & B = 1, & C = 1 & \rightarrow & & 0 & 1 & 1 \\
A = 1, & B = 0, & C = 1 & \rightarrow & & 1 & 0 & 1 \\
A = 1, & B = 1, & C = 0 & \rightarrow & & 1 & 1 & 0 \\
\end{array}
$$

The Karnaugh map shows quite clearly that no simplification is possible since there are no adjacent boxes to group together. The resulting logical expression from the map is then

$$P = \overline{A}\cdot\overline{B}\cdot\overline{C} + \overline{A}\cdot B\cdot C + A\cdot B\cdot\overline{C} + A\cdot\overline{B}\cdot C$$

Example 6-10.   Obtain a logical expression for the function W described by Table 6-2.

Table 6-2.

X	Y	Z	W
0	0	0	0
0	0	1	0
0	1	0	1
0	1	1	1
1	0	0	1
1	0	1	0
1	1	0	1
1	1	1	1

Solution: A Karnaugh map for the truth table given is shown in Figure 6-24.

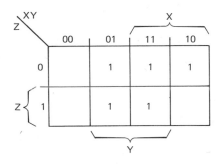

Figure 6-24.   Karnaugh map for Example 6-10.

There are five 1's on the truth table that are directly read off in binary and plotted on the Karnaugh map. A simple expression can be read off the map, this being

$$W = Y + X\overline{Z}$$

Numbered Box Designation. To help make the operation more systematic we can assign a number to each line of the truth table and to each box of the Karnaugh map corresponding to the binary value of the three-variable term. Table 6-3 shows this designation, as does Figure 6-25a.

From the truth table the output P is a logical-1 for lines 0, 3, 5 and 6; therefore, on the map of Figure 6-25b, 1's are placed in the corresponding box positions.

Using the number Karnaugh map (as in Figure 6-25a) thus allows direct transfer from the truth table to the Karnaugh map in a simple manner.

Table 6-3. *Truth Table Showing Row Numerical Designation*

Numerical Value	A	B	C	P
0	0	0	0	1
1	0	0	1	0
2	0	1	0	0
3	0	1	1	1
4	1	0	0	0
5	1	0	1	1
6	1	1	0	1
7	1	1	1	0

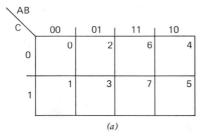
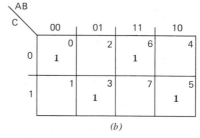

Figure 6-25.   Karnaugh map with box number designation.

Example 6-11.   Prepare a Karnaugh map for the following truth table (Table 6-4).

Table 6-4.

	X	Y	Z	W
0	0	0	0	1
1	0	0	1	0
2	0	1	0	1
3	0	1	1	1
4	1	0	0	0
5	1	0	1	0
6	1	1	0	1
7	1	1	1	1

Solution: The logical-1's from the truth table are mapped into boxes 0, 2, 3, 6 and 7 in Figure 6-26.

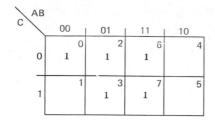

Figure 6-26.   Karnaugh map for Example 6-11.

The use of numbered designations becomes even more helpful for four-variable Karnaugh maps. A Karnaugh map showing this designation is that of Figure 6-27.

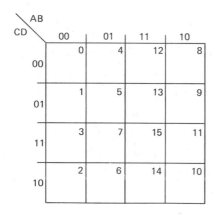

Figure 6-27.   Four-variable Karnaugh map with number designation.

Example 6-12.   Prepare a Karnaugh map corresponding to the logical function of Table 6-5.

From the truth table the function T is logical-1 for the row designations 0, 2, 3, 4, 6, 10, 12, and 13. Plotting 1's on a Karnaugh map for these box designations results in the map of Figure 6-28.

Canonical Form. Each of the rows of the truth table (or each box of a Karnaugh map) represents the *canonical* form for expressing a logical term. For a three-variable function each canonical term contains three variables; there are eight altogether. For a four-variable function there are 16 canonical terms of four variables each. There are two basic expansions of Boolean functions. One, the *disjunctive canonical expansion* (D.C.E.), also referred to as the *expanded sum of products* or *minterm expansion* is, for example,

$$D = AB\overline{C} + \overline{A}\overline{B}C + A\overline{B}C$$

Table 6-5. *Truth Table for Example 6-12*

	A	B	C	D	T
0	0	0	0	0	1
1	0	0	0	1	0
2	0	0	1	0	1
3	0	0	1	1	1
4	0	1	0	0	1
5	0	1	0	1	0
6	0	1	1	0	1
7	0	1	1	1	0
8	1	0	0	0	0
9	1	0	0	1	0
10	1	0	1	0	1
11	1	0	1	1	0
12	1	1	0	0	1
13	1	1	0	1	1
14	1	1	1	0	0
15	1	1	1	1	0

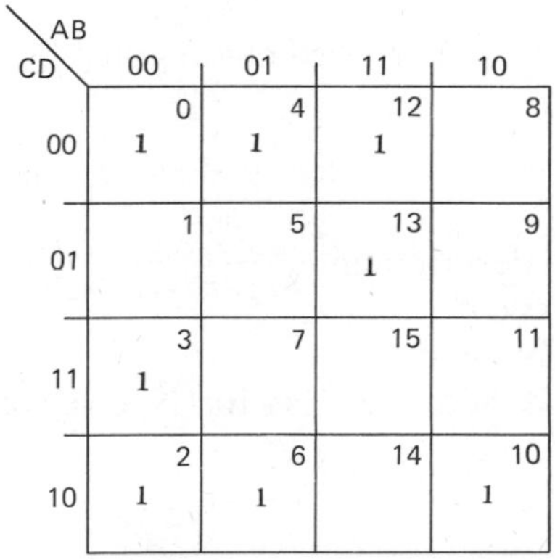

Figure 6-28.   Karnaugh map for Example 6-12.

The other is the *conjunctive canonical expansion* (C.C.E.) also referred to as the *product of sums or maxterm expansion*, given, for example, by

$$D = (\overline{A} + \overline{B} + \overline{C})(A + \overline{B} + \overline{C})(A + \overline{B} + C)$$

For the present we only note that the minterm form is the desired form to obtain a NAND logic expression and the maxterm form is suitable to manipulate into a NOR logic expression. One additional shorthand notation will prove helpful. Rather than write out the complete Boolean expression from a truth table, the row number designation may be stated as follows. For Example 6-11, the minterms expression can be specified as

$$W = \Sigma\,(0, 2, 3, 6, 7)$$

meaning that the sum of the Boolean terms of rows 0, 2, 3, 6, and 7 form the Boolean expression for W, which in this case would be

$$W = \overline{X}\,\overline{Y}\,\overline{Z} + \overline{X}\,Y\,\overline{Z} + \overline{X}\,Y\,Z + X\,Y\,\overline{Z} + X\,Y\,Z$$

Exercise 6-5. Prepare a truth table and Karnaugh map for the logic circuit to provide an even parity bit for octal codes.

Exercise 6-6. Prepare a four-variable Karnaugh map for the Boolean function expressed by the minterms.

$$S = \Sigma\,(0, 3, 4, 7, 9, 12, 14)$$

and obtain the simplest expression from the map.

6-3. Sample Design Problems

Design Procedure.   A logic circuit design may be carried out in a step-by-step procedure as follows:

1. Obtain verbal description of problem with clearly defined logic definitions.
2. Prepare logic truth table from verbal descriptions.
3. Map from logic table onto Karnaugh map.
4. Obtain simplified logic expression from map.
5. Manipulate to desired logic form if necessary (as for NAND or NOR gate implementation).
6. Draw logic circuit diagram.

A few examples should show how this is used.

Example 6-13.   Design a logic circuit to provide the odd parity bit for an 8421 BCD code unit.

Solution: A truth table for obtaining the odd parity bit (P) for the 8421 code is prepared as shown in Table 6-6.

The minterms from the table for the function P can be stated as

$$P = \Sigma\,(0, 3, 5, 6, 9)$$

Table 6-6.   *Truth Table for BCD Odd-Parity Bit Generator*

	A (8)	B (4)	C (2)	D (1)	Odd Parity Bit (P)
0	0	0	0	0	1
1	0	0	0	1	0
2	0	0	1	0	0
3	0	0	1	1	1
4	0	1	0	0	0
5	0	1	0	1	1
6	0	1	1	0	1
7	0	1	1	1	0
8	1	0	0	0	0
9	1	0	0	1	1

The minterm function can be easily plotted on a Karnaugh map using box numerical designation as shown in Figure 6-29. From the Karnaugh

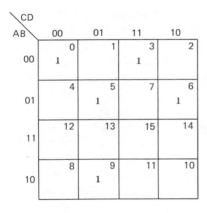

Figure 6-29.   Karnaugh map for Example 6-13.

map it is immediately obvious that with no adjacent boxes no simplification can be obtained. The logic expression can be read as

$$P = \overline{A}\,\overline{B}\,\overline{C}\,\overline{D} + \overline{A}\,\overline{B}CD + \overline{A}B\overline{C}D + \overline{A}BC\overline{D} + A\overline{B}\,\overline{C}D$$

The expression could be written in the factored form

$$P = \overline{A}\,\overline{B}(\overline{C}\,\overline{D} + CD) + AB(\overline{C}D + C\overline{D}) + A\overline{B}\,\overline{C}D$$
$$= \overline{A}\,\overline{B}(\overline{C}\,\overline{D} + CD) + \overline{A}B(\overline{C}D + C\overline{D}) + A\overline{B}\,\overline{C}D$$

Using the last expression, a NAND gate implementation could be obtained as shown in Figure 6-30.

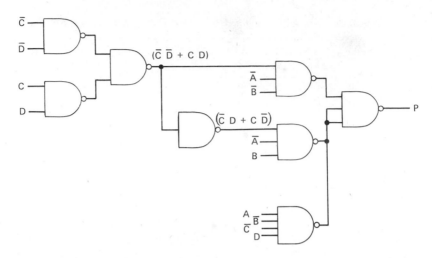

Figure 6-30.   Logic diagram for Example 6-13.

Full-Adder Circuit.   An important logical circuit is the full-adder circuit used in the arithmetic section of a computer, for example. When adding two binary numbers, X and Y, the sum resulting for each bit position of addition depends on the bits X and Y *in that position* and also any carry from the next lower position of the number. Only the units position (2^0) has no carry to add. All other positions required addition of the X bit, Y bit, *and* carry-in (C_i) bit from the next lower position. Thus, a full adder has three inputs to be summed. The full adder must also provide two outputs—a sum (S) output and a carry-out (C_o), this being the carry to be added into the next higher position of the number. A truth table for the full adder is shown in Table 6-7. The table is obtained by summing the three input bits (X, Y, C_i) with a resulting sum of 1 for an odd number of

Table 6-7.   *Truth Table for Full-Adder Operation*

X	Y	C_i	S	C_o
0	0	0	0	0
0	0	1	1	0
0	1	0	1	0
0	1	1	0	1
1	0	0	1	0
1	0	1	0	1
1	1	0	0	1
1	1	1	1	1

1 bits and 0 otherwise. The carry-out is a 1 for input combinations having two or three bits of 1.

As a next step note the Karnaugh maps for the full-adder circuit as obtained from the truth table. There are two separate Karnaugh maps — one for each output function (see Figure 6-31).

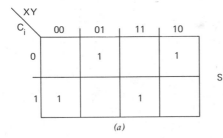

(a)

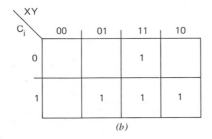

(b)

Figure 6-31.   Karnaugh maps for full-adder. (*a*) Sum map. (*b*) Carry-out map.

From the maps we note that the sum function allows no simplification by grouping adjacent 1's. The carry-out function can be simplified by grouping adjacent 1's. As a start, the resulting logical expressions can be obtained from the maps.

$$S = \overline{X}\overline{Y}C_i + \overline{X}Y\overline{C}_i + XYC_i + X\overline{Y}\overline{C}_i$$
$$C_o = YC_i + XC_i + XY$$

A logic implementation using NAND gates only is shown in Figure 6-32.

Full-Subtractor Circuit.   Another logic circuit that can be associated with an arithmetic unit is the full subtractor. Two binary numbers are subtracted so that in each bit position we obtain the difference of $(X - Y) - B_i$, where B_i is the borrow-in from the next lower position of the binary number.

A truth table for the subtractor is shown in Table 6-8 with D, the difference between X and the sum of Y and B_i, and B_o, the borrow-out for the next higher position.

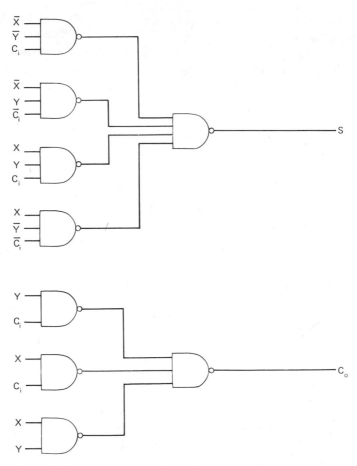

Figure 6-32.   Logic diagram of full-adder.

Table 6-8.   *Truth Table for Full-Subtractor*

X	Y	B_i	D	B_o
0	0	0	0	0
0	0	1	1	1
0	1	0	1	1
0	1	1	0	1
1	0	0	1	0
1	0	1	0	0
1	1	0	0	0
1	1	1	1	1

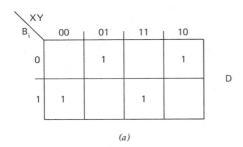

(a)

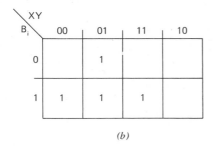

(b)

Figure 6-33.   Karnaugh maps for full-subtractor. (a) Difference map. (b) Borrow-
out map.

From the truth table the Karnaugh maps obtained are those of Figure
6-33. The logical expressions for the difference (D) and borrow-out (B_o)
may be obtained as follows

$$D = \overline{X}\,\overline{Y}B_i + \overline{X}Y\overline{B}_i + XYB_i + X\overline{Y}\,\overline{B}_i$$
$$B_o = \overline{X}B_i + \overline{X}Y + YB_i$$

The logical expressions may be reworked to the form

$$D = B_i(XY + \overline{X}\,\overline{Y}) + \overline{B}_i(X\overline{Y} + \overline{X}Y)$$
$$B_o = B_i(\overline{X} + Y) + \overline{X}Y$$

Figure 6-34 shows the logical circuit of the full subtractor for the last
expressions above. A careful observation of the difference expression or
Karnaugh map shows that with B_i replaced by C_i the sum or difference
terms are identical.

Exercise 6-7.   Design a logic circuit to provide an output when any two
or three of four switches are closed.

Exercise 6-8.   Design a logic circuit to provide an even parity bit for the
excess-three code.

Exercise 6-9.   Design the logic circuit of a three-bit comparator which
provides a 1 output whenever the three input bits are *not all* the same.

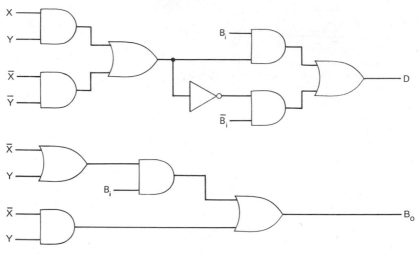

Figure 6-34.   Full-subtractor logic circuit.

6-4.   Code Converter Logic Design

As another example of logic design of a more advanced nature a few code converter logic circuits will be designed in this section. In addition a new idea, that of *don't care* terms will be introduced.

2*421 to BCD Code Converter.   A first example will be a logic converter circuit to convert the 2*421 code into the 8421 (BCD) code. A truth table showing the corresponding code terms for both codes is provided in Table 6-9.

Table 6-9.   *2*421 and 8421 code equivalencies*

Decimal Number	A (2*)	B (4)	C (2)	D (1)	W (8)	X (4)	Y (2)	Z (1)
0	0	0	0	0	0	0	0	0
1	0	0	0	1	0	0	0	1
1	0	0	1	0	0	0	1	0
3	0	0	1	1	0	0	1	1
4	0	1	0	0	0	1	0	0
5	1	0	1	1	0	1	0	1
6	1	1	0	0	0	1	1	0
7	1	1	0	1	0	1	1	1
8	1	1	1	0	1	0	0	0
9	1	1	1	1	1	0	0	1

A block diagram of the logic converter is shown in Figure 6-35. For any of the four-bit 2*421 code values as input the logic circuit will provide the equivalent BCD (8421) code value as described in Table 6-9. For example, inputs of ABCD of 1101, respectively, should result in outputs of WXYZ of 0111, respectively.

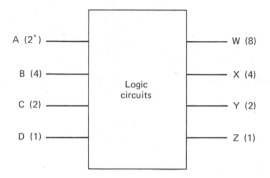

Figure 6-35.   Block diagram of 2*421 to BCD converter.

Having obtained a truth table the next step is to prepare Karnaugh maps for each of the output variables, that is, one map for W, one for X, one for Y, and one for Z, as shown in Figure 6-36. Expressed as minterms the Karnaugh plot can be obtained directly from the truth table from

$$W = \Sigma\,(8, 9)$$
$$X = \Sigma\,(4, 5, 6, 7)$$
$$Y = \Sigma\,(2, 3, 6, 7)$$
$$Z = \Sigma\,(1, 3, 5, 7, 9)$$

From the Karnaugh maps the following logical expressions are obtained:

$$W = A\overline{B}\overline{C}$$
$$X = \overline{A}B$$
$$Y = \overline{A}C$$
$$Z = \overline{A}D + \overline{B}\overline{C}D$$

A logic circuit of the code converter is shown in Figure 6-37.

BCD (8421) to Excess-Three Code Converter.   A second example is a converter to go from the 8421 BCD code to the excess-three code. Table 6-10 is the logic truth table showing equivalent code values.

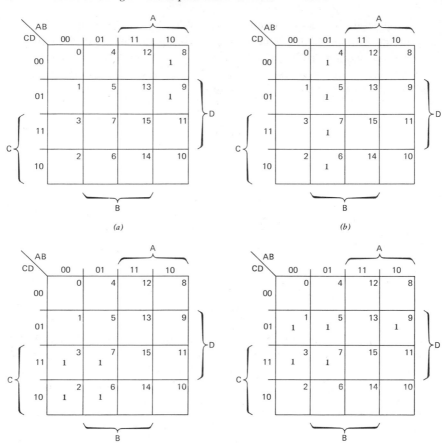

Figure 6-36.   Karnaugh maps for 2*421 to BCD code converter. (*a*) W map. (*b*) X map. (*c*) Y map. (*d*) Z map.

The minterm expressions from the truth table are

$$W = \Sigma\,(5, 6, 7, 8, 9)$$
$$X = \Sigma\,(1, 2, 3, 4, 9)$$
$$Y = \Sigma\,(0, 3, 4, 7, 8)$$
$$Z = \Sigma\,(0, 2, 4, 6, 8)$$

The Karnaugh maps for the converter are shown in Figure 6-38. From the Karnaugh maps the following expressions can be obtained.

$$W = A\overline{B}\overline{C} + \overline{A}BD + \overline{A}BC$$
$$X = \overline{A}\overline{B}C + \overline{B}\overline{C}D + \overline{A}BC\overline{D}$$
$$Y = \overline{A}C\overline{D} + \overline{B}\overline{C}D + \overline{A}CD$$
$$Z = \overline{A}\overline{D} + B\overline{C}\overline{D}$$

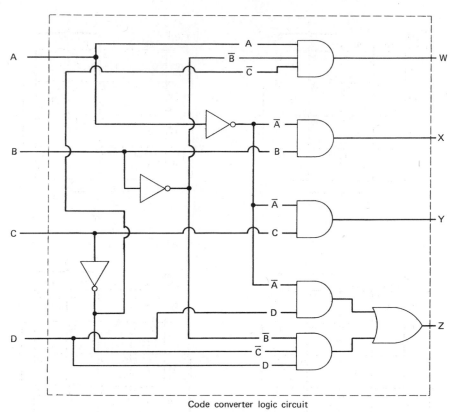

Code converter logic circuit

Figure 6-37.   2*421 to 8421 code converter.

Table 6-10.   *Truth Table of BCD and Excess-Three Codes*

Decimal Number	BCD				Excess-three			
	A (8)	B (4)	C (2)	D (2)	W	X	Y	Z
0	0	0	0	0	0	0	1	1
1	0	0	0	1	0	1	0	0
2	0	0	1	0	0	1	0	1
3	0	0	1	1	0	1	1	0
4	0	1	0	0	0	1	1	1
5	0	1	0	1	1	0	0	0
6	0	1	1	0	1	0	0	1
7	0	1	1	1	1	0	1	0
8	1	0	0	0	1	0	1	1
9	1	0	0	1	1	1	0	0

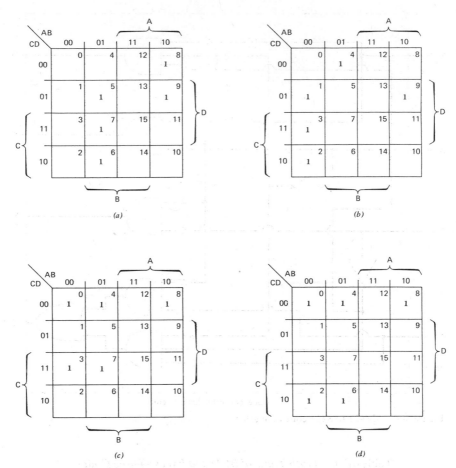

Figure 6-38.   Karnaugh maps for BCD to excess-three code converter. (*a*) W map. (*b*) X map. (*c*) Y map. (*d*) Z map.

Don't Care Terms.   When designing the code converter logic circuits the output functions were considered only for the ten possible combinations of code numerical values. There are, in these cases, six other combinations of the four variables that were not considered at all. Since these six other combinations of input should never occur it seemed appropriate to ignore them. This will be seen as shortsighted because, although nothing other than the desired input combinations can occur, we can make use of the nonoccurring states, as we shall now describe.

Returning to the previous example, converting BCD code to excess-three, notice in Figure 6-39 that there are 16 boxes for each Karnaugh

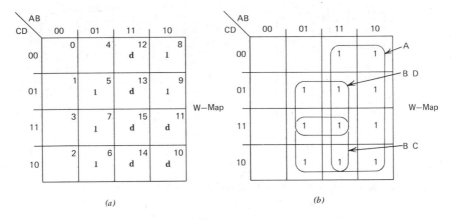

Figure 6-39.   Karnaugh maps showing use of don't-care condition.

map. For ten of these the function (as given by the truth table) is either 0 or 1. For the other six boxes, however, we really *don't care* whether the box is assigned a 0 or a 1 since these conditions will not occur. If we truly don't care then we could assign each or these six remaining boxes as *either* 0 or 1. In the past example they were supposedly ignored, but actually they were considered to be 0. What we now propose is to be more concerned with assigning 1 or 0 to each of the don't care boxes. Figure 6-39*a* shows the initial map condition for the output variable W. From the map there are five boxes that are 1, five boxes that are 0 and six boxes marked as *d* for *don't care*. In the previous consideration these six don't care boxes were assumed to be all 0 and the map function obtained was

$$W = A\overline{B}\overline{C} + \overline{A}BD + \overline{A}BC$$

Using the don't care terms it may be possible to obtain a simpler relation. For example, choosing all six boxes of don't care as 1 results in the Karnaugh map shown in Figure 6-39*b*. Grouping these 1's as shown results in the logical expression

$$W = A + BC + BD = A + B(C + D)$$

which is much simpler than the expression for W above. We have taken advantage of the six states that are of no concern (and shouldn't occur). Notice carefully that the ten conditions that are of interest do still result in 1 or 0 outputs for W, as specified by the truth table. Using the don't care concept in the remaining output variables leads to the Karnaugh maps of Figures 6-40 to 6-42 for the variables X, Y, and Z, respectively.

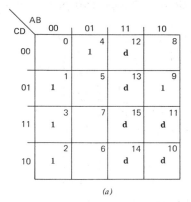
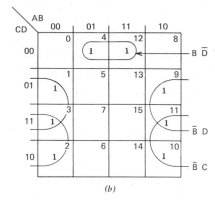

Figure 6-40.   Karnaugh maps using don't-care conditions for X.

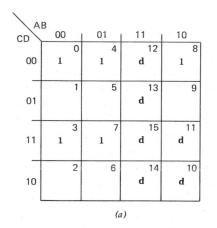
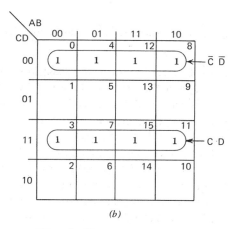

Figure 6-41.   Karnaugh maps using don't-care conditions for Y.

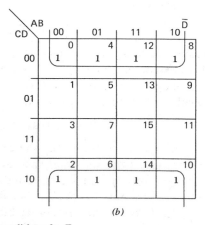

Figure 6-42.   Karnaugh maps using don't-care conditions for Z.

180

The resulting equations (including the W expression) are

$$W = A + B(C + D)$$
$$X = B\overline{D} + \overline{B}(C + D)$$
$$Y = CD + \overline{C}\overline{D}$$
$$Z = \overline{D}$$

A logic circuit for the above logic expressions is shown in Figure 6-43.

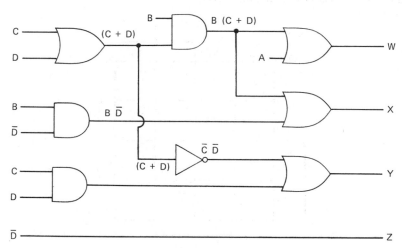

Figure 6-43.   BCD to excess-three code converter logic circuit.

Exercise 6-10.   Design a code converter for excess-three code to BCD.
(Use don't care conditions to help simplify.)

Exercise 6-11.   Design a BCD to 2*421 code converter using don't care
conditions to help simplify logic expressions.

PROBLEMS

§6-1   1. Write the simplest logical expression for the following Karnaugh maps
(Figure 6-44).
2. Draw a Karnaugh map for the following expressions. Obtain a simplified expression from the map where possible.

(a) $ABC + A\overline{B}C + \overline{A}BC + \overline{A}\overline{B}C$
(b) $XY\overline{Z} + X\overline{Y}Z + X\overline{Y}\overline{Z} + XYZ$

3. Write the simplest Boolean expression for the Karnaugh maps of
Figure 6-45.

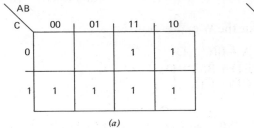
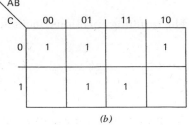

(a)   (b)

Figure 6-44.   Karnaugh maps for Problem 6-1.

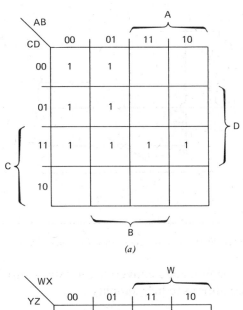

(a)

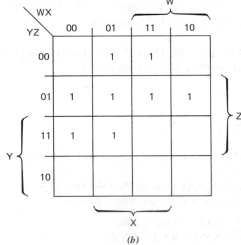

(b)

Figure 6-45.   Karnaugh maps for Problem 6-3.

§6-2   4. Prepare a truth table and Karnaugh map for a logic circuit to provide output when any one of all three signals are present for three inputs.

5. Prepare a four-variable Karnaugh map for the Boolean function expressed by the minterms

$$W = \Sigma(1, 5, 6, 7, 14, 15)$$

Obtain simplest logical expression from map.

§6-3   6. Develop the logic expressions to provide an output when only one or two inputs are present for a four-input circuit.

7. Develop the logic expressions to provide an odd parity bit for the 2*421 code.

8. Design a four-bit comparator which provides an output whenever the four input bits are *different*.

§6-4   9. Design a code converter for BCD to 5421 code. Use don't care conditions to help simplify.

Section Two

COMPUTER CIRCUITS AND BLOCKS

0111

Computer logic gates and multivibrators

7-1. Introduction

The field of computer circuits is changing and growing at a very quick rate. Initially, computer circuitry (or logic circuits) was ingeniously made using relays and switches. The first computers had little or no memory and operated from a wired or fixed program only. When the memory feature was added, making it possible to store programs, the entire concept of computer utilization changed. Relays were no longer used because they were slow, large, and had poor mechanical reliability. Vacuum tubes (triodes and diodes) came into use for a short time. They too have been quickly replaced because of the size factor, amount of power used (heater power alone is considerable for a computer with a few thousand tubes), and reliability. Solid-state components entered the computer field (and many other fields) and quickly took complete control. Switching transistors, switching diodes, tunnel diodes, field-effect transistors, zener diodes, silicon-controlled rectifiers, unijunction transistors, power transistors, and so on, all have the advantages of the solid-state device — small size, no heater power (and no warm-up time), and high reliability. Initially, these components proved themselves very useful to the military because of weight (size) and power for use in sea and aerospace operation. Once accepted and used, the initial high cost was overcome, and these components were universally accepted in the civilian consumer market because of their high reliability. Figure 7-1a shows some practical computer circuits as built on printed circuit connector boards. Circuits similar to those studied in this chapter are shown.

In the past few years a further advance in solid-state electronics has again changed the character of computer circuits. Integrated circuits (ICs), containing complete circuits or even groups of circuits, have been

187

made in a single manufacturing process. The general designation for these new "components" is microelectronics (see Figure 7-1*b*). They are of a few orders of magnitude smaller than discrete circuits (as a whole) and have very good reliability. New computer systems on the market are now using microelectronic circuits almost exclusively. At present, a few different types of microelectronic circuits are available, and research to develop better circuits results in continual changes in the circuit configuration and basic components. Chapter 8 deals exclusively with a variety of logic gates and multivibrator circuits manufactured as IC units.

Because semiconductor (solid-state) devices are very popular and will be encountered in practice, they will be used to describe typical building

Figure 7-1.   Computer circuits. (*a*) Computer circuits built on printed circuit boards (courtesy of Digital Electronics, Westbury, N.Y.). (*b*) Computer circuits built with microelectronics (integrated) components.

blocks. Computer OR gates and AND gates are made of diode and resistor combinations, with the diode as the gating or logic element. Inverter circuits require an active device, the transistor in this case, to negate, to complement, or to invert a signal. A NAND gate or NOR gate made of a combination of diodes, resistors, and transistors, with the diode again the logic element and the transistor the inverting component, is covered.

The three basic multivibrator circuits — bistable, monostable, and astable are covered as is the Schmitt trigger circuit. These are basic versions of the circuits built using discrete components. Basic circuit concepts are developed in this chapter.

7-2. Diode AND, OR Gates

Diode Operation.   A review of the diode characteristic is provided before considering it's use in logic circuits. Ideally, the diode acts like a short-circuit when *forward-biased* and an open-circuit when *reverse-biased* (see Figure 7-2).

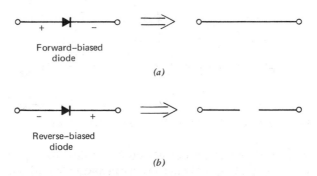

Forward–biased
diode

(*a*)

Reverse–biased
diode

(*b*)

Figure 7-2.   Ideal action of diode. (*a*) Forward-biased diode. (*b*) Reverse-biased diode.

A volt-ampere characteristic of the ideal diode is shown in Figure 7-3*a*. When reverse-biased, the diode current is zero, corresponding to infinite resistance. When forward-biased, the diode voltage drop is zero, corresponding to zero resistance.

A practical diode characteristic is shown in Figure 7-3*b*. It differs from the ideal diode in the forward direction in two main factors. A voltage of typically a few tenths of a volt (about 0.3 volt for germanium and 0.7 volt for silicon) results when the diode is forward-biased. In addition, the diode has an average dc resistance of, typically, a few ohms to tens of

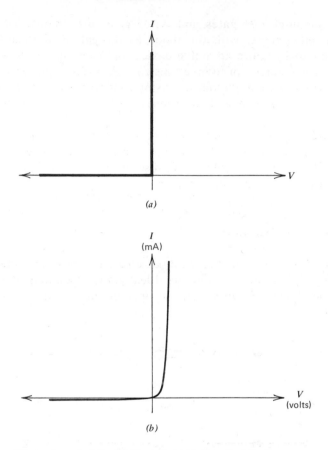

Figure 7-3.   Diode characteristic. (*a*) Ideal diode. (*b*) Practical diode.

ohms. The conventional current direction is the flow of positive charge in the direction of the diode symbol arrow (from anode to cathode).

When a practical diode is reverse-biased it comes very close to ideal behavior. Rather than exactly zero current in the reverse direction there is a small leakage current, typically a few microamperes for germanium and as little as a few nanoamperes for silicon devices.

Diode Circuit Action.   A single-input diode gate performs no logic since the output follows the input, but it will still demonstrate the diode's electrical operation in a circuit (Figure 7-4*a*). When the input is at 0 volts, the + 10-volt supply voltage forward-biases the diode through a resistor connected to the anode side of the diode. The diode is forward-biased with a few tenths of a volt across it. Current through the diode is limited

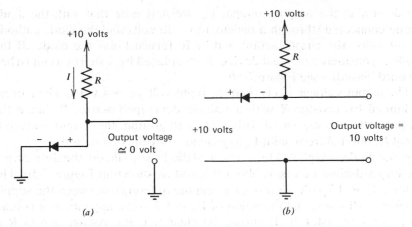

Figure 7-4.   Diode circuit action. (*a*) Output for diode gate with 0-volt input. (*b*) Diode gate with +10-volt input.

by the resistor to less than 10/R. The output voltage taken from the anode to ground is then nearly 0 volts.

With an input of +10 volts (Figure 7-4*b*), the diode is not forward-biased, no current flows through the resistor R, and no voltage drop is developed across R. Thus, the output voltage is the supply voltage, +10 volts.

To be sure that the operation of a diode in a single dc circuit is understood, consider the circuit of Figure 7-5*a*. An input of +4 volts is applied.

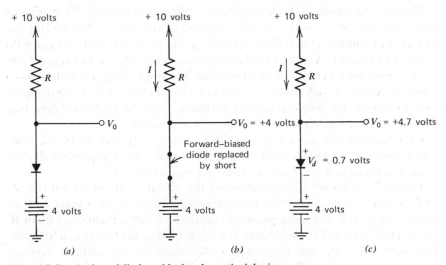

Figure 7-5.   Action of diode as ideal and practical device.

To determine the output voltage, V_0, we first note that with the diode anode connected (through a resistor) to $+10$ volts and the diode cathode at $+4$ volts, the circuit action will be to forward-bias the diode. If the diode is considered an ideal device, it is replaced by a short-circuit (when forward-biased) — see Figure 7-5b.

The output voltage, V_0, is then the input voltage, $+4$ volts. The current is limited by resistor R with a voltage developed across R. Since the output voltage is measured with respect to ground, the output voltage V is not IR but that from point V_0 to ground, $+4$ volts in this case.

If the diode is replaced by a practical diode, say silicon, the drop across the forward-biased diode is about 0.7 volt as shown in Figure 7-5c. The voltage V_0 is 4.7 volts in this case and the difference between the supply voltage, $+10$ volts, and the value of V_0, $+4.7$ volts, appears as a voltage drop across resistor R. It should be clear that the voltage across R is 5.3 volts, in this case, without any specification of R or calculation of I. The voltage drop across R in the present circuit is *fixed* by the voltage drops across the supply and input batteries and a fixed voltage is dropped across the diode. The current I is determined by the choice of R and generally the value of R is chosen to limit the current I.

Diode Logic Gates.   We have already considered logic operation with AND and OR gates in Chapters 5 and 6. Logic levels of 0 and 1 are applied as input to a logic gate with the output either 0 or 1. Recall that for an AND gate all inputs must be 1 for the output to be 1, and for the OR gate any input of 1 results in a 1 output.

Figure 7-6a shows a diode logic gate. We will determine what type of logic gate it is after analyzing the operation of the circuit. The circuit has two input terminals, each diode providing an input. All voltages are with respect to ground. A more usual circuit diagram is shown in Figure 7-6b. In this diagram it is to be understood that the single output terminal has a voltage measured *with respect to ground* and that the $+V$ voltage designation indicates the positive battery terminal with the understanding that the negative battery terminal is connected to ground.

Consider the circuit of Figure 7-7a having supply voltage of $+6$ volts and resistor R of 1K. Assume the diode as ideal for the present discussion. The input voltage levels will be $+6$ volts and 0 volts.

Figure 7-7b shows the operation of the circuit with one input 0 volts and the other $+6$ volts. With the cathode of diode D_2 at 0 volts and the anode connected to a more positive voltage ($+6$ volts) through resistor R, diode D_2 is forward-biased. Since the ideal voltage drop across a forward-bias is 0 volts, the anode voltage is the same as the cathode voltage, 0 volts. The anode of D_2 is then seen to be reverse-biased, with the $+6$

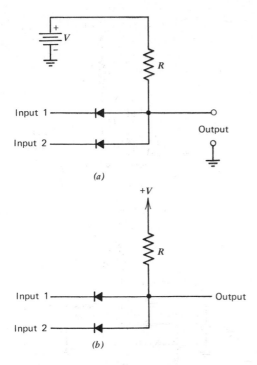

(a)

(b)

Figure 7-6.   Diode logic circuit.

volts input (at cathode) more positive than the 0 volts at the diode anode. Current flows through the resistor R and forward-biased diode D_2. The value of the current is limited by resistor R to (in this example)

$$I = \frac{V}{R} = \frac{6V}{1K} = 6 \text{ mA}$$

If the output voltages of $+6$ volts and 0 volts were connected to diodes D_2 and D_1, respectively, then diode D_1 would conduct (be forward-biased) and diode D_2 would be reverse-biased. The output voltage would still be 0 volts because of forward-biased diode D_1 connected to the 0-volt input. If both diodes are connected to 0 volts (see Figure 7-7c), then both diodes are forward-biased, the output voltage is 0 volts, and the current through R splits up equally between the two conducting diodes.

Finally, if both inputs are $+6$ volts, the output will be $+6$ volts. Figure 7-7d shows that with $+6$ volts at a diode cathode and, at most, $+6$ volts at the diode anode, the diode is not forward-biased but is nonconducting. With no current flow, the output voltage is $+6$ volts.

A summary of the circuit operation is provided in Table 7-1, which is a *voltage truth table* showing the circuit operation for all possible conditions of the two input voltages, $+6$ volts and 0 volts.

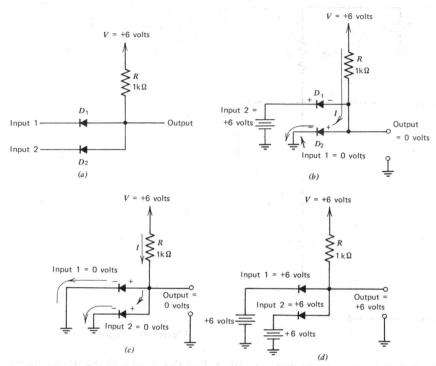

Figure 7-7.   Practical logic circuit.

Table 7-1.   *Voltage Truth Table for Circuit of Figure 7-7a*

Input 1	Input 2	Output
0 volts	0 volts	0 volts
0 volts	+6 volts	0 volts
+6 volts	0 volts	0 volts
+6 volts	+6 volts	+6 volts

If the diode is considered a practical device, the main difference from the above consideration is that the voltage drop across a forward-biased diode is V_d, which is typically 0.7 volt for silicon and 0.3 volt for germanium diodes. Thus, the output voltage would be +0.7 volt (for silicon diode) instead of the ideal 0-volt value in Table 7-1.

We can determine the logic operation of the circuit just considered by defining the logic levels. If the choice is

$$\text{logical-1} \equiv +6 \text{ volts}$$
$$\text{logical-0} \equiv 0 \text{ volts}$$

then the circuit of Figure 7-7a is an AND gate, as verified by Table 7-2 and is obtained from Table 7-1 by replacing the voltage levels by the logic levels defined above.

Table 7-2. *Logic Truth Table of AND gate*

Input 1 A	Input 2 B	Output C
0	0	0
0	1	0
1	0	0
1	1	1

The diode gate just considered can have more inputs, if desired, by simply adding a diode for each additional input. Figure 7-8 shows a four-input gate.

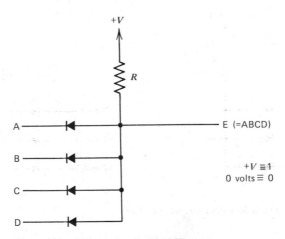

Figure 7-8.   Four-input diode AND gate.

Operation with Various Inputs. To understand the operation of the diode circuit of Figure 7-8, let us consider its operation with a variety of input voltages. Although this is not the usual operation as a logic gate, it will reinforce understanding the operation of the circuit. Figure 7-9a shows a logic gate with various input voltages. Assuming ideal diode operation, the output voltage will be +2 volts with only diode D_2 conducting. All the other diodes are reverse-biased, as shown in Figure 7-9b.

Figure 7-10a shows a second example of various input voltages to a three-input logic gate. Only diode D_1 will conduct in this example. Figure 7-10b shows the resulting operation with the output of −8 volts.

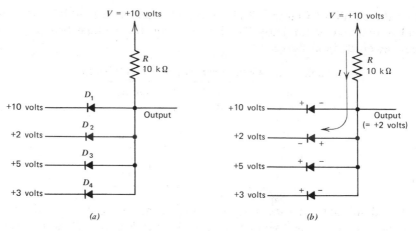

Figure 7-9.   Operation of diode circuit with various input voltages.

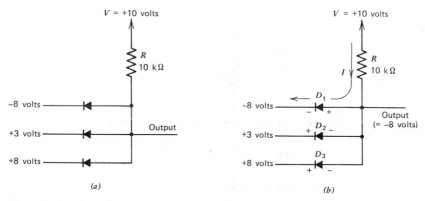

Figure 7-10.   Diode logic gate circuit operation.

We now can state the circuit operation for all these cases as follows:

> For a logic circuit as shown in Figure 7-8 the output voltage always follows the *lower of the input voltages.*

The input voltage that is least positive or most negative will set the output voltage level, all other inputs then reverse-biasing those diodes. In a logic gate typically only two voltage levels are defined and in this case we would state that the output is the value of the lower (less positive) of the two voltage levels, whenever it occurs as input.

A second form of a diode logic gate is shown in Figure 7-11. The diodes are now connected with cathodes common to the output and the resistor to a negative supply voltage. Using input voltage levels of 0 volts and +10

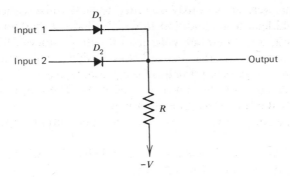

Figure 7-11.   Diode logic gate.

volts we shall determine the output voltage for all combinations of input voltage.

Figure 7-12*a* shows one input of + 10 volts and the other of 0 volts. The output follows the *more positive voltage* in this circuit connection and the output is shown to be + 10 volts. Diode D_1 is then forward-biased, conducting current through resistor R. Diode D_2 is reverse-biased, with the + 10 volts at the cathode more positive than the 0 volts at the anode.

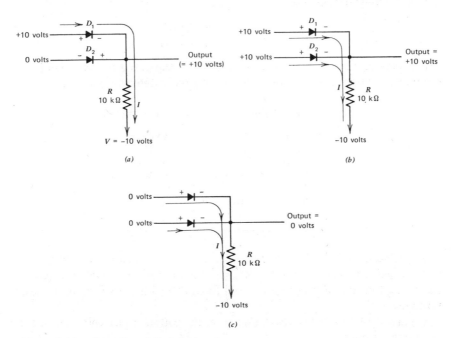

Figure 7-12.   Operation of diode logic gate.

If the output were erroneously assumed to be 0 volts, it should be seen that this would lead to a condition in which diode D_1 had an anode voltage of +10 volts and a cathode voltage of 0 volts—a forward-biased voltage with 10 volts across the forward-biased diode. This cannot happen and the output voltage is *not* 0 volts in the present case.

Figure 7-12b shows both inputs at +10 volts. The output is then +10 volts with both diodes conducting as shown.

Figure 7-12c shows both inputs at 0 volts. The output is then 0 volts as shown.

The above discussion is summarized in Table 7-3, which is a voltage truth table for the circuit of Figure 7-11.

Table 7-3.   *Voltage Truth Table for Figure 7-11*

Input 1	Input 2	Output
0 volts	0 volts	0 volts
0 volts	+10 volts	+10 volts
+10 volts	0 volts	+10 volts
+10 volts	+10 volts	+10 volts

Using the logic definitions of

$$+10 \text{ volts} \equiv \text{logical-1}$$
$$0 \text{ volts} \equiv \text{logical-0}$$

the circuit of Figure 7-11 is an OR gate, as indicated in logic Table 7-4 developed from Table 7-3 (using the above logic definitions).

Table 7-4.   *Logic Truth Table of OR Gate*

Input 1 A	Input 2 B	Output C
0	0	0
0	1	1
1	0	1
1	1	1

Operation with Various Input Voltages. If a logic gate as in Figure 7-13 is operated with various input voltages, the operation can be summarized be saying that the output voltage will follow the *more positive* of the input voltages.

Figure 7-14 shows the logic circuit with various input voltages and the resulting output voltage.

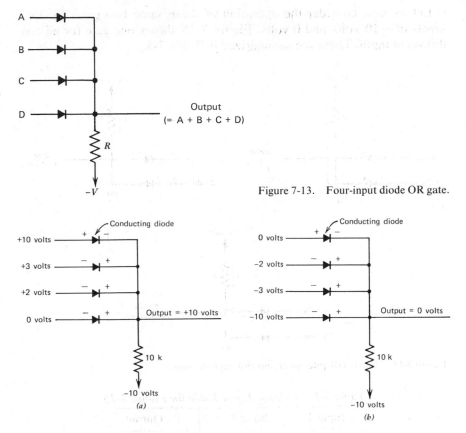

Figure 7-13.   Four-input diode OR gate.

Figure 7-14.   Operation for various input voltages.

Positive-Negative Logic.   The two logic circuits considered were shown to perform as AND and as OR gates. Actually, which gate is AND and which OR depends on the logic level definitions. There are two basic logic definitions that can be made.

Positive Logic: The more *positive* voltage is defined as logical-1.

Negative Logic: The more *negative* voltage is defined as logical-1.

So far we have used the logical definitions of

$$+ 10 \text{ volts} \equiv \text{logical-1}$$
$$0 \text{ volts} \equiv \text{logical-0}$$

which is a positive logic definition. For this logic definition the circuit of Figure 7-7a is an AND gate and that of Figure 7-11 is an OR gate.

Let us now consider the operation of these same two gates for logic levels of -10 volts and 0 volts. Figure 7-15 shows one gate for all conditions of input. These are summarized in Table 7-5.

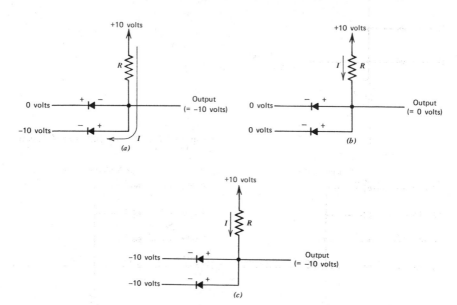

Figure 7-15.   Diode OR gate operations (for negative logic).

Table 7-5.   *Voltage Truth Table for Figure 7-15*

Input 1	Input 2	Output
0 volts	0 volts	0 volts
0 volts	-10 volts	-10 volts
-10 volts	0 volts	-10 volts
-10 volts	-10 volts	-10 volts

Using negative logic definitions of

$$0 \text{ volts} \equiv \text{logical-0}$$
$$-10 \text{ volts} \equiv \text{logical-1}$$

The logic truth table derived from Table 7-5 and the above definitions show the circuit to be an OR gate. The same circuit is thus a positive logic AND gate or negative logic OR gate. In any digital system it would be one or the other type of gate so that no confusion would exist. If, however, in one system the given circuit (Figure 7-7a) is an AND gate and in another the circuit is an OR gate it should be immediately evident that they are using positive and negative logic definitions, respectively, and that both are correct.

The operation of the circuit of Figure 7-11 with voltage levels of 0 volts and -10 volts is shown for all possibilities of input in Figure 7-16.

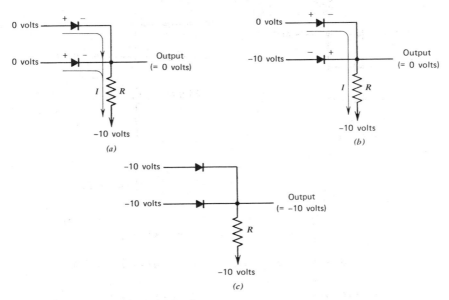

Figure 7-16.   Operation of logic circuit.

A summary of this operation is provided in Table 7-6. Using this truth table and negative logic definitions a resulting logic truth table will show this circuit to be an AND gate. Thus, the same circuit (Figure 7-11) is a positive logic OR gate or negative logic AND gate.

Table 7-6.   *Voltage Truth Table for Figure 7-16*

Input 1	Input 2	Output
0 volts	0 volts	0 volts
0 volts	-10 volts	0 volts
-10 volts	0 volts	0 volts
-10 volts	-10 volts	-10 volts

A summary of the corresponding positive logic gates and negative logic gates is provided in Figure 7-17. If positive logic is used, the gates of Figure 7-17a operate as AND and OR gates as shown. For a negative logic operating system, the gates are logically defined in Figure 7-17b.

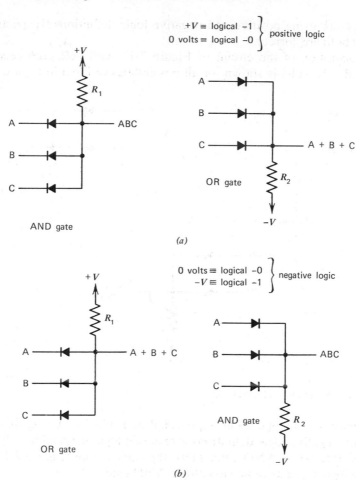

Figure 7-17.   Positive and negative logic gates. (*a*) Positive logic gates. (*b*) Negative logic gates.

Exercise 7-1.   Prepare voltage and logic truth tables for a negative logic OR gate (refer to Figure 7-7*a*) for voltage levels of 0 volts and −6 volts.

Exercise 7-2.   For the circuit of Figure 7-11 prepare voltage and logic truth tables using negative logic definitions. Supply voltage is $V = -6$ volts and input voltage levels are 0 volts and −6 volts. What type of logic gate is indicated by the logic truth table?

Multistage Logic.   Up to now we have discussed ideal operation of diode logic gates each considered separately. When logic is performed using

AND and OR gates, a number of practical factors of circuit operation such as loading have to be considered. In any actual logic system the number and type of logic gates interconnected are limited. Some of the limiting factors are voltage level and desired operating speed. We will use the positive logic gates of Figure 7-17a to show how some of the practical circuit limitations come about. Interconnecting two logic gates could result in cascades (series) connection of two AND gates, two OR gates, AND-OR gates or OR-AND gates. Practical operation of each of these will be considered in these discussions — particularly silicon diodes with forward-biased drops of 0.7 volt.

AND-AND Connection. Figure 7-18a shows two positive logic AND gates connected in series. If all inputs are +6 volts, the output is then +6 volts. If, as shown in Figure 7-18b, one input is 0 volts, the output of the second AND gate (point D) is as much as 1.4 volts resulting from forward-biased voltage drops of 0.7 volt across two diodes in series. As a practical factor then, connecting AND gates in series is limited by the

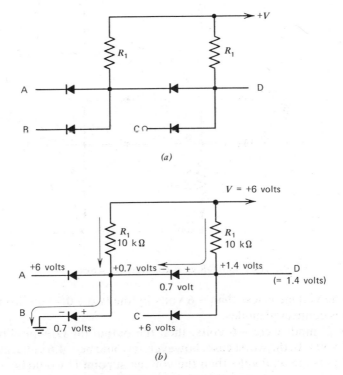

Figure 7-18.   Two AND gates connected in series.

condition of the diode drops adding up, so that instead of an ideal output voltage of 0 volts, in this case the voltage was $+1.4$ volts as practical voltage corresponding to logical-0. What voltage level is "too high" is dependent on a number of other circuit considerations, but it should be clear that a practical limit does exist. Here it could be stated that two AND gates in series is the most allowed and that any logical connection would have to reflect this limitation on the logical design.

OR-OR Connection. Figure 7-19a shows two positive logic OR gates connected in series. If one of the first inputs is $+6$ volts and the other input is 0 volts, as shown in Figure 7-19b, the output voltage is not $+6$

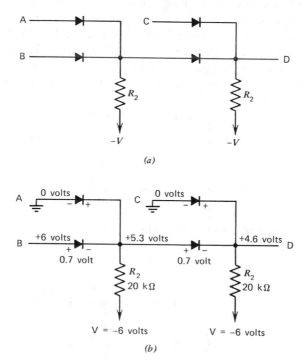

Figure 7-19.   Two OR gates connected in series.

volts. The voltage is less than $+6$ volts by the two $+0.7$ volt drops across the series connected diodes.

If the C input were $+6$ volts, then the output (at D) would be raised to $+5.3$ volts. In the worst case, however, it would be $+4.6$ volts, as shown. If the inputs are all 0 volts then the voltage at point D would be -0.7 volt due to a 0.7-volt drop across the C-input diode.

Thus, the output voltage at point D could be either -0.7 for logical-0 or $+4.6$ or $+5.3$ for logical-1. Again the decision of how many OR gates may be connected in series depends on additional circuit factors. We can already see that with two AND gates connected in series the logical-0 voltage could rise to 1.4 volts, and with two OR gates in series the logical-1 voltage could drop to $+4.6$ volts. We might then expect that we are near the practical limit in which the two voltage levels resulting from practical operation are the same and the circuit no longer operates properly.

OR-AND Gate. Figure 7-20a shows a connection of an OR gate followed by an AND gate. To properly investigate all combinations of input we can use a voltage truth table—for three input variables there are 2^3 or eight combinations. Some of these are similar in terms of circuit operation and we will point out those cases. We could have used this more systematic procedure in the above cases of AND-AND and OR-OR but

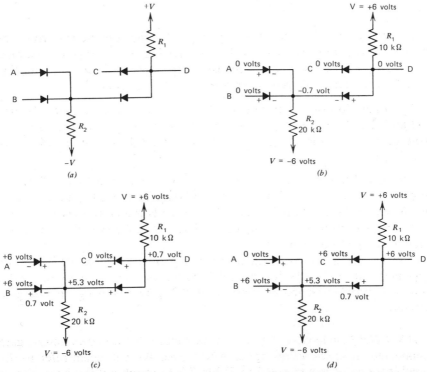

Figure 7-20.   Operation of OR-AND gates in series. (*a*) Logic gates. (*b*) Row 0 conditions (row 1 similar). (*c*) Row 2 conditions (rows 4 and 6 similar). (*d*) Row 3 conditions (rows 5 and 7 similar).

chose to show the less hit-and-miss way of checking all circuit operation. Table 7-7 shows the start of setting down all eight combinations to be investigated.

Table 7-7. *Voltage Truth Table To Use in Completely Checking the Circuit of Figure 7-20a*

Row Numbers	A	B	C	D
0	0	0	0	
1	0	0	+6	
2	0	+6	0	
3	0	+6	+6	
4	+6	0	0	
5	+6	0	+6	
6	+6	+6	0	
7	+6	+6	+6	

Figure 7-20*b* shows the circuit operation for the conditions of row 0 of Table 7-7 (row 1 operation is similar). Somewhat suprisingly, the resulting voltage at point D is 0 volts because of the voltage drop across an OR gate diode and the voltage rise across an AND gate diode.

The operation of the circuit for the conditions of row 2 (see Figure 7-20*c*) is similar to the conditions in rows 4 and 6. In all three cases the voltage output of the OR gate is +5.3 volts and the output at point D is +0.7 volt.

The operation for the conditions of row 3 shown in Figure 7-20*d* is similar to that of rows 5 and 7. The voltage at the OR gate output is +5.3 volts and the voltage at point D is +6 volts in all three cases.

The above discussion is summarized in Table 7-8, which is the completed voltage truth table.

The results of output voltage being either 0 volts or +0.7 volt for logical-0 and +6 volts for logical-1 indicates that there is very little practical problem in connecting an AND gate following an OR gate circuit.

AND-OR Connection. The circuit of Figure 7-21*a* shows an OR gate connected in series following an AND gate. We will again refer to the combinations of inputs listed in Table 7-7 to check out the operation of this circuit connection.

Table 7-8. *Voltage Truth Table (Complete for Figure 7-20)*

Row Number	A	B	C	D
0	0	0	0	0
1	0	0	+6	0
2	0	+6	0	+0.7
3	0	+6	+6	+6
4	+6	0	0	+0.7
5	+6	0	+6	+6
6	+6	+6	0	+0.7
7	+6	+6	+6	+6

Row 0: Figure 7-21*b* shows that for all inputs at 0 volts, the AND gate output is +0.7 volt and output at point D is 0 volts, the same as ideally expected. Rows 2 and 4 have similar operation.

Row 1: Figure 7-21*c* shows the conditions for row 1. The AND gate output is +0.7 volt and output at point D is +5.3 volts. Rows 3 and 5 have similar operation.

Row 7: Figure 7-21*d* shows the circuit conditions corresponding to row 7. The AND gate diodes are reverse-biased, and the output is +5.3 volts, as shown.

Row 6: The operation for this particular set of conditions (Figure 7-21*e*) was left for last since it presents a particular loading problem as will now be shown. Diodes D_1 and D_2 are reverse-biased and have no direct effect on the output voltage. Neglecting D_4 for the moment, an equivalent of the remaining circuit is shown in Figure 7-21*f*. The voltage at point D is determined by the voltage divider set up by resistors R_1 and R_2.

We can solve for the current I as follows:

$$I = \frac{V - (-V) - V_{D_3}}{R_1 + R_2} = \frac{2V - V_{D_3}}{R_1 + R_2} \qquad (7\text{-}1)$$

For the values of Figure 7-21 this would give

$$I = \frac{2(6) - 0.7}{10 + 20} = \frac{11.3V}{30K} = 0.377 \text{ mA}$$

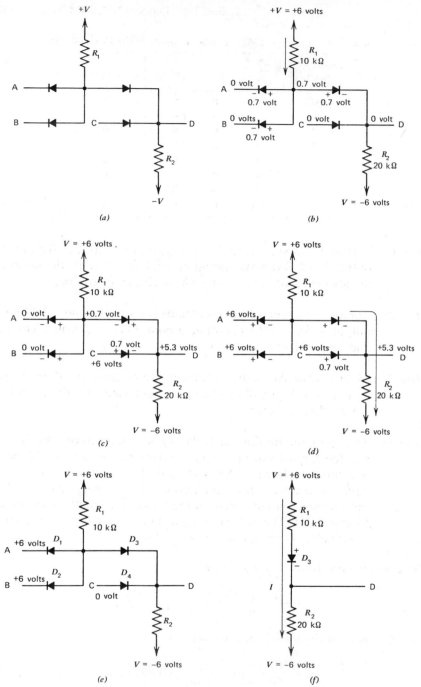

Figure 7-21. AND-OR gate connection. (*a*) Circuit connection. (*b*) Row 0 conditions (rows 2 and 4 similar). (*c*) Row 1 conditions (rows 3 and 5 similar). (*d*) Row 7 conditions. (*e*) Row 6 conditions. (*f*) Divider action.

The voltage drop across the R_2 resistor is IR_2. The output voltage at point D is this voltage drop minus the voltage supply

$$V_0 = IR_2 - V \tag{7-2}$$

which, for $R_2 = 20K$ and $V = 6$ volts gives

$$V_0 = (0.377 \text{ mA})(20K) - 6 = 7.54 - 6 = 1.54 \text{ volts}$$

Using circuit analysis, the voltage at point D can be calculated by the single equation

$$V_0 = \frac{R_2}{R_1 + R_2} (2V - V_d) - V \tag{7-3}$$

where the drop across the diode is V_d.

Using Equation 7-3 we get

$$V_0 = \frac{20}{10 + 20} (2 \times 6 - 0.7) - 6 = \frac{20}{30}(11.3) - 6 = 7.5 - 6 = 1.5 \text{ volts}$$

We obtain an output of about 1.5 volts — and the output should be at the logical-1 condition ($= 6$ volts, ideally). What has happened? Equation 7-3 shows the divider action of resistors R_1 and R_2. For the output voltage, V_0, to approach the supply voltage value of 6 volts the value of R_2 must be much larger than the value of R_1. If, for example, the component values had been $R_1 = 1K$, and $R_2 = 10K$ the voltage V_0 using Equation 7-3 would be

$$V_0 = \frac{10}{10 + 1}(2 \times 6 - 0.7) - 6 = \frac{10}{11}(11.3) - 6 = 10.2 - 6 = 4.2 \text{ volts}$$

Even this value is less than the ideal voltage expected. This shows that an OR gate may significantly load down an AND gate and in particular this loading shows up for a specific condition of inputs. In other words, the circuit will provide correct output in a number of cases but will fail in some condition of the inputs, which is enough to make the entire operation invalid. Of course, suitable selection of R_2 and R_1 will provide a properly operating circuit for all input conditions and this is what is expected in designing logical circuits. Before leaving this particular loading problem we might consider what happens if, as above, values are selected for satisfactory operation, but in connecting the logical circuit two OR gates are connected to an AND gate output. Figure 7-22a shows the circuit connection and Figure 7-22b shows the equivalent circuit.

As shown, the circuit can be reduced to that of Figure 7-21f with R_2 replaced by $R_2/2$. With two OR gates connected, the equivalent value of $R_2/2$ forms a voltage divider with R_1, and the output voltage is thus lower

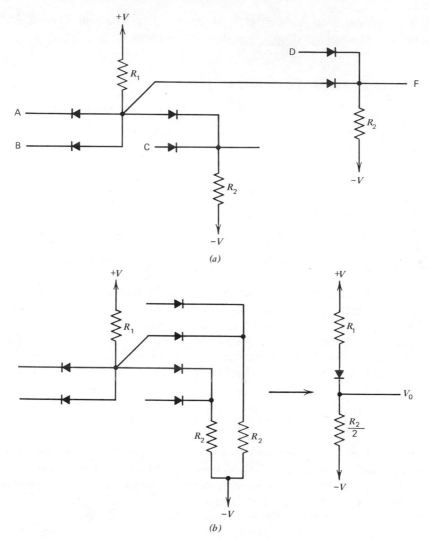

Figure 7-22.   Loading of AND gate by two OR gates.

in value. To calculate the value of output voltage we need only replace R_2 in Equation 7-3 by $R_2/2$ which for $R_1 = 1$K, and $R_2 = 10$K results in an output voltage of

$$V_0 = \frac{5}{1+5}(11.3) - 6 = 9.44 - 6 = 3.44 \text{ volts}$$

instead of the value of 4.2 volts for one OR gate connected. Thus, even if the circuit values provide proper operation for even one OR gate connected, they may not be sufficient with two or more OR gates connected to an AND gate output. Loading problems may exist with diode AND, OR gates, and we will see how this problem is handled using NOR or NAND gates later on.

Consider $R_1 = 1K$, $R_2 = 10K$, as circuit components for completing the voltage truth table for the AND-OR connection of Figure 7-21a. Table 7-9 shows the completed truth table.

Table 7-9. *Voltage Truth Table for AND-OR Connection of Figure 7-21a*

Row Number	A	B	C	D	
0	0	0	0	0	
1	0	0	+6	+5.3	
2	0	+6	0	0	
3	0	+6	+6	+5.3	
4	+6	0	0	0	
5	+6	0	+6	+5.3	
6	+6	+6	0	+4.2	(depends on R_1 and R_2 values)
7	+6	+6	+6	+5.3	

Additional Circuit Considerations. To provide least loading of the AND-OR connection, R_2 should be chosen very large and R_1 very small in value. There exists, however, practical limitations on these values, as is now described.

Why not make R_2 large? We could certainly decide to make the output voltage sufficiently high. R_2 cannot be made indiscriminately large because of speed of operation restriction. There is a small amount of stray capacitance (C) at the output of the gate due to wiring, diodes, and so on. If we represent the gate simply as in Figure 7-23, we can see the effect of R_2.

Figure 7-23 shows the equivalent of part of the AND-OR connection with the addition of stray capacitance that occurs due to wiring.

When the two inputs go low (to 0 volts), the output should also go to 0 volts. However, the OR gate diodes get reverse-biased and the output will drop to 0 volts as the capacitor discharges through R_2. Thus the R_2C time constant will determine how fast the output goes down to 0 volts. For a C of 100 $\mu\mu$F and R_2 of 100 kΩ, the time constant is

$$R_2C = (100 \times 10^{-12})(100 \times 10^3)$$
$$= 10 \times 10^{-6}$$
$$= 10 \,\mu\text{sec}$$

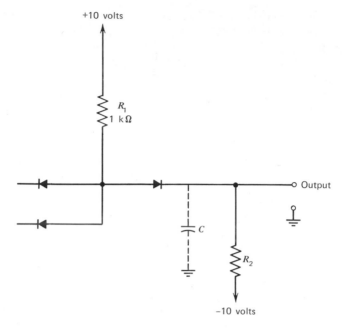

Figure 7-23.   Diode AND-OR gate with stray capacitance included.

If it took four time constants to reach a sufficiently low voltage, the gate could not be operated faster than every 40 μsec, or at 25 kHz. The values chosen were particularly high, but a limit on the size of R_2 should be apparent.

Looking back at the circuit, we find there is another way to keep the AND gate from being loaded down. If R_1 is made small compared to R_2, the output voltage level could still be kept high. But this solution also has its drawbacks. Consider the current through the input diodes for $R_1 = 1$ kΩ. The maximum value is slightly less than 10 volts/1 kΩ or 1 mA. If R_1 is decreased to 100 Ω to improve the output voltage level, the diode must carry almost 10 mA. Obviously we cannot decrease R_1 too much without putting undue restrictions on the choice of the logic diodes. Preferably the diodes and circuits should operate with as little power as possible since so many will be needed in the computer. So we are left with the conclusion that in using AND and OR gates the number of logic gates in cascade is limited. One solution to this problem is to use inverters to prevent too much loading. The inverter is basically an amplifier and therefore builds up the signal again so that the loading is eliminated as will be considered next.

Exercise 7-3.   Prepare a voltage truth table for the circuit of Figure 7-21*a* using $R_1 = 1.5\text{K}, R_2 = 10\text{K}, V_d = 0.6$ volts, and $V = \pm 5$ volts.

Exercise 7-4.   Prepare a voltage truth table for the following connection of negative logic OR-AND gates in series (Figure 7-24).

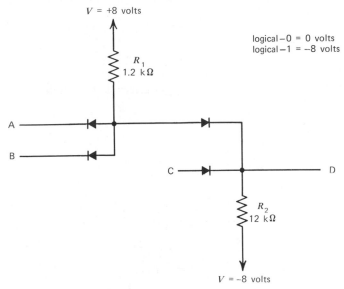

Figure 7-24.   Negative logic OR-AND gate connection for Exercise 7-4.

7-3.   Transistor Inverter Circuit

The logical inversion operation converts a logical-1 to logical-0 and vice versa. Circuits to perform the inversion operation can be made using active devices such as transistor FET. We will find that in addition to providing inversion, a transistor circuit will also help reduce loading effects, as noted in the preceding section.

A review of transistor characteristics with emphasis on the features of importance to switching circuits will be helpful at this time. For logic use the transistor circuit must represent the states 0 or 1, so that they are well distinguished. This corresponds to the transistor being operated fully ON and fully OFF. Ideally, we can compare the transistor output to an ideal switch. When fully ON the transistor should appear as a short circuit, and when fully OFF it should appear as an open circuit. A common-emitter characteristic will more clearly define the transistor deviations from ideal and the basic operation as a switching element. A typical transistor collector characteristic is shown in Figure 7-25. A load line corresponding to the circuit and component values of Figure 7-26*a* is shown in the characteristic.

Studies involving the transistor as a linear amplifier would concentrate on the operation within the linear region of the characteristic covered by

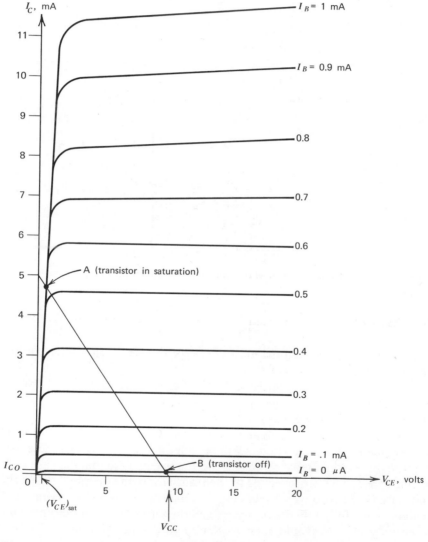

Figure 7-25.   Transistor common-emitter collector characteristics.

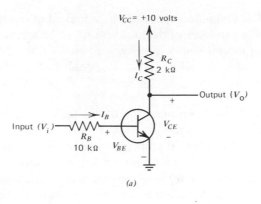

(a)

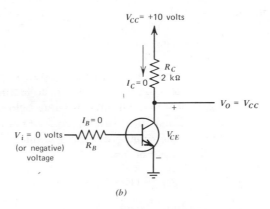

(b)

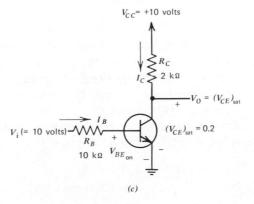

(c)

Figure 7-26. Transistor inverter circuit. (*a*) Circuit. (*b*) Transistor OFF. (*c*) Transistor ON.

215

the load line. For computer operation as a logical inverter circuit, however, only the two extremes of the load line are of concern. A transistor in a logical inverter circuit should be operated either fully ON or *saturated* (point A) or completely OFF (point B) as shown on the load line of Figure 7-25a.

Transistor OFF. To understand the transistor and circuit operation in cutoff a partial circuit diagram is shown in Figure 7-26b.

The input voltage is either 0 volts or some small negative voltage. For the NPN transistor this corresponds to a base voltage that holds the transistor off. There is then no base current and the base emitter appears as an open circuit corresponding to a reverse-biased diode. With no base current no collector current is caused to occur and, as shown, $I_c = 0$ and the voltage drop across R_C is also 0 volts. The output voltage is the supply voltage value, $+V_{CC}$, which in this case is 10 volts. Notice that as an inverter circuit 0-volt input results in $+10$-volt output so that the output is logically opposite the input.

The circuit now has the transistor operating at point B of Figure 7-25. There is a small amount of leakage current from collector to base that would result in the voltage dropping slightly in value below $+V_{CC}$. However, for the typical silicon transistor this leakage, even at relatively high temperatures, is less than a microampere. For a value of R_C of 1K and I_{CO} of 1 μA the voltage drop would be

$$V_{CO} = I_{CO} \cdot R_C = 1\text{K} \times 1\mu\text{A} = 1 \text{ mV}$$

Thus, we can expect the effect of leakage current on typical switching transistor circuits to be quite negligible and we will neglect it in our discussions.

Transistor ON. Figure 7-26c shows an input of $+10$ volts and the conditions with the transistor ON and in saturation. If the input voltage is sufficiently large to result in a base-emitter voltage above about 0.4 volt for silicon transistors, the transistor will *begin* to turn on. The base-emitter will then reach a level around 0.7 volt (for silicon) which will remain fairly constant for a range of input base current value. We will generally use the value of base-emitter on-voltage

$$(V_{BE})_{\text{on}} = 0.7 \text{ V, Si}$$
$$= 0.3 \text{ V, Ge}$$

The input voltage shown in Figure 7-26c is fixed at 10 volts and the base emitter at $(V_{BE})_{\text{on}} = 0.7$ volt. The base current I_B is then determined by the base resistor value as given by the equation

$$I_B = \frac{V_i - (V_{BE})_{on}}{R_B}\qquad (7\text{-}4)$$

which, with the present values is

$$I_B = \frac{10 - 0.7}{10\text{K}} = \frac{9.3\text{ V}}{10\text{K}} = 0.93\text{ mA}$$

Notice from Figure 7-25 that a base current between 0.5 and 0.6 mA is sufficient to drive the transistor into saturation. Current in excess of that amount will be stored as charge in the base of the transistor, but the operating point voltage (point A) remains the saturated value. In other words, any base current in excess of the minimum needed to just saturate the transistor will only provide that with some nominal allowance in base resistor value, supply voltage value, and so on, the transistor will still be operating in saturation.

Typical range of values of transistor collector-emitter voltage in saturation are:

$$(V_{CE})_{\text{sat}} = 0.1\text{ V} - 0.3\text{ V}$$

The value can range from about 0.05 V to near 1 volt and is somewhat dependent on the level of collector current, but the above approximate values are reasonable for most transistors used in switching circuits.

From Figure 7-26c the equation of the collector-emitter (output) section of the circuit provides for calculating the collector current from

$$I_C = \frac{V_{CC} - (V_{CE})_{\text{sat}}}{R_C}\qquad (7\text{-}5)$$

which for the present values would result in

$$I_C = \frac{10 - 0.2}{2\text{K}} = \frac{9.8\text{ V}}{2\text{K}} = 4.9\text{ mA}$$

Notice point A in Figure 7-25 showing the saturated operating point at about

$$\left.\begin{array}{l}(V_{CE})_{\text{sat}} = 0.2\text{ volt}\\ I_C = 4.9\text{ mA}\end{array}\right\}\text{ at point A}$$

We should observe an important circuit factor from the calculations of I_B and I_C. Both were calculated independently of the other. Should not calculation of one value provide the other if the transistor current gain

(h_{FE}) is known? The answer to this question is quite definitely NO. Transistor current gain has value only within the linear region of operation of the transistor. When operated in saturation the value of current gain has no meaning. Consider the present circuit with base current of 0.98 mA and collector current of 4.9 mA. If the base current were made twice as large by reducing R_B to 5 kΩ, the base current would double to $I_B = 1.96$ mA. What of I_C? Assuming (V_{CE})$_{sat}$ remains at about 0.2 volt, the collector current would still be 4.9 mA. Obviously the ratio of I_C/I_B is *not* the current gain h_{FE} defined only in the linear range of device operation.

The ratio is, however, an indication of a circuit gain as it is determined mostly by circuit voltages and resistances and only very slightly by the transistor. We can thus define a circuit current gain or *circuit beta* by:

$$\boxed{\beta_C \equiv \frac{I_C}{I_B}} \tag{7-6}$$

where, β_C = circuit beta (current gain) and I_B and I_C are calculated from Equations 7-4 and 7-5, respectively, for the circuit of Figure 7-26a.

An important observation can now be made. For the value of β_C to have significance, the transistor *must* be in saturation. As a check to determine that this is so we need only compare the actual transistor current gain, h_{FE} with the circuit current gain, β_C.

If, h_{FE} is greater than β_C in value this assures us that indeed the transistor will be in saturation.

For example, a base current of 0.98 mA in the circuit of Figure 7-26a and transistor current gain of $h_{FE} = 10$ would result in a collector current of

$$I_C = h_{FE} \cdot I_B = 10(0.98 \text{ mA}) = 9.8 \text{ mA}$$

Since $I_C = 4.9$ mA is the maximum collector current for the present circuit, occurring with the transistor in saturation, we see that more than enough base current is provided to drive the transistor into saturation.

Example 7-1.   For the circuit of Figure 7-26a and values of $V_{CC} = +6$ volts, (V_{CE})$_{sat} = 0.1$ volt, (V_{BE})$_{on} = 0.7$ volt, $R_B = 8.2$K, $R_C = 1.2$K and $h_{FE} = 15$, determine whether the transistor is driven into saturation by an input of $V_i = +6$ volts.

Solution: 1. Using Equation 7-4

$$I_B = \frac{V_i - (V_{BE})_{on}}{R_B} = \frac{6 - 0.7\text{V}}{8.2\text{K}} = 0.647 \text{ mA}$$

2. Using Equation 7-5

$$I_C = \frac{V_{CC} - (V_{CE})_{\text{sat}}}{R_C} = \frac{6 - 0.2 \text{ V}}{1.2\text{K}} = 4.83 \text{ mA}$$

3. Using Equation 7-6

$$\beta_C = \frac{I_C}{I_B} = \frac{4.83}{0.647} = 7.47$$

4. Since $h_{FE} = 15$ and $\beta_C = 7.47$, we see that $h_{FE} > \beta_C$ and conclude that the transistor is indeed operating in saturation for the input of $+6$ volts.

The logical operation of the inverter circuit of Figure 7-26a can be shown using the following logical definitions

$$\text{logical-1} = +10 \text{ V}$$
$$\text{logical-0} = 0 \text{ V}$$

For an input of 0 volts the transistor is OFF and output is $+10$ volts. For an input of $+10$ volts the transistor is ON and output is near 0 volts. In logical terms, the input and output are always opposite and the circuit thus acts as a logical inverter.

Idealized Transistor Inverter Operation. When the action of a transistor inverter is considered it is often possible to view the transistor as an ideal switch. If the transistor is OFF, it draws no current through the collector emitter terminals (assuming leakage current is neglected) and appears to be an open-circuit, as shown in Figure 7-27a. If the transistor is ON, then the voltage from the base emitter may be considered fixed at about 0.7 volt (for silicon). The collector-emitter voltage may be considered as 0 volt (neglecting the value of $(V_{CE})_{\text{sat}}$, typically 0.2 volt) and appears to be a short circuit as shown in Figure 7-27b.

Two Voltage Supply Inverter Circuit. An additional voltage supply is sometimes included in an inverter circuit, as shown in Figure 7-28 to provide an extra margin in holding the transistor OFF. Again we will consider the operation by separately examining the conditions of transistor ON and OFF. A practical circuit is shown in Figure 7-29a.

Transistor ON. Figure 7-29b shows the inverter circuit with input of $+6$ volts and the transistor driven into saturation. The equations of circuit operation are easily obtained by considering the input base-emitter section and then the output collector-emitter section of the circuit.

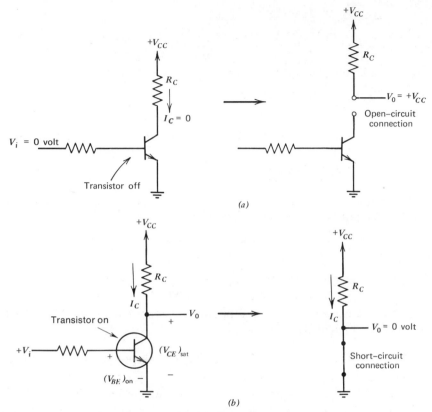

Figure 7-27.   Transistor inverter as ideal device.

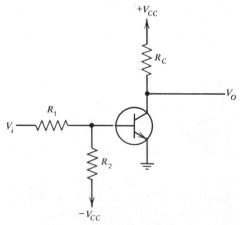

Figure 7-28.   Two voltage supply inverter circuit.

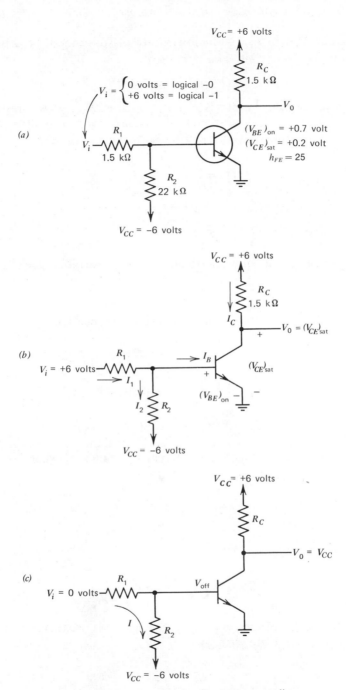

Figure 7-29. Practical inverter circuit using two supplies.

Input Section.   With $V_i = +6$ volts, the transistor should be driven into saturation. The base-emitter voltage will be

$$(V_{BE})_{on} = +0.7 \text{ volt}$$

The voltages at both terminals of each resistor, R_1 and R_2 are fixed by either the supply voltage or the $(V_{BE})_{on}$ voltage drop so that we can calculate the current through each resistor separately as follows

$$\boxed{I_1 = \frac{V_i - (V_{BE})_{on}}{R_1}} \qquad (7\text{-}7)$$

$$\boxed{I_2 = \frac{(V_{BE})_{on} - (-V_{CC})}{R_2} = \frac{(V_{BE})_{on} + V_{CC}}{R_2}} \qquad (7\text{-}8)$$

The base current, as shown in Figure 7-29b, is the difference of I_1 and I_2

$$\boxed{I_B = I_1 - I_2} \qquad (7\text{-}9)$$

The calculations for the circuit of Figure 7-29a result in

$$I_1 = \frac{+6 - 0.7 \text{ V}}{7.5\text{K}} = 0.716 \text{ mA}$$

$$I_2 = \frac{+0.7 + 6 \text{ V}}{22\text{K}} = 0.305 \text{ mA}$$

$$I_B = I_1 - I_2 = 0.716 - 0.305 = 0.411 \text{ mA}$$

Output Section.   The collector current can be calculated when the transistor is in saturation from

$$\boxed{I_C = \frac{+V_{CC} - (V_{CE})_{sat}}{R_C}} \qquad (7\text{-}10)$$

For the circuit of Figure 7-29a we get

$$I_C = \frac{6 - 0.2 \text{ V}}{1.5\text{K}} = 3.87 \text{ mA}$$

Check on Saturation Condition.   As a check to be sure that the transistor is in saturation, calculate β_C from

$$\boxed{\beta_C = \frac{I_C}{I_B}} \qquad (7\text{-}11)$$

where I_C and I_B are given by Equations 7-9 and 7-10.

If $h_{FE} > \beta_C$, then the transistor is in saturation. For the present circuit

$$\beta_C = \frac{3.87}{0.411} = 9.42$$

and since $h_{FE} = 25$, we see that $h_{FE} > \beta_C$ so that the circuit does drive the transistor properly into saturation with $V_i = 6$ volts. In fact, we have a safety margin of more than two, that is

$$\text{overdrive ratio} \equiv \frac{h_{FE}}{\beta_C} = \frac{25}{9.42} = 2.45$$

meaning that the base current is 2.45 times more than is needed to just saturate the given transistor ($h_{FE} = 25$) for the amount of collector current calculated above. It should be pointed out that higher collector currents would require more base drive to maintain the transistor in saturation, and that for the present transistor the collector current could be increased (by reducing R_C or by drawing external current into the collector) up to 2.45 times the present value with the transistor remaining in saturation.

Practically, an overdrive of at least two is reasonable to insure that with the nominal tolerances of components, power supply voltages, and transistor parameters the circuit remains in saturation (for the logical-1 input voltage).

Transistor OFF. With input of $V_i = 0$ volts the transistor will be held OFF by a negative base-emitter voltage calculated as follows (see Figure 7-29c).

$$I = \frac{V_i - (-V_{CC})}{R_1 + R_2}$$

$$\boxed{V_{\text{OFF}} = IR_2 + (-V_{CC}) = \frac{R_2}{R_1 + R_2}(V_i + V_{CC}) - V_{CC}} \qquad (7\text{-}12)$$

Using this for the circuit of Figure 7-29c we get

$$V_{\text{OFF}} = \frac{22}{7.5 + 22}(0 + 6) - 6 = \frac{22}{29.5}(6) - 6 = 4.47 - 6 = -1.5 \text{ volts}$$

The voltage from base to emitter is thus -1.5 volts and for an *npn* transistor this polarity voltage will hold the transistor off.

Noise Margin. A noise margin value may now be defined. Notice above that with 0-volt input the base-emitter voltage was about -1.5 volts. How much positive voltage could be applied at the input before the transistor begins to turn on? The noise margin is defined as that input voltage that just begins to turn the transistor on. For silicon transistors a base emitter of about 0.4 volt just begins to turn on the transistor and using that value as V_{OFF} we can use Equation 7-12 to calculate V_i:

$$V_{OFF} = 0.4 \text{ V} = \frac{R_2}{R_1 + R_2}(V_i + V_{CC}) - V_{CC}$$

Solving for V_i we get

$$\boxed{V_i = \frac{0.4(R_1 + R_2) + R_1 V_{CC}}{R_2} = \text{Noise Margin}} \qquad (7\text{-}12a)$$

For the circuit of Figure 7-29a we would get

$$\text{Noise Margin (N.M.)} = \frac{0.4(7.5 + 22) + 7.5(6)}{22}$$

$$\text{N.M.} = \frac{11.8 + 45}{22} \cong 2.6 \text{ volts}$$

This means that the input voltage could go as high as 2.6 volts before the transistor will begin to turn on. It may be that circuit design calls for an input of near 0 volts as logical-0 input. However, "noise" voltages may result from pickup on the signal lines, ground lines, and so on. If the noise voltage at the circuit input is less than the noise margin voltage above, then the transistor will still remain off.

If only a single voltage supply is used, as in the circuit of Figure 7-25a, the OFF voltage is 0 volts and the only noise margin is the 0.4 volt required to just start turning the transistor on. For the circuit of Figure 7-29a noise margins of a few volts are possible providing much better noise margins.

As a simplification of Equation 7-12 we could consider the noise margin as that input voltage that results in a base-emitter voltage of 0 volts. This would result in the simplified version of Equation 7-12a.

$$\boxed{\text{Noise Margin} = \frac{R_1}{R_2} V_{CC} \qquad (V_{OFF} = 0 \text{ V})} \qquad (7\text{-}12b)$$

For the circuit of Figure 7-29a we would get

$$\text{N.M.} = \frac{7.5}{22}(6) = 2.04 \text{ V}$$

Example 7-2.   Calculate the noise margin and check the saturation condition for the *pnp* transistor inverter circuit and values of Figure 7-30.

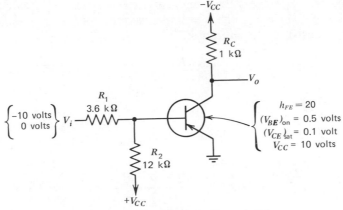

Figure 7-30.   Transistor inverter circuit for Example 7-2.

Solution: For the OFF condition of the transistor we can calculate the approximate noise margin using Equation 7-12*b*.

$$\boxed{\text{Noise margin} = \frac{R_1}{R_2}(V_{CC})}$$

$$= \frac{3.6}{12}(6) = 1.8 \text{ V}$$

(for *pnp* operation the input voltage must go *negative* by 1.8 volts to begin to turn the transistor on).

For the ON condition we calculate the base and collector currents using Equations 7-7 to 7-10.

$$I_1 = \frac{V_i - (V_{BE})_{\text{on}}}{R_1} = \frac{10 - (0.5) \text{ V}}{3.6\text{K}} = 2.64 \text{ mA}$$

$$I_2 = \frac{(V_{BE})_{\text{on}} + V_{CC}}{R_2} = \frac{0.5 + 10 \text{ V}}{12\text{K}} = 0.875 \text{ mA}$$

$$I_B = I_1 - I_2 = 2.64 - 0.975 = 1.765 \text{ mA}$$

$$I_C = \frac{V_{CC} - (V_{CE})_{\text{sat}}}{R_C} = \frac{10 - 0.1 \text{ V}}{1\text{K}} = 9.9 \text{ mA}$$

The circuit β calculated using Equation 7-11 is

$$\beta_C = \frac{I_C}{I_B} = \frac{9.9}{1.765} = 5.6$$

Since $h_{FE} = 20$ is greater than β_C, the transistor is in saturation.

Exercise 7-5. For the circuit and values in Figure 7-31, calculate the circuit noise margin and check whether an input of 5 volts is sufficient to drive the transistor into saturation.

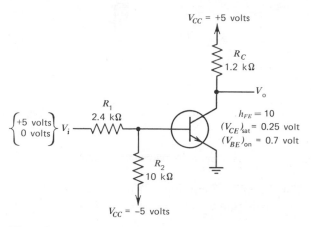

Figure 7-31.   Transistor inverter circuit for Exercise 7-5.

7-4.   DCTL Logic Circuits

In Section 7-2 we considered some loading problems that exist when connecting AND and OR gate circuits. As a practical device, a circuit containing an AND gate or OR gate followed by an inverter has much less loading problem and, in fact, the amount of load can be more precisely defined. An AND-Inverter circuit is, as covered in Chapters 5 and 6, a NAND gate, and an OR-Inverter circuit is a NOR gate. As we have seen, the NAND or NOR gate alone is sufficient for obtaining all logical operations desired. Thus, in place of three separate circuits — AND, OR, Inverter, a single logical block is used (either NAND or NOR).

NPN NAND Gate Using Diode-Capacitor-Transistor Logic (DCTL). A NAND gate can be formed by connecting an *npn* inverter after a positive logic AND gate as shown in Figure 7-32.

The circuit is referred to as a Diode-Capacitor-Transistor Logic or DCTL circuit. Analysis of the circuit operation can be covered separately for the transistor ON and for the transistor OFF. A practical version of positive logic DTL NAND gate is shown in Figure 7-33*a*.

The capacitor serves to speed up the operation of the circuit. It is included in the circuit for completeness but, as will be seen, the capacitor

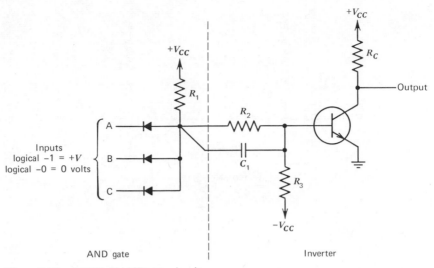

AND gate

Inverter

Figure 7-32.   DCTL NAND gate circuit.

is not included in analysis of the circuit operation since it has no effect on the direct current operating conditions. Speed of circuit operation is discussed separately later in this chapter.

Transistor OFF. If any input to the circuit of Figure 7-33a is logical-0, the transistor of that circuit should be held in cutoff. Since typically one NAND gate circuit is used as input to another, the logical-0 voltage will not be 0 volts but that of a saturated transistor. Figure 7-33b shows a practical value of logical-0 as input to one diode of the NAND gate circuit under consideration. The positive supply voltage, through resistor R_1, provides bias voltage to forward-bias diode D_1 with current through resistor R_1, conducting diode D_1 and the saturated collector emitter of the transistor providing the input signal.

The voltage at the junction of R_1, R_2, and D_1 is held fixed at a value of

$$V'_i = V_d + (V_{CE})_{sat} \qquad (7\text{-}13)$$

which for the present circuit is

$$V_i = 0.7 + 0.2 = 0.9 \text{ V}$$

The voltage V'_i and the negative supply voltage through resistors R_2 and R_3 provide an OFF voltage at the transistor base emitter calculated as follows:

$$V_{OFF} = \frac{R_3}{R_2 + R_3}(V'_i + V_{CC}) - V_{CC} \qquad (7\text{-}14)$$

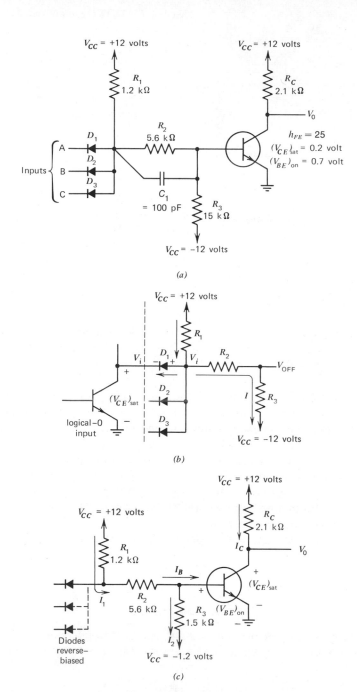

Figure 7-33. Practical DCTL NAND gate circuit.

For the present circuit we calculate

$$V_{OFF} = \frac{15}{5.6+15}(0.9+12)-12 = 9.4-12 = -2.6 \text{ V}$$

For an *npn* transistor, as in Figure 7-33*a*, the negative base-emitter voltage does provide for holding the transistor cutoff.

A noise margin can be calculated, as was done for the inverter circuit. We must calculate a value of input voltage (at the input to diode D_1, for example) which results in a base-emitter voltage of 0.4 volt, just enough to start biasing the transistor ON.

Referring to the input voltage as the more general value V_i [instead of $(V_{CE})_{sat}$, which would occur if any noise voltage is neglected] we have

$$V_i' = V_i + V_d \tag{7-15}$$

which replaces V_i' in Equation 7-14 and with $V_{OFF} = 0.4$ V

$$0.4 \text{ V} = \frac{R_3}{R_2+R_3}(V_i+V_d+V_{CC})-V_{CC}$$

$$V_i = \frac{0.4(R_2+R_3)+R_2V_{CC}-(R_2+R_3)V_d}{R_3}$$

$$\boxed{\text{N. M.} = \frac{(0.4-V_d)(R_2+R_3)+R_2V_{CC}}{R_3}} \tag{7-16a}$$

If we neglect the diode drop, V_d, and use a base-emitter voltage of 0 V to calculate the noise margin, Equation 7-16*a* can be expressed more simply

$$\boxed{\text{N. M.} \cong \frac{R_2}{R_3}V_{CC} \quad \left(\begin{matrix} V_{OFF}=0 \text{ V} \\ V_d=0 \text{ V} \end{matrix}\right)} \tag{7-16b}$$

Calculating the noise margin in both cases:
For Equation 7-16*a*,

$$\text{N. M.} = \frac{(0.4-0.7)(5.6+15)+5.6(12)}{15}$$

$$= \frac{-6.16+62.3}{15} = 3.75 \text{ V}$$

For Equation 7-16*b*,

$$\text{N. M.} \cong \frac{5.6}{15}(12) = 4.48 \text{ V}$$

From the exact noise margin expression we determine that an input of 3.75 volts will only begin to turn the transistor on. If the approximate expression is used, the value is quite a bit larger. It should be used only for quick check and not when exact calculation is needed.

Transistor ON. If *all* inputs are logical-1 (+ 12 volts) and all input diodes are reverse-biased, the transistor should be driven on in saturation. Figure 7-33c shows the partial circuit resulting in the transistor being in saturation.

With the transistor on, the base-emitter voltage is fixed and the base current can be calculated as follows:

$$I_1 = \frac{V_{CC} - (V_{BE})_{\text{on}}}{R_1 + R_2} \qquad (7\text{-}17)$$

$$I_2 = \frac{V_{CC} + (V_{BE})_{\text{on}}}{R_3} \qquad (7\text{-}18)$$

$$I_B = I_1 - I_2 \qquad (7\text{-}19)$$

The calculations for the circuit of Figure 7-33 result in

$$I_1 = \frac{12 - 0.7 \text{ V}}{1.2 + 5.6} = 1.66 \text{ mA}$$

$$I_2 = \frac{12 + 0.7 \text{ V}}{15\text{K}} = 0.845 \text{ mA}$$

$$I_B = I_1 - I_2 = 1.66 - 0.845 = 0.815 \text{ mA}$$

The collector current obtained from the collector-emitter loop voltage drops is

$$I_C = \frac{V_{CC} - (V_{CE})_{\text{sat}}}{R_C} \qquad (7\text{-}20)$$

and we calculate

$$I_C = \frac{12 - 0.2 \text{ V}}{2.1\text{K}} = 5.63 \text{ mA}$$

Checking the circuit beta against the transistor current gain

$$h_{\text{FE}} > \beta_C = \frac{I_C}{I_\beta} \quad \text{for saturation}$$

which is

$$25 > \frac{5.63}{0.815} = 6.9$$

and the transistor *is* driven into saturation.

Example 7-3. A DCTL NAND gate circuit is designed as in Figure 7-32 having the following circuit and transistor values: $R_1 = 1.8$ K, $R_2 = 5.1$ K, $R_3 = 18$ K, $R_C = 2.4$ K, $V_{CC} = 8$ V, $h_{FE} = 20$, $(V_{BE})_{on} = 0.7$ V, $(V_{CE})_{sat} = 0.1$ V. The logical inputs are: logical-1 $= +8$ V, logical-0 $= 0$ V. Check the circuit operation for the conditions of transistor ON and transistor OFF. Determine the noise margin and overdrive ratio.

Solution: *For the transistor OFF:*   Using Equation 7-14

$$V_{OFF} = \frac{R_3}{R_2 + R_3}(V_i' + V_{CC}) - V_{CC}$$

$$= \frac{18}{5.1 + 18}(0.7 + 0.1 + 8) - 8 = 5.9 - 8 = -2.1 \text{ V}$$

The noise margin calculated from Equation 7-16*a* is

$$\text{N. M.} = \frac{(0.4 - V_d)(R_2 + R_3) + R_2 V_{CC}}{R_3} = \frac{(0.4 - 0.7)(5.1 + 18) + 5.1(8)}{18}$$

$$= \frac{-0.3(23.1) + 5.1(8)}{18} = 1.88 \text{ V}$$

For the transistor ON: Using Equations 7-17 to 7-20

$$I_1 = \frac{V_{CC} - (V_{BE})_{on}}{R_1 + R_2} = \frac{8 - 0.7}{1.8 + 5.1} = \frac{7.3 \text{ V}}{6.9 \text{ K}} = 1.06 \text{ mA}$$

$$I_2 = \frac{V_{CC} + (V_{BE})_{on}}{R_3} = \frac{8 + 0.7}{18} = \frac{8.7 \text{ V}}{18 \text{ K}} = 0.48 \text{ mA}$$

$$I_B = I_1 - I_2 = 1.06 - 0.48 = 0.58 \text{ mA}$$

$$I_C = \frac{V_{CC} - (V_{CE})_{sat}}{R_C} = \frac{8 - 0.1 \text{ V}}{2.4 \text{ K}} = 3.3 \text{ mA}$$

Checking for saturation operation

$$\text{is} \quad h_{FE} = 20 > \beta_C = \frac{I_C}{I_B} = \frac{3.3}{0.58} = 5.7$$

Yes; therefore transistor is in saturation.

$$\text{Overdrive ratio} = \frac{h_{FE}}{\beta_C} = \frac{20}{5.7} = 3.5$$

Exercise 7-6. For *npn* positive logic NAND gate of Figure 7-32 calculate the noise margin and check for saturation operation for circuit values of: $R_1 = 1.5$ K, $R_2 = 3.9$ K, $R_3 = 24$ K, $R_C = 1.8$ K, $V_{CC} = \pm 9$ V, $(V_{BE})_{on} = 0.7$ V, $(V_{CE})_{sat} = 0.2$ V, $h_{FE} = 15$, $V_d = 0.7$ V.

The logic operation of the NAND circuit may be obtained by preparing voltage and logic truth tables for a logic-inverter circuit as in Figure 7-32. Using the practical circuit of Figure 7-33a the truth tables are provided in Tables 7-10 and 7-11.

Table 7-10.   *Voltage Truth Table*

A	B	C	Output
0	0	0	+ 12
0	0	+ 12	+ 12
0	+ 12	0	+ 12
0	+ 12	+ 12	+ 12
+ 12	0	0	+ 12
+ 12	0	+ 12	+ 12
+ 12	+ 12	0	+ 12
+ 12	+ 12	+ 12	0

Table 7-11.   *Logic Truth Table*

A	B	C	Output
0	0	0	1
0	0	1	1
0	1	0	1
0	1	1	1
1	0	0	1
1	0	1	1
1	1	0	1
1	1	1	0

logical-1 = + 12 V
logical-0 = 0 V

The logic table shows that if A, B, and C are all 1, then the output is 0, which is the operation of a NAND circuit. Figure 7-32 is a positive logic NAND gate circuit.

7-5.   Integrated Logic Circuit Manufacturing

Computer logic circuits are mainly manufactured as integrated circuit (IC) devices. Up to now the circuits considered were shown as discrete component circuits. The individual resistors and transistors are separately selected and connected together to build the logic circuit. With IC logic circuits one buys a complete logic gate. The circuit component values and transistor parameters have already been selected and, in fact, the circuit is fully connected, operational, and fully tested. For all this the price of IC logic units is quite low and thus quite popular with logic circuit users.

Integrated circuits can be manufactured in the same way as individual transistors. The monolithic silicon manufacturing is most popular and various types of logic gates made by this technique will be considered. There also exists special microminiature processes such as hybrid techniques combining thin-film and monolithic manufacture and hybrid techniques such as those used by IBM in their solid logic technology (SLT) circuit manufacture and DEC in their flip-chip construction technique. Our attention will be directed to the monolithic gates presently most popular and commercially available at low cost.

A number of factors about the differences of using IC or discrete logic circuits will soon be quite evident. First, we will not analyze the circuit operation in order to *calculate* currents and voltages within the circuit because the circuit is already built and we cannot change any component. In fact, without a microscope we cannot even *see* any component and this would be possible *only if* the case were cut open, which is not at all easy to do. In effect then an IC circuit is provided to the user as the proverbial electronic "black box." *It really doesn't matter what is inside the unit but only how it may be used.* In learning about the different logic types it will prove helpful to discuss the internal circuit operation—but with the thought that this will help to understand better how to *use* the device from the available input and output terminals.

A number of facts about IC units in general might be interesting before going into different logic types of gates. Packaging and connection of IC units are of interest to the user. Figure 7-34 shows a number of IC packages including transistor-type cans, flat packs, and in-line packages. Notice that, typically, 8-, 10-, or 14-pin leads are provided to permit connection of supply voltages, input and output signals. As will be indicated later, these units may contain more than one logic gate. Typically, two 4-input logic gates or four 2-input logic gates could all be provided in one package. It is, of course, necessary that the manufacturer provide complete information on logic levels and all connection pins so that the unit may be properly used. For example, Figure 7-35 shows a typical logic unit containing two 3-input NOR gates. The power supply voltage for both gates is provided at pin 10 (the tab on the can) and ground is connected to pin 5. Four pins are used for three inputs and outputs of each logic NOR gate. Logic levels are $+V_{CC}$ and 0 volts, where V_{CC}, is typically 3 to 6 volts.

Boards used to connect discrete component units are not the best possible for IC units. There are no individual components to connect but only multipin units. Sockets are available for each package type and these are then placed on a connector board so that the IC unit need only be plugged in. In final form the connector boards are printed circuit cards that connect the supply voltages to each IC unit and interconnect the logic inputs and outputs as desired (see Figure 7-36). For testing individual IC logic units a test unit such as that of Figure 7-37 allows plug-in of an IC unit. The tester provides internal voltage supply and a low voltage meter allowing the unit to be made operational and checked statically. Dynamic signal operation is obtained by connecting inputs by means of plug-in connector leads. Notice that this arrangement allows connections

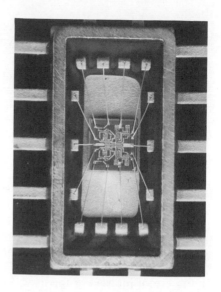

(a)

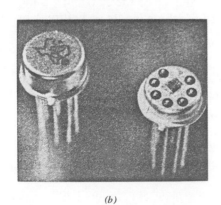

(b)

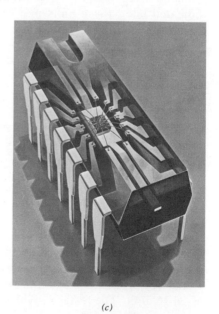

(c)

Figure 7-34. Various logic circuit packages. (a) Fourteen-pin in-line. (b) Ten-pin can. (c) Fourteen-pin flat pack.

234

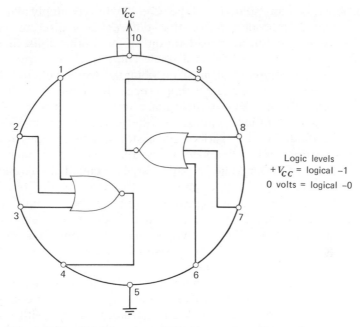

Figure 7-35.   Dual three-input NOR gates packaged in ten-pin can.

Figure 7-36.   IC units interconnected on printed circuit card.

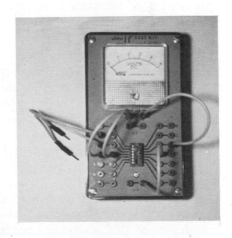

Figure 7-37.   Test board for IC units.

235

to be made without any soldering of the IC unit, which is simply plugged in.

Another quite important factor that differentiates discrete and IC circuits is the manufacturing considerations of monolithic units. Since the complete circuit is to be made on a single chip, much as a transistor is manufactured, all components must be obtained from the same manufacturing procedure. The manufacturing process for monolithic silicon IC circuits is basically the same used to make transistors. There are additional *masking and diffusing* steps, but the process best provides p-n junctions for diodes or the various transistor junctions. Resistors are obtained as sections of lightly doped *p* or *n* areas. We know from practice that resistances of larger values require larger areas of the circuit chip and are thus undesirable. In fact, most resistors may require an area of, say, 2 to 10 times more than a single transistor requires. A suitable circuit for IC manufacture then uses transistors and diodes and as few resistors (of low value) as possible. This is obviously different from the approach in discrete component circuits, where resistors are generally as small and cheaper than a single transistor unit. Capacitors are made on monolithic IC chips using back-biased *p-n* junctions, which provide values of only a few hundred picofarads at most. Capacitors are thus almost completely avoided in IC circuits. Again no such restriction occurs with discrete component circuits. Inductors, not found in digital IC units, are not in discrete IC units either.

Figure 7-38 shows a blow-up of the inside of an IC chip with transistor and resistor areas indicated.

A discussion on the manufacture of a monolithic silicon IC circuit is provided in the following paragraphs so that you may become aware of the "inside" of an IC unit.

Monolithic IC Manufacturing Process.   The manufacturing process used to make monolithic IC circuits is similar to that in the manufacture of transistors. One exception is that for IC manufacture many more steps are necessary — about 40 major process steps. A pure or intrinsic semiconductor material is grown to about 6 to 8 inches in length and 1/2 to 1 inch in diameter. A number of slices or slabs are then cut from this piece with each slice about 6 mils in thickness (6/1000 of an inch). The basic semiconductor slab and individual slices made from it are shown in Figure 7-39.

A multistep process is then used to prepare hundreds of identical circuits on a single slice (1 inch diameter by 6 mils thickness). At the completion of this multistep process each slice contains hundreds of individual circuits. The silicon slice or wafer is then cut into individual dice, each die containing identical logic circuits. Thus many complete IC

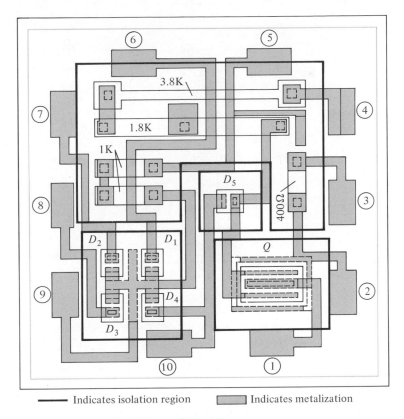

— Indicates isolation region   ▨ Indicates metalization

Figure 7-38.   Details of IC monolithic chip.

units are manufactured in one continuous manufacturing process. At this point the cost per die is quite inexpensive—a few cents usually. The largest part of the total cost comes in handling the individual die—testing and packaging.

Steps in Manufacturing Process.   The sequence of steps in the manufacturing process are generally classified as

1. Surface preparation
2. Epitaxial growth
3. Diffusion
4. Metallization

Since it is quite important to isolate each circuit on the wafer, *surface preparation* is first carried out to provide a layer onto which the circuits are developed. *Epitaxial growth* is the process of depositing a layer of

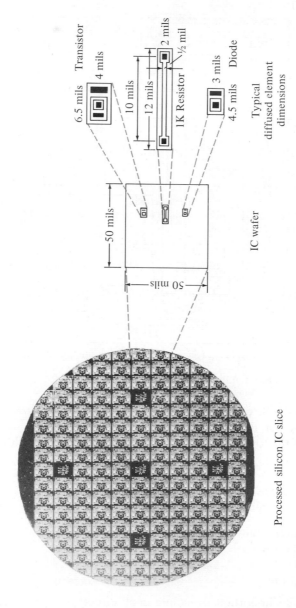

Transistor

6.5 mils

4 mils

10 mils

12 mils

2 mils

½ mil

1K Resistor

3 mils

4.5 mils

Diode

Typical
diffused element
dimensions

50 mils

IC wafer

50 mils

Processed silicon IC slice

Figure 7-39.   Processed IC chip.

238

material having special electrical characteristics. A number of *diffusion* steps are then done to produce the resistor, diode, and transistor components. Finally, a *metallization* operation is performed to interconnect all the individual components of each circuit on the wafer. A single wafer now exists containing the hundreds of individual circuits.

Preliminary testing is then done to determine which of the circuits are operational. After slicing the wafer into individual die, only those that "work" are carried to the testing and packaging steps that follow.

Surface Preparation. The basic wafer is typically a 1 inch by 6 mil slab of silicon. It is a relatively high resistivity (5 to 10 ohm-cm) *p*-type single crystal substrate. Each slice or wafer is lapped smooth on both sides and then one side is polished mirror smooth. Many wafers are cut and prepared from a single bar of silicon material and the success of each wafer depends on the uniformity of the material characteristics over the entire wafer surface. Since many slices will be processed at the same time, the controls for achieving desired results must be consistently considered.

Epitaxial Growth. A thin layer of additional single crystal silicon is grown on the polished surface of the silicon slice. During this growth process minute amounts of *n*-type dopant (impurity atoms) are added to achieve a desired low resistivity. The epitaxial layer is from 0.5 to 2 mils thick and has a resistivity of about 0.1 to 0.5 ohm-cm.

The epitaxial layer provides a good surface for forming the collector of a transistor as is usually done. The opposite type *p*-substrate will act to isolate the separate *n*-areas formed to make the components in later steps. After the epitaxial layer is formed, the entire surface of the wafer is protected by a layer of silicon dioxide (SiO_2) formed by exposing the wafer to an oxygen atmosphere at about 1000°C. The SiO_2 material acts to prevent any outside impurities from entering the epitaxial layer below it and thus acts as a protective layer.

Masking. A very intricate and important part of the fabrication process is the use of many photographically formed masks that provide the basic pattern for forming the circuit. Many masks are used in one fabrication process and all must align perfectly.

A mask or plate is first drawn by a draftsman from the engineer's sketches and information. These plates are made in large sizes (of many feet) and are then reduced to about 1 inch by photographic techniques. This part of the process is quite carefully controlled and the photographic equipment is usually mounted on a large solid bed of concrete that is isolated from the surrounding area to prevent normal vibrations from affecting the quality of the photographic process. A set of masks that are used in the various steps in the manufacturing process may be used repeatedly to provide a wafer of many hundreds of circuits. The procedure of photoetching is used to form the mask pattern on the wafer material (Figure 7-40). A mask is placed over the wafer and a photoresist coating on the wafer surface is exposed to ultraviolet light. A chemical is then used to etch away the unexposed surface leaving only the surface

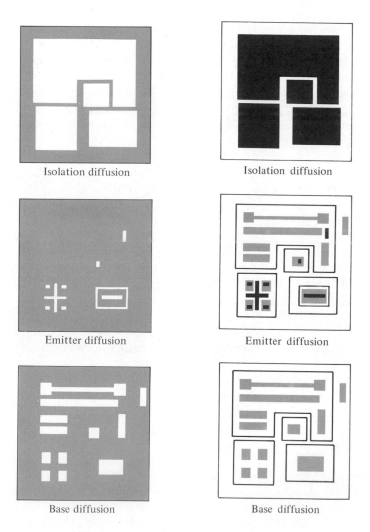

Isolation diffusion   Isolation diffusion

Emitter diffusion   Emitter diffusion

Base diffusion   Base diffusion

Figure 7-40.   Masking of IC chip.

pattern desired. The surface pattern is then prepared for a diffusion operation as will be described next.

Diffusion. As in the process of single transistor manufacture, the diffusion operation is the doping of part of the device structure with either *p*- or *n*-type impurity. The diffusion is carried out by passing a gas of the impurity or dopant over the multiunit wafer under controlled temperature and pressure conditions. The impurity diffuses into the solid structure for a period of time until the desired depth of diffusion is achieved. The SiO_2 layer acts to block any diffusion of impurity through it, whereas the masked and etched surface allows diffusion to take place.

Although there are many steps in the manufacturing process, there are a few basic diffusion steps that will show the general operation. The diffusion steps may be classified as isolation diffusion, base diffusion, and emitter diffusion, as will be described (See Figure 7-41).

1. Isolation diffusion. Figure 7-41 shows a single die cross-section.

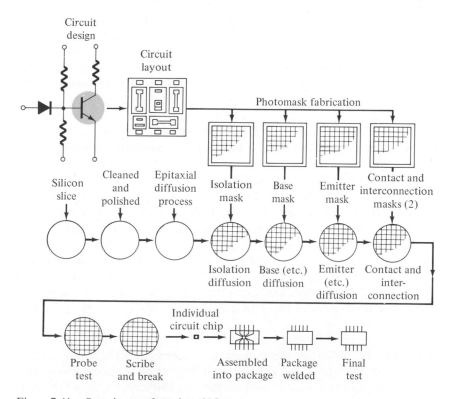

Figure 7-41.   Steps in manufacturing of IC.

(Although we speak of a single die, the procedure described is being carried out simultaneously for all the dice on the wafer). In the isolation diffusion, the *p*-type dopant is allowed to penetrate the *n*-type epitaxial layer until it reaches the *p*-type substrate. The remaining "islands" are then isolated from each other and each will eventually result in a separate component — resistor, diode, or transistor.

A new oxide layer is now formed to cover over the surface and another photoetching operation is performed to prepare the die for the next diffusion.

2. Base diffusion. During the base diffusion step the circuit resistors, diode anodes, and transistor base structures are formed. The *p*-type impurities are allowed to diffuse through the masked and etched areas. The value of the resistor is determined by the resistivity of the *p*-type material and its area and length. To obtain resistor values of only a few hundred ohms requires using a large amount of the die area. Proportionately, the resistor uses much more area of the die than the transistor or diode, and the die size is dependent more on the resistors than on the diodes and transistors. Again the surface is protected by an oxide coating and a photoetching operation is performed to prepare for the emitter diffusion.

3. Emitter diffusion. The diode cathodes and transistor emitters are formed at this step. The *n*-type impurity is allowed to diffuse into the structure at the open area (windows). The diffusion depth is controlled carefully. Although capacitors have not been discussed yet they are formed by using a reverse-biased diode. This technique only allows small capacitor values — in the range of hundreds of picofarads. Where larger size resistors or capacitors are needed, a thin-film technique is used to separately manufacture the resistors and capacitors and then the two different chips — one containing diodes and transistors, the other resistors and capacitors — are combined into one package called a hybrid assembly.

Often the circuit can be cleverly designed so that few resistors and capacitors are required, with the major circuit components being made of transistors and diodes. This is then suitable for monolithic manufacture. Notice that diodes and transistors are cheaper and require less area to manufacture than resistors and capacitors, and therefore a circuit design using a few transistors in place of a resistor is often preferable for this construction process.

Metallization. With all the components formed on the many similar dice areas of the wafer, the next operation is again a photoetching, this time to open up the windows to provide the connections between components. All the interconnections are made in one step by vacuum deposition of a thin film of aluminum over the entire wafer. A final masking and etching clears away any unnecessary connection areas leaving only the desired interconnection pattern.

Depending on the manufacturing requirements, either selected sections or all of the wafer circuits are tested for operational circuits. Those that fail are marked off (usually by a blob of ink on that die area). The wafer is then scribed by a diamond-tipped tool and separated into individual chips. Up to now the cost of production is quite low, possibly a few dollars for the single wafer. Once individual die are obtained, the handling and testing and packaging costs enter the picture. Each die is fully tested, mounted on a leader and encapsulated in either a transistorlike can (with many leads) or in a flat pack.

7-6.   IC Logic Circuits

Having considered some general aspects of manufacturing IC units we shall now discuss a number of specific digital logic IC circuits. Those presently most popular which will be considered are

1. DTL – Diode-Transistor Logic
2. RTL – Resistor-Transistor Logic
3. TTL – Transistor-Transistor Logic
4. ECL – Emitter-Coupled Logic

As would be expected, each type of logic circuit has certain advantages and disadvantages so that no one type as yet is preferred over the others. At present TTL is most popular. However, RTL is inexpensive and ECL is the fastest. These distinctions will be pointed out as each logic type is covered. They are all made as monolothic IC circuits and are similarly packaged.

There are numerous factors to be considered in selecting the type of IC circuit to use in a particular system. Logically, the circuits may be considered alike (NOR or NAND gates).

As a partial summary of the important factors used in selecting a circuit type we have (not necessarily in order of importance):

1. Cost
2. Power dissipation
3. Speed of operation
4. Noise immunity

DTL – Diode-Transistor Logic.   The integrated circuit DTL logic gate is somewhat similar to the DCTL circuit covered as a discrete device. We shall consider a few variations of DTL gates. Figure 7-42*a* shows a DTL

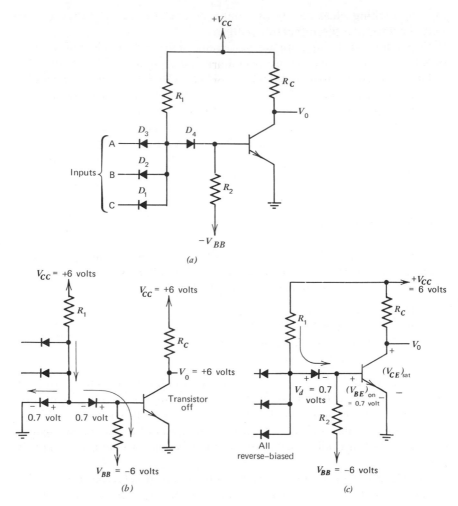

Figure 7-42.   DTL circuit with two voltage supplies. (*a*) Basic circuit. (*b*) Transistor OFF. (*c*) Transistor ON.

circuit using two voltage supplies. Notice the use of diode D_4 to replace a resistor and capacitor in the previous DCTL circuit. Whenever possible, IC circuits should be made with diodes and transistors in place of resistors and capacitors. As shown, the circuit has a number of disadvantages. First, it requires two supply voltages where only a single supply would be most desirable. The circuit has poor noise margin (noise immunity) as shown. Figure 7-42*b* shows the operation with one (or more) diode inputs at 0 volts. The junction point of diodes D_1, D_4, and resistor R_1 is held at about $V_{D_1} = 0.7$ volt. With the same value voltage drop across coupling diode D_4 the voltage at the base of the transistor is 0 volts, which holds the transistor OFF but with little noise margin left. The negative supply does not help to improve the noise margin in this circuit, but is provided to help speed up turn off of the transistor.

Figure 7-42c shows the circuit conditions for the transistor driven ON. With all inputs logical-1 (+ 6 volts), the input diodes are all open (reverse-biased) and the transistor is driven ON with resulting output voltage of $(V_{CE})_{\text{sat}}$. We shall only note how the circuit operates. Exact calculations are not necessary since we cannot change anything in any case (remember the complete circuit is a single enclosed chip).

A more practical form of the DTL circuit is shown in Figure 7-43a. Only a single voltage supply is used. Two diodes are used for coupling to provide greater noise immunity, as will be shown.

With two diodes the input voltage needed to drive the DTL circuit transistor ON must result in a base-emitter voltage exceeding about 0.4 volt. We calculate

$$V_{\text{noise}} + (V_{CE})_{\text{sat}} + V_{d_2} - V_{d_4} - V_{d_5} \geqslant 0.4 \text{ V}$$

to begin to drive the transistor ON. The noise immunity is then

$$V_{\text{noise}} = V_{d_4} + V_{d_5} - V_{d_2} - (V_{CE})_{\text{sat}} + 0.4$$

$$\text{Noise Immunity} = 0.7 + 0.7 - 0.7 - 0.1 + 0.4 = 1 \text{ V}$$

The extra coupling diode required an additional drop of 0.7, which brought the noise margin up to about 1 volt for the DTL circuit.

Figure 7-43b shows the condition of all inputs logical-1 with all input diodes reverse-biased and the transistor driven ON. We expect that the circuit is properly designed and that $V_0 = (V_{CE})_{\text{sat}}$ for the transistor ON. Notice that the voltage at the junction of R_1 and coupling diode D_4 is about 2.1 volts [$= V_{d_4} + V_{d_5} + (V_{BE})_{\text{ON}}$] and that the input voltage must be greater than about 2 volts for the logical-1 level. Practical values of 3.6 to about 6 volts are typical.

One of the more popular DTL circuits is the Fairchild Series 930. Figure 7-44a shows this more practical IC version of a DTL circuit. Notice that the circuit includes an input transistor to replace one of the input offset diodes in the conventional DTL circuit (as in Figure 7-43a). The transistor added provides turn-on drive to the output inverter transistor allowing increased loading. In addition, the input transistor acts as a current source allowing a smaller base to ground resistor so that a negative supply voltage is not needed for quick transistor turn-off.

Figure 7-44b shows one input (or more) at 0 volts with the resulting

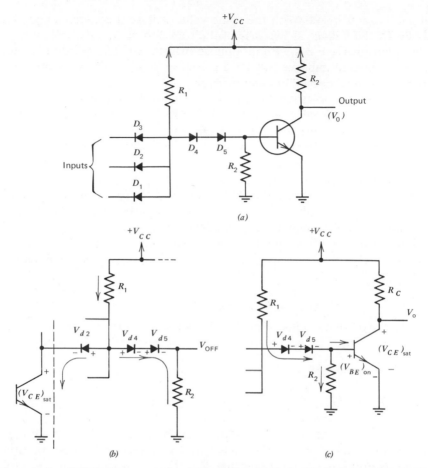

Figure 7-43.   DTL logic gate — single supply version. (*a*) Basic circuit. (*b*) Transistor OFF. (*c*) Transistor ON.

output high ($+5$ volts). The voltage after the input diode is about $+0.7$ volt. In order to drive transistor Q_1 on, the base voltage must be more positive than the emitter. For this to occur the base would have to exceed about 1.4 volts $[V_{d_3} + (V_{BE})_{on}]$. This is not the case in Figure 7-44*b* and transistor Q_1 is OFF as is transistor Q_2 (base voltage is 0 volts). The output is $+5$ volts as shown.

Figure 7-44*c* shows the conditions for the output being driven low. The inputs are all high ($+5$ volts) and, as shown, transistors Q_1 and Q_2 are driven ON. The output is low, $(V_{CE})_{sat}$.

The circuit is a positive logic NAND gate. Figure 7-44*d* shows a logic diagram of a dual four-input gate packaged as a 14-pin in-line unit. The

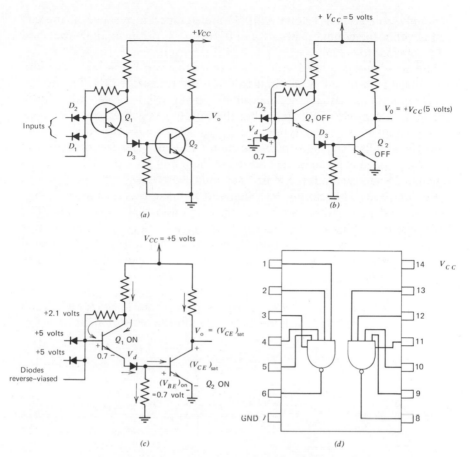

Figure 7-44.   Fairchild 930 DTL circuit. (*a*) Fairchild 930 DTL gate. (*b*) Output high. (*c*) Output low. (*d*) Logic pin connections.

numbered pins allowed connection information in using the two separate NAND gate circuits. For example, the supply voltage for both gates is $+ V_{CC}$ connected to pin 14 and ground (GND) connected to pin 7. One gate has four inputs at pins 1, 2, 4, and 5 with output at pin 6. Pin 3 is the extender point at the junction of the four input diode anodes. It allows connecting additional input diodes if needed.

Some specified ratings for the unit are

$$\text{noise immunity} = 1 \text{ volt}$$
$$\text{power dissipation} = 8 \text{ mW}$$
$$\text{fan-out} = 8$$
$$\text{propagation delay} = 25 \text{ nsec}$$

Supply voltage is $+5$ volts ($\pm 10\%$) and temperature range of the circuit is either the commercial range of $0°$ to $+75°C$ or the military specified range of $-55°$ to $+125°C$.

The *noise immunity* of 1 volt means that at least a 1-volt noise or pick-up voltage is required at an input to drive the transistor ON. The *power dissipation* of 8 mW is the maximum power used by the unit (both circuits). A *fan-out* of 8 means that the output of each gate can be connected to up to 8 similar types of logic gates. *Propagation delay* is the time for a pulse signal to pass through the logic gate (more detail on switching speed is given later) and the present unit provides a delay to the signal of 25 nanoseconds (25×10^{-9} seconds).

For the 930 DTL circuit, less demand is made on resistor tolerance, fan-out, and power dissipation than in conventional DTL circuits. The DTL circuit of Figure 7-44 therefore has the advantages of single power supply, lower power dissipation, larger drive capability, higher speed operation, and better noise immunity than the conventional circuits of Figures 7-42 or 7-43.

Resistor-Transistor Logic (RTL).   A resistor-transistor logic (RTL) circuit is shown in Figure 7-45. Each logic input requires a resistor and transistor.

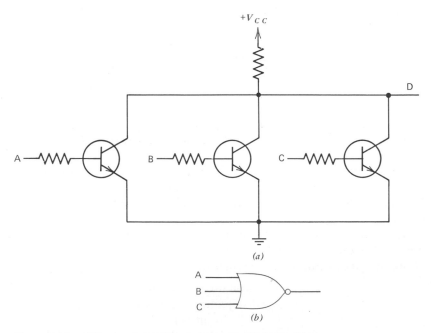

Figure 7-45.   RTL circuit. (*a*) Circuit schematic. (*b*) Logic diagram.

The circuit shown is a 3-input positive logic NOR gate. For positive logic the definitions used are $+V_{CC}$ = logical-1, 0 V = logical-0.

If any input is logical-1 ($+V_{CC}$), the transistor connected to that input will be driven into saturation. This is shown in Figure 7-46a. The input of $+V_{CC}$ volts will drive the transistor into saturation placing the output voltage at $(V_{CE})_{sat}$ or about 0 volts. Any one or more transistors in saturation will result in the output being near 0 volts. Only if all transistors are OFF (all inputs 0 volts) is the output at $+V_{CC}$ volts. In terms of logical operation, the output is logical-0 if A, B, or C, or any combination of these is logical-1 so that the circuit acts as a NOR gate.

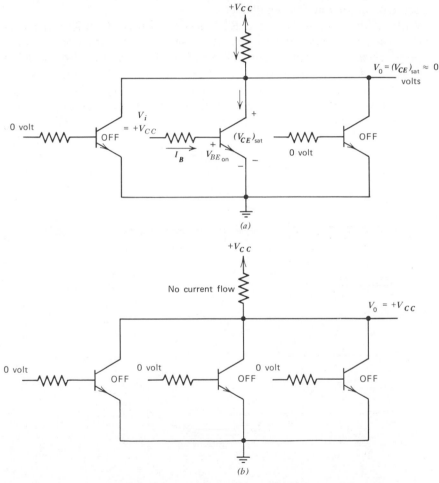

Figure 7-46.   Operation of RTL circuit. (a) Output 0 volts. (b) Output $+V_{CC}$ volts.

The use of RTL circuits will be limited by a number of factors, however. Noise immunity is quite poor. Referring to Figure 7-46*b*, a transistor is held OFF by only the amount of base-emitter voltage required to drive the transistor ON. For a required value of about 0.4 volts, and with V_i typically 0.1 volt (from the output of a saturated transistor), the noise immunity available is only 0.3 volt (300 mV). In addition, this value is quite sensitive to temperature, the noise immunity degrading rapidly with temperature increase.

The voltage level required to switch an RTL circuit also shifts considerably with operating temperature and fan-out. Speed of operation as measured by turn-on and turn-off delay times of the RTL circuit are also affected by fan-in and fan-out changes.

With all these limitations the RTL has the only advantage that it is one of the least expensive to buy at present. It only requires a single supply voltage, typically about 3 to 5 volts. The circuit is also available in a modified version (resistor values higher) in which the required power dissipation is quite low. This milliwatt RTL circuit typically dissipates about 2 mW of power, which is attractive when thousands of gates are used in a system.

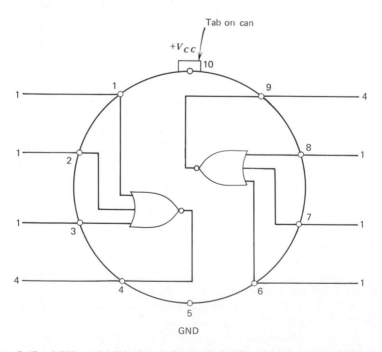

Figure 7-47.   Milliwatt RLT logic unit (Motorola 718G) – dual three-input NOR gates.

The following summarizes the RTL circuit.

Advantages: low cost, simple IC manufacture, single voltage supply, low milliwatt operation.

Disadvantages: low noise immunity, slow speed, temperature sensitive in a number of operating factors.

As an example of a low power (milliwatt) RTL logic gate, the loading diagram of Figure 7-47 shows a Motorola dual 3-input unit. The unit is packaged in a 10-pin can. The numbers in sequence around the can (counter-clockwise from 1 to 10) are the pin designations. Notice the tab is right by pin 10 to allow identifying the pins on the actual unit. The view shown is from the bottom or pin side of the can. For example, one of the NOR gates has three inputs at pins 1, 2, and 3 with the NOR gate output at pin 4.

The numbers shown outside the can are loading factors for the milliwatt RTL circuits. The inputs of a logic gate each represent a loading of 1 on whatever circuit is connected to it. The output of the NOR gate is shown to be capable of fan-out of 4. This means that it could be used to provide input signal to four inputs of load 1.

Some important factors specified by the manufacturer for the above logic unit are:

Supply voltage:	$V_{CC} = 3.6$ V $\pm 10\%$
Temperature range:	$+15°$ to $55°$C
Power dissipation:	3 mW
Noise immunity:	300 mV
Average propagation delay:	25 nsec

Transistor-Transistor Logic (TTL).   The fastest of the saturated-type logic circuits (those which drive the ON transistor into saturation) is the transistor-transistor logic circuit also called TTL or T^2L. A basic TTL NAND gate is shown in Figure 7-48a. Notice the unusual feature of this IC circuit-multiple emitters on a single transistor. To help explain the operation of the basic TTL gate let us consider a discrete version of the same gate first (see Figure 7-48b). Using positive logic the definitions are logical-1 $= V_{CC}$, logical-0 $= 0$ volt.

In summary, any input of logical-0 (0 volts) will result in that input transistor being driven ON, resulting in output inverter transistor Q_4 being held OFF and the output being $+ V_{CC}$. Only if all inputs are logical-1 $(+ V_{CC})$ are all input transistors held OFF with the result that output transistor Q_4 is driven ON (in saturation) and the output is near 0 volts (logical-0). This action describes the operation of a positive logic NAND gate (output is logical-0 *only if* inputs A AND B AND C are *all* logical-1).

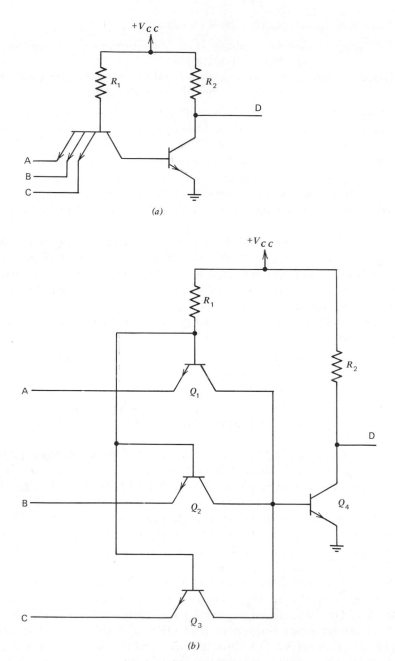

Figure 7-48.   Transistor-transistor logic, basic circuit. (*a*) Basic TTL circuit. (*b*) Discrete component form of TTL circuit.

To consider some circuit detail we will cover the case of at least one input logical-0 with output logical-1 and the case of all inputs logical-1 with output logical-0.

Output Transistor OFF. Figure 7-49a shows the circuit detals with one or more inputs at 0 volts and the output transistor OFF. In particular, two inputs are 0 volts. Transistors are forward-biased by the $+V_{CC}$ voltage through resistor R_1 since the emitters of those transistors are at lower potential. The input of $+V_{CC}$ to input B causes that transistor to remain OFF since there is not sufficient voltage to forward-bias that transistor base emitter. With transistors Q_1 and Q_3 biased ON (and in saturation,

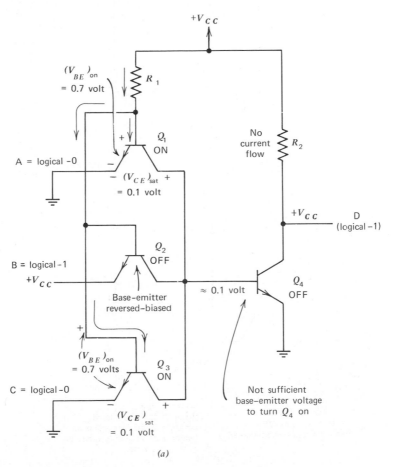

(a)

Figure 7-49. Operation of basic TTL discrete form circuit. (a) Output transistor (Q_4) OFF.

where R_1 has been chosen by the manufacturer to allow sufficient base current to saturate an ON input transistor), the voltage at the base of transistor is $(V_{CE})_{sat}$ or about 0.1 volt. This voltage is not sufficiently positive to drive Q_4 ON, so that Q_4 remains OFF and with no collector current in Q_4, the output voltage resulting is $+V_{CC}$ (logical-1 level). In summary, any one or more inputs of 0 volts results in output of $+V_{CC}$.

Output Transistor ON. Figure 7-49*b* shows all inputs logical-1 $(+V_{CC})$

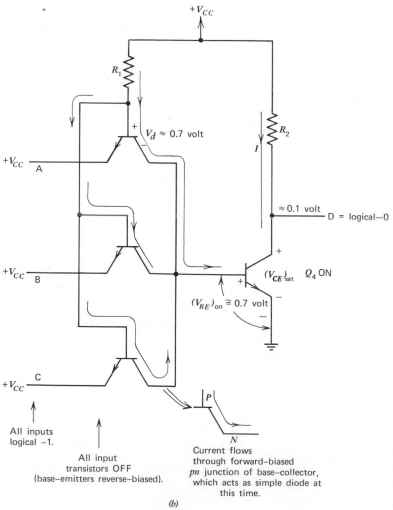

(b)

Figure 7-49.   (b) Output transistor (Q_4) ON.

with the result that all input transistors are biased OFF. The base-emitter junction is reverse-biased and appears as an open circuit. As shown in the figure, a current does flow from the plus supply through R_1 through the base collector of each transistor. At this time with the base emitter open and no transistor action taking place, the collector-emitter junction is merely a p-n junction, as shown in Figure 7-49b, permitting current flow in the base to collector direction only. The voltage drop across the base collector is fixed at about 0.7 V, as for any silicon p-n junction. Transistor Q_4 is biased into saturation with the output voltage about 0.1 volt.

The operation of the IC circuit in Figure 7-48a is exactly the same as just described for the discrete circuit form. The only difference is that the IC unit is actually one input transistor with multiple emitters. Although the basic TTL circuit of Figure 7-48a can be operated as a logic circuit, it has poor noise immunity as well as other poor circuit features.

A modified version of a TTL circuit, and one that is widely used as the circuit actually implemented in IC manufacture, is shown in Figure 7-50. The logic operation of this circuit is that of a positive logic NAND gate. To consider the two main cases of circuit operation we must consider the case of one or more inputs logical-0 with output $+ V_{CC}$ and the case of all inputs $+ V_{CC}$ with output near 0 volts. Voltage and logic truth tables for the previous circuit and for the circuit of Figure 7-50 are provided for two inputs in Tables 7-12 and 7-13 to show the positive logic NAND operation.

Table 7-12. *Voltage Truth Table*			Table 7-13. *Logic Truth Table*		
A	B	Output	A	B	Output
0 V	0 V	$+ V_{CC}$	0	0	1
0 V	$+ V_{CC}$	$+ V_{CC}$	0	1	1
$+ V_{CC}$	0 V	$+ V_{CC}$	1	0	1
$+ V_{CC}$	$+ V_{CC}$	0 V	1	1	0

To examine the circuit operation we will separately consider operation for output logical-1 and for output logical-0.

Output Logical-1. With one or more inputs at 0 volts, the output will be $+ V$ as shown in Figure 7-51a. With one input (or more) at 0 volts input, transistor Q_1 is biased ON by the $+ V_{CC}$ through resistor R_1. The collector voltage of Q_1 is about 0.1 volt, which is too low to forward-bias Q_2, which is then OFF. Since no current then flows through R_3, the voltage at the

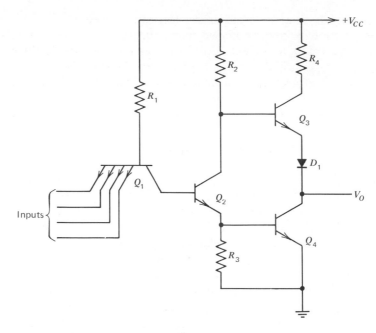

Figure 7-50.   TTL NAND gate circuit, practical version.

base of Q_4 is 0 volts with Q_4 then OFF. The $+V_{CC}$ voltage through R_2 drives Q_3 ON with resulting voltage at the output $+V$, somewhat less than $+V_{CC}$ by the saturated voltage drop across Q_3 and the voltage drop across diode D_1. Diode D_1 serves to prevent transistor Q_3 from turning ON until Q_4 has turned OFF when the circuit switches state.

Output Logical-0. If all inputs are $+V$ (logical-1) the output will be near 0 volts, as shown in Figure 7-51b. Transistor Q_1 is biased OFF by the inputs. Transistor Q_2 is then driven ON and the current flow through R_3 provides sufficient voltage to drive Q_4 ON. The output voltage is then pulled down to about 0.1 volt.

With Q_4 and Q_2 ON the voltage at the collector of Q_2 is about 0.8 volt $[(V_{BE})_{on} = 0.7 \text{ V plus } (V_{CE})_{sat} = 0.1 \text{ V}]$. With the collector Q_4 voltage at about 0.1 volt the base Q_3 voltage would have to be greater than about 1.2 volts $[(V_{CE})_{sat} + V_{C_1} + 0.4]$. Since the base Q_3 voltage is less, transistor Q_3 is held OFF.

Typical TTL circuitry has a power dissipation of about 14 mW, propagation delay of 3 nsec, noise immunity of 400 to 500 mV. In addition, individual component requirements with the IC circuit are not very stringent, which leads to good yields in production.

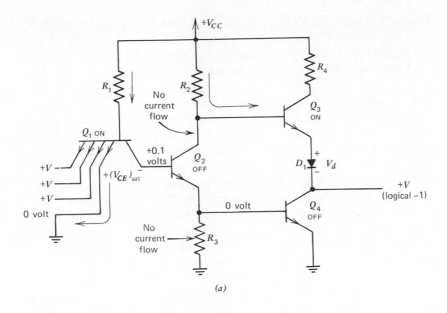

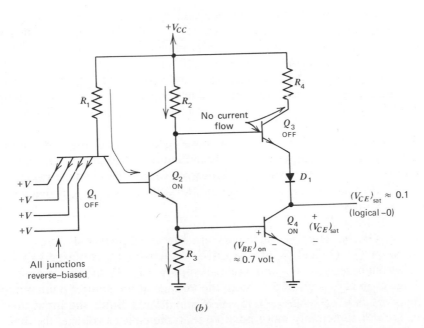

Figure 7-51. Operation of practical TTL circuit. (a) Output $+V$ (logical-1). (b) Output near 0 volts (logical-0).

257

Figure 7-52 shows a TTL logic gate packaged in a 14-pin flat-pack. The Texas Instrument (TI) Company's SN5410 shown is a triple 3-input positive NAND gate. The circuit for one gate is shown, as is the unit pin-connection diagram and some typical circuit values.

Emitter Coupled Logic (ECL).   Emitter-coupled logic (ECL) was developed as early as 1963 by the Motorola Corporation. The ECL or current mode logic (CML) circuit is basically a nonsaturating, very high speed logic gate. Figure 7-53 shows the basic Motorola ECL circuit (called MECL for Motorola Emitter Coupled Logic) and logic symbol. The circuit will be shown to be a positive logic NOR gate having, in addition, an inverted NOR output-on OR output. Each input is made through a transistor and each output is taken from an emitter-follower driver. The circuit as shown requires a bias transistor to obtain the proper nonsaturated operation and the circuit appears to require three voltage supplies. (It will be shown that only one supply voltage and an additional bias driver circuit will be sufficient to replace the three indicated supplied). The circuit shown has the property that logic levels are determined by resistor values (which are relatively stable) instead of the transistor characteristics.

The bias transistor sets a reference voltage at the emitter point of the transistors and current flows through R_{C_2} and R_E. If the input voltages are all less than the set emitter voltage, the input transistors remain OFF with no current through R_{C_1} and the NOR output *high*. If any one input goes *high* driving that input transistor ON, the NOR output goes *low*. The circuit operates as a positive logic NOR gate at the D output terminal. The $\bar{D}$ output will be shown to be opposite D thus acting as an OR output.

To see how the circuit operates in more detail consider the two operating conditions—D output *high* (logical-1) and D output *low* (logical-0). As a practical circuit consider the Motorola version and voltage values of Figure 7-54a. Notice the addition of emitter follower stages to provide the outputs of the gate.

NOR Output High. If all inputs are low as shown in Figure 7-54b transistors Q_1, Q_2 and Q_3 are all OFF. Transistor Q_4 is biased ON by V_{BB} through resistor R_E and voltage supply V_{EE}. With a base-emitter voltage drop across Q_4 of 0.75 volt, the voltage at the emitter point of the transistors is -1.9 volts ($-1.15 - 0.75 = -1.9$ V). Since the input voltages are not sufficiently more positive than the emitter voltage, the input transistors are each OFF. A current flows through R_{C_2}, transistor Q_4, and R_E with a resulting voltage drop set by the value of R_{C_2}, of 0.8 volt

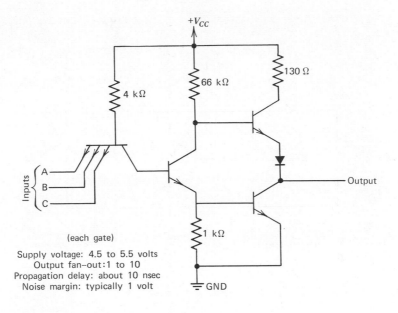

(each gate)
Supply voltage: 4.5 to 5.5 volts
Output fan–out: 1 to 10
Propagation delay: about 10 nsec
Noise margin: typically 1 volt

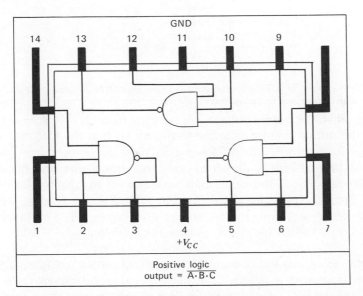

Positive logic
output = $\overline{A \cdot B \cdot C}$

Figure 7-52. Texas Instrument SN5410 triple 3-input positive NAND gate using TTL circuitry.

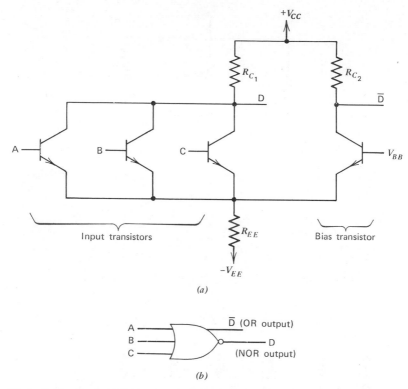

Figure 7-53.   Basic ECL circuit. (*a*) Circuit diagram. (*b*) OR/NOR logic symbol.

across R_{C_2}. The OR output voltage is less by the base-emitter drop of 0.75 through the output emitter-follower transistor so that the OR output is presently -1.55 volts $(-0.8-0.75=-1.55$ V).

No collector current is drawn by the input transistors and the only current through R_{C_1} is the very small base current for the NOR output emitter follower. Neglecting the slight voltage drop across R_{C_1}, the output voltage is less than 0 volts by the base-emitter voltage drop of the NOR emitter-follower output transistor—so that the NOR output is -0.75 volts.

NOR Output Low. If any one input is *high*, as shown in Figure 7-54*c*, that input transistor is driven ON and Q_4 is thereby driven OFF. In Figure 7-54*c* input C goes *high* to -0.75 volt driving Q_3 ON and raising the voltage at the emitter point to -1.5 volts $(-0.75-0.75=-1.5$ V). The emitter voltage going positive decreases the base-emitter voltage drop across Q_4 and Q_4 turns OFF. The current through emitter resistor R_E now comes through resistor R_{C_1} instead of R_{C_2} and the drop of about

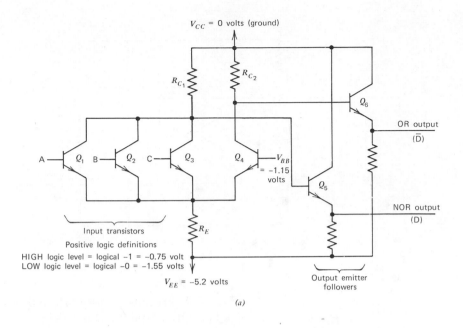

(a)

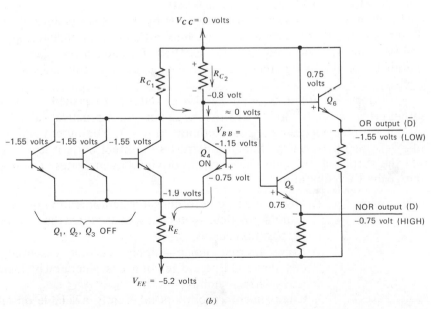

(b)

Figure 7-54. Practical version of ECL logic circuit. (*a*) Motorola ECL circuit. (*b*) NOR output *high*.

261

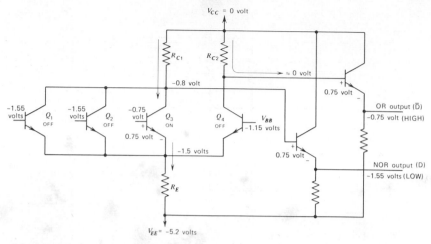

(c) NOR output *low*.

-0.8 volt across R_{C_1} (set by the value of R_{C_1}) results in the NOR output being -1.55 volts (*low* logic level). The OR output is about 0.75 volt below 0 volts or -0.75 volt (*high* logic level).

The voltage levels selected, which are set by the resistor values of the circuit, provide that the transistors are biased ON but not in saturation. Emitter-coupled logic circuits, such as that of Figure 7-54c can only operate properly driving other gates of the exact same circuit and voltage levels.

The typical circuit uses emitter-follower outputs to provide a large output drive capability and therefore a large fan-out. A practical value for fan-out without degrading speed is about 20 to 25. The output-emitter followers also perform the function of restoring direct current levels so that the output of one gate may directly drive following gates. To summarize the ECL operation:

Advantages: 1. High speed—due to nonsaturated operation of transistor's practical switching speeds of less than 5 nsec propagation delays.
                 2. Low internal noise—supply current essentially constant and little noise voltage is generated by logic gates when switching.
                 3. Complementary outputs inherently available on all gates.

Disadvantages: 1. Low noise margin—typically 300 mV.
                 2. Need of bias driver to supply V_{BB} voltage.

Bias Driver. To be complete a schematic of a bias driver used to supply the $V_{BB} = -1.15$ volts is shown in Figure 7-55. The circuit uses a temperature-compensated voltage divider network to set the regulated output voltage V_{BB} at -1.15 volts. Notice that the circuit uses the supply voltage V_{EE} so that with the addition of a bias driver only V_{EE} is required as supply voltage for the operation of ECL circuits.

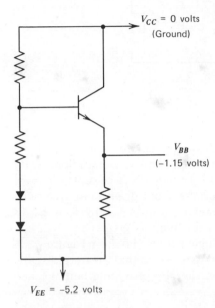

Figure 7-55.   Bias driver circuit.

Field Effect Transistor (FET) Logic Gates.   The use of field effect transistors as logic elements has gained significantly. This growth is most impressive in the production of large-scale integration (LSI) circuits, which provide multigate circuits to carry out complete logic or subsystem operations. More on LSI devices will be given later. For the moment we are interested in the operation of FET logic gates. Figure 7-56 shows a simple logic gate using FET devices as input. The FET acts as in inverter, similar to the way a transistor would. Using logic levels of $+V_{CC} =$ logical-1 and 0 volts = logical-0 the circuit of Figure 7-56 performs as a positive logic NOR gate. With all inputs at 0 volts the FETS are all OFF and the output voltage at D is $+V_{CC}$. If any one (or more) input is $+V_{CC}$, a FET is driven ON lowering the output voltage to near 0 volts.

As an integrated circuit there is only one resistor required in Figure 7-56. Even this can be eliminated and replaced by a transistor, as shown in Figure 7-57.

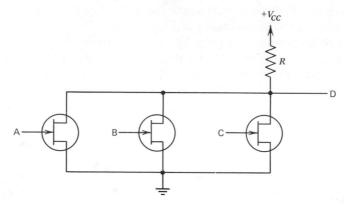

Figure 7-56.   Positive logic NOR gate using FETs.

Essentially, FET Q_4 acts as a fixed resistor. Recall that the channel of a FET has a resistance, typically a few hundred ohms to a few kilohms. By connecting the drain and gate, the channel pinch effect is kept relatively constant and the device looks like a resistor from drain to source. The space savings in IC manufacture by making a chip having four FETs instead of three and a resistor is quite worthwhile.

A practical circuit version of a FET logic gate is shown in Figure 7-58. The circuit uses complementary FET transistors so that the output signal is always provided by an active device, thereby providing better speed

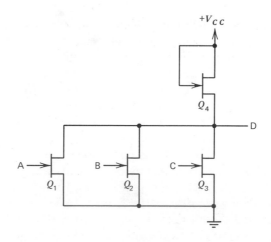

Figure 7-57.   FET logic gate using only FET devices.

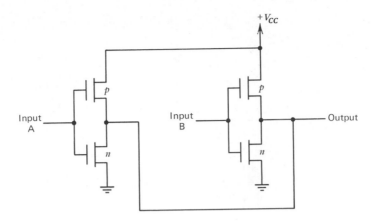

Figure 7-58.   FET logic gate with complementary operation.

and loading operation. The circuit shows that p-channel and n-channel MOSFETs (Metal Oxide Semiconductor FETs) are used. If either input A or B (or both) are $+V_{CC}$, the n-channel FET is driven ON placing the output point near 0 volts. (Also, the p-channel FET's are biased OFF). If both input A AND B are 0 volts, the p-channel FETs are biased ON (and n-channel FETs OFF) with the output voltage $+V_{CC}$ through the conducting p-channel FETs.

The MOSFET provides logic circuits that are particularly situated for moderate speed (around 1 MHz), low power, high impedance, and very well suited to IC production.

General Designation of Logic Circuits.   The different types of logic circuits can be considered as one of the group types:

1. current sourcing
2. current sinking
3. current mode

The terminology of source and sink may be considered analogous to a kitchen faucet as being the "source" and the place where the water goes as the "sink." Electrically, the source provides the current and the sink receives current.

Current Sourcing. As an example of a current sourcing operation consider the action in Figure 7-59a. When connecting the output of one logic gate as input to a second logic gate current flows from the output of the first gate into the input of the second gate. The first stage acts as a

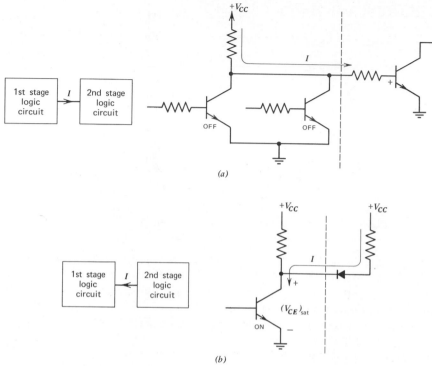

Figure 7-59.   Sourcing and sinking operations. (*a*) Current sourcing. (*b*) Current sinking.

current source. The general characteristics of a current sourcing gate are:

1. Logic current flows into inputs.
2. Drive current flows out of outputs.
3. Gate performs positive NOR function.

Referring to the types of logic circuits covered we find that the following are current sourcing circuits:

$$\left.\begin{array}{l}\text{RTL logic gate}\\\text{FET logic gate}\end{array}\right\}\quad\text{Current Source Circuits}$$

Current Sinking. If the interconnection of logic gates results in the first logic stage drawing current from the second logic stage as in Figure 7-59*b*, the gate operates as a current sinking circuit. The first logic stage acts as a current sink pulling current from the second stage input as general characteristics of current sinking circuits:

1. Logic current flows out of inputs.

2. Outputs *sink* drive current.
3. Gate performs positive NAND function.
4. Highest voltage noise immunity.

Of the circuits covered two are current sinking circuits:

$$\left.\begin{array}{l}\text{DTL logic gates}\\ \text{TTL logic gates}\end{array}\right\}\quad\text{Current Sinking Circuits}$$

Current Mode. Current mode is not as easy to specify since current could flow either into or out of inputs. It is still possible to specify some characteristics such as:

1. Logic current is small and flows in for high input impedance.
2. Gate performs OR/NOR functions.
3. Fastest logic form-nonsaturating.

Compatability. The reason for mentioning these operation catagories is that when different logic types (DTL, TTL, RTL, etc) are used it is possible to use one type to operate another type *only* if they are the same circuit category. That is, since DTL and TTL are both current sinking it would be possible to use one to drive the other (assuming voltage levels correspond). It would not at all be possible to feed a TTL output as input to an RTL circuit since the TTL output would want to draw current for the following gate's input, whereas the RTL requires the preceding gate to feed current. Current-mode being nonsaturating would not be possible to operate directly with either saturated current sourcing or sinking type logic circuits.

PROBLEMS

§7-2   1. Draw the circuit diagram of a negative logic AND gate with 3 inputs.
      2. Using voltage levels of -8 volts and 0 volts prepare voltage and logic truth tables for the circuit of Problem 1.
      3. Prepare voltage and logic truth tables for the circuit and voltages indicated in Figure 7-60. What is the logic operation of the circuit?
      4. Prepare a voltage truth table for a connection of negative logic OR gate with two inputs (A, B) feeding a negative logic AND gate with one other input (C). The supply voltage is $V_{CC} = 12$ V, OR gate resistor is 2 K and the AND gate resistor is 4 K. Inputs are 0 V and -12 V.
      5. Prepare a voltage truth table for the circuit of Figure 7-21a using $R_1 = 1.8$ K, $R_2 = 5.6$ K, $V_d = 0.7$ V, and $V = \pm 4$ V with voltage inputs of 0 V and $+4$ V.

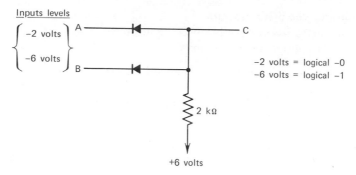

Figure 7-60.   Circuit for Problem 7-3.

§7-3   **6.** Check the operation of the inverter circuit of Figure 7-26a for values of $V_{CC} = +5$ V, $(V_{CE})_{sat} = 0.3$ V, $R_B = 8.6$ K, $R_C = 1$ K, and $h_{FE} = 20$, $V_i = +5$ V, $(V_{BE})_{on} = 0.7$ V.

7. Draw *pnp* inverter circuit having two supply voltages.

8. For the circuit of Figure 7-31 with values below calculate the circuit noise margin and check whether the transistor is driven into saturation for input of $V_i = 4$ volts: $R_1 = 2.4$ K, $R_2 = 27$ K, $V_{CC} = \pm 4$ V, $(V_{CE})_{sat} = 0.1$ V, $(V_{BE})_{on} = 0.7$ V, $h_{FE} = 25$, $R_C = 2$ 1 K.

§7-4   **9.** For the positive logic NAND gate of Figure 7-32 calculate the noise margin and check the saturation operation for circuit values of: $R_1 = 1.2$ K, $R_2 = 4.7$ K, $R_3 = 18$ K, $R_C = 2.4$ K, $V_{CC} = \pm 6$ V, $(V_{BE})_{on} = 0.75$ V, $(V_{CE})_{sat} = 0.15$ V, $h_{FE} = 12$.

10. Draw a negative logic *pnp* NAND gate circuit.

§7-5   **11.** List the general steps in producing IC circuits.

12. Describe the steps of monolithic IC manufacture.

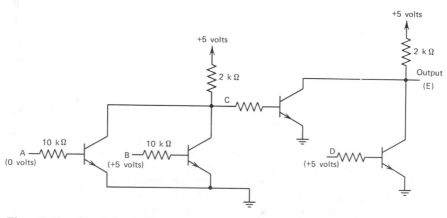

Figure 7-61.   Circuit for Problem 7-17.

§7-6   13. Draw a circuit diagram of a DTL gate and define positive logic levels.
14. Draw the circuit diagram of a TTL positive logic NAND gate and define voltage and logic levels.
15. Show the circuit connection of two 3-input RTL NOR gates in series.
16. What is the output voltage of the IC circuits in Figure 7-61?
17. Draw the circuit diagram of two 2-input ECL circuits with the output of one feeding the second.

1000

Multivibrator circuits

The two basic digital units are logic circuits and multivibrator circuits. In the present chapter we shall consider the basics of the multivibrator circuits—bistable (or flip-flop), monostable (or single-shot), and astable (or clock). These units are now used almost exclusively as IC units and a variety of the latest types available will be considered. In addition, the Schmitt trigger circuit and a number of special IC units are considered.

8-1. Bistable Multivibrator Circuits (Flip-Flop)

The bistable multivibrator or flip-flop circuit is used for such applications as storage stage, counter stage, or shift register stage. A characteristic of all multivibrator circuits is the availability of two outputs from the basic circuit, these outputs being logically inverse. To differentiate between these two outputs they are typically designated as 1 and 0 or, TRUE and FALSE, or A and $\overline{A}$, and so on. The main point of the designation is to indicate that the outputs are logically opposite and to mark one output as the reference output (1, TRUE, or A).

Another means of specifying the state of the outputs of the multivibrator outputs is the use of the designations SET and RESET. When referring to the output conditions of a multivibrator circuit the definitions of SET and RESET are the following:

$$
\begin{aligned}
&\text{SET:} \quad &&\text{TRUE} \quad &&\text{output is logical-1} \\
& &&\text{FALSE} \quad &&\text{output is logical-0} \\
&\text{RESET:} \quad &&\text{TRUE} \quad &&\text{output is logical-0} \\
& &&\text{FALSE} \quad &&\text{output is logical-1}
\end{aligned}
$$

Bistable Multivibrator (Flip-Flop).   The flip-flop circuit, being the most important of the multivibrator circuits, will be covered first. To provide some basic consideration of this circuit's operation a simple form of bistable circuit is shown in Figure 8-1a using two inverters. The inverters

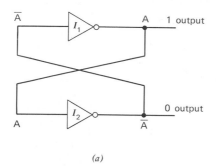

(a)

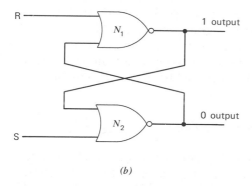

(b)

Figure 8-1. Logic connection of flip-flop. (a) Two-inverter flip-flop circuit. (b) RESET and SET operation of flip-flop.

are essentially connected in series, with two output points, as indicated. The two outputs are labelled 1-output and 0-output, or A and $\overline{\text{A}}$, respectively. If the A output is a logical-1, then inverter I_2 will provide $\overline{\text{A}}$ as a logical-0. Since $\overline{\text{A}}$ is connected as input to inverter I_1, it will cause the output of that stage to be a logical-1, as assumed. Thus, the state of logical conditions, or the voltages they represent, forms a stable situation with A-output logical-1, and $\overline{\text{A}}$-output logical-0 (SET state). If some external means is used to cause the A signal to change to logical-0, then, through inverter I_2, A would change to logical-1. The $\overline{\text{A}}$ input of logical-1 would then result in A being logical-0, as initially proposed. Thus, the circuit will also remain in a stable condition if the A-output is logical-0, and $\overline{\text{A}}$-output is logical-1 (RESET state). In effect then, the circuit has two stable operating states, acting as a memory of the last state it was placed into. Some external means is necessary, however, to cause the circuit to change state.

Figure 8-1*b* shows the use of NOR gates connected in series with additional inputs providing signals to cause the circuit to change state. The inputs are marked R for *reset* and S for *set*. Recall that a NOR gate provides logical-0 output if any one of its inputs is logical-1. A logical-1 input to the S terminal will cause the output of N_2 to be logical-0. Assuming that no input is connected to the R terminal at this time, the inputs to N_1 are both logical-0 with output of logical-1. The result of a *set* input signal then, is to cause the circuit to become SET, where the SET state was previously defined as 1-output $=$ logical-1, and 0-output $=$ logical-0. Similarly, the application of only a logical-1 to the R input will cause the 1-output to become logical-0 and 0-output logical-1, which is the RESET state of the circuit. It should be obvious that simultaneous application of logical-1 signals to both S and R inputs is ambiguous, forcing both outputs to the logical-0 condition. This would not be an accepted operation of this circuit in which the two output signals should be always logically opposite. If the R and S inputs are both logical-0, then the circuit remains in whatever state it was last placed into.

RS Flip-Flop.   A basic version of the flip-flop circuit is the RS or RESET-SET flip-flop. A block version of this circuit is given in Figure 8-2*a*, showing R and S input terminals, and 1 and 0 output terminals. As was previously considered, the application of a SET signal to the S-input terminal will cause the circuit to become SET (1-output $=$ logical-1 and 0-output $=$ logical-0). A detailed circuit diagram is shown in Figure 8-2*b* with circuit inputs and outputs indicated. Positive logic voltage definitions, of $+V$ $-$ logical-1, and 0 V $=$ logical 0, are used. If an input of logical-1 is applied to the R terminal, for example, the $+V$ volts will provide a turn-on voltage through resistor R_4 to the base of transistor Q_2, causing that transistor to turn ON. With Q_2 ON, the 1-output voltage is near 0 volts (actually $(V_{CE})_{\text{sat}}$, for transistor Q_2), and transistor Q_1 is held OFF through the cross-coupling connection of resistor R_2 from the collector of Q_1 to the base of Q_2. With Q_1 OFF and Q_2 ON the circuit is in the RESET state.

Similarly, an input of logical-1 applied to the S terminal will drive transistor Q_1 ON, thereby forcing Q_2 OFF and placing the circuit in the SET state. Notice that the signal to switch the circuit need only be applied momentarily — long enough for the cross-coupling voltage to turn the opposite transistor OFF. Once this condition is reached removal of the original input signal will leave the circuit in its present state. On the other hand, it should be clear that as long as a logical-1 signal is maintained at the input the circuit cannot change state since this input signal holds the circuit "locked." This is important when the circuit has additional means of input triggering, as will shortly be discussed.

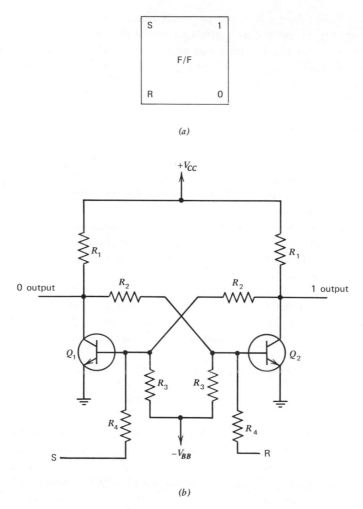

Figure 8-2.   RS flip-flop. (*a*) Block symbol of RS flip-flop. (*b*) RS flip-flop circuit diagram.

Typically, a signal level of logical-1 will be applied for a short amount of time to either SET or RESET the circuit. The logical-1 input to S or R then goes to logical-0 so that with no logical-1 input signal present the circuit is "free" to change state. The operation of the circuit can be defined for the two distinct conditions of transistor Q_2 ON, and transistor Q_2 OFF. (These circuit conditions are exactly the same for transistor Q_1 since the circuit is symmetrically set up). Figure 8-3*a* shows a partial circuit diagram involved in driving transistor Q_2 ON. If, as assumed for the moment, transistor Q_1 goes OFF, then transistor Q_2 is driven ON by a

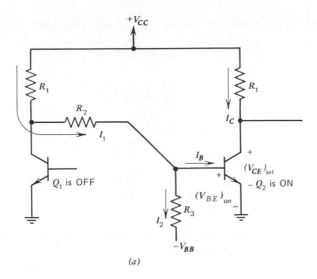

(a)

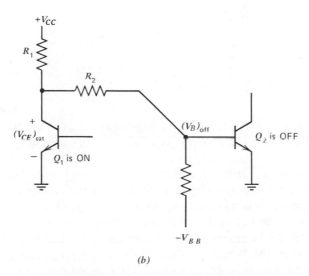

(b)

Figure 8-3.   Partial circuits of RS flip-flop. (a) Transistor Q_2 ON, partial circuit diagram. (b) Transistor Q_2 OFF, partial circuit diagram.

resulting base current. As in the previous discussion on transistor inverters, the conditions for the transistor being driven into saturation are that sufficient base current drive be provided so that at minimum transistor current gain (h_{FE}) the amount of maximum collector current can be handled by the transistor while leaving it in the saturated state. The equations developed for the diode-transistor logic case (see Chapter 7) apply here:

$$I_1 = \frac{V_{CC} - (V_{BE})_{\text{on}}}{R_1 + R_2} \tag{8-1}$$

$$I_2 = \frac{V_{BB} + (V_{BE})_{\text{on}}}{R_3} \tag{8-2}$$

$$I_B = I_1 + I_2 \tag{8-3}$$

$$I_C = \frac{V_{CC} - (V_{CE})_{\text{sat}}}{R_1} \tag{8-4}$$

$$h_{FE} > \beta_C = \frac{I_C}{I_B} \tag{8-5}$$

Similarly, the circuit conditions for holding transistor Q_2 OFF (when transistor Q_1 goes ON) are indicated in the partial circuit diagram of Figure 8-3b. The equations for determining the base OFF voltage and noise margin (see Chapter 7) are:

$$(V_{BE})_{\text{off}} = \frac{R_3}{R_2 + R_3}[(V_{CE})_{\text{sat}} + V_{BB}] - V_{CC} \tag{8-6}$$

$$\text{Noise Margin} = V_i\big|_{(V_{BE})_{\text{off}} = 0\text{V}} = \frac{R_2}{R_3}(-V_{BB}) \tag{8-7}$$

With transistor Q_1 ON [collector voltage at $(V_{CE})_{\text{sat}}$], the voltage divider of R_2 and R_3 to $-V_{BB}$ will provide, typically, a negative voltage at the base of transistor Q_2 to cause transistor Q_2 to be held in the OFF condition. Notice that with Q_2 OFF the collector voltage of Q_2 will rise up toward V_{CC} and through cross-coupling resistor R_2 from the collector of Q_2 to the base of Q_1 and will result in the base drive to hold Q_1 ON.

Referring back to Figure 8-2, an input of logical-1 ($+V_{CC}$) applied to the R input terminal will provide a drive voltage (and current) to cause transistor Q_2 to turn ON. When Q_2 is fully ON, its saturated collector voltage will then cause transistor Q_1 to be held OFF through the cross-coupling connection. If the input signal to R is now removed, the circuit will remain with transistor Q_2 ON and Q_1 OFF — this being the **RESET** condition of the circuit. Similarly, a logical-1 input to the S input terminal will result in transistor Q_1 being driven ON, in turn holding transistor Q_2 OFF — this being the SET condition of the circuit. It should be clear from the circuit connection that leaving either the **RESET** or SET input signal as logical-1 will hold the circuit locked in that state. Notice, also, that simultaneous application of logical-1 signals to the R and S terminals will drive both transistors ON leaving the circuit in an ambiguous state. If both signals are then removed "simultaneously," the state resulting for the circuit would be unpredictable, depending on the particular transistors used, the manner of connections, and so on. In usual operation, then, the inputs to an RS flip-flop are both logical-0, either one going to logical-1 momentarily when it is desired to either SET or RESET the circuit.

Another version of RS flip-flop uses capacitive coupling of the input signal to the R or S terminals. This allows the input sign to remain logical-1, while not locking the circuit in the state it was placed. In fact, this type of operation causes the circuit to change state only when the input signal *changes* state (say from 1 to 0) so that switching occurs for a specified change of state in the input signal.

Before seeing how the input triggering is done, consider the differentiator circuit of Figure 8-4a. If the RC time constant of the circuit is short compared to the time interval (T) of the input pulse, the output waveform

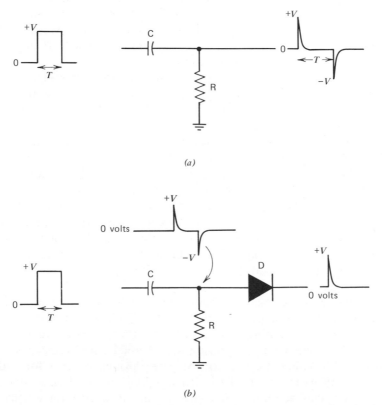

Figure 8-4.   Waveshaping circuits. (*a*) Differentiating circuit. (*b*) Pulse shaping circuit.

obtained is positive and negative voltage spikes, as shown in Figure 8-4a. Since the voltage across a capacitor cannot change instantaneously, a voltage step in the positive voltage direction (leading edge of pulse) will result in a positive voltage spike. When the input pulse goes negative by V volts on the trailing edge of the input pulse, a negative voltage spike results. The addition of a diode connected to block the negative spike allows only the positive spike to pass through the diode. The result of the RC-diode waveshaping circuit then is to convert a pulse signal to a positive polarity spike occurring when the input pulse goes from a less positive to a more positive voltage. The voltage amplitude of the spike is about the same as the magnitude of voltage change of the input pulse.

We can now consider the operation of a SET-RESET flip-flop using trigger circuitry to allow the circuit to be operated by a change of input voltage (ac input triggering or pulse edge-triggering) rather than the use of dc voltage level triggering as previously considered. Whereas the dc voltage level type of SET or RESET triggering required the input voltage to go to the 1 level and then return to the 0 level so as not to hold the circuit locked, the ac triggering will cause the circuit to become SET or RESET only when the input voltage changes in voltage level (in a positive voltage direction, for the present example).

Figure 8-5 shows a *pnp* RS flip-flop using ac type triggering. When an input pulse applied to the S input, for example, goes positive, the action of the input triggering network is to provide a positive spike at the base of transistor Q_2, this causing Q_2 to momentarily be turned OFF. When Q_2 turns OFF, the voltage at the collector of Q_2 drops toward $-V_{BB}$ which, through the cross-coupling resistor R_2, drives transistor Q_1 ON. With Q_1 ON, the voltage at the collector of Q_1 is near 0 volts, which through the other cross-coupling resistor R_2 will provide a positive base voltage to transistor Q_2, thereby holding that transistor OFF. The action initiated by the positive voltage spike now results in the circuit remaining in the transistor state $-Q_2$ OFF and Q_1 ON$-$the SET state of the circuit. Similarly, a positive-going pulse input to the R trigger network will result in Q_1 being turned OFF and, thereby, Q_2 ON$-$this being the RESET state of the circuit.

Referring to the circuit, it should be obvious that the input pulse remaining at the more positive voltage level will not hold the circuit locked in either operating state since only the *positive-going voltage change* will result in any triggering signal appearing at the base of a transistor. DC voltage levels do not pass through a capacitor and do not cause any fixed action of the RS flip-flop circuit. (For an *npn* flip-flop circuit it can be shown that edge-triggering occurs for a negative-going voltage change).

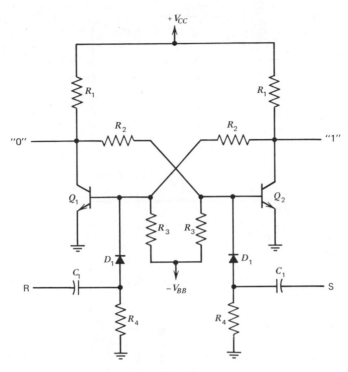

Figure 8-5.   AC operated RS flip-flop.

T-Type Flip-Flop.   One of the more common types of flip-flop circuit is the T-type or Triggered flip-flop. This circuit is also called a complementing flip-flop or Toggle flip-flop, since its action is to change state every time an input pulse is applied to the single T-input terminal. Figure 8-6*a* shows a block symbol of the T flip-flop and Figure 8-6*b* shows the circuit details using *npn* transistors.

A pulse applied to the T-input terminal is coupled through both input circuit capacitors. The input pulse is differentiated into positive and negative voltage spikes, which appear at the two junction points of resistor (R_4), diode (D_1), and capacitor (C_1). The connection of the R_4 resistors to appropriate collector terminal points provides a *steering* action at each of these junction points. Assume, as in Figure 8-7 that transistor Q_1 is OFF and Q_2 is ON. The collector voltage of transistor Q_1 provides a $+V$ voltage level around which the positive and negative spikes vary as shown in the figure. For ON transistor, Q_2, the collector voltage level is near 0 volts with the positive and negative going voltage spikes varying around the 0-volt level. Notice, now, that the cathode

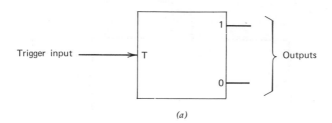

(a)

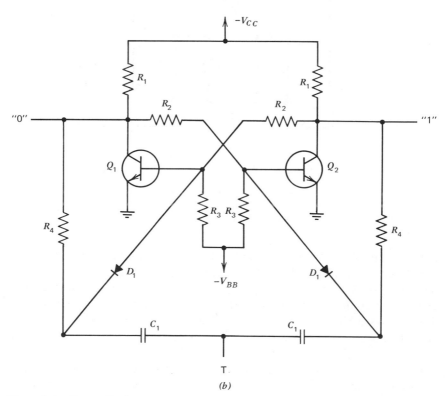

(b)

Figure 8-6.   T-type flip-flop. (*a*) T flip-flop, block symbol. (*b*) T flip-flop, circuit diagram.

voltage of the diode connected to the base of transistor Q_1 never goes
below 0 volts, and with the diode anode voltage at some negative voltage
holding transistor Q_1 OFF, the negative spike does not pass through the
diode. On the other side of the circuit, however, the negative-going
voltage spike will drive that diode ON providing a negative going voltage
pulse at the base of transistor Q_1 as shown in Figure 8-7. Thus, the action

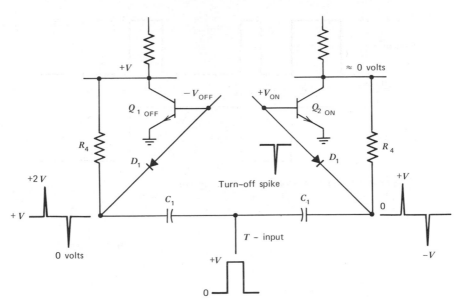

Figure 8-7.   Partial circuit showing steering action.

of the steering resistors (R_4) is to pass a negative spike to the base of the conducting transistor only (that transistor having a collector voltage of near 0 volts). By this steering voltage action the ON transistor will receive the negative voltage spike turning the ON transistor OFF.

On the next negative-going voltage change of the input trigger signal the ON transistor (Q_1 at that time) will be turned OFF and Q_2 will turn ON, the circuit again changing stage. In summary, then, the triggered flip-flop will change state whenever a specified voltage polarity change occurs — typically, negative-going for *npn* transistors and positive-going for *pnp* transistors.

Figure 8-8 shows an input pulse train waveform and the resulting output voltage from the 1-output side of the flip-flop circuit. Notice that the circuit changes state *only* on every negative-going voltage change of the input pulse signal.

RST Flip-Flop.   A versatile multivibrator circuit combines the SET, RESET, and Toggle features in a single unit called an RST flip-flop. The R input (see Figure 8-9) provides direct RESET operation, the S input provides direct SET operation, and the T input provides toggle or complementing operation.

When a logical-1 input is applied to the R input the circuit will be RESET. If the logical-1 signal is maintained at the R terminal, the circuit

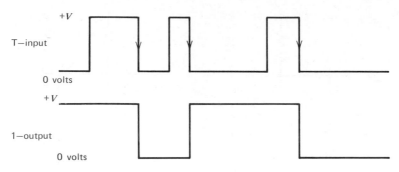

Figure 8-8.   Typical waveforms for T-type flip-flop.

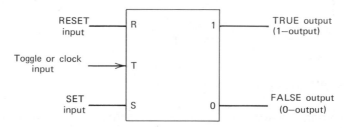

Figure 8-9.   RST flip-flop.

will be held locked in the RESET state. Even if a clock signal is applied to the T input, the circuit will remain RESET. Similarly a logical-1 input only to the S terminal will hold the circuit locked in the SET state. Only if both R and S inputs are logical-0 can the T input signal operate the flip-flop (which is the usual operating state). With R and S inputs logical-0, a clock input to the T terminal will complement the stage output for every clock pulse received.

8-2.   IC Flip-Flops

JK Flip-Flop.   The RS and RST flip-flops considered so far were shown as discrete circuits. They can also be obtained as IC units. The JK flip-flop in Figure 8-10 is shown to be an IC unit. That is, no circuit detail need be covered and operating descriptions are made for the logic block symbol shown in Figure 8-10.

The J and K input terminals are used to provide information or data inputs. When a trigger pulse is then applied the circuit changes state

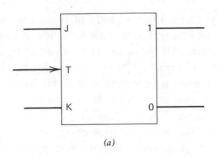

(a)

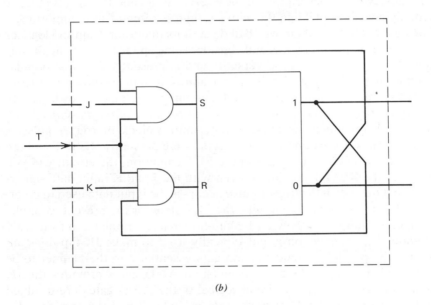

(b)

J	K	Output State
0	0	No change
0	1	RESET
1	0	SET
1	1	Toggle

(c)

Figure 8-10. Basics of JK flip-flop. (a) Logic symbol of JK flip-flop. (b) JK flip-flop made using RS flip-flop plus gating. (c) JK flip-flop truth table.

corresponding to the input logic signals at the J and K terminals. A JK circuit can be built in integrated circuit form using DTL, TTL, or even ECL logic manufacture. All these circuits have the same basic operating features. It is not at all important here to consider the circuit details and, in fact, one only purchases a complete unit in IC form and has little to do with the details of circuit operation. It is important to be aware of the differences in using these different logic types, in knowing whether they use current sourcing, sinking, or emitter-coupled logic, in details of speed of operation, noise margin, power supply voltage, and so on. These factors, however, are descriptive of the overall circuit and the details of what actually goes into building the actual circuit is often of little importance. For the JK flip-flop, then, we shall discuss its operation from the logic or block diagram point of view, and consider some applications using the circuit. The JK circuit is quite versatile and is presently the most popular version of the flip-flop circuit. The J and K terminals shown in Figure 8-10*a* are the data input terminals, the inputs being logical-1 or logical-0. *These data inputs do not, however, change the state of the flip-flop circuit*, which will remain in its present state until a clock or trigger pulse is applied. Thus, for example, if the circuit were presently RESET and the input data is such as to result in the SET condition, the circuit will still maintain the RESET condition, even with the J and K input data signals applied. Only when the trigger pulse occurs is the input data used to determine the new state of the circuit — the SET state for the present example.

Figure 8-10*b* shows how an RS flip-flop may be modified to form a JK flip-flop. This connection is not typically used to make JK flip-flops, although the practical circuit version acts essentially in the manner to be described. Using an RS flip-flop and two AND gates provides the JK operation. With the trigger input logical-0, the AND gates are disabled and the circuit will maintain its present state. When the trigger pulse occurs (becomes logical-1), the circuit operation still depends on the other inputs to the AND gates. Since each AND gate had one input fed back from the outputs of the circuit, at least one of the AND gates has a logical-1 in addition to the logical-1 of the CLOCK signal (when it occurs). Finally, we have the J and K inputs to each of the respective AND gates. There are four possible combinations of the J and K inputs. In order to consider the complete operation of the circuit each of the possible conditions is listed in the truth table of Figure 8-10*c*. If both J and K inputs are logical-0 then both AND gates are disabled and the circuit remains in the same state (no change takes place). If the J input is logical-1 and K input is logical-1, and further if the 1-output is logical-1, then the CLOCK pulse going to the logical-1 level will provide all logical-1 inputs to the AND gate connected to the R input so that the circuit ends up in the RESET state. If the K input is logical-0 and J input logical-1, and further, if the 0-output is logical-1, then the occurrence of the CLOCK pulse will cause the circuit to be SET. Finally, if both J and K inputs are logical-1, the action of the CLOCK pulse becoming logical-1 is to toggle or complement the circuit. If the 0-output were logical-1 (circuit RESET), the CLOCK pulse occurring would result in the circuit being SET, thereby causing it to change state. Similarly, with 1-output logical-1, the occurrence of a CLOCK pulse would result in a RESET signal, thereby changing the circuit state. Thus, the circuit will toggle (change state) from whichever condition it happens to be in upon application of the CLOCK pulse. In this last case, with J and K inputs both logical-1, the circuit operates as a T flip-flop and can be used as such. When opposite data input signals are applied, such as J and K inputs, the CLOCK pulse will shift the data into the present flip-flop state, with the stage acting as a shift register stage. Thus, the JK flip-flop can be used as a shift-register stage, toggle stage for counting operations or, generally, as a control logic stage.

Using positive logic (0 volts as logical-0 and $+V$ as logical-1, for example), the circuit triggers when the CLOCK goes from the logical-0 to logical-1 condition—this is referred to as *positive edge*-triggering, since the circuit is triggered at the time the voltage goes positive (from 0 volts to $+V$ volts). Opposed to this, the circuit used in the T flip-flop discussion (Figure 8-6) triggered when the voltage went from $+V$ volts to 0 volts—this being *trailing-edge* logic triggering. The manufacturer's information sheets should indicate the type of triggering required to operate the particular circuit so that it may be properly used.

Figure 8-11 shows a logic symbol as found in a manufacturer's specification sheets. Instead of a single J and a single K input, AND gates are provided to allow three inputs for each so that some logical operation is possible as an additional feature of the IC unit. In this way the J input is logically $J = J1 \cdot J2 \cdot J3$, while the K input is logically $K = K1 \cdot K2 \cdot K3$. Notice that the internal connection of the output states back to the input section, as shown in Figure 8-10b, is not indicated, although such operation is internally provided. The action of the combinational J or K signals is the same as described in the truth table of Figure 8-10c. The opposite output terminals are indicated here as Q and $\overline{Q}$ instead of 1 and 0 to correspond to the particular manufacturer's designation, although the meaning is the same. Upon application of a CLOCK pulse the circuit will change state as determined by the J and K input signals. DC CLOCK-triggering occurs at a specific voltage change of the CLOCK pulse. After the CLOCK input threshold voltage has been passed, the gated inputs are locked out (meaning that they do not affect the circuit output state until another CLOCK pulse occurs).

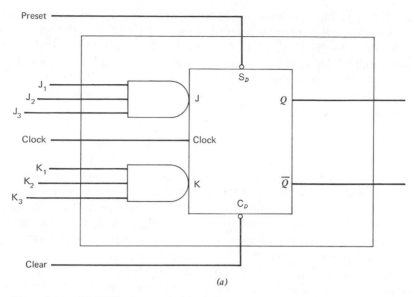

Figure 8-11.   IC JK flip-flop symbol, including direct set (S_D) and clear (C_D).

When we refer to the triggering as being edge-triggered we mean that the new state of the circuit will be brought about on the edge of the triggering pulse (when trigger pulse changes from the logical-1 to logical-0 level, for example). The data at the input terminals is shifted into the present flip-flop stage at the time the trigger edge occurs. Any change in the data after the trigger pulse edge has passed has no further effect on the stage state until another trigger pulse edge (of proper slope) is received.

Figure 8-11 also shows preset and clear input terminals. This should be understood to correspond to direct SET and direct RESET, respectively. These are direct action inputs meaning that a Lo level direct SET signal will immediately cause the circuit to SET. The JK terminals are referred to as *synchronous* inputs, whereas the clear and preset inputs are referred to as *asynchronous* inputs. By asynchronous we imply direct circuit action caused by either C_D or S_D signals without regard to any trigger or synchronizing signal. These direct action inputs correspond in operation to the R and S inputs discussed previously, whereas the J and K inputs are not direct acting but require the CLOCK pulse to bring about any change, that change corresponding to the J and K input data at the time the trigger pulse (or synchronizing) occurs.

RTL JK Flip-Flop.   A flip-flop unit that has a slightly different operating truth table (but is still referred to as a JK flip-flop) is shown in Figure

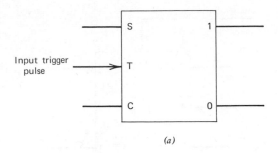

(a)

S	C	Output
0	0	Toggle
0	1	RESET (or clear)
1	0	SET
1	1	No change

(b)

Figure 8-12.   RTL JK flip-flop. (*a*) Block symbol. (*b*) Operating truth table.

8-12*a*. As the operating truth table of Figure 8-12*b* shows, the difference between the present flip-flop and the JK unit of Figure 8-10 is the conditions for toggle and no change. For the RTL unit the conditions of both S and C inputs logical-0 provide for toggle operation *when a trigger pulse is applied*. If both S and C data inputs are logical-1, then a trigger pulse will cause no change of state.

Although the difference between the JK flip-flop, as covered in Figure 8-10, corresponding to the type built using DTL or TTL logic units, and that of Figure 8-12, which was built using RTL logic units, is slight, it has to be mentioned so that the proper logic operation of each is clearly seen.

The RTL JK flip-flop unit can also have direct preset (PS) and preclear (PC) inputs as shown in Figure 8-13.

D Flip-Flop.   Another version of flip-flop circuit is that called a D or Delay flip-flop (see Figure 8-14). This designation should indicate that the circuit output is the same as the circuit input that appeared one CLOCK pulse time previously. Essentially it is a JK flip-flop with only

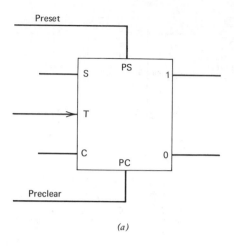

(a)

PS	PC	1	0	Remarks
0	0	NC	NC	NC = No change
0	1	1	0	1 output goes Hi
1	0	0	1	0 output goes Hi
1	1	1	1	(undesireable condition)

Note: Lo or 0 input on PS or PC causes circuit action.

(b)

Figure 8-13. RTL JK flip-flop with direct SET and CLEAR operation.

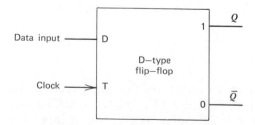

Figure 8-14. Logic symbol of D-type flip-flop.

one data input (to assure the conditions of J and K always being opposite). Thus, the D flip-flop is a shift-stage with a single data input that is shifted by the CLOCK (trigger) pulse into the present stage—the new output being determined by the data present at the time of the shift operation only.

Master-Slave (M/S) Flip-Flops.   One of the more popular IC flip-flop circuits is the master-slave (M/S) connection used as either RS or JK flip-flop. The master slave circuit contains two different flip-flop units, the one receiving the input data referred to as the *master* flip-flop and a second circuit that operates from the master flip-flop referred to as the *slave* flip-flop. The circuit output is obtained from the slave flip-flop. Figure 8-15 shows a simple representation of this connection. Although there are internally two flip-flop units, the outside connections provide J and K inputs along with the single CLOCK signal and the complementary output terminals marked Q and $\overline{Q}$.

Before going into the details of the M/S operation it would be appropriate to first comment on why this circuit connection exists. To do this we must have a short discussion of trailing- and leading-edge logic opera-

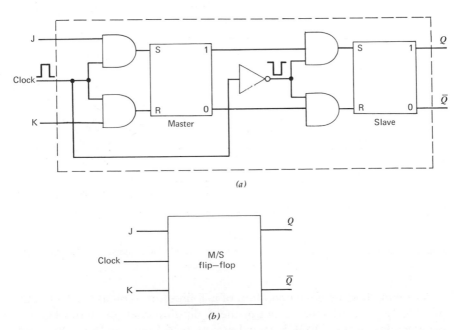

(a)

(b)

Figure 8-15.   Clocked master-slave (M/S) flip-flop. (a) Clocked M/S flip-flop. (b) Logic representation of a single M/S flip-flop.

tion. Figure 8-16 shows a pulse waveform with an indication of what is meant by a leading edge and a trailing edge. For positive logic operation the leading edge occurs when the CLOCK pulse goes from the logical-0 to the logical-1 state. The leading edge of the CLOCK pulse is then a positive-going edge and the CLOCK signal is logical-1 just after the leading edge of the signal occurs. The pulse edge at which the CLOCK returns to the logical-0 level is referred to as the trailing edge of the pulse, as shown in Figure 8-16*a*.

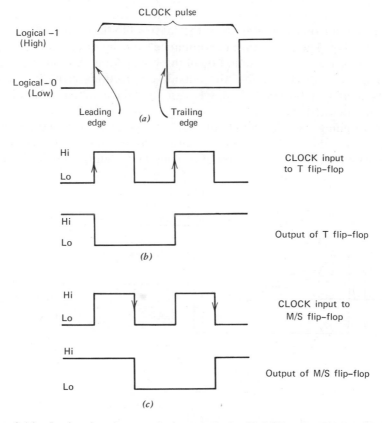

Figure 8-16.   Logic triggering waveforms. (*a*) Basic CLOCK pulse. (*b*) Leading edge triggering. (*c*) Trailing edge logic.

Assuming leading-edge operation of a T flip-flop (such as the JK circuit previously covered), the output of the T flip-flop changes state when the leading edge of the CLOCK signal occurs (see Figure 8-16*b*). One main disadvantage with this type of triggering is that the CLOCK signal causing the change will remain present (logical-1) for some time during which the flip-flop will first be in one state and then in the complement state, all with the same CLOCK pulse present. This occurs because the CLOCK pulse first must become logical-1 before the flip-flop begins to change state. During the time the flip-flop requires to change state, the outputs are the initial flip-flop state and the CLOCK logical-1. After the flip-flop changes state, the outputs are the complement state of the flip-flop with CLOCK still logical-1. This ambiguity may lead to false operations within the circuits using the same flip-flop output signals and CLOCK signal. The condition of two signals changing state (CLOCK and flip-flop output) in which one may be delayed in happening, provides what is referred to as a *race* condition.

Figure 8-16c shows the use of trailing-edge logic showing CLOCK input (such as used with the M/S flip-flop circuit considered previously) and resulting output waveform. The flip-flop circuit changes state when the input CLOCK changes from the logical-1 to logical-0 condition. In this case the CLOCK goes to logical-0 at the time it causes the circuit state to change. Thus, the triggering CLOCK pulse should be logical-0 at the time the new circuit state is reached. In this case there is *no ambiguity of state* and no race condition.

The use of two flip-flops in the Master-slave circuit provides the trailing-edge triggering operation with no resulting race condition. In fact, the shift or transfer of data occurs when the CLOCK signal reaches the logical-1 voltage *level* and does not occur at the edge of the CLOCK pulse. This means that the CLOCK waveform need not be of specified sharpness or magnitude and that the *M/S circuit operates on voltage level rather than voltage change.*

Referring back to Figure 8-15, assume, for example, that the Q and Q outputs are presently logical-0 and logical-1, the RESET condition. Assume further, that the J and K inputs are logical-1 and logical-0, respectively, which will result in the SET circuit state after the CLOCK pulse occurs. Just before the CLOCK pulse the conditions are then:

> Master state — RESET
> Slave state — RESET
> J input — logical-1
> K input — logical-0

When the CLOCK goes to the logical-1 level, the AND gate with J input of logical-1 results in the master flip-flop being SET. Since the inverted CLOCK signal (now logical-0) is used to operate the slave flip-flop, the slave outputs remain in the RESET state. Thus, the master state presently is SET but the slave output remains RESET. When the CLOCK input then goes to the logical-0 level, the inverted CLOCK signal goes to the logical-1 level now shifting the SET conditions from the master into the slave flip-flop—whose outputs now assume the SET state. Since only the slave output is referred to as the M/S flip-flop output, the change of state occurs when the input CLOCK changes (from the logical-1) to the logical-0 level. The triggering of the M/S flip-flop occurs after the CLOCK goes to logical-0 so that no race problem exists. Although the circuit requires two flip-flop units, it has very good operational features which make it very popular for building counters and shift-registers in computer operation.

8-3.   Monostable Multivibrator (Single-Shot)

As a characteristic property of a multivibrator circuit the monostable provides opposite state output signals. As the name implies, however, the outputs are stable in only one of the two possible states (SET and RESET). Figure 8-17a shows a logic block symbol of a single-shot circuit in the stable RESET state (1-output—logical-0; 0-output—logical-1). The

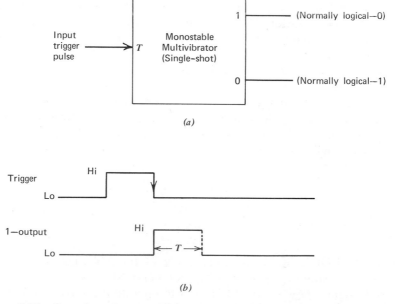

Figure 8-17.   Operation of monostable multivibrator (single shot). (*a*) Single-shot logic symbol. (*b*) Input trigger and 1-output waveforms.

input trigger signal is a pulse that operates the circuit in an edge-triggered manner. Figure 8-17b shows a typical input trigger pulse and corresponding output waveform (assuming triggering on the trailing edge of the trigger pulse). The 1-output is normally Lo (RESET state). When a negative-going voltage change triggers the circuit, the 1-output goes Hi (SET state), which is the unstable circuit state. It will remain Hi only for a fixed time interval, T, which is determined basically by a timing capacitor whose value may be selected externally. Thus, the output state remains the SET state only for a preselected time T, after which the output returns to the RESET state, where it remains until another trigger pulse is applied.

Referring to the waveform of Figure 8-17b, the output of the single shot can be viewed as a delayed pulse whose negative-going edge occurs at some set time, T, *after* the trigger pulse. Figure 8-18 shows a number of additional actions possible using a single-shot circuit. For example, it is possible to accept a train of narrow pulses as trigger signal and provide as output a corresponding train of wider pulses as shown in Figure 8-18a. If the pulses received are quite narrow, then they may be widened to a pulse interval, T, where T is, of course, less than the interval between trigger pulses. Any input pulse received during the timing interval T will be ignored by the usual single-shot circuit.

Figure 8-18b shows a series of wide input pulses and corresponding narrow output pulses from the single-shot circuit. Notice that for the present example the narrow pulse is initiated by the negative-going edge (Hi to Lo) of the input trigger signal. Figure 8-18c shows how the single-shot may be used to provide only a single pulse when the trigger signal is a number of pulses. This is quite useful, for example, if the input pulses are obtained from a mechanical switch. When the switch is moved to change the signal from Hi to Lo the contact bounce will usually result in a number of transitions between Lo and Hi states. If the switch signal is used directly, one throw of the switch may result in one, two, three, or more Hi to Lo transitions—which would result in erroneous system action. Using the single shot, only a single pulse is provided—even with the multiple input pulses shown, as long as the interval of contact bounce is less than the pulse interval, T, of the single shot.

A single-shot circuit diagram is shown in Figure 8-19. A basic difference between this single-shot circuit and that of the bistable multivibrator of Figure 8-2 is the cross-coupling component capacitor, C_T. Normally, transistor Q_2 is held ON and transistor Q_1 is held OFF through cross-coupling resistor R_2. A trigger pulse applied through a differentiating and diode clipping circuit provides a negative spike to turn transistor Q_2 OFF. Through the direct cross-coupling of resistor R_2 transistor Q_1 is

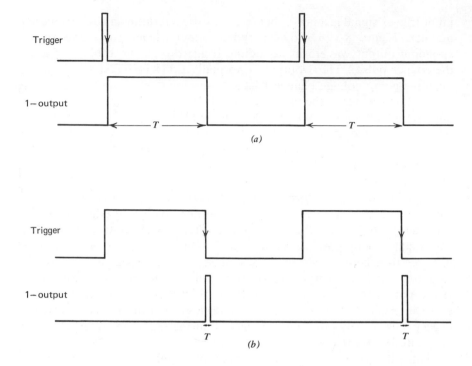

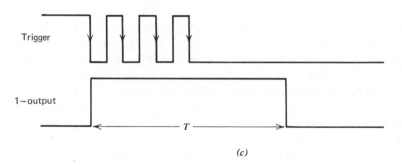

Figure 8-18.   Some pulse shaping actions of single-shot circuit. (*a*) Pulse shaping—widening a narrow pulse. (*b*) Pulse shaping—narrowing a wide pulse. (*c*) Blocking unwanted pulses.

turned ON. Transistor Q_2 is held OFF during a timing interval determined essentially by components R_T and C_T, as will be shown. After a fixed time interval, T, transistor Q_2 turns ON thereby causing transistor Q_1 to turn OFF, and the circuit is back in a stable operating state.

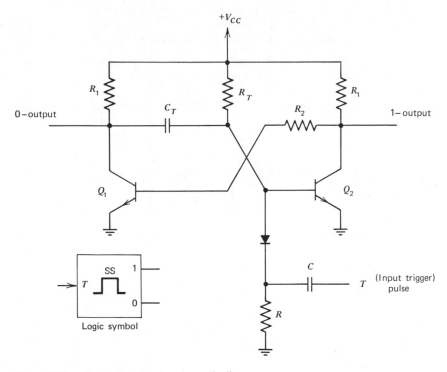

Figure 8-19.   Single-shot circuit, schematic diagram.

Both 1 and 0 outputs are available—these being in the RESET condition until the circuit is triggered, the outputs going to the SET condition for a period of time, T, dependent on the circuit timing components, C_T and R_T. A more detailed consideration of the circuit operation will now be made for the cases of normally RESET (stable state) and temporarily SET (unstable state).

RESET State (stable state of circuit). Figure 8-20a shows the circuit conditions during the normally stable (or RESET) state of the circuit. Transistor Q_1 is OFF and transistor Q_2 is ON. A positive turn-on voltage is applied to the base of transistor Q_2 from the supply voltage through resistor R_T. The base-emitter voltage of Q_2 is then $(V_{BE})_{ON}$, which is about 0.7 volt. The collector-emitter voltage of Q_2 is $(V_{CE})_{sat}$ which is approximately 0.1 volt. The 1-output is then near 0 volts, the output Lo level.

The low saturation voltage of Q_2 is coupled to the base of Q_1, and being less than the required transistor Q_1 turn-on voltage, Q_1 is held OFF. This condition, of Q_2 ON and Q_1 OFF (the RESET state), will be main-

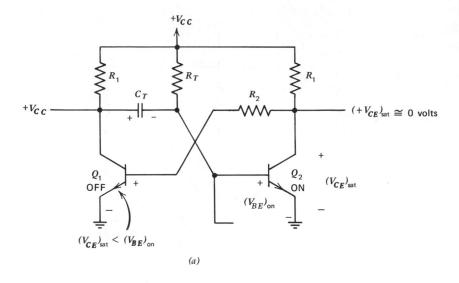

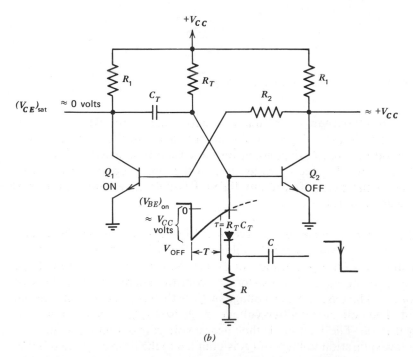

Figure 8-20.   Partial circuits for RESET and SET states. (*a*) RESET state (stable state of circuit). (*b*) SET state (unstable state of circuit).

tained as long as no trigger pulse is applied and the circuit is thus stable in this operating state. Capacitor, C_T is charged up to about V_{CC} volts with $+V_{CC}$ volts on the terminal connected to the collector of OFF transistor Q_1 and $(V_{BE})_{ON}$ at the terminal connected to the base of ON transistor Q_2.

SET State (unstable state of circuit). A trigger pulse applied to the T input (see Figure 8-20b) is differentiated and clipped so that a negative spike appears at the base of Q_2, temporarily turning Q_2 OFF. If Q_2 remains OFF long enough for its collector voltage to rise toward $+V_{CC}$, transistor Q_1 will then turn ON because of the cross-coupled voltage through R_2. When transistor Q_1 switches ON its collector voltage drops from $+V_{CC}$ to near 0 volts. Since the voltage across a capacitor cannot change instantaneously, the drop of about V_{CC} volts at the Q_1 collector terminal is matched by a corresponding drop of about V_{CC} volts at the Q_2 base terminal. The voltage *across* the capacitor remains the same instantaneously, but the base Q_2 voltage goes from slightly above 0 volts negative by about V_{CC} volts. Thus, a negative voltage now is present due to the coupling of capacitor, C_T, and Q_2 will remain OFF (and Q_1 ON), even if the initiating spike no longer remains.

The base voltage of Q_2, however, will not remain at the negative hold-off value since capacitor C_T will discharge through resistor R_T with the Q_2 base voltage rising exponentially toward $+V_{CC}$ with time constant, $R_T C_T$. Figure 8-20b shows the base voltage waveform. When the voltage does rise to $(V_{BE})_{ON}$, transistor Q_2 will again go ON and thereby turn Q_1 OFF. Once the circuit returns out of the unstable state, capacitor C_T charges again to prepare for the next timing operation.

With the base waveform going from about $-V_{CC}$ to $+V_{CC}$ voltage and the time interval ending when the voltage reaches $(V_{BE})_{ON}$, analysis of the charging operation provides a time interval which is approximately

$$\boxed{T \cong 0.7\, R_T C_T} \tag{8-8}$$

Typically, R_T is set at a fixed value since it also provides base drive current to Q_2, when ON. The connections for C_T are then provided so that an external capacitor may be connected in parallel to adjust the circuit time value, T. Figure 8-21 shows a few of the circuit waveforms as described in the discussion above.

Example 8-1. Draw the pulse waveform of the 1-output from a single-shot circuit as in Figure 8-19 for a 100 kHz square wave used as trigger input. Circuit timing components are $R_T = 10K$ and $C_T = 100$ pF.

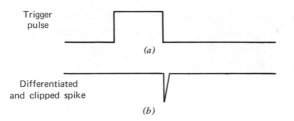

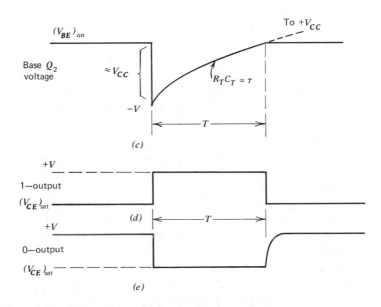

Figure 8-21.   Monostable multivibrator circuit waveforms.

Solution: $T = 0.7R_T C_T = 0.7(10 \times 10^3)(100 \times 10^{-12}) = 0.7\ \mu\text{sec}$

$$\frac{1}{f} = \frac{1}{100 \times 10^3} = 10\ \mu\text{sec (CLOCK period)}$$

Solution is shown in Figure 8-22.

Example 8-2.   A trigger signal of 12.5 kHz is used to operate a *pnp* transistor monostable circuit having $R_T = 7.5$ K and $C_T = 0.001\ \mu\text{F}$. Draw the 1-output waveform.

Solution: $T = 0.7R_T C_T = 0.7(7.5 \times 10^3)(0.001 \times 10^{-6}) = 5.25\ \mu\text{sec}$

$$\frac{1}{f} = \frac{1}{12.5 \times 10^3} = 80\ \mu\text{sec (CLOCK period)}$$

Solution is shown in Figure 8-23.

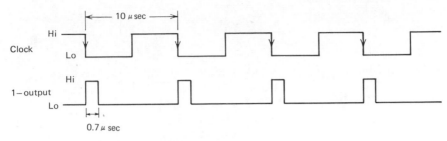

Figure 8-22.   Solution of Example 8-1.

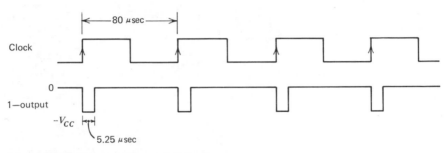

Figure 8-23.   Solution of Example 8-2.

IC Single-Shot Units.   A single-shot circuit can be obtained as an IC unit which is fully built, except for the timing components. Appropriate terminals are provided with the unit to which timing resistor (R_X) and capacitor (C_X) must be connected (see Figure 8-24a).

The manufacturer's specification sheet would contain information on logic levels, triggering mode (leading-edge or trailing-edge triggering), and on how the single-shot time interval (T) is determined (either an equation or a graph is provided).

Figure 8-24b shows some additional logic gates provided by one manufacturer as part of the single-shot IC unit. The extra logic provides more versatility with single-shot applications. If inputs 1 and 2 are grounded (logical-0), a logical-1 input to the AND gate results. Then input 3 can trigger the single-shot by going to logical-0 so that the AND gate output (trigger input) goes from Hi to Lo and fires the single shot. If, however, input 3 is left Hi (no connection), either input 1 or 2 going Hi will cause the single-shot to be triggered (on the leading edge of this input signal).

A few examples of single-shot applications are shown in Figure 8-25. Figure 8-25a shows a delayed pulse generator providing an output pulse of any desired pulse width (T_2) delayed by any desired pulse delay (T_1). The circuit waveforms in Figure 8-25b show the resulting output delayed pulse.

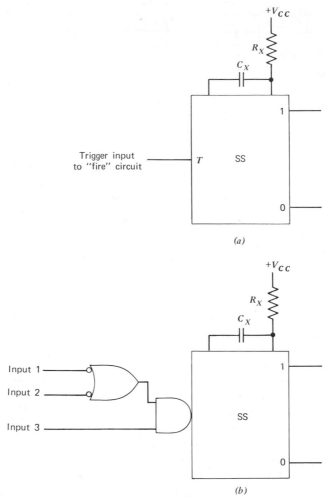

Figure 8-24.   IC single-shot circuit.

Another application is shown in Figure 8-26. The circuit of Figure 8-26*a* shows how the single-shot unit can be connected to provide non-retriggerable operation. This is useful when it is desired to block multiple pulses, as from a mechanical switch having contact bounce. The waveforms of Figure 8-26*b* show that the first negative transition triggers the single shot, but that succeeding pulses do not trigger the unit until the single-shot timing interval, T, is over. This trigger-blocking action is obtained by connecting the 0-output back to the logic gate input, as in Figure 8-26*a*. When the 1-output is Hi (during pulse interval), the 0-

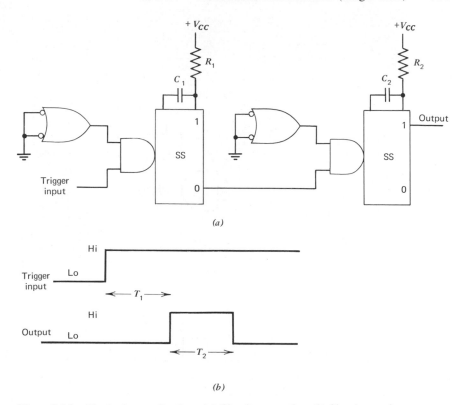

(a)

Figure 8-25.   Single-shot applications. (a) Circuit connection. (b) Circuit waveforms.

output is then Lo, forcing the OR gate output to be Hi. The trigger input signal then going Lo does not cause any change in the OR gate output and will only be able to operate the single-shot when the 0-output goes back Hi after the pulse interval is over.

Another means of obtaining single-shot operation without need of a special single-shot unit is possible using a NAND gate and timing components as shown in Figure 8-27. The RC differentiator network causes the output to drop to 0 volts when the input goes from 0 volts to $+V$. Then the gate input appears as a decaying voltage, as shown in Figure 8-27b. When the gate input drops below a threshold level the output returns to $+V$ and the pulse interval, T, set by the values of R and C, is over. It should be noted, however, that this circuit connection only works if the output pulse interval T is less than the input pulse interval T_1. This is because on the negative edge of the input pulse the output would go to $+V$, even if the pulse interval T were not completed due to the resulting negative spike as shown in Figure 8-27b.

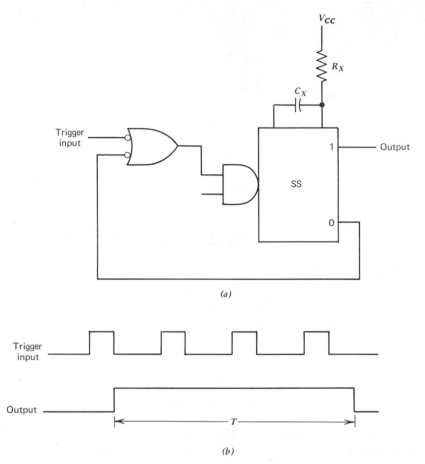

Figure 8-26.   Non-retriggerable operation of single shot. (*a*) Circuit connection. (*b*) Circuit waveforms.

A circuit connection that uses NAND gates and allows the output pulse T to be longer than the input pulse interval T_1 is shown in Figure 8-27c. The addition of a connection of output signal as an input to NAND gate N_1 prevents the input trigger signal from further affecting the output until the timing interval (set by R and C) is over. Circuit waveforms are shown in Figure 8-27d.

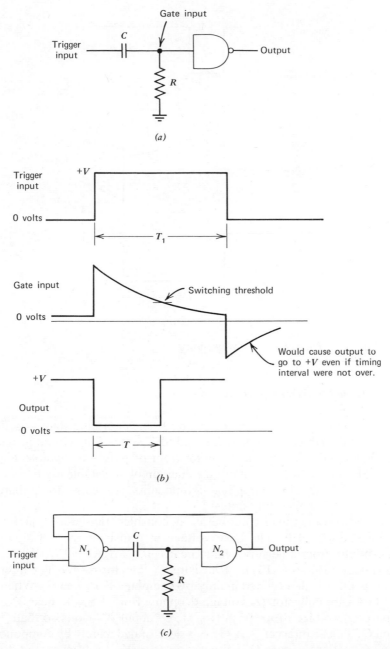

Figure 8-27. Single shot using NAND gate, where $T < T_i$. (a) Circuit. (b) Waveforms. (c) Circuit.

303

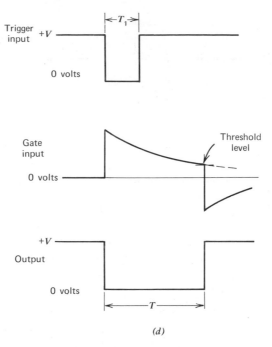

Figure 8-27.   (*d*) Waveforms.

8-4.   Astable Multivibrator (CLOCK)

A third version of multivibrator has no stable operating state — oscillating back and forth between RESET and SET states. The circuit provides a CLOCK signal for use as a timing train of pulses to operate digital circuits. Figure 8-28 shows a circuit diagram of an astable multivibrator. Notice that both cross-coupling components are capacitors, thereby allowing *no* stable operating state.

In order to study the circuit operation, consider transistor Q_1 just turning ON and Q_2 OFF. The base voltage of transistor Q_2 will then rise exponentially from a negative value near $-V_{CC}$ toward $+V_{CC}$. When the base voltage reaches $(+V_{BE})_{on}$, transistor Q_2 then turns ON. The interval that Q_2 is OFF is determined mainly by components R_2 and C_2. When Q_2 turns ON with collector Q_2 voltage dropping from $+V_{CC}$ to near 0 volts, the base Q_1 voltage drops from $(V_{BE})_{ON}$ by about V_{CC} volts so that Q_1 is turned OFF. The interval Q_1 is OFF is determined mainly by components R_1 and C_1. After the base Q_1 voltage rises to $(+V_{BE})_{on}$, transistor Q_1 turns ON, Q_2 then is turned OFF and the operation will continue to repeat

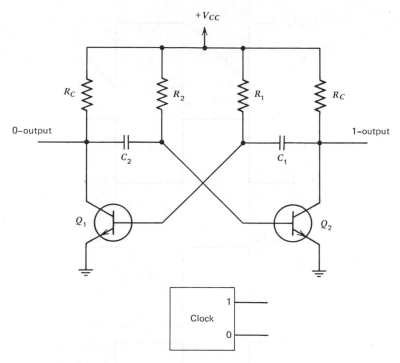

Figure 8-28.   Astable multivibrator circuit and logic symbol.

indefinitely (as long as supply voltage $+V_{CC}$ is present). Figure 8-29 shows base collector waveforms, as examples of the astable operation.

The frequency of the astable circuit can be determined as follows:

$$f = \frac{1}{T_1 + T_2} = \frac{1}{0.7R_1C_1 + 0.7R_2C_2}$$

$$\boxed{f = \frac{1.4}{R_1C_1 + R_2C_2}}$$

(8-9)

If the resistors and capacitors used are of equal value the frequency of the CLOCK is

$$f = \frac{1}{2T} = \frac{1}{2(0.7)RC} = \frac{1}{1.4RC}$$

$$\boxed{f = \frac{0.7}{RC}}$$

(8-10)

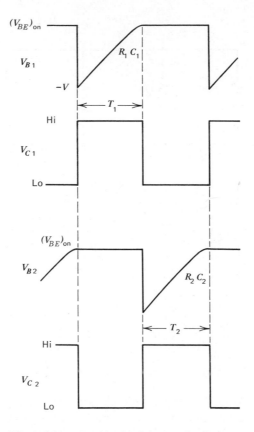

Figure 8-29.   Astable circuit base and collector waveforms.

Example 8-3.   An astable multivibrator has component values $R_1 = R_2 = 10$ K, $C_1 = C_2 = 120$ pF. Calculate the oscillator CLOCK frequency.

Solution: $\quad f = \dfrac{0.7}{RC} = \dfrac{0.7}{(10 \times 10^3)(120 \times 10^{-12})} = 0.584 \times 10^6 = 584 \text{ kHz}$

IC Astable Units.   The circuit of Figure 8-30a shows how two single-shot units can be connected to form an astable multivibrator. If the values of R and C for each unit are the same, then a clock signal having equal Hi and Lo intervals is obtained. The circuit output waveform shows that a pulse train is provided (opposite at the output terminals).

When power is first turned on, one single-shot triggers the other. Then each unit continuously triggers the other, after a delay time, and a continuous output pulse train results.

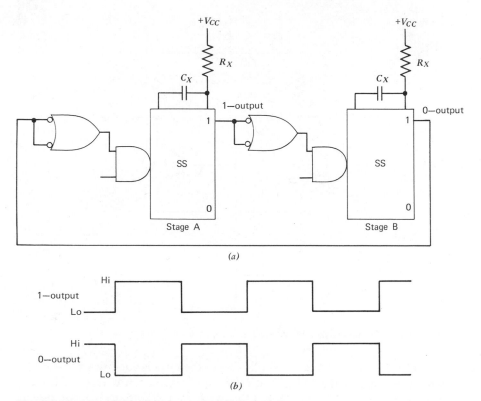

Figure 8-30.   Astable multivibrator, using IC single shots.

8-5. Schmitt Trigger Circuit

A circuit that is somewhat like the multivibrator circuits previously considered is the Schmitt trigger circuit shown in Figure 8-31. The Schmitt trigger is used for waveshaping purposes. Basically, the circuit has two opposite operating states as do all the multivibrator circuits. The trigger signal, however, is not typically a pulse waveform but a slowly varying alternating current voltage. The Schmitt trigger is *level sensitive* and switches the output state at two distinct triggering levels, one called a lower trigger (LTL) and the other an upper trigger level (UTL). The circuit generally operates from a slowly varying input signal such as a sinusoidal waveform and provides a digital output—either the logical-0 or logical-1 voltage level. To appreciate how the circuit operates we shall separately consider the conditions that determine the UTL and LTL voltages.

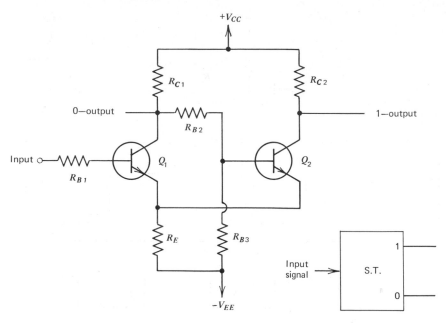

Figure 8-31.   Schmitt trigger circuit and block symbol.

UTL Consideration.   Figure 8-32*a* shows the circuit conditions that determine the value of the UTL. With the input signal below this UTL value transistor Q_1 is OFF and Q_2 is ON. With Q_1 OFF there is base current drive to saturate Q_2. Figure 8-32*b* shows a partial circuit diagram to determine the voltage at the common emitter connection, V_E. If, for the moment, we assume that the value $(V_{CE})_{sat}$ is 0 volts (actually at 0.2 volt, typical) then resistors R_{C_2} and R_E form a voltage divider between supplies V_{CC} and V_{EE}, so that the emitter voltage can be calculated:

$$V_{E_1} \cong \frac{R_E}{R_{C_2} + R_E}(V_{CC} + V_{EE}) - V_{EE} \qquad (8\text{-}11)$$

In order to drive transistor Q_1 ON then, all that is necessary is that the base Q_1 voltage exceed the value of emitter voltage by the transistor base-emitter ON voltage, $(V_{BE})_{on}$. We may thus determine the value of the UTL voltage as

$$\text{UTL} = V_{E_1} + (V_{BE})_{on} \qquad (8\text{-}12)$$

where, V_{E_1} is given by Equation 8-11. It should be noted that the values of R_{C_1}, R_{B_2} and R_{B_3} should be partly selected to provide sufficient base drive to insure that transistor Q_2 is saturated, as was assumed.

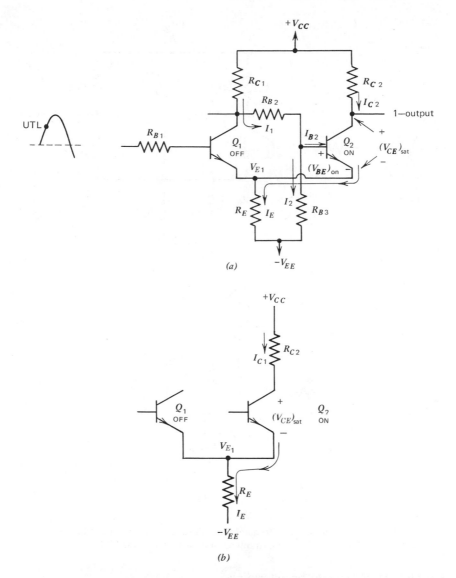

Figure 8-32.   Circuit considerations to determine UTL. (*a*) Full circuit conditions to determine UTL. (*b*) Partial circuit to conditions to determine UTL voltage.

LTL Consideration.   Figure 8-33*a* shows the circuit conditions before the LTL voltage switches the circuit. In order to turn Q_1 OFF it is necessary to drop below the base voltage that keeps Q_1 ON. Again a simple voltage divider exists as shown in Figure 8-33*b*. Assuming $(V_{CE})_{sat}$ is 0 volts, the

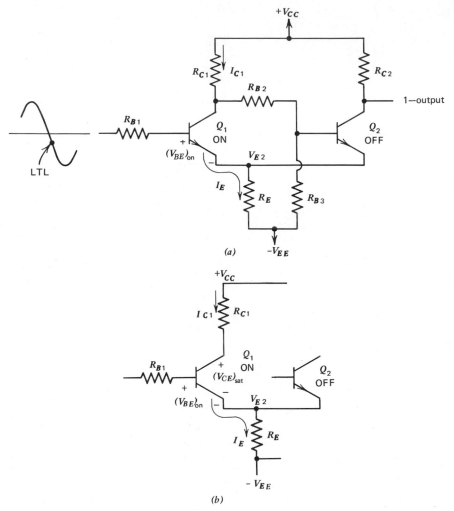

Figure 8-33.   Circuit considerations to determine LTL. (*a*) Full circuit conditions to determine LTL. (*b*) Partial circuit conditions to determine LTL.

emitter voltage can now be determined:

$$V_{E_2} = \frac{R_E}{R_{c_1} + R_E} (V_{CC} + V_{EE}) - V_{EE} \qquad (8\text{-}13)$$

The voltage at the base of Q_1 is more positive by the value of $(V_{BE})_{on}$ so that the LTL can be calculated:

$$\text{LTL} = V_{E_2} + (V_{BE})_{on} \qquad (8\text{-}14)$$

If the input voltage drops below the value of the LTL specified by Equations 8-13 and 8-14, transistor Q_1 will turn OFF and Q_2 will turn ON, the other operating state of the Schmitt trigger circuit.

Regenerative Operation.   In discussing the conditions to determine the firing voltage levels for UTL and LTL we passed over an important aspect of the circuit operation, namely, its regenerative switching action. This means that even for a slowly varying input signal the output waveform (see Figure 8-34) is sharply sloped, changing from a Lo to Hi (or

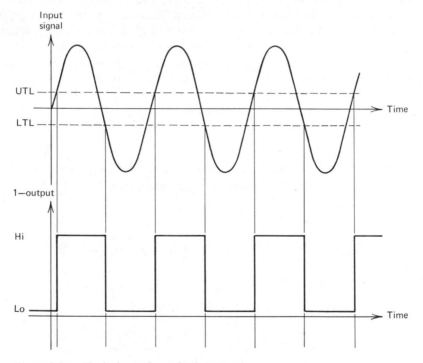

Figure 8-34.   Typical waveforms for Schmitt trigger.

Hi to Lo) voltage state very rapidly. In other words, once the switching action is started it continues very quickly until the output voltages have changed state. The regenerative action to be discussed provides a feedback of the output signal to reinforce the action of the input signal, further accelerating the change initiated by the input voltage.

Referring to Figure 8-32*a* with Q_1 OFF and Q_2 ON, the input going above the UTL voltage will begin turning Q_2 ON. As Q_2 goes ON, the collector Q_2 voltage drops thereby beginning to turn Q_2 OFF. In addition, the input voltage to the base of Q_1 is coupled to the common emitter as Q_1 goes ON, this positive-going voltage at the emitter helping to further drive Q_2 OFF. Thus, Q_2 is quickly driven OFF and Q_1 ON.

When the input voltage drops below the LTL (see Figure 8-33a), Q_1 begins to turn OFF. The collector Q_1 voltage then rises toward V_{CC}, this action beginning to turn Q_2 ON. As Q_2 turns ON, the emitter voltage rises and further drives Q_1 OFF so that the circuit regeneratively switches state.

The typical waveform of Figure 8-34 shows a sinusoidal waveform input and squared waveform output. Notice that the output signal frequency is exactly that of the input signal, except that the output has sharply shaped slope and remains at the Lo or Hi voltage level until it switches. One example of a Schmitt trigger application is converting a sinusoidal signal into one that is useful with digital circuits. Signals such as a 60-Hz line voltage, or a slowly varying voltage obtained from a magnetic pickup are squared up for digital use. Another possibility is using the Schmitt trigger to provide a logical signal which indicates whenever the input goes above a threshold level (UTL).

Example 8-4. For the Schmitt trigger circuit of Figure 8-31 with the following component values, determine the values of UTL and LTL .
$R_{c_1} = 2.4\text{K}, R_{c_2} = 1.5\text{K}, R_E = 2\text{K}, V_{CC} = V_{EE} = 10\text{ V}$
$R_{B_1} = R_{B_2} = 10\text{K}, R_{B_3} = 18\text{K}.$

Solution: $V_{E_1} = \dfrac{R_E}{R_{c_2} + R_E}(V_{CC} + V_{EE}) - V_{EE} = \dfrac{2}{1.5 + 2}(10 + 10) - 10$

$$= 1.4\text{ V}$$

$$\text{UTL} = V_{E_1} + (V_{BE})_{\text{on}} = 1.4 + 0.7 = 2.1\text{ V}$$

$$V_{E_2} = \dfrac{R_E}{R_{c_1} + R_E}(V_{CC} + V_{EE}) - V_{EE} = \dfrac{2}{2.4 + 2}(10 + 10) - 10$$

$$= -0.9\text{ V}$$

$$\text{LTL} = V_{E_2} + (V_{BE})_{\text{on}} = -0.9 + 0.7 = -0.2\text{ V}$$

Example 8-5. For the circuit of Example 8-4 draw the output waveform for an input signal of 12 volts, rms at 60 Hz. Indicate trigger levels and time base.

Solution: The sinusoidal signal has peak amplitude

$$V_P = 1.4\,V_{\text{rms}} = 1.4(12) = 16.8\text{ V}$$

Trigger level points are: UTL = 2.1 V
                             LTL = −0.2 V

For f = 60 Hz, T = $1/f$ = 1/60 = 16.67 msec/cycle, waveforms are shown in Figure 8-35.

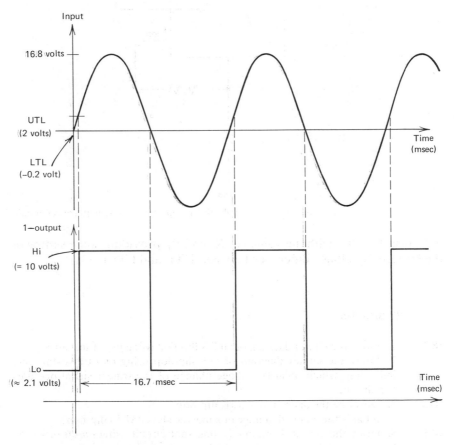

Figure 8-35.   Waveform for solution of Example 8-5.

IC Schmitt Trigger Units. Figure 8-36, without going into circuit detail, shows how an emitter-coupled logic NOR gate (MECL) can be connected to operate as a Schmitt trigger circuit. The advantage of such connection is the possibility of obtaining Schmitt trigger circuit operation using only a NOR gate and two external resistors. The particular arrangement, shown for a Motorola NOR gate, can only be done using an emitter-coupled logic unit. In the present circuit the UTL and LTL points are essentially

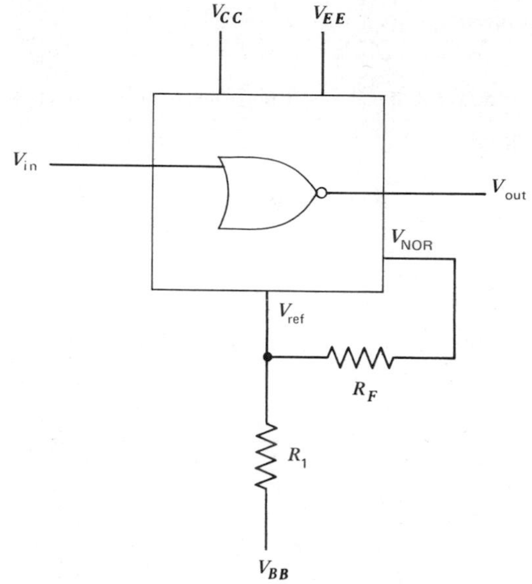

Figure 8-36.   Connection of MECL logic gate as a Schmitt trigger circuit.

both near 0 volts, with the values of R_1 and R_F providing some setting of the hysteresis voltage (difference between UTL and LTL).

PROBLEMS

§8-1   **1.** Draw the circuit diagram of an RS flip-flop using *pnp* transistors.

2. Draw the circuit diagram of a T flip-flop using *pnp* transistors and indicating which polarity voltage change of the trigger signal operates the circuit.

§8-2   **3.** Describe the operation of a JK flip-flop.

4. What is the main advantage of a master-slave (M/S) flip-flop?

§8-3   **5.** Draw the circuit diagram of a one-shot circuit using *pnp* transistors. Define output logic levels and show which polarity voltage change triggers the circuit.

6. Draw the output waveform from the TRUE (1) side of a one-shot circuit using *pnp* transistors for an input CLOCK signal of 10 kHz. The timing component values are $R_T = 10$ K and $C_T = 1000$ pF.

§8-4   **7.** What is the frequency of an astable multivibrator circuit having timing component values of $R_T = 2.7$ K and $C_T = 750$ pF.

8. Draw the TRUE output voltage signal of an *npn* Schmitt trigger circuit for the input trigger signal of 5 volts, rms at 60 Hz. Circuit trigger levels are: UTL = +5 volts, LTL = 0 volts.

1001

Counter and data transfer registers

Multivibrator circuits have many applications in computers. The bistable multivibrator is the most useful of the multivibrator circuits being used in counters that provide timing for various computer operations, in counters that perform arithmetic operations, in shift-registers that move binary data between computer units, and as a basic information storage stage. The astable multivibrator provides clock signals to operate the counters, shift-registers, and other parts of the computer. Monostable multivibrator circuits are used to shape various signals so that a fixed-delay interval is obtained, or to lengthen pulses that are too narrow, or to narrow pulses that are too wide.

This chapter will deal with the multivibrator and logic units as block symbols, that is, with the interconnection of the basic building units as block diagrams without any consideration of the detail circuitry that actually forms the unit. This level of computer study is called logic design and only the logical operation of the blocks is required in order to carry out any design. Both discrete-type and IC building blocks will be covered, although major emphasis is on IC units since most design is done using ICs.

9-1. Basic Binary Ripple Counter

A binary counter is generally made using bistable multivibrator circuits so that each input pulse applied to the counter causes the count to advance (or decrease). A basic counter circuit is shown in Figure 9-1 using two triggered (T-type) flip-flop stages. Each clock pulse applied to the T-input causes the stage to toggle. The 1 and 0 output terminals are always logically opposite. If the 1-output is logical-1 (SET), the 0-output is then logical-0. If the 1-output is logical-0 (RESET), then the 0-output is logical-1.

315

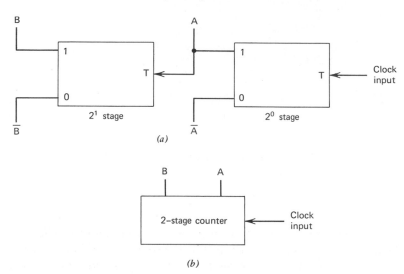

Figure 9-1.   Basic two-stage binary counter.

The clock input causes the flip-flop to toggle or change state once each clock pulse. Figure 9-2a shows the clock input signal and 1-output signal. Notice that the circuit used in this case toggles on the trailing edge of the clock signal (when logic signal goes from 1 to 0). Referring back to Figure 9-1, the 1-output of the first stage (called the 2^0 stage or unit's position stage) is used here as the toggle input to the second stage (called the 2^1 or two's position stage). The 1-outputs from the two successive stages are marked A and B, respectively, to differentiate them. Notice, that the 0-output of each stage is marked with a negation bar over the letter designation, so that whatever logical state A is at, $\overline{A}$ is the opposite logical state.

Since the 1-output (A signal) from the first stage triggers the second stage, the second stage changes state only when the 1-output of the first stage goes from logical-1 to logical-0, as shown in Figure 9-2b. An arrow is included on the waveform of stage A as a reminder that it triggers stage B only on a trailing edge (1 to 0 logical change). Notice that the output waveform of succeeding stages operates half as fast. To see that this circuit operates as a binary counter a table can be prepared to show the 1-output state of each stage after each clock pulse is applied. Table 9-1 shows this operation for the circuit of Figure 9-1.

To see how a counter is made using more stages consider the 4-stage counter of Figure 9-3. The counter is simply made with the 1-output of each stage connected as the toggle input to the succeeding stage. With four stages the counter cycle will repeat every sixteen clock pulses. In

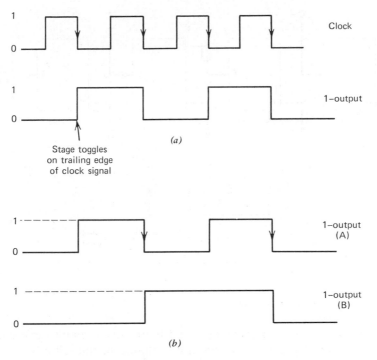

Figure 9-2.   Toggle action of counter stage.

Table 9.1.   *Count Table for 2-Stage Binary Counter of Figure 9-1*

Input Pulses	2^1 Output (B)	2^0 Output (A)
0	0	0
1	0	1
2	1	0
3	1	1
4 (or 0)	0	0

general there are 2^n counts with an n-stage counter. For the four stages used here the count goes 2^4, or 16 steps. As a rule, for a binary counter

$$\text{Number of counts} = N = 2^n$$

where, n = number of counter stages. A six-stage counter ($n = 6$) would then provide a count that repeats every $N = 2^6 = 64$ counts. A ten-stage counter ($n = 10$) would recycle every $N = 2^{10} = 1024$ counts

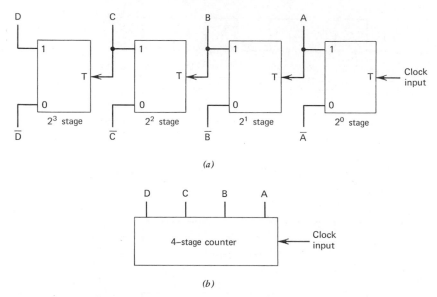

Figure 9-3.   Four-stage binary counter.

Returning to the 4-stage counter of Figure 9-3, a count table can be prepared as in Table 9-2. Arrows are included in the table to act as a reminder that a change from 1 to 0 results in a succeeding stage being toggled. Notice in Table 9-2 that the 2^0 stage toggles on every clock pulse, the 2^1 stage toggles every two clock pulses, the 2^2 stage toggles every four clock pulses. This implies that we can associate a weighting value to the stage output. The 2^3 stage output can be considered of value eight, the 2^2 output equals four, 2^1 output equals two, and 2^0 equals one. We see then that the binary states of the counter can be read as a number equal to the pulse input count. After the counter reaches the count 1111, which is the largest count obtained using four stages, the next input pulse causes the counter to go to 0000 and a new count cycle repeats.

It should be obvious that the count sequence is an increasing binary count for each input clock pulse. Thus, the counter is also referred to as a count-up binary counter. The resulting output waveform for each stage is shown in Figure 9-4.

Count-Down Counter.   A simple change of connection is all that is needed to make a count-down counter as shown in Figure 9-5. The 0-output of each stage is now used as trigger input to the following stage. *We still use the 1-output as indication of the state of each stage* as shown in the count table (Table 9-3). Starting with the counter RESET (1-output of *each*

Table 9-2.   *Count-Up Operation (Four Stages)*

Input Pulses	2^3 Output (D)	2^2 Output (C)	2^1 Output (B)	2^0 Output (A)
0	0	0	0	0
1	0	0	0	1
2	0	0	1	0
3	0	0	1	1
4	0	1	0	0
5	0	1	0	1
6	0	1	1	0
7	0	1	1	1
8	1	0	0	0
9	1	0	0	1
10	1	0	1	0
11	1	0	1	1
12	1	1	0	0
13	1	1	0	1
14	1	1	1	0
15	1	1	1	1
16 (or 0)	0	0	0	0

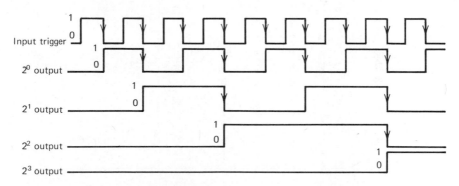

Figure 9-4.   Waveforms of four-stage count-up counter.

stage is logical-0), the first input pulse causes stage A to toggle from 0 to 1. The trigger pulse to stage B being taken from the 0-output of stage A goes from 1 to 0 at this time, so that stage B is also toggled. The 0-output of stage B (B going from 1 to 0) causes stage C to be toggled, which then causes stage D to toggle. Table 9-3 shows, then, that the count goes to 1111. The next input pulse toggles stage A. Since the signal $\overline{A}$ (used to toggle stage B) now goes from 0 to 1, stage B (and C and D) remain the

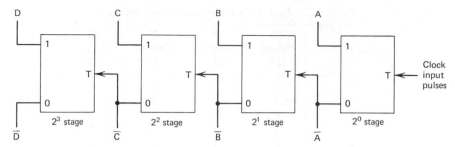

Figure 9-5.   Four-stage count-down binary counter.

Table 9-3.   *Count Table of 4-Stage Count-Down Counter of Figure 9-5*

Input Pulse	D	C	B	A	Decimal Output Count
0	0	0	0	0	0 (or 16)
1	1	1	1	1	15
2	1	1	1	0	14
3	1	1	0	1	13
4	1	1	0	0	12
5	1	0	1	1	11
6	1	0	1	0	10
7	1	0	0	1	9
8	1	0	0	0	8
9	0	1	1	1	7
10	0	1	1	0	6
11	0	1	0	1	5
12	0	1	0	0	4
13	0	0	1	1	3
14	0	0	1	0	2
15	0	0	0	1	1
16	0	0	0	0	0 (or 16)
	1	1	1	1	15

same, the count now being 1110. Thus, the count has decreased as a result of the input trigger pulse. In fact, the count will continue to decrease by one binary count for each input trigger pulse applied. Table 9-3 shows that the count will decrease to 0000 after which it will go to 1111 to repeat another count cycle. Using four stages, the count-down counter provides a full cycle of

$$N = 2^n = 2^4 = 16 \text{ counts}$$

but in a decreasing count mode of operation.

A counter could be used as a simple arithmetic operator providing addition when used as a count-up counter and subtraction when used as a count-down counter. A 6-stage counter would allow counts up to 111111 or 63. If the counter were reset and then 9 pulses applied, the count would go to 001001 (or 9). If, then, another 9 pulses were applied the counter (continuing from 001001) would go to the count 010010 (or 18). Thus, the counter acts as an adder or accumulator for a train of pulses. It should be stated, however, that although this might be suitable for some special application, general-purpose computers use other addition schemes which usually allow parallel addition of two binary numbers as will be discussed in Chapter 11.

Exercise 9-1.   Draw the logic diagram of a 5-stage count-up counter and prepare a count table.

Exercise 9-2.   Draw the logic diagram of a 5-stage count-down counter and show 1-output waveform of each stage and clock waveform.

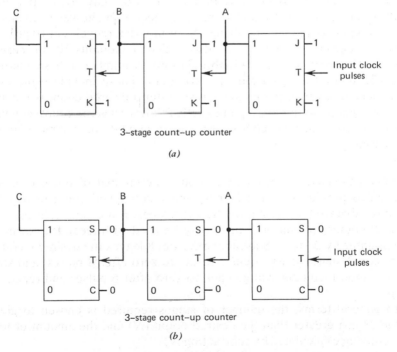

3-stage count-up counter

(a)

3-stage count-up counter

(b)

Figure 9-6.   Binary ripple counters using IC JK flip-flops. (*a*) Using DTL or TTL type JK flip-flops. (*b*) Using RTL type JK flip-flops.

Binary Ripple Counter Using JK Flip-Flops.   Although no new theory is involved there are some details to consider in using JK flip-flops as counter stages. We must, however, differentiate between DTL- and TTL-type JK flip-flops that toggle when both J and K inputs are logical-1 and RTL-type flip-flops that toggle when both S and C inputs are logical-0. Figure 9-6 shows 3-stage count-up counters. Figure 9-6*a* shows a counter using JK flip-flops which require a logical-1 signal (or no input connection) to all J and K inputs. Figure 9-6*b* shows a logical-0 (no connection) to all S and C inputs.

Exercise 9-3.   Draw a 3-stage count-down counter using RTL flip-flops.

Exercise 9-4.   Repeat Exercise 9-3 for DTL- or TTL-type JK flip-flops.

9-2.   Modulus Counters

The counters discussed in section 9-1 allowed only counts that were multiples of $2^n - 4$, 8, 16, and so on. It is necessary, however, to be able to use counters of any count value. A counter that recycles in 10 pulses is called a decade counter. It is also called a modulus-10, or base-10 counter (Mod-10 counter, for abbreviation). A number of basic methods have been used to build modulus counters. These include using pulse feedback to advance the counter, reset after a desired count is reached, and logic gating so that the count exactly follows a desired count sequence. Each of these will be considered and a number of sample counters discussed.

Feedback Counters.   For a desired count the number of stages needed is chosen to provide the next higher binary count and count feedback is used to advance the counter by the extra steps. For example, to count 6 a 3-stage counter (count of 2^3 or 8) may be used with feedback advancing the counter by 2 steps. Subtracting 2 from 8 leaves the desired 6 counts. Just as a 3-stage binary counter resets to zero after 8 pulses, and starts over, a mod-6 counter will go back to zero after 6 pulses and repeat the count.

In general terms, the number of stages required is chosen to give a value 2^n just greater than the desired count (N) and the amount of feedback advance calculated by subtracting N.

$$\text{Number of feedback advance pulses} = 2^n - N$$

For $N = 6$ we used 3 stages ($n = 3$) and the amount of count advance was

$$\text{Number of feedback advance pulses} = 2^3 - 6 = 8 - 6 = 2$$

For a mod-24 counter ($N = 24$) we would need a 5-stage counter ($n = 5$) with count advance

$$\text{Number of feedback advance pulses} = 2^5 - 24 = 32 - 24 = 8$$

Figure 9-7 shows a possible mod-6 counter using feedback advance. Since each pulse input to the 2^1 stage advances the count by 2, the use of feedback to the 2^1 input gives the desired amount of count advance. The count advances to 4 at which time the one-shot circuit is triggered by the 2^2 stage 0-output going from 1 to 0. As the waveforms of Figure 9-7 show, the feedback pulse toggles the 2^1 stage an extra time advancing the counter by 2. Table 9-4 shows the count sequence with a new cycle repeating after 6 input pulses.

Table 9-4.   *Count Table for Mod-6 Counter of Figure 9-7*

Input Pulse	2^2 Stage 1-Output	2^1 Stage 1-Output	2^0 Stage 1-Output	
0	0	0	0	
1	0	0	1	
2	0	1	0	
3	0	1	1	One count
4	1	0	0	cycle
Due to feedback Pulse	1	1	0	
5	1	1	1	
6 (or 0)	0	0	0	

Mod-25 Counter. A counter that recycles every 25 counts requires 5 stages ($2^5 = 32$) with a count advance of

$$\text{Count advance} = 2^n - N = 32 - 25 = 7 \text{ pulses}$$

To advance the count by 7, the 2^0 (1), 2^1 (2), and 2^2 (4) stages can be advanced once ($1 + 2 + 4 = 7$). Figure 9-8 shows the counter circuit and Table 9-5 provides the count sequence of a mod-25 counter.

Mod-12 Counter. A mod-12 ($N = 12$) counter requires 4 stages ($2^4 = 16$) with count advance of 4:

$$\text{Count advance} = 2^n - N = 16 - 12 = 4$$

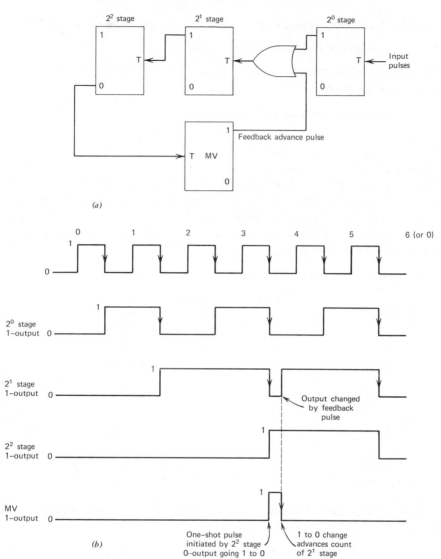

Figure 9-7.   Mod-6 counter using feedback advance pulse.

To advance the count by 4 a feedback pulse can be applied to the 2^2 stage once as shown in the circuit of Figure 9-9*a*. During one count cycle the last counter stage changes from 1 to 0. The next to the last stage, however, changes from 1 to 0 twice during a count cycle. Thus, Figure 9-9*b* shows another way to advance the counter by 4 counts — twice add 2 to the count. That is, the feedback pulse obtained from the next to the

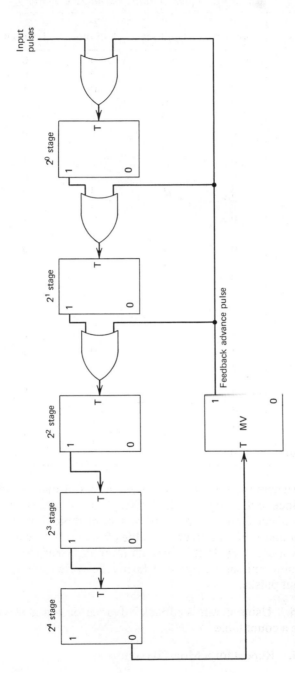

Figure 9-8. Mod-25 feedback counter.

Table 9-5.   *Count Table of Mod-25 Counter*

Input Pulses	2^4 1-output	2^3 1-output	2^2 1-output	2^1 1-output	2^0 1-output
0	0	0	0	0	0
1	0	0	0	0	1
2	0	0	0	1	0
3	0	0	0	1	1
4	0	0	1	0	0
5	0	0	1	0	1
6	0	0	1	1	0
7	0	0	1	1	1
8	0	1	0	0	0
9	0	1	0	0	1
10	0	1	0	1	0
11	0	1	0	1	1
12	0	1	1	0	0
13	0	1	1	0	1
14	0	1	1	1	0
15	0	1	1	1	1
16	1	0	0	0	0
Feedback advance pulse	1	0	1	1	1
17	1	1	0	0	0
18	1	1	0	0	1
19	1	1	0	1	0
20	1	1	0	1	1
21	1	1	1	0	0
22	1	1	1	0	1
23	1	1	1	1	0
24	1	1	1	1	1
25 (or 0)	0	0	0	0	0

last stage triggers the one-shot twice during a full count cycle. Since the count advance pulse triggers the 2^1 stage, it advances the count by 2 each time—a net count advance of 4. Count tables for the counters of Figure 9-9*a* and 9-9*b* are given in Tables 9-6 and 9-7, respectively. Both tables show a count cycle that repeats after 12 count pulses. Each, however, has a different count sequence during the cycle, although both *recycle* after 12 input pulses.

Exercise 9-5.   Using count feedback advance design a Mod-10 counter and prepare a count table.

Exercise 9-6.   Repeat for a Mod-20 counter.

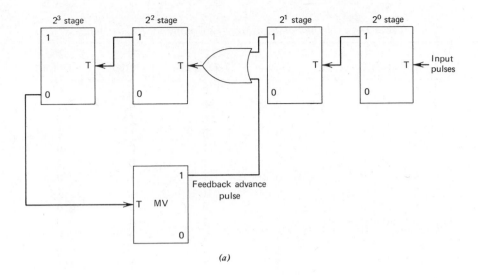

(a)

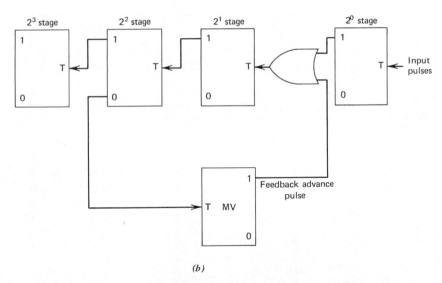

(b)

Figure 9-9. Mod-12 counter using feedback advance. (*a*) Count advanced once by four.
(*b*) Count advanced twice by two.

Table 9-6. *Count Table for Mod-12 Counter of Figure 9-9a*

Input Pulses	2^3 1-Output	2^2 1-Output	2^1 1-Output	2^0 1-Output
0	0	0	0	0
1	0	0	0	1
2	0	0	1	0
3	0	0	1	1
4	0	1	0	0
5	0	1	0	1
6	0	1	1	0
7	0	1	1	1
8	1	0	0	0
Feedback advance	1	1	0	0
9	1	1	0	1
10	1	1	1	0
11	1	1	1	1
12 (or 0)	0	0	0	0

Table 9-7. *Count Table for Mod-12 Counter of Figure 9-9b*

Input Pulses	2^3 1-Output	2^2 1-Output	2^1 1-Output	2^0 1-Output
0	0	0	0	0
1	0	0	0	1
2	0	0	1	0
3	0	0	1	1
4	0	1	0	0
Feedback advance	0	1	1	0
5	0	1	1	1
6	1	0	0	0
7	1	0	0	1
8	1	0	1	0
9	1	0	1	1
10	1	1	0	0
Feedback advance	1	1	1	0
11	1	1	1	1
12 (or 0)	0	0	0	0

The type of feedback circuit discussed presently has a number of special factors for consideration, some of which may be considered disadvantageous.

1. The counter requires a one-shot stage adjusted to provide a pulse of width shorter than one clock interval at the highest clock rate. The pulse from the one-shot unit, however, cannot be too short since it must allow the counter "enough" time after the count increases to that count which results in the feedback pulse. If, say, the feedback pulse were to trigger the circuit 1 μsec after the pulse is initiated, then the counter stage must be capable of operating at a 1 MHz rate (1/1 μsec = 1 MHz). This timing consideration and the addition of a one-shot unit may be considered a disadvantage.

2. Binary count sequence does not always correspond to decimal count of input pulse during a cycle. When the feedback pulse advances the count correspondence is lost. If, however, one only desires an indication of when 12 pulses have occurred without regard to the counter state at each step, then the resulting count sequence is satisfactory.

Counter Reset for Binary Equivalent Count.   Another technique to develop various modulus counters, and which removes the second disadvantage mentioned above by providing a binary equivalent count, uses logic decoding and counter reset. Simply stated, the count advances in binary sequence and is reset after it reaches a specific count state as sensed by a decoding logic gate. For example, consider a Mod-10 (decade) counter.

Mod-10 Counter. Figure 9-10 shows a decade counter (using discrete component flip-flops) having a binary count that is always equivalent to the input pulse count. The circuit is essentially a binary ripple counter which could count up to 16. We desire however, a circuit operation in which the count advances from 0 to 9 and then resets to 0 for a new cycle. This reset is accomplished at the desired count as follows:

1. With counter RESET (count = 0000), the counter is ready to start a count cycle.
2. Input pulses advance counter in binary sequence up to count of 9 (count = 1001).
3. The next count pulse advances the count to 10 (count = 1010). A logic NAND gate decodes the count of 10 providing a level change at that time to trigger the one-shot unit, which then resets all counter stages. Thus, the pulse after the counter is at count = 9 effectively results in the counter going to count = 0 (RESET state), and a full cycle is complete.

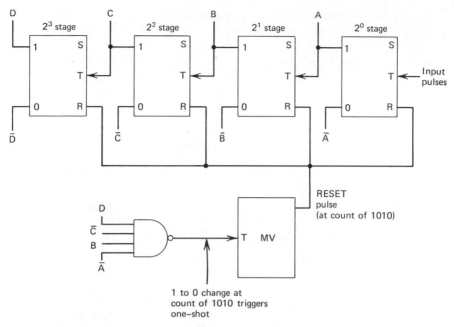

Figure 9-10.   Decade counter using count reset.

Table 9-8 provides a count table showing the binary count equivalent to the decimal count of input pulses. The table also shows that the count goes momentarily from nine (1001) to ten (1010) before resetting to zero (0000). The NAND gate provides an output of 1 until the count reaches ten. The count of ten is decoded (or sensed in this case) by using logic inputs that are all 1 at the count of ten. When the count becomes ten the NAND gate output goes to logical-0 providing a 1 to 0 logic change to trigger the one-shot unit, which then provides a short pulse to reset all counter stages. The one-shot pulse need only be long enough so that the slowest counter stage resets. Actually, at this time only the 2^1 and 2^3 stages need be reset but all stages are reset to insure that a new cycle starts at the count 0000.

BCD Counter. As a simple extension of the decade counter of Figure 9-10 a series of decade counters providing BCD binary output and decimal display is shown in Figure 9-11. Input pulses are applied to a decade counter which provides an output of BCD on four lines. These outputs are also used to operate a decimal display light so that the decimal value of the BCD count is displayed. The one-shot pulse from this counter unit can be used as count pulses to a second identical decade

Table 9-8.   *Count Table of Decade Counter of Figure 9-10*

Input Pulses	D	C	B	A
0	0	0	0	0
1		0	0	1
2	0	0	1	0
3	0	0	1	1
4	0	1	0	0
5	0	1	0	1
6	0	1	1	0
7	0	1	1	1
8	1	0	0	0
9	1	0	0	1
10	1	0	1	0
↓	↓	↓	↓	↓
0	0	0	0	0

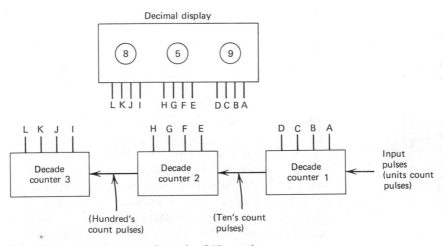

Figure 9-11.   Decade counter for scale-of-10 counting.

counter. Since a pulse occurs every tenth input pulse the second decade counter counts by tens and the displayed decimal value is the ten's position count. The binary output of the second decade counter drives the ten's position display light. Similarly, the one-shot output of the second decade counter occurs once every hundred input pulses and is used to trigger a third decade counter representing the hundred's count.

Mod-24 Counter. Another example of a counter that provides a count in binary sequence, resetting at a specified count is the mod-24 counter of Figure 9-12. This counter is made using TTL logic components. A five-stage ripple counter is shown (which can count up to 31). An output of each stage is used to decode the count of 24 — with NAND gate N1.

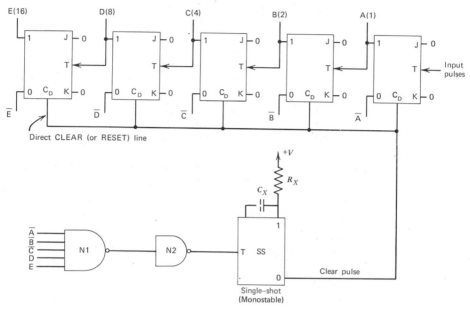

Figure 9-12.   Mod-24 counter using TTL units.

The output of N1 goes lo on the count of 24 (11000). The one-shot triggered by gate N2 then provides a lo level signal for a time determined by the external R_x and C_x components. This pulse is applied to the direct CLEAR input (C_D) of each stage causing each state to be reset. The binary count thus progresses from zero (00000) to 23 (10111) and then resets on the next input pulse (going momentarily to the 24 count state).

Mod-12 Counter Using TTL Logic Units. A counter that recycles after 12 pulses is the Mod-12 counter of Figure 9-13 built using TTL logic units. A 4-stage JK counter steps up to the count of $11_{10}(1011)$. The next clock pulse advances the count to $12_{10}(1100)$, NAND gate N1 goes low and gate N2 goes high triggering the single-shot unit. Components C_x and R_x externally set the duration of the pulse used to operate the direct clear (C_D) of each stage. The input to C_D going low causes the stage to be reset so that the counter is reset and a new cycle may now start. Circuit waveforms in Figure 9-13 show how the counter is reset when the single-shot unit is triggered.

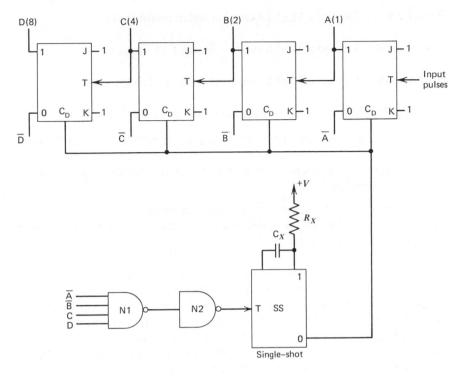

(a) Logic connection

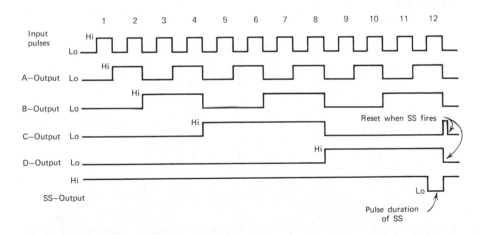

Figure 9-13.   Mod-12 counter using TTL logic. (a) Logic Connection. (b) Circuit waveforms.

Exercise 9-7.   Design a Mod-18 counter using count reset.

Exercise 9-8.   Design a Mod-6 counter using TTL logic units.

Exercise 9-9.   Design a Mod-15 counter using TTL logic units.

Two disadvantages of the counters considered presently are

1. Count must advance to a temporary state before going to the reset state.
2. Circuit uses a single-shot unit and special timing adjustment on pulse duration.

It is possible to build a counter that does not need a single shot and goes directly from the last count to the reset state and such direct reset counters will now be considered.

Direct Reset Counters.   The above two disadvantages can be removed by using some logic to implement a circuit that provides a desired count sequence, exactly. A few examples should help show how counters can be built to exactly follow a prescribed count table. The counters will be designed using only IC units—either RTL logic units or TTL (or DTL) logic. The techniques used are about the same in either case, although the resulting circuits are somewhat different.

Mod-6 Counter. The count table of a mod-6 counter is specified in Table 9-9.

Table 9-9.   *Mod—6 Count Table*

Count	C	B	A
0	0	0	0
1	0	0	1
2	0	1	0
3	0	1	1
4	1	0	0
5	1	0	1
6 (or 0)	0	0	0

One count cycle (brace spanning counts 0 through 5)

Looking at the output of stage A we see that it complements on each input pulse. Stage B toggles each time stage A changes from 1 to 0, except when C is logical-1 at which time stage B remains reset. Stage C can be seen to remain reset each time stage A changes from 1 to 0, except when B is logical-1. This information is used to design a mod-counter using JK flip-flops as shown in Figure 9-14a. The counter waveforms are shown in Figure 9-14b.

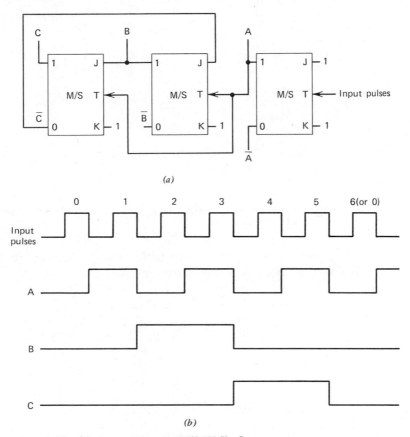

(a)

(b)

Figure 9-14. Mod-6 counter using M/S JK flip-flops.

Mod-12 Counter. The count table of a mod-12 counter using TTL flip-flops is provided in Table 9-10. Four counter stages are needed as shown in Figure 9-15. The triggering of each stage is obtained as follows:

1. Stage A toggled each input pulse.
2. Stage B toggled each time A goes 1 to 0.
3. Stage C toggled each time B goes 1 to 0, except when D is logical-1.
4. Stage D is reset each time B goes 1 to 0, except when C = 1 allows stage D to be toggled.

Table 9-10.   *Count Table for Mod-12 Counter*

Count	D	C	B	A
0	0	0	0	0
1	0	0	0	1
2	0	0	1	0
3	0	0	1	1
4	0	1	0	0
5	0	1	0	1
6	0	1	1	0
7	0	1	1	1
8	1	0	0	0
9	1	0	0	1
10	1	0	1	0
11	1	0	1	1
12 (or 0)	0	0	0	0

Figure 9-15 shows the mod-12 counter operated as the above details specify.

Mod-10 (Decade) Counter. The count table of a decade counter is given in Table 9-11. Four counter stages are needed.

Table 9-11.   *Mod-10 (Decade) Count Table*

Count	D	C	B	A
0	0	0	0	0
1	0	0	0	1
2	0	0	1	0
3	0	0	1	1
4	0	1	0	0
5	0	1	0	1
6	0	1	1	0
7	0	1	1	1
8	1	0	0	0
9	1	0	0	1
10 (or 0)	0	0	0	0

The required triggering of each counter stage can be done as specified below:

1. Stage A is toggled each input pulse.

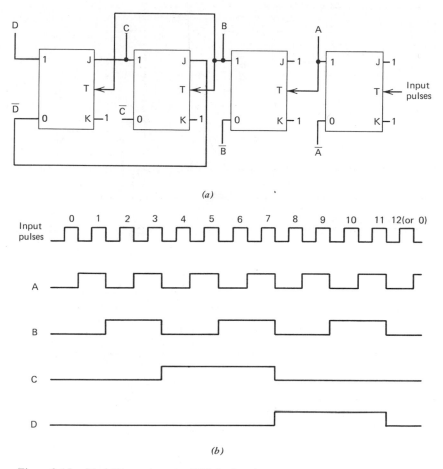

Figure 9-15.   Mod-12 counter using TTL logic units.

2. Stage B is toggled each 1 to 0 change of A, except when D is logical-1, when stage B remains reset.
3. Stage C is toggled each time B goes 1 to 0.
4. Stage D is reset each time stage A changes from 1 to 0, except when B and C are both logical-1.

In order to obtain BC using NAND gates, two NAND units were needed as shown in Figure 9-16 of a mod-10 counter using TTL or DTL logic. Perhaps the only feature in designing the counter was using the A signal as trigger to stage D. If it is noted that going from the count 9 to 10 (or 0) only stage A changes (stage D change is due to stage A as trigger signal) then there is no other choice of trigger signal for stage D.

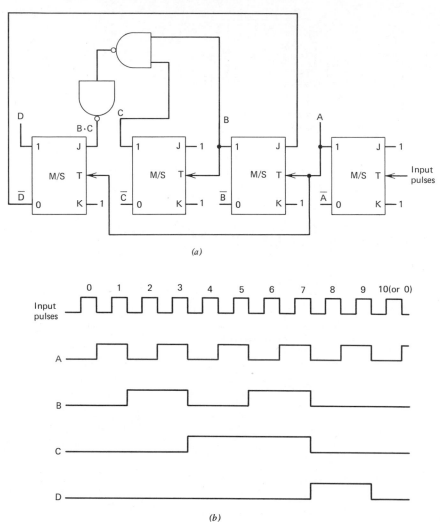

(a)

(b)

Figure 9-16.   Decade counter using M/S JK flip-flops and TTL (or DTL) logic.

Using RTL logic units to build the same decade counter results in the circuit of Figure 9-17. It should be clear that all examples provided here are not necessarily the only circuits that can give the desired operation. They are quite typical and provide good examples to present useful design techniques.

Stage A in Figure 9-17 is toggled each input pulse, stage B is toggled each time A goes 1 to 0, except when D is logical-1, and stage C is toggled each time B goes 1 to 0. Stage D is reset each time A goes 1 to 0, except

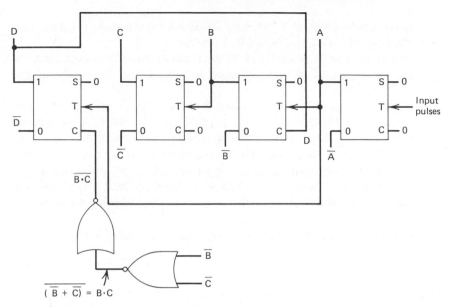

Figure 9-17.   Decade counter using RTL logic units.

when B and C are both logical-1. Using RTL NOR gates, the logic signal $\overline{BC}$ provides a logical-1 signal causing stage D to be cleared except when $\overline{BC}$ is logical-0 when both B and C outputs are logical-1 and S and C inputs of logical-0 result in stage D being toggled (to logical-1).

Mod-5 Counter. The desired count table for a mod-5 counter is given in Table 9-12. Our design requires careful consideration of the count table.

Table 9-12.   *Count Table for Mod-5 Counter*

Count	C	B	A	
0	0	0	0	
1	0	0	1	One cycle
2	0	1	0	of mod-5
3	0	1	1	counter
4	1	0	0	
5 (or 0)	0	0	0	

1. Looking down the column representing the state of the A flip-flop stage for each input pulse we may note that the stage complements each input pulse except when the C stage output is 1. The K input is

accordingly a logical-1, whereas the input to terminal J is taken from the $\overline{C}$ output which is logical-0 at count of 4.

2. The operation of stage B can be determined from the count table by noting that stage B complements each time the A signal changes from 1 to 0.

3. Stage C toggles when both A and B change from 1 to 0 on the fourth input pulse. However, stage C toggles again on the fifth input pulse when neither stage A nor stage B change state. It will thus be necessary to use the input signal to toggle stage C. From the count table we see that the input signal can reset stage C every pulse except the fourth. If the J-input is then logical-1, the stage will toggle this one count step. The resulting mod-5 counter is shown in Figure 9-18.

Mod-7 Counter. A mod-7 count table is given in Table 9-13. From the

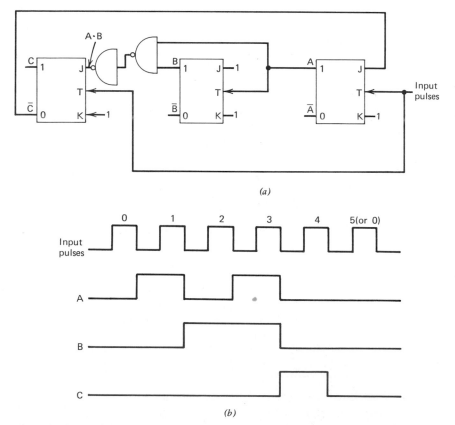

(a)

(b)

Figure 9-18.   Mod-5 counter.

Table 9-13.   *Count Table for Mod-7 Counter*

Count	C	B	A	
0	0	0	0	
1	0	0	1	
2	0	1	0	
3	0	1	1	One count cycle
4	1	0	0	
5	1	0	1	
6	1	1	0	
7 (or 0)	0	0	0	

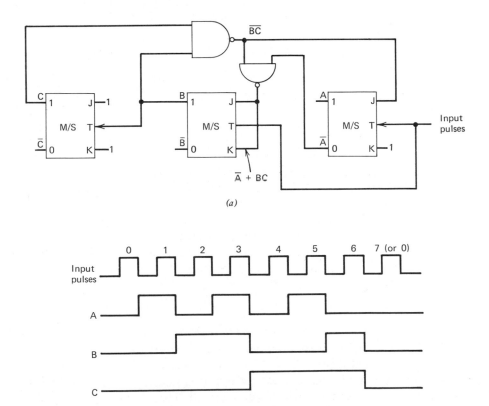

Figure 9-19.   Mod-7 counter.

count table the following facts are obtained:

1. Stage A is toggled each input pulse except when B and C are both logical-1.
2. Stage B is toggled when A is logical-1 or when BC is logical-1: when $A + BC$ is logical-1.
3. Stage C is toggled each time B goes from 1 to 0.

The resulting counter circuit and circuit waveforms are shown in Figure 9-19.

Exercise 9-10.   Design a mod-9 counter using TTL JK flip-flops.

Exercise 9-11.   Repeat Exercise 9-10 for a mod-20 counter.

Exercise 9-12.   Repeat Exercise 9-10 for a mod-18 counter.

Exercise 9-13.   Repeat Exercise 9-10 for a mod-15 counter.

9-3.   Shift and Transfer Registers

In addition to operation in counters, flip-flop stages are also used extensively in forming a chain of units or register to hold and transfer binary data. If data is moved serially (one bit at a time) the flip-flops are connected as a shift registers. Shift registers may be designed to move the data to the right or left (from the most significant bit to least significant bit, or vice versa). Data may be also transferred in *parallel* (all bits at the same time) for fastest operation.

Using JK flip-flops to build a shift register, the J and K inputs are data inputs and the T input is the trigger pulse or shift pulse. Using JK flip-flops to build a parallel transfer register the preclear (C_D) and preset (S_D) inputs provide data inputs.

Shift Registers.

Shift-Left Register. A four-stage shift-left register is shown in Figure 9-20. The individual stages are JK flip-flops made using RTL units in Figure 9-20a and TTL (or DTL) units in Figure 9-20b. Notice that in both cases the data input consists of opposite binary signals, the TRUE (1-output) or reference data signal going to the S (or J) input and the opposite data signal (FALSE or 0-output) going to the C (or K) input. These opposite data input signals represent a logical-1 if S (or J) input is logical-1 and logical-0 if C (or K) input is logical-1.

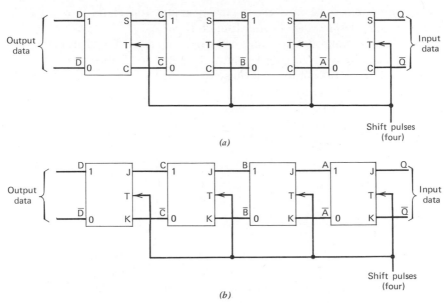

Figure 9-20.   Shift-left registers. (a) RTL units. (b) TTL (or DTL) units.

The shift pulse is applied to each stage, operating each simultaneously. When the shift pulse occurs (level changes from 1 to 0) the data input at terminals S (or J) and C (or K) is shifted into that stage. Each stage is set or reset corresponding to the input data at the time the shift pulse occurs. Thus, the input data bit (Q) is shifted into stage A by the first shift pulse. At the same time the data of stage A (A logic signal) is shifted into stage B, and so on for the following stages. At each shift pulse, data stored in the register stages shifts left by one stage. New data is shifted into stage A, whereas the data present in stage D is shifted out (to the left) for use by some other shift register or computer unit.

For example, consider starting with all stages reset (all 1-outputs logical-0) and applying a steady logical-1 input as data input to stage A. Table 9-14 shows the data in each stage after each of four shift pulses.

Table 9-14.   *Operation of Shift-Left Register*

Shift Pulse	D	C	B	A
0	0	0	0	0
1	0	0	0	1
2	0	0	1	1
3	0	1	1	1
4	1	1	1	1

Notice in Table 9-14 how the logical-1 input first shifts into stage A and then shifts left to stage D after four shift pulses.

As another example, consider shifting alternate 0 and 1 data into stage A starting with all stages logical-1. Table 9-15 shows the data in each stage after each of four shift pulses.

Table 9-15.   *Operation of Shift-Left Register*

Shift Pulse	D	C	B	A
0	1	1	1	1
1	1	1	1	0
2	1	1	0	1
3	1	0	1	0
4	0	1	0	1

Finally, as a third example of shift register operation, consider starting with the count in step 4 of Table 9-15 and applying four more shift pulses while placing a steady logical-0 input as data input to stage A. Table 9-16 shows this operation.

Table 9-16.   *Operation of Shift-Left Register*

Shift Pulses	D	C	B	A
0	0	1	0	1
1	1	0	1	0
2	0	1	0	0
3	1	0	0	0
4	0	0	0	0

Considering the data in stage A as least-significant (2^0) digits (LSD) and that in stage D as most-significant digits (MSD), shift-left register operation provides data starting with the MSD bit. A few points should be made clear in regard to shift register operation.

1. The number of shift pulses should be the same as the number of shift register stages.
2. Changes in the shift stages take place simultaneously but only when the shift pulse occurs.
3. Data shift into a register stage only depends on what logic levels *were* present at input terminals S and C (or, J and K) at the time the shift pulse occurs. Changes that then take place resulting from data shifted will not affect the next stage until the next shift pulse occurs.

4. The M/S-type flip-flop operates so that input data present when the shift pulse goes high (logical-1) is moved into the master flip-flop stage. Any data after that time has no effect until the next shift pulse. This data, however, appears at the output only when the shift pulse goes low (logical-0), at which time the data shifted into the master stage appears as output from the slave stage.

Shift-Right Register. Sometimes it is necessary to shift the least significant digit first, as when addition is to be carried out serially. In that case a shift-right register is used such as in Figure 9-21. Input data is applied

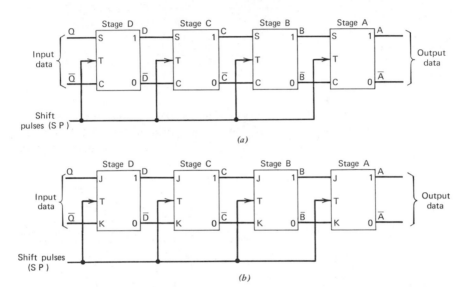

Figure 9-21.   Shift-right registers. (*a*) RTL units. (*b*) TTL (or DTL) units.

to stage D and shifted right. The shift operation is the same as discussed previously except that data transfers to the right. Table 9-17 shows the action of shifting all logical-1 inputs into an initially reset shift register.

Table 9-17.   *Shift-Right Operation*

Shift Pulse	D	C	B	A
0	0	0	0	0
1	1	0	0	0
2	1	1	0	0
3	1	1	1	0
4	1	1	1	1

In addition to shifting data into a register, data is also shifted out of a register. Table 9-18 shows register operation for an initial value of 1101. Notice that the output from stage A contains the binary number, each bit (starting initially with the LSD) appearing at the output of each shift step. In the present example it was assumed that logical-0 was shifted as input data so that after four shift pulses have occurred the data has passed through the register and the stages are left reset after the fourth shift pulse.

Table 9-18.   *Data Shifted out of Shift-Right Register*

Shift Pulse	D	C	B	A
0	1	1	0	1
1	0	1	1	0
2	0	0	1	1
3	0	0	0	1
4	0	0	0	0

Shift-Around Register. When it is necessary to shift data out of a register without losing the initial data a shift-around connection can be used. Figure 9-22 shows TTL stages in a shift-right, shift-around register

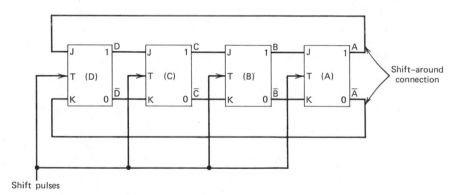

Figure 9-22.   Shift-right, shift-around register.

connection. All that was needed was connection of the output of stage A as input to stage D. Then, as four shift pulses move the binary data into stage A, the data being shifted out of stage A is shifted into stage D and returns into the register. Table 9-19 shows the result of shifting the binary number 1101 through (and around) the shift register.

Notice that after four shift pulses have occurred the initial value is again in the shift register. To see how any action has taken place other than just

Table 9-19.   *Shift-Around Action with Shift-Right Register*

Shift Pulse	D	C	B	A
0	1	1	0	1
1	1	1	1	0
2	0	1	1	1
3	1	0	1	1
4	1	1	0	1

shifting the number around the register, consider two shift register stages as in Figure 9-23. Each register, shown in block form, is a four-stage shift-right register. Externally connecting the A and $\overline{A}$ outputs of register 1 back to the data input of the same register results in it acting as a shift-around register. The logic signal appearing at output A (and $\overline{A}$) is also shifted into register 2. Table 9-20 shows the operation starting with 1101 in register 1 and 0000 in register 2. If the shift-around of register 1 were not used and data input were left unconnected (logical-0), then after four shift pulses the data originally in register 1 would be in register 2, with register 1 then reset.

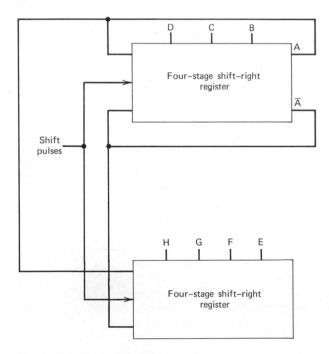

Figure 9-23.   Two shift-right registers.

Table 9-20.   *Operation of Shift Registers of Figure 9-23*

Shift Pulse	D	C	B	A	H	G	F	E
0	1	1	0	1	0	0	0	0
1	1	1	1	0	1	0	0	0
2	0	1	1	1	0	1	0	0
3	1	0	1	1	1	0	1	0
4	1	1	0	1	1	1	0	1

Shift-In, Shift-Around Operation. Going further we can see how a shift register can be operated so that at one time data is shifted in whereas data is shifted out (and around) at another operating time. Figure 9-24 shows a four-state shift register and the necessary logic to switch from shift-in to shift-out, shift-around operation.

Four JK stages form the basic shift-right register. The output data is available for connection to another register and is also connected to logic

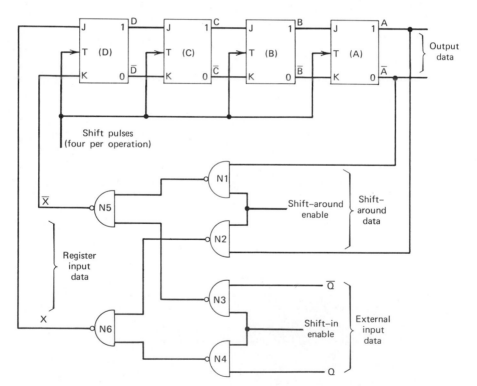

Figure 9-24.   Operation of shift-right register in shift-in and shift-around modes.

NAND gates N1 and N2. External data input to the register (Q and Q) is connected to logic NAND gates N3 and N4. The shift-in enable must be present (logical-1) for external data to be shifted into the register. If the shift-around enable signal is present instead, then the output data (A and $\overline{A}$) is to be shifted back into the register. Only one mode of operation should take place during one shift cycle (four shift pulses) so that both enable pulses are not logical-1 at the same time. The output of NAND gates N5 and N6 are the external input data or the shift-around data, depending on which enable signal is present.

An operating cycle might proceed as described in the following discussion. For shift-in cycle:

1. Shift-in enable signal becomes logical-1 (shift-around signal remaining logical-0).
2. Four shift pulses cause external input data, Q and $\overline{Q}$, from another shift register, to be shifted into the present four-stage shift register. The same four shift pulses are used to operate both external register and present register so that data is shifted *synchronously*.
3. Shift-in enable signal goes low (logical-0), and cycle is over.

To see how the gating operates:

1. With shift-around enable at logical-0, output of gates N1 and N2 are both logical-1, regardless of A and $\overline{A}$ data signals. Thus, the shift-around data is disabled from affecting the input data (X and $\overline{X}$) at this time.
2. With shift-in enable at logical-1, output of gates N3 and N4 depends on Q and $\overline{Q}$ data. If, for example Q = 1 (and $\overline{Q}$ = 0), then the N3 output is logical-0 and N4 output is logical-1. Following the gating the output of N5 is then logical-0 and N6 is logical-1. In effect then, for Q = 1, $\overline{Q}$ = 0, we have X = 1, $\overline{X}$ = 0 so that the register input follows the external data input, as desired.
3. If, instead, the shift-around enable were logical-1 (and shift-in enable logical-0), then the outputs of A and $\overline{A}$ would determine the values of X and $\overline{X}$, respectively.

For shift-around cycle:

1. The shift-around enable signal becomes logical-1 (shift-in enable signal remains logical-0).
2. Four shift pulses cause register output data at A and $\overline{A}$ to be shifted back into the register.
3. Shift-around enable signal goes low and cycle is over.

A number of examples of how larger-sized shift registers are operated will be left to appropriate areas of application, such as the arithmetic unit, input-output units, memory unit, and control unit.

Exercise 9-14. Draw the diagram of a five-stage shift-left register using RTL units.

Exercise 9-15. Draw the diagram of a six-stage shift-right register using TTL (or DTL) logic units.

Parallel Data Transfer. So far the only means of moving data from a register in one computer location to another used shift registers and the data was transferred serially. This is common in some input-output units and special purpose computer units. However, most modern digital computers provide parallel operation so that all data bits in a register are transferred at the same time. Using the clock pulse as the basic step in our consideration, a shift register having 20 stages would require 20 shift pulses to move a full stored data word (20 bits). Using a clock time of 1 μsec, for example, the time needed to transfer a 20-bit word serially would be 20 μsec. The same data word could be transferred in parallel in one clock pulse time, or 1 μsec, quite a bit faster. The cost of this faster operating rate is handling more signal lines and more logic gating as will now be shown. It should be clear, however, that the greater cost and complexity of parallel operation is more than offset by the faster operating speed in most modern computers.

Figure 9-25a shows the connection of a four-stage register into which data may be transferred in parallel. The basic operation of this register is the clearing of all stages by a clear pulse and then the transfer of all input data bits by a single transfer pulse. To fully understand the operation of a single stage we must recall that the S_D and C_D inputs are direct set and clear inputs (also called asynchronous inputs). For TTL units the operation of these terminals provides that a high (logical-1) input has no effect on the stage operation. With clear and transfer lines normally low (logical-0) as shown in Figure 9-25a the outputs of all NAND gates are held high. When the clear pulse occurs it resets all stages when the clear line goes low and then back high to "free" the stages for other operations. After this the transfer pulse goes high enabling all transfer gates. Any gate having a data bit of logical-1 then provides a low signal to cause that stage to directly set so that its 1-output is then logical-1. Those gates having input data of logical-0 hold the respective S_D input high with no change taking place. The net result is that input data of logical-1 SET their stages and input data of logical-0 leave their stages RESET so that a parallel transfer of the complete data word (all bits) results.

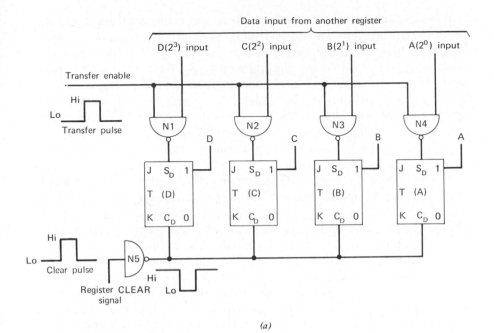

(a)

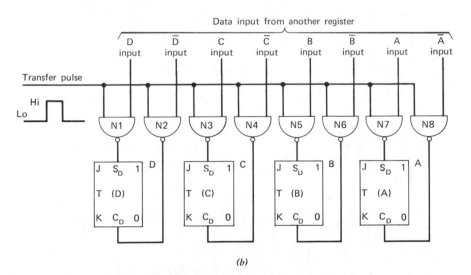

(b)

Figure 9-25. Parallel transfer register. (a) Using CLEAR and transfer pulses. (b) Using single transfer pulse.

It should be obvious that before clear and transfer pulses occur the input data to the four NAND gates and the output data from the 1-output terminals of the register stages can be different. After the clear and transfer pulses the two are then identical, the input data having been transferred into the register for storage or use by that register. After the transfer pulse ends the input data can change without affecting the register stored data since the logic gates are disqualified from operating (all outputs held high by low transfer enable signal). Notice that J, K, and T inputs were not required for the present operation and that no connection is used in the present circuits.

Using a few more logic gates as shown in Figure 9-25b allows a single transfer pulse to accomplish the full data transfer. Opposite outputs of each input bit are required. The transfer pulse being normally low holds the output of all NAND gates high thereby leaving the register stages "free" to operate (if J, K, and T terminals were used). When the transfer pulse occurs (goes high) those gates with logical-1 inputs would result in logical-0 outputs to either S_D or C_D terminal thereby setting or resetting, respectively, the appropriate stage. Since data bit inputs are opposite, D and $\bar{D}$, or, C and $\bar{C}$, etc., have one logical-1, the other logical-0. If, for example D input = 1 and D input = 0, then N1 output is low and N2 output is high so that stage D is then SET. If, for example, C input = 0 and $\bar{C}$ input = 1, then the stage C S_D signal is high and C_D signal is low so that stage C is RESET (C output = 0).

Figure 9-26 shows how the logic can be modified to eliminate the need

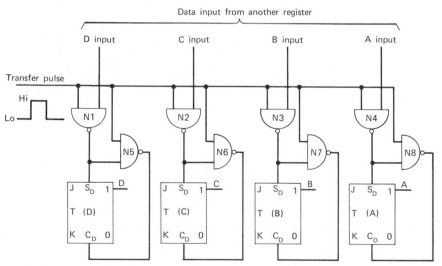

Figure 9-26.   Parallel transfer gating.

for two transfer input lines per bit, by providing inversion of S_D and C_D signals. Operation is otherwise the same as the register of Figure 9-25. It should be clear that with S_D and C_D for each stage depending on the data-input to a stage the transfer pulse will result in either setting or resetting of the stage to occur and the stage output will depend on the input data bit for that stage.

Serial-Parallel Transfer Operation.   You might have wondered by now whether it is possible to operate a register in both serial (shift) and parallel modes of operation. Figure 9-27 shows just such a circuit arrangement. The input data is transferred in parallel when the parallel transfer pulse occurs or serially when four shift pulses occur. It should be clear that both operations should not take place at the same time. Compare Figure 9-27 with Figures 9-26 and 9-21 to see that the present unit operates exactly as each transfer method discussed separately.

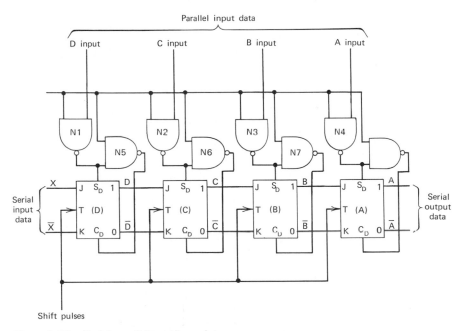

Figure 9-27.   Serial-parallel transfer register.

Exercise 9-16.   Draw the logic diagram of a three-stage shift-left register with parallel data transfer using TTL units.

9-4.   Counters and Decoding Techniques

When a counter is used to provide a number of controlled steps in a computer operation it is necessary to obtain individual pulses for each count step. For a mod-6 counter it is desired that six separate pulses be formed so that only one is present at each count step. One way to obtain this operation is to gate the counter outputs so as to decode each count value. Figure 9-28*a* shows a mod-6 counter with six decoding gates to select the individual counts. The mod-6 counter is the same as in Figure 9-14. The present discussion deals with the six three-input NAND gates used as decoder gates. At the count of zero (000) the inputs to gate N1 are all high and the CS0 (counter step number 0) output signal is then logical-0. Checking the other gates will show that at least one input (for this count) is logical-0 with output of gates N2 to N6 all logical-1. When the clock advances the counter to 001 the output of gate N1 goes high and the output of gate N2 goes low, the only low output of the six gates for the count of 001.

A better picture of what results from the counter-decoder connection is shown in the circuit waveforms of Figure 9-28*b*. The clock signal steps the counter resulting in the waveform shown for the counter outputs A,

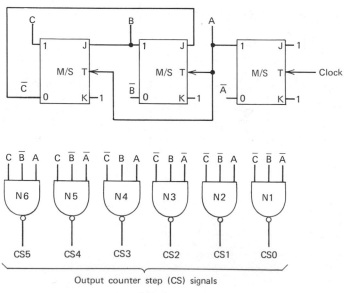

Output counter step (CS) signals

(*a*)

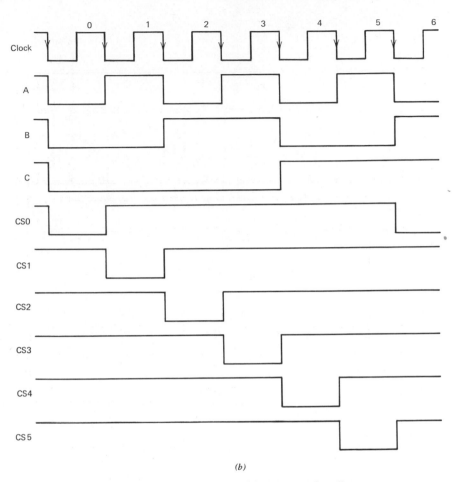

(b)

Figure 9-28.   Mod-6 counter with count step decoding.

B, and C. These signals (along with their complement signals A, B, and C available from the counter stages) are decoded by the six NAND gates. Notice that each clock step output of the gates is low in sequence. First CS0 goes low for a count interval. Then CS1 goes low for the next count interval, and so on to CS5. The decoded clock step signals provide a group of timing signals that can be used by other computer circuits.

Another method used to provide a group of timing signals similar to those in Figure 9-28*b* is used in the counter of Figure 9-29*a*. Actually, the circuit is a shift-around, shift-left register. If, however, the register operation is started with all stage output logical-0, except stage A (which is

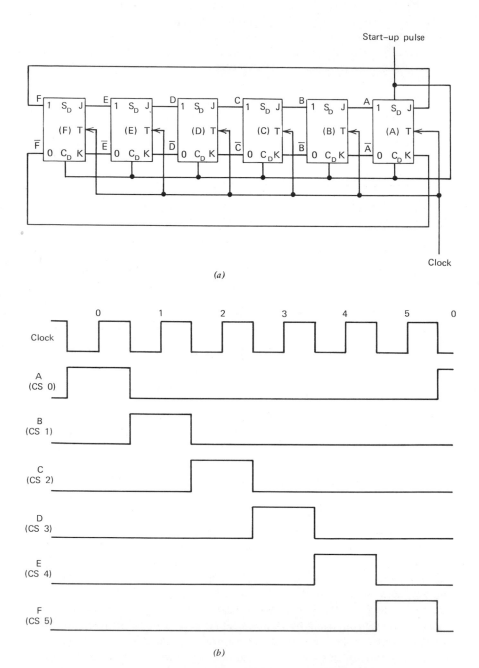

Figure 9-29. Six-stage ring counter and output waveforms.

logical-1), then as the single 1 is shifted down the register each stage output becomes logical-1 for only one count interval and does so in a fixed sequence. The operation of shifting a logical-1 around in a "ring" leads to the circuit being referred to as *ring counter*. The resulting output waveforms from the unit which can be used as clock step signals is directly obtained from the individual stage outputs. The stage A output can be used as CS0, the first clock step, the stage B output as CS1, the second step, and so on. No additional decoding is needed.

Comparing Figures 9-28 and 9-29 we can notice a few differences.

1. Decoder counter requires only *n* stages for 2^n count steps. If, for example, a count of eight steps is needed ($2^3 = 8$), then a three-stage counter is sufficient. However, eight three-input decoding gates are also needed.
2. If a ring counter is used to provide *N* count steps, then *N* counter stages are required. An eight-step count sequence requires eight counter stages — but no decoding gates are necessary.
3. The decoder counter can be reset at the start or it can begin operating at any step and will then provide sequential clock step signals. The ring counter *must* be initially started up so that there is only one stage in SET, the others all being RESET. Any power interruption or disturbance might also cause the single 1 to be "lost" or extra 1's to appear. In normal operation, however, no such action should take place. Figure 9-29*a* shows a start-up pulse results in stage A being SET and all other stages being RESET. The clock pulses then start the ring counter going and the stage outputs provide sequential clock step timing signals. A circuit that operates as a compromise between the full decode using a counter and no decode of a ring counter is shown in Figure 9-30*a*. The stages are connected as a shift-around register. However, the shift data is inverted on shift-around. The inversion results from the connection of 1-output to K input and 0-output to J input, opposite that for shifting directly between stages. The resulting count table in Figure 9-30*b* shows an eight-step cycle for the four counter stages. With four stages a regular counter will have 2^4 or 16 count steps, and a ring counter will have only four steps. The present connection is a compromise having eight count steps. To decode each step it is only necessary to use two inputs per decode gate as shown in Figure 9-30*c*, which is less decoding than with a regular four-stage counter but more than for a ring counter. The eight sequential decoded count steps are shown in Figure 9-30*d*.

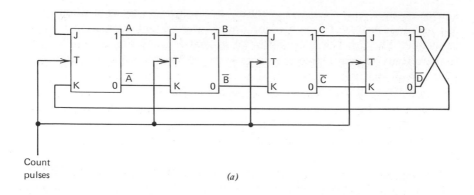

(a)

Count pulse	A	B	C	D
0	0	0	0	0
1	1	0	0	0
2	1	1	0	0
3	1	1	1	0
4	1	1	1	1
5	0	1	1	1
6	0	0	1	1
7	0	0	0	1
8 (or 0)	0	0	0	0

(b)

$\overline{A}$, $\overline{D}$ — CS0

A, $\overline{B}$ — CS1

B, $\overline{C}$ — CS2

C, $\overline{D}$ — CS3

A, D — CS4

$\overline{A}$, B — CS5

$\overline{B}$, C — CS6

$\overline{C}$, D — CS7

(c)

Figure 9-30. Inverting ring counter with decode gating. (a) Counter. (b) Count table. (c) Decode gating.

358

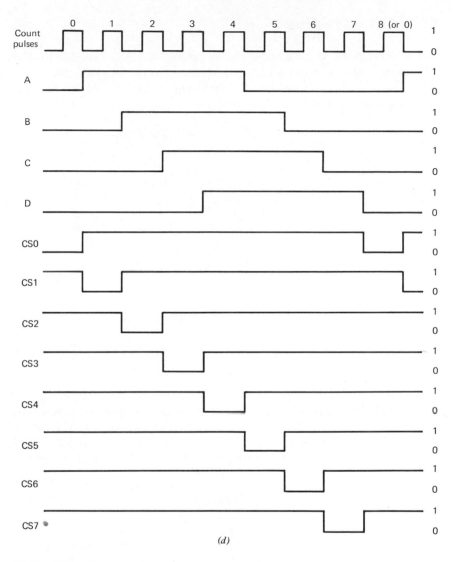

(d) Circuit waveforms.

Exercise 9-17.   Draw the logic diagram of a three-clock step decoder counter. Use TTL logic units.

Exercise 9-18.   Draw the logic diagram of a three-count step ring counter using TTL logic units.

9-5. BCD Code Counters

A number of BCD code counters are considered in this section to show additional techniques and more advanced counters. As examples to consider, Table 9-20 lists the 8421, excess-three, and 2*421 BCD codes (discussed in Chapter 4).

Table 9-20. *Code Table for a Few BCD Codes*

Decimal Digit	8421 Code				Excess-Three Code				2*421 Code			
	D	C	B	A	D	C	B	A	D	C	B	A
0	0	0	0	0	0	0	1	1	0	0	0	0
1	0	0	0	1	0	1	0	0	0	0	0	1
2	0	0	1	0	0	1	0	1	0	0	1	0
3	0	0	1	1	0	1	1	0	0	0	1	1
4	0	1	0	0	0	1	1	1	0	1	0	0
5	0	1	0	1	1	0	0	0	1	0	1	1
6	0	1	1	0	1	0	0	1	1	1	0	0
7	0	1	1	1	1	0	1	0	1	1	0	1
8	1	0	0	0	1	0	1	1	1	1	1	0
9	1	0	0	1	1	1	0	0	1	1	1	1
$\overline{10}$ (or $\overline{0}$)	$\overline{0}$	$\overline{0}$	$\overline{0}$	$\overline{0}$	$\overline{0}$	$\overline{0}$	$\overline{1}$	$\overline{1}$	$\overline{0}$	$\overline{0}$	$\overline{0}$	$\overline{0}$

The 8421 BCD code is provided by a decade counter, as was previously considered. An excess-three code counter can be designed by considering the necessary triggering of each counter stage to operate as specified in Table 9-20. A possible logic circuit is that of Figure 9-31a using RTL logic units. Using Table 9-20 the triggering required can be developed as described below.

1. Stage A alternates 1 to 0 and need only be toggled by the input count pulses.
2. Stage B toggles each time A goes 1 to 0 and additionally when the count goes from 9 to 10 (or 0). This latter condition causes somewhat of a problem. Referring to Table 9-20, B changes from 0 to 1 when the count goes from 9 to 10 but there is no obvious signal that can be used to provide a trigger at that time *which does not* block the triggering otherwise required. A technique that would not have been at all obvious but that is worth considering is shown in Figure 9-31a. Using available RTL NOR gates the logic gates perform the following logic operation.

$$B \text{ trigger} = A_d + B \cdot C \cdot \text{Input clock}$$

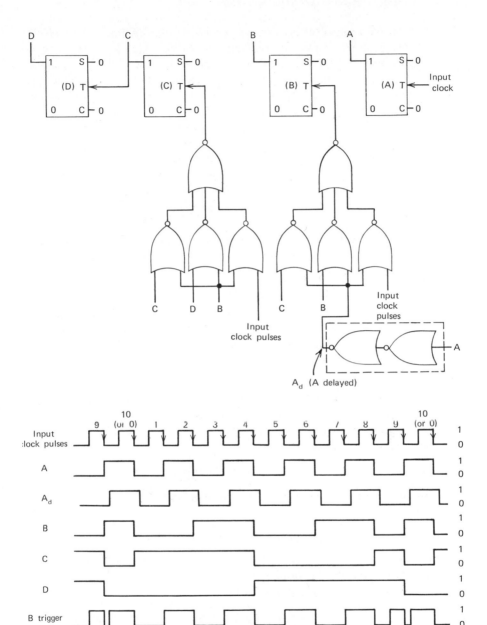

(b)

Figure 9-31. Excess-three counter.

where, A_d is the A output delayed by the switching time of two NOR stages. It must be pointed out that the clock which triggers stage A from 0 to 1 on the 9 to 10 step is used to provide the 1 to 0 change to trigger stage B. However, if A goes to 1 before the clock has sufficient time to cause the B stage to trigger, the counter will not perform as expected. To provide sufficient time the A signal used is delayed by the typical delay time of two NOR gates so that the B trigger signal goes to 1. The waveforms of Figure 9-31*b* should show more clearly how the delayed A signal and B trigger signal operate.

3. A similar problem exists when stage C is triggered by the logic signal.

$$C \text{ trigger} = B + C{\cdot}D{\cdot}\text{Input clock}$$

No delay problem exists here and the B change from 1 to 0 toggles stage C as does, additionally, the clock 1 to 0 change when $C = 1$ and $D = 1$.

4. Stage D is toggled each time C goes 1 to 0.

The 2*421 counter shown in Figure 9-32*a* is built using M/S JK flip-flops and TTL (or DTL) logic NAND gates. Figure 9-32*b* shows the resulting waveforms. The circuit operation is fairly straightforward, as described below.

1. Stage A toggles each clock pulse.
2. Stage B is toggled whenever A goes 1 to 0 and additionally when the clock goes 1 to 0 and $D = 0$, $C = 1$ (at count step 4 to 5). Delay of the A signal is required as provided by two NAND gates in series. The B trigger signal is

$$B \text{ trigger} = A + C{\cdot}\overline{D}{\cdot}\text{Input Clock}$$

3. Stage C is toggled when B goes 1 to 0 and additionally at step 4 to 5. The C trigger signal is

$$C \text{ trigger} = B + C{\cdot}\overline{D}{\cdot}\text{Input Clock}$$

No delay of B was necessary since stage B is already triggered at a delayed time after the clock goes 1 to 0.

4. Stage D is toggled by C going 1 to 0.

9-6.   Parallel (Clocked) Counters

A parallel or clocked counter is one in which all state changes occur simultaneously with the clock pulse, each stage change depending on its

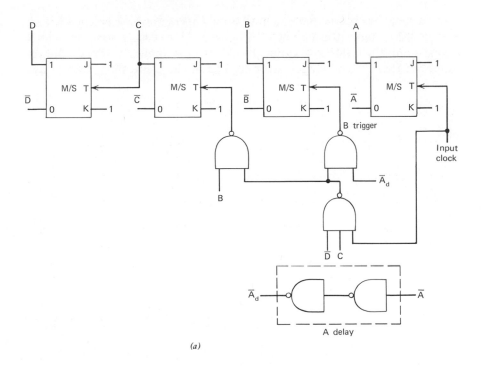

(a)

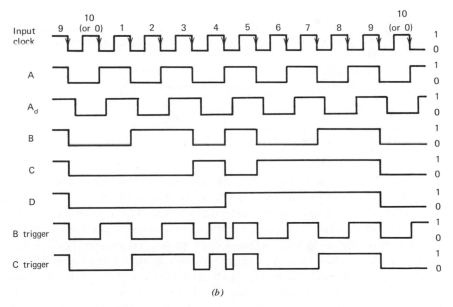

(b)

Figure 9-32.   2*421 counter.

logic gating. For an example, a mod-8 binary counter will be considered. Using RTL logic, the circuit of Figure 9-33 operates with the clock signal connected through gating to the trigger input of every counter stage. In this way all stages are triggered at the same time. Each stage

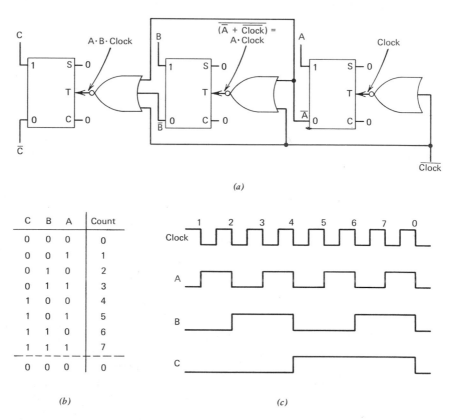

(a)

(b)

(c)

Figure 9-33.   Mod-8 parallel binary counter.

will then toggle, or not, depending on the state of the logic signals connected to it. Recall that a ripple counter requires a lower order stage to change state before any higher stage can change. There is thus a necessary time for the state changes to ripple down to the highest order state dependent on the switching delay in each stage. The accumulated delay over a large number of stages results in slower operating speed of the counter. Using the synchronized triggering technique as in Figure 9-33 all stages are triggered simultaneously so that the switching delay of the slowest stage is the total counter delay. Obviously, the cost of the extra gating to obtain parallel operation is part of the price for achieving faster counter operation.

1. The input stage of the mod-8 counter is triggered by the clock input signal and toggles on each pulse.

$$T_A \text{ (trigger signal of stage A)} = \text{Clock}$$

2. Stage B has as a trigger signal

$$T_B \text{ (trigger signal of stage B)} = \overline{(\overline{A} + \overline{\text{Clock}})} = A \cdot \text{Clock}$$

When A is 1, the clock signal going 1 to 0 triggers stage B.

   Referring to the count table in Figure 9-33b we see that this is the desired counter operation — that is, with $A = 1$ the next clock 1 to 0 change will cause the T_B signal 1 to 0 change. With $A = 0$, no change in T_B occurs.

3. State C trigger signal is

$$T_C = A \cdot B \cdot \text{Clock}$$

The table in Figure 9-33b shows that when both $A = 1$ and $B = 1$ stage C toggles on the next clock pulse.

The waveforms of Figure 9-33c are basically the same as for a ripple counter.

Mod-7 Counter. Parallel counters of any base can be built using logic inputs to J or K terminals to block some stage from changing thereby reducing the binary count. Figure 9-34 shows a mod-7 counter including count table and waveforms. Starting with count 001, the counter sequences normally up to 111 as shown. To eliminate the 000 count and thus obtain a seven-step sequence the condition of 111 is used to gate NAND gate N1 so that at the count of 111 the output of the gate goes low (logical-0). With J input logical-1 and K input logical-0 (at this count step) the next clock pulse will SET stage A. Since stage A is already SET at this time it remains $A = 1$. The other two stages are RESET at this time so that the count goes to 001. The count sequence thereby recycles every seven clock pulses providing a mod-7 counter.

Since all stages are triggered in synchronism with the clock, the speed of the counter is limited only by the slowest stage.

Mod-10 Parallel Counter. Another example of a parallel counter is the decade counter of Figure 9-35. Using a similar technique to that shown in Figure 9-34 the four counter stages are all gated so that they trigger when the clock goes 1 to 0 for synchronous operations. A NAND gate decodes

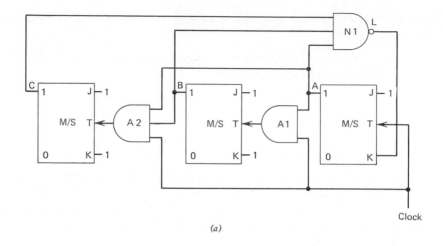

(a)

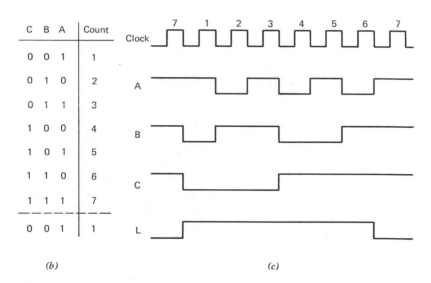

C	B	A	Count
0	0	1	1
0	1	0	2
0	1	1	3
1	0	0	4
1	0	1	5
1	1	0	6
1	1	1	7
0	0	1	1

(b)   (c)

Figure 9-34.   Mod-7 parallel counter.

the count of 1111 providing a logic-0 at that time so that at the next clock pulse the count becomes 0110, thereby avoiding six count steps with a resulting count cycle of ten steps.

The counter, although recycling after ten clock pulses, does not provide a BCD sequence that is usually desired. A decade counter providing an 8421 BCD count sequence can be built as a parallel counter as shown in Figure 9-36. Notice that each stage is triggered synchronously by the

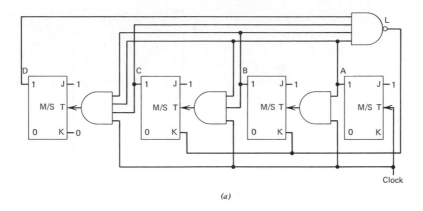

(a)

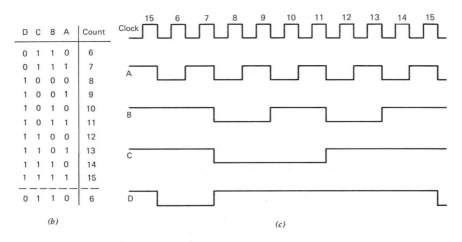

(b)   (c)

Figure 9-35.   Mod-10 parallel counter.

clock pulse. Stage B is triggered by the clock each time A = 1 except when D = 1 ($\overline{D}$ = 0) as specified in the count table of Figure 9-36b. Stage D is not triggered on every clock pulse when A = 1. The J input logic signal, however, is logical-0 except at the count of 0111, so that stage D is held reset except at step 0111 when stage D is toggled by the clock pulse.

When more than three or four stages are used, the additional input gating needed to provide a gated clock pulse results in more gating than other types covered previously. When speed is important, however, the added cost is then justified.

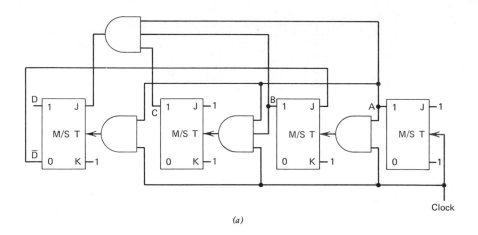

(a)

D	C	B	A	Count
0	0	0	0	0
0	0	0	1	1
0	0	1	0	2
0	0	1	1	3
0	1	0	0	4
0	1	0	1	5
0	1	1	0	6
0	1	1	1	7
1	0	0	0	8
1	0	0	1	9
0	0	0	0	0

(b)

Figure 9-36.   Decade parallel counter with 8421 BCD count sequence.

9-7.   Up-Down Counter

When it is necessary to provide both count-up and count-down operation, it is possible to obtain both using a single up-down counter. A straight forward example is shown by the three-stage up-down binary ripple counter in Figure 9-37. Recall that using 1-output as trigger to the

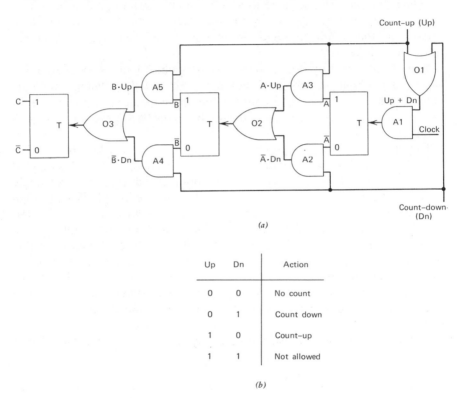

(a)

Up	Dn	Action
0	0	No count
0	1	Count down
1	0	Count–up
1	1	Not allowed

(b)

Figure 9-37.   Three-stage up-down binary ripple counter.

following stage gives count-up action, although using the 0-output gives count-down action. In Figure 9-37 a clock signal is supplied to operate the counter as well as two control signals. The Table in Figure 9-37b shows that with both $Up = 0$ and $Dn = 0$ no action results even with the clock signal present. If $Up = 0$ and $Dn = 1$ then AND gates A2 and A4 are enabled providing a 0-output signal as trigger for the following stage — this giving count-down operation. With $Up = 1$ and $Dn = 0$, AND gates A3 and A5 are enabled and the 1-output signals provide count-up operation.

Both Up = 1 and Dn = 1 are not allowed and the two possible operating conditions are mutually exclusive. Stage A is triggered by the clock for either Up = 1 or Dn = 1 and not at all if both are logical-0. One problem with the present gating arrangement is that a false trigger pulse may occur when the Up or Dn enable pulse turns off. For example, if A = 1 and the Up signal turns off (goes 1 to 0), a 1 to 0 change results at the B stage trigger input causing the stage to toggle. In an operating situation where the counter accumulates a count and then switches to count-down operation, the count-up enable signal switching off may completely upset the counter state.

A more practical up-down counter is shown in Figure 9-38 using RTL logic units. The logic design of such a counter is helped using a table as shown in Figure 9-38a. The count value and present state binary count are shown. Recall that in either count-up or count-down operation stage A is directly toggled.

Using RTL flip-flops, a stage is SET with S = 1 and C = 0, RESET with S = 0 and C = 1, no change for both S = 1 and C = 1, and is toggled when S = 0 and C = 0. Starting at the count of 000 the necessary logic signals to get to count to 001 on a count-up operation is to hold both stage C and B reset. This requires providing $C_C = 1$ and $C_B = 1$ (C_C = C input of stage C, C_B = C input of stage B). The S_C and S_B at this time can be considered a don't care (d) signal, that is, it really doesn't matter at this time if S_C and S_B are logical-1 or logical-0. If, for example, S_C is logical-0 then the clock pulse will cause stage C to be cleared (which it already is). With $S_C = 1$ (and $C_C = 1$) no change will result when the clock pulse occurs — but since stage C is 0 and should next be 0 no change was necessary.

A count of 001 clock pulse should cause stage B to change to 1 so that

Count	Present state			Up				Down			
	C	B	A	S_C	C_C	S_B	C_B	S_C	C_C	S_B	C_C
0	0	0	0	d	1	d	1	1	0	1	0
1	0	0	1	d	1	1	0	d	1	d	1
2	0	1	0	d	1	1	d	d	1	0	1
3	0	1	1	1	0	0	1	d	1	1	d
4	1	0	0	1	d	d	1	0	1	1	0
5	1	0	1	1	d	1	0	1	d	d	1
6	1	1	0	1	d	1	d	1	d	0	1
7	1	1	1	0	1	0	1	1	d	1	d

(a)

Figure 9-38.   Three-stage parallel up-down counter. (a) Logic table.

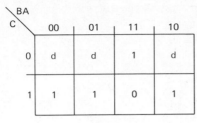

BA C	00	01	11	10
0	d	d	1	d
1	1	1	0	1

$(S_C)_{Up} = \overline{A \cdot B \cdot C} = \overline{A} + \overline{B} + \overline{C}$

BA C	00	01	11	10
0	1	1	0	1
1	d	d	1	d

$(C_C)_{Up} = \overline{A \cdot B \cdot \overline{C}} = \overline{A} + \overline{B} + C$

BA C	00	01	11	10
0	d	1	0	1
1	d	1	0	1

$(S_B)_{Up} = \overline{A} + \overline{B}$

BA C	00	01	11	10
0	1	0	1	d
1	1	0	1	d

$(S_B)_{Dn} = \overline{A} + B$

BA C	00	01	11	10
0	1	d	d	d
1	0	1	1	1

$(S_C)_{Dn} = \overline{\overline{A} \cdot \overline{B} \cdot C} = A + B + \overline{C}$

BA C	00	01	11	10
0	0	1	1	1
1	1	d	d	d

$(C_C)_{Dn} = \overline{\overline{A} \cdot \overline{B} \cdot \overline{C}} = A + B + C$

BA C	00	01	11	10
0	1	d	1	0
1	1	d	1	0

$(C_B)_{Up} = A + \overline{B}$

BA C	00	01	11	10
0	0	1	d	1
1	0	1	d	1

$(C_B)_{Dn} = A + B$

(b)

(b) Karnaugh maps.

371

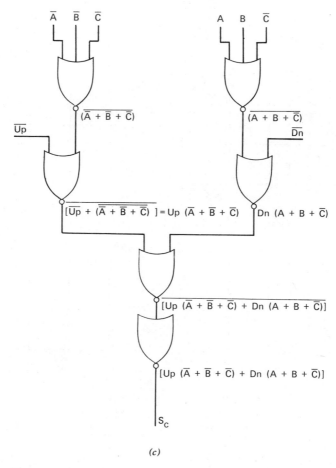

(c)

Figure 9-38. *(c)* Logic gating for S_c.

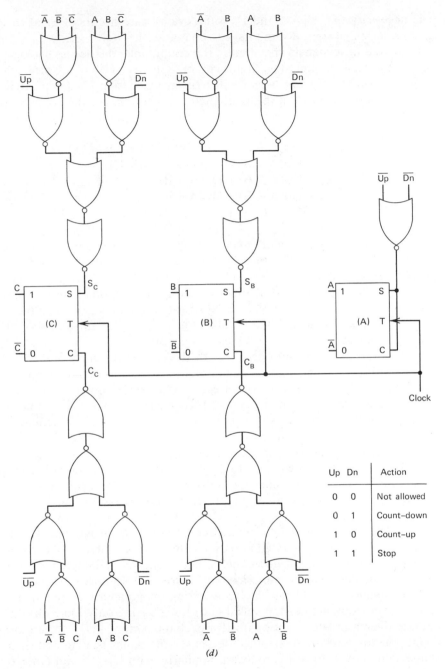

Figure 9-38. (*d*) Full counter circuit.

373

it is necessary that $S_B = 1$ and $C_B = 0$. A don't care occurs at S_C at this time because that stage doesn't have to change at this step.

Using the logic signals specified in the count table, the necessary logic signals for each counter stage input can be obtained. Use of a Karnaugh map as shown in Figure 9-38b will help in the design. A set of logic expressions obtained from the Karnaugh maps to operate the counter is as follows:

$$S_C = Up(\overline{A} + \overline{B} + \overline{C}) + Dn(A + B + \overline{C})$$
$$C_C = Up(\overline{A} + \overline{B} + C) + Dn(A + B + C)$$
$$S_B = Up(\overline{A} + \overline{B}) + Dn(A + \overline{B})$$
$$C_B = Up(\overline{A} + B) + Dn(A + B)$$
$$S_A = C_A = UpDn$$

To see how this gating is obtained the logic signals for S_C is covered in detail in Figure 9-38c. The basic pattern to be used requires two logic NOR gates to obtain the (S_C) up signal and two more for the (S_C) signal. These are ORed using a NOR-inverter gating connection. Thus, each S and C input signal requires six logic NOR gates as shown in the complete counter circuit of Figure 9-38d. A signal is used to gate stage A so that count action will not take place if $Up = 1$ and $Dn = 1$.

The present counter can operate with the clock constantly present at the trigger input of each stage. The counter action is controlled by the Up and Dn logic signals as specified in Figure 9-38d. With only the Up signal high, for example, the counter begins advancing the count by one for each clock pulse. When the Dn signal then goes high the count immediately stops and further clock pulses have no effect on the counter stage. In fact, when $Up = 1$ and $Dn = 1$ the S and C inputs to all stages are logical-1 so that no change takes place due to the clock pulse. No situation of Up or Dn control signal changing causing a false triggering of the counter results with the present circuit (as long as both Up and Dn are not logical-0).

BCD Decade Up-Down Counter. Because of its great popularity, the circuit of an 8421 code (BCD) parallel up-down counter is shown in Figure 9-39. The design follows the procedure just covered and only the results of the design are summerized in Figure 9-39. In operation the Up and Dn signals are both logical-1 preventing the counter from changing state. If, for example, the Up signal goes low (leaving only Dn high) the counter decreases the count by one for each input clock pulse. When the count goes to zero the next pulse decreases the count to nine and then sequentially down toward zero again. Similarly, with $Up = 1$ and $Dn = 0$ the count then sequences up to nine and then back to zero.

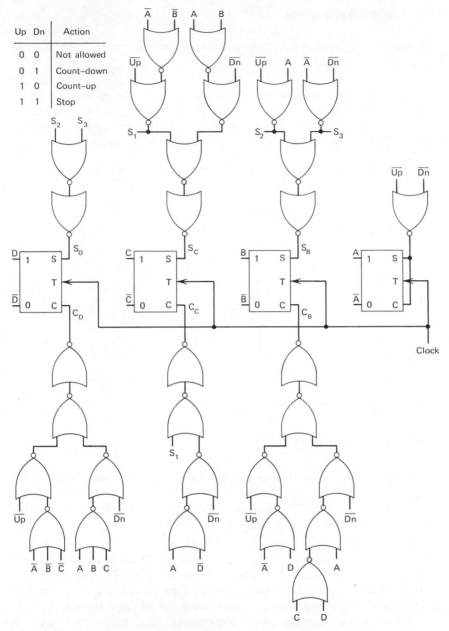

Up	Dn	Action
0	0	Not allowed
0	1	Count–down
1	0	Count–up
1	1	Stop

Figure 9-39.   BCD up-down parallel counter.

9-8.   Counter Applications

It might be helpful at this time to consider some practical applications using various types of counters.

Octal Counter. An octal counter can be built using groups of three-stage counters. Each three-stage group can provide a count from 000 to 111 or from 0 to 7 in octal. If Nixie display lights are used, the counter binary outputs can be used, as shown in Figure 9-40, to provide an octal display.

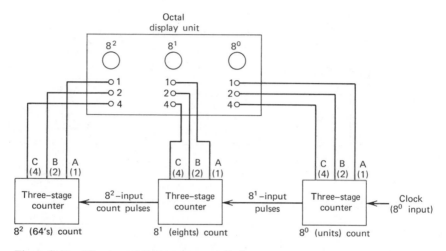

Figure 9-40.   Three-octal digit counter and display.

The first (8^0) counter is operated by the input clock and advances sequentially through the eight count states 000 to 111, one count step for each input clock pulse. The decimal display operated by the stage outputs of this counter section will display the numeric 0 to 7 sequentially following the binary count of the three output lines.

When the first octal count stage goes from 7 to 0 the 8^1 counter section is advanced by one count pulse up to a total count of 77 for the two octal sections. Similarly, each time the 8^1 stage goes from 7 to 0 the 8^2 section is advanced by one count up to a total count for all three sections of 777.

Using nine stages in groups of three allows an octal equivalent count from 000 to 777 as read directly on the display lights. (The individual stage outputs can be read as octal-coded binary if no display lights are used.)

Decade Counter. An arrangement similar to that just covered can be used to form a decade counter. Using three decade counter sections as shown in Figure 9-41 will allow a count up to 999 as indicated on the decimal display lights. A clock pulse triggers the first (10^0) stage which

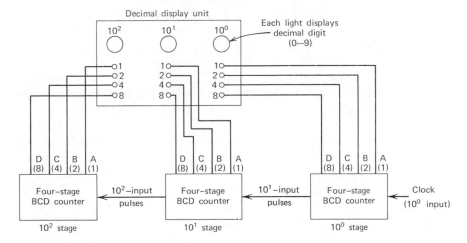

Figure 9-41.   Three-decimal digit counter and display.

counts from 0000 to 1001 in BCD code. The four output lines of that stage connect to a Nixie light display unit, which converts the BCD input to an equivalent decimal numeral display. Each time the BCD count goes from 1001 to 0000 a single pulse triggers the next BCD counter advancing its count by one. Although the second (10^1) stage is identical to the other stages its count and decimal display digit changes once every ten clock pulses giving it a weight of 10 (so that it represents the 10^1 position).

A pulse from the 10^1 stage that occurs when the 10^1 count goes from 9 to 0 is used to trigger the 10^2 stage. The overall count goes from decimal 000 to 999 and then back to 000.

Counter Gate Control. In many applications it is necessary to start and stop a counter from operating. This is typically done by disabling the clock pulses used to trigger the counter. A simple means of gating is shown in Figure 9-42.

The clock signal as shown contains a continuous train of pulses. With the gate input logical-0 the output of the AND gate remains logical-0 and no counter input pulses result. When the gate signal goes to logical-1 it enables the AND gate so that a number of clock pulses appear at the

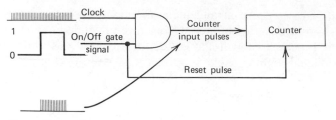

Figure 9-42.   Counter gate control.

counter input causing the count to increase. The number of counter pulses received depends on the time interval of the gate signal (and on the clock rate itself).

Frequency Counter. Numerous techniques are used to provide a gate pulse. Figure 9-43 shows a single shot being triggered on by a start signal. The gate interval of the single shot is fixed by the circuits own time constant, providing a fixed gate interval. Using the single-shot 1-output normally logical-0 to hold the counter reset, the counter would then count up clock pulses for the fixed gate interval.

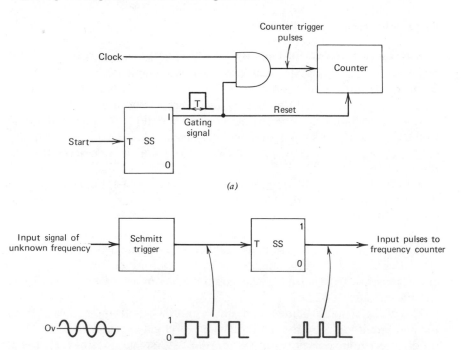

Figure 9-43.   Gate signal of set pulse width.

This scheme would provide operation as a digital frequency meter. By proper scaling of the counter and gate interval the resulting count should be seen to depend on the clock rate. If the gate interval were set at, say 1 msec (10^{-3} seconds), then a count of 675 would correspond to the counter receiving 675 clock pulses in 0.001 sec, which is equivalent to a clock rate of

$$\frac{675 \text{ pulses}}{0.001 \text{ seconds}} = 675 \times 10^3 \text{ cycles per second} = 675 \text{ kHz}$$

The counter could be a 3-stage decade counter as shown in Figure 9-41 so that the numeric display between 000 and 999 can be read as the clock rate of the input signal in kHz. It should be clear now that by varying the single shot gate signal interval could result in changing the frequency scale of the digital meter. For example, increasing the interval to 0.01 seconds would change the scale to hundreds of cycles. A count of 675 would then result if the clock rate were

$$\frac{675 \text{ pulses}}{0.01 \text{ seconds}} = 67,500 \text{ pulses per second} = 67.5 \text{ kHz}$$

If the input signal is not a digital-type clock pulse train it must first be converted to a pulse-like signal. Figure 9-43*b* shows how a Schmitt trigger may be used to square up the slowly varying input signal to provide a more suitable signal. In addition, a single shot could then be used (if necessary) to shape the clock pulse to a narrow pulse width as shown.

Example 9-1.   If the input signal resulted in a count of 755 using a gate interval of 0.1 msec, what is the frequency of the input signal?

Solution: $\dfrac{755 \text{ pulse}}{0.1 \text{ msec}} = 7550 \times 10^{-3} \text{ pulses per second}$

$$= 7550 \text{ kHz} = 7.55 \text{ MHz}$$

A similar technique to that just discussed could be used to determine the interval of an input signal. Figure 9-44 shows the gating arrangement. Using a Schmitt trigger circuit to square up the input signal and a toggle flip-flop to provide a pulse width exactly set to one cycle of the input signal results in a gate signal whose width is the same as the interval of one cycle of input signal. A clock is used having a rate much faster than that of the input signal whose interval is to be measured. If the reference clock rate is an accurate 1 MHz and the input signal results in an interval of 10 msec, the counter would read

$$10^6 \frac{\text{pulses}}{\text{second}} \times (10 \times 10^{-3}) \text{ seconds} = 10,000$$

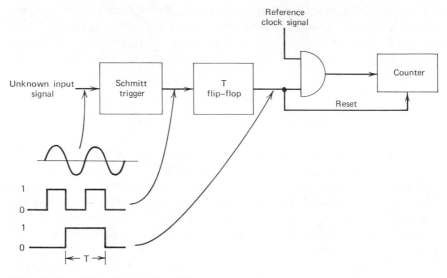

Figure 9-44.   Measuring signal period.

A resulting count of 10,000 would then indicate an interval of one cycle of the input signal of 1 msec. Similarly, a count of 1000 would be interpreted as 1 msec and a count of 825 would be read as 0.825 msec or 825 μsec. Thus, a clock rate of 1 MHz sets a time scale of 1 μsec (per count step).

Example 9-2.   What clock rates are needed to provide interval scale settings of (a) 5 μsec; (b) 1 msec? What would a count of 500 be interpreted as for each scale setting?

Solution:

(a)

$$f = \frac{1}{T} = \frac{1}{5\,\mu\text{sec}} = \frac{10^6}{5} = 200\,\text{kHz}$$

A clock rate of 200 kHz would provide a time scale of 5 μsec. For a count of 500 the input signal interval is

$$500 \times 5\,\mu\text{sec} = 2500\,\mu\text{sec} = 2.5\,\text{msec}$$

(b) A clock rate of

$$f = \frac{1}{T} = \frac{1}{1\,\text{msec}} = 1\,\text{kHz}$$

would give a 1 msec scale factor. For a count of 500, the input signal interval is

$$500 \times 1 \text{ msec} = 500 \text{ msec} = 0.5 \text{ sec}$$

Digital Voltmeter. Another possible application using a counter is a digital voltmeter. (See Figure 9-45.) The heat of the system is a circuit

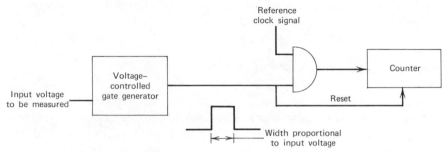

Figure 9-45.   Digital voltmeter.

that provides a pulse whose width is proportional to the input voltage to be measured. Thus, an input voltage of, say, 1 mV might result in an output pulse width of 1 msec and an input voltage of 50 mV might then result in an output pulse width of 50 msec. Using this output signal to gate an accurate reference clock signal the resulting count can be interpreted as the value of input voltage. Using a 1 MHz clock a count of 50,000 (in 50 msec) would then be read as 50 mV.

Example 9-3.   A digital voltmeter circuit using a 10 MHz clock has a voltage-controlled gate generator that provides a width of 10 msec per volt of input signal. What is the meter scale and what voltage would a count of 750 be equivalent to?

Solution: Counting at 10×10^6 pulses per second

$$T = \frac{1}{f} = \frac{1}{10 \times 10^6} = 0.1 \text{ msec per pulse}$$

In 10 msec the pulse count would be

$$\frac{10}{0.1} = 100$$

A count of 100 is then equivalent to 1 volt of input signal and the scale factor is

$$\frac{1}{100} \text{ volts/count step} = 0.01 \text{ volts/count step}$$

A count of 750 steps then corresponds to

$$750 \text{ steps} \times \frac{1}{100} \frac{\text{volts}}{\text{step}} = 7.5 \text{ volts}$$

It should be clear that the accuracy of such a meter depends most critically on the linearity of the voltage to pulse width converter circuit. More detail on such analog (voltage) to digital conversion is covered in Chapter 13.

9-9.   Digital Timer (Clock)

Another counter application, but one that will be covered in more detail, is that of a digital timer or clock which would provide decimal display of hours, minutes, and seconds. A simplified diagram of the required circuitry is shown in Figure 9-46. The clock pulses for the unit is taken from the 60-Hz voltage supply line. A Schmitt trigger circuit is used to square up the input sinusoidal waveform. The 60 Hz is divided in frequency by a mod-60 counter whose output is then at 1 cycle per second.

Using a mod-60 counter made of mod-10 and mod-6 counters in series the counter output as observed on a decimal display light (such as a Nixie light or a 7-segment light) is a decimal number that goes sequentially from 00 to 59 and then recycles to 00.

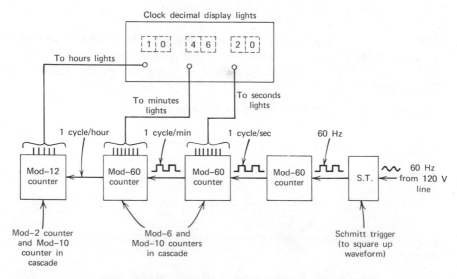

Figure 9-46.   Simplified block diagram of electronic clock.

A duplicate mod-60 counter is triggered once a minute by the output of the second counter. Each time the second counter recycles from 59 to 00 it triggers the minute counter. The minute counter also provides a sequential count from 00 to 59, recycling then to 00.

Finally, a pulse from the minute counter which occurs when the count goes from 59 to 00 triggers the mod-12 hour counter. An arrangement whereby the counter goes from 01 to 12 and then recycles to 01 provides a count of the hour.

The circuit as indicated here is to provide a representative example of how counters can be incorporated into a larger operating unit. It should be pointed out that the present cost of building such a system is relatively expensive and that mechanical clocks that move a fixed number display to provide minutes and hours is far cheaper and more common to find.

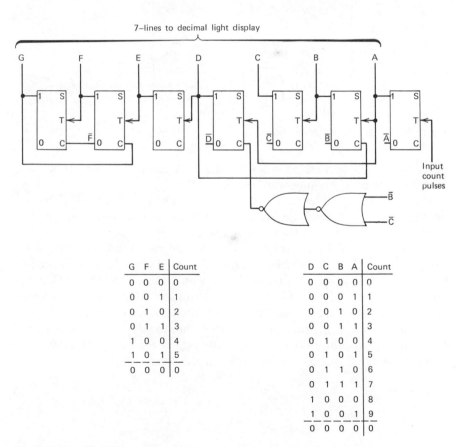

G	F	E	Count
0	0	0	0
0	0	1	1
0	1	0	2
0	1	1	3
1	0	0	4
1	0	1	5
0	0	0	0

D	C	B	A	Count
0	0	0	0	0
0	0	0	1	1
0	0	1	0	2
0	0	1	1	3
0	1	0	0	4
0	1	0	1	5
0	1	1	0	6
0	1	1	1	7
1	0	0	0	8
1	0	0	1	9
0	0	0	0	0

Figure 9-47.   Mod-60 counter.

In any case an electronic clock is an elegant circuit to study and fits in nicely with the present topic of interest.

Each of the three mod-60 counters can be built using a mod-10 and mod-6 counter as has already been covered. Figure 9-47 shows two such counters connected in a mod-60 count configuration and the resulting output count sequence. The seven output lines are in BCD code (8421 code) and can be used directly to excite a display light unit having a built-in decoder circuit. If only a light unit is used, an additional IC decoder unit is required.

A mod-12 counter used to provide the hour count is shown in Figure 9-48. Notice the count table showing the count sequence 1 to 12. In

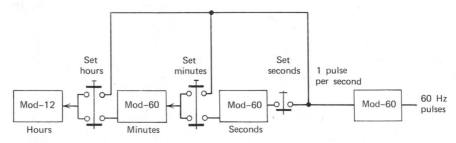

Figure 9-48.   Mod-12 counter for hours.

order to obtain the desired count sequence a combination of ripple and parallel counter techniques were used.

The complete counter unit so far shown can be built using IC units. In addition one could build the Schmitt trigger unit and dc power supply for the IC circuit using discrete components.

The decode and light display can be bought as a complete unit or as separate units that are fully built. One additional consideration is setting the clock when power is first turned on and some random clock time appears. Figure 9-49 shows how push buttons can be arranged to allow interrupting the normal pulse flow and using the 1 pulse per second signal to advance each of the time counters to obtain the desired clock reading. Pressing the push buttons to sequentially adjust the hours, minutes, and seconds counters will allow synchronizing the clock.

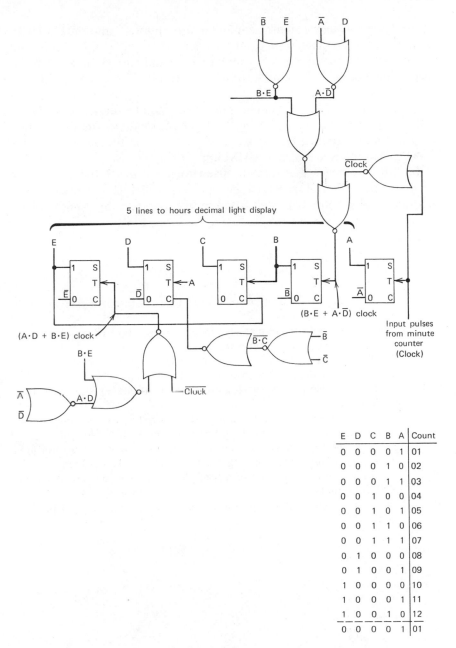

5 lines to hours decimal light display

(A·D + B·E) clock

B·E

(B·E + A·D̄) clock

Input pulses
from minute
counter
(Clock)

E	D	C	B	A	Count
0	0	0	0	1	01
0	0	0	1	0	02
0	0	0	1	1	03
0	0	1	0	0	04
0	0	1	0	1	05
0	0	1	1	0	06
0	0	1	1	1	07
0	1	0	0	0	08
0	1	0	0	1	09
1	0	0	0	0	10
1	0	0	0	1	11
1	0	0	1	0	12
0	0	0	0	1	01

Figure 9-49. Sychronizing count of clock timer.

385

Summary

Basic parts of every digital computer are counters and data transfer registers. Flip-flop stages may be toggled to provide either count-up or count-down operation. The number of a unique count is 2^n for n stages; for example, 8 counts with 3 stages (2^3), 32 counts with five stages (2^5).

When other than a binary count is desired, count feedback, count reset, or direct reset techniques may be used. These modulus (mod) counters are found quite frequently, the most common being the decade counter that can be purchased as a single MSI unit.

The bistable stages may also be used to make up shift registers for serial data transfer and transfer registers for parallel data transfer. Combinations of these are also built to provide serial data input and parallel data output or vice versa.

PROBLEMS

§9-1   **1.** Draw the block diagram of a five-stage count-down register using TTL-type JK flip-flops.

§9-2   **2.** Draw the logic diagram of a feedback advance mod-18 counter.

3. Design a mod-14 counter using count reset.

4. Design a mod-5 counter using direct reset for JK flip-flops.

5. Design a mod-18 direct reset counter using JK flip-flops.

§9-3   **6.** Draw the logic diagram of a four-stage shift-left register using TTL JK flip-flops.

7. Draw the logic diagram of a four-stage register with parallel transfer of input data and shift-right of output data using TTL JK flip-flops.

8. Draw the logic diagram of a three-stage shift-right register for input data and parallel transfer of output data using TTL JK flip-flops.

§9-4   **9.** Draw the logic diagram of a four-clock step decoder counter using TTL logic units.

10. Draw the logic diagram of a four-step ring counter using TTL logic units.

Section Three

COMPUTER UNITS

1010

Computer timing and control

10-1. General

Although a computer seems to "think" and act automatically, in actuality it only performs very simple steps in a set order. The control unit is the part of the computer that provides the basic timing signals to operate all units of the computer. Although the stored program directs the main flow of operations to be performed, the control unit still provides for all the little steps that must be taken for each command executed.

The difference between a "wired" operation and the operation with a stored program should be appreciated. By "wired" we mean those that are carried out automatically by special circuits of the computer. For example, the multiply and divide operations may be wired so that a single multiply or divide command starts the operation and all the little steps needed to carry out the command are provided by the control unit. If the computer had only add or subtract commands, the multiply and divide could still be performed as a number of steps of a stored program. The difference is mainly speed of execution, the wired operation being faster.

The control unit may vary considerably from one computer to another depending on what commands are wired and the type of internal memory, whether serial or parallel operations are performed, and so on. Although details of a control unit can become involved, there are basic parts that may be studied. These include counters, diode matrices, decoding gates, and registers. When all operation is controlled by a master clock (astable oscillator, for example), the computer operates synchronously. If synchronous operation is too slow (it requires waiting a set time interval to begin the next step), asynchronous operation is used where the next step occurs immediately after the present one is completed. Before considering the overall operation of a control unit, some of the basic parts will be studied.

389

10-2. Timing Signals

In any computer it is necessary to provide a group of timing signals which are present in a set sequence and which may then be used to gate various computer circuits. These gating signals provide an automatic means of stepping the computer circuits through a fixed routine to carry out all the necessary smaller steps to execute an instruction. Timing signals are obtained using counters and decoding logic gates. Some consideration of developing timing signals has already been covered in Chapter 9. We will now expand on the material presented with the emphasis on the timing property of the signals under consideration.

Using a three-stage counter provides for counting 2^3 or eight count steps. The count step is read as the binary value of the counter stage outputs. These logic signals can be decoded using logic gates so that a separate count step signal is present for each count value. Figure 10-1 shows a three-stage binary counter with logic decode. The counter steps from 000 to 111 in binary sequence on each clock pulse. Eight decoding gates are used, each to detect a different step of the counter. For example, at the count of 000 the input $\overline{A} = 1$, $\overline{B} = 1$, $\overline{C} = 1$ cause CS0 to be high (logical-1) all other gates remaining logical-0 at that time. (Check each gate inputs to see that at this count step at least one gate input is logical-0 and only the CS0 gate has all inputs logical-1.) The gating will thus decode each count value so that only one gate provides logical-1 for each count step. The gates are numbered CS0 to CS7 corresponding to count step 0 to count step 7 of the counter. The logic waveforms show how the count step signals provide sequential output pulses. As timing signals we can use CS0 to gate certain computer circuits and CS1 to gate other circuits knowing that step CS0 will occur before step CS1 occurs. Thus, we can connect these timing signals to various places in the computer to achieve an operation that requires a sequence of steps.

For an example, consider the gating of Figure 10-2. The block-logic diagram is quite simplified but should provide some understanding of how count step pulses are used. At CS0 the data transfer register is cleared (reset). At CS1 input data is parallel transfered into the data transfer register. Although ten data lines and gates are needed only one is symbolically shown in Figure 10-2. During steps CS2 and CS3 no change in the register shown takes place. It should be clear that at these steps other operations in separate circuits of the computer could be taking place. At CS4 a clock, having a frequency which results in ten pulse during a count step, is gated as shift pulses to serially transfer data out of the register.

Another example of a counter and decoder logic is the five-step sequence generator of Figure 10-3. As shown, a count sequence of five steps is

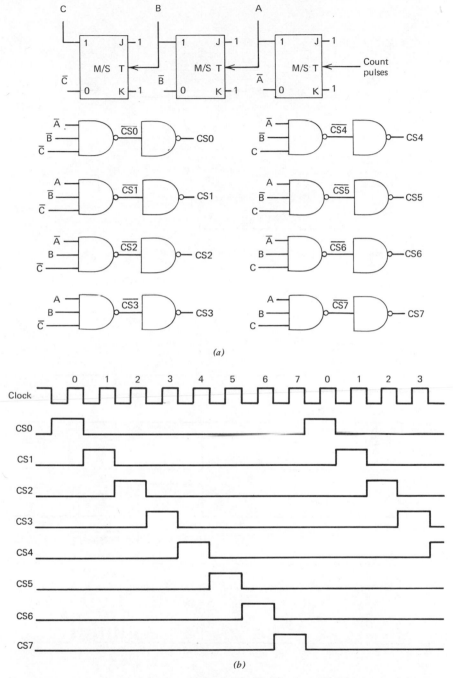

Figure 10-1. Three-stage binary counter with logic decode. (*a*) Logic circuit. (*b*) Circuit waveforms.

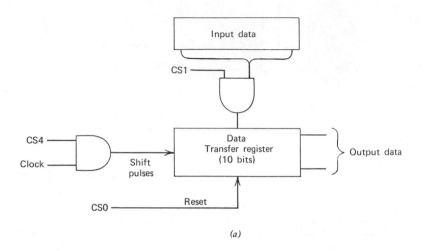

(a)

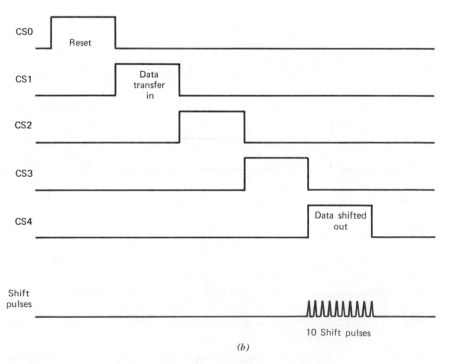

(b)

Figure 10-2. Sample operation using count step pulses.

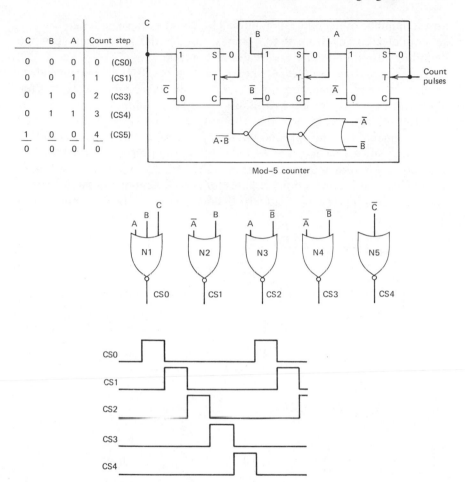

C	B	A	Count step	
0	0	0	0	(CS0)
0	0	1	1	(CS1)
0	1	0	2	(CS3)
0	1	1	3	(CS4)
1	0	0	4	(CS5)
0	0	0	0	

Figure 10-3.   Five-step counter and decoding logic.

generated using a mod-5 counter (built with RTL units) and five logic decode gates. In the present example the count steps (specified in the count table shown) are decoded using five logic NOR gates. If $A = 0$, $B = 0$, and $C = 0$, for example, the output of gate N1 is $CS0 = 1$. When the count gets to 010, for example, the conditions $A = 0$ and $\bar{B} = 0$ are sufficient to provide $CS2 = 1$. Looking at the count table we note that C is 1 only on step 4 and inverting C in gate N5 provides the CS4 pulse (which could have been taken directly off the counter stage C output).

The five count steps provide timing signals for computer operations. The present five-step counter showed that sometimes it is possible to save

on the number of decode gate inputs. The count pattern generally used—
sequential stepping from 0 to 5—may not be the most suitable when
decoding into timing signals is the desired output.

A modified ring counter is shown in Figure 10-4; it can provide a
sequence of ten count step signals using only five count stages and ten
logic gates each with only two inputs. The JK flip-flop are connected as
a shift-right register. Notice that the outputs from stage A are reversed
when connected as shift-around to stage E. Thus, a 0 in stage A is shifted
as a 1 into stage E. This pattern of shifting to the right and bit reversal on
shift around is shown for each of the ten cycle steps in the table of Figure
10-4. This simple connection provides ten distinct count steps and furthermore these steps can be uniquely decoded using only two inputs to a

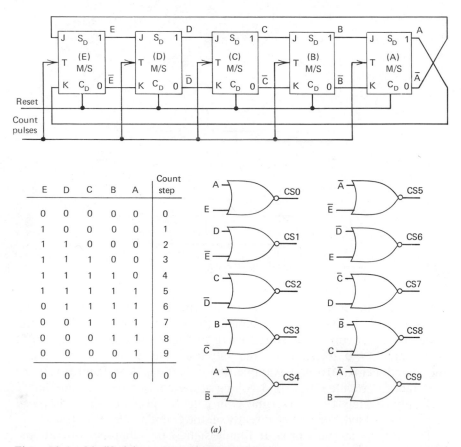

Figure 10-4.   Modified ring counter with ten-step count.

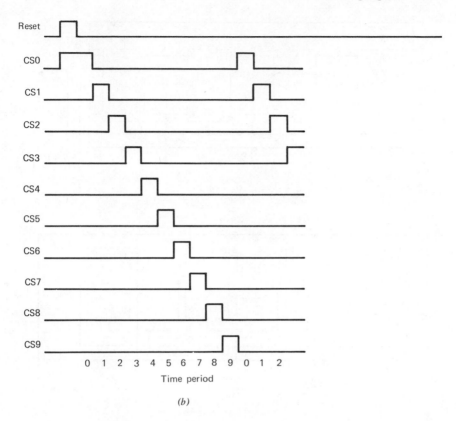

(b)

NOR gate. The decoding shown in Figure 10-4a will provide the count step pulses shown in Figure 10-4b.

To initiate to counter a reset pulse clears all five stages placing the count at 00000. When the reset pulse is over the counter will then sequence through CS0 to CS9 cyclically providing ten steps for use as timing signals.

The same ten count step signals could be obtained using a ten-stage shift-around register with a single 1 as data. However, the choice of only five stages with ten two-input gates is probably a more reasonable logic circuit. In addition, each stage of the present logic circuit changes stage only once every five clock pulses so that a higher clock rate is possible with the present circuit.

If a ring counter is to be used the logic connections shown in Figure 10-5 might be a suitable choice. The ring counter in Figure 10-5a is basically a shift register shifting a single logical-1 around to provide a

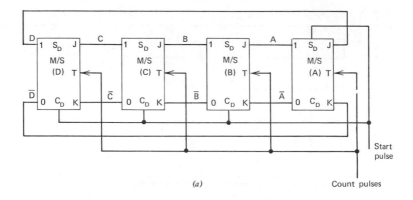

(a)

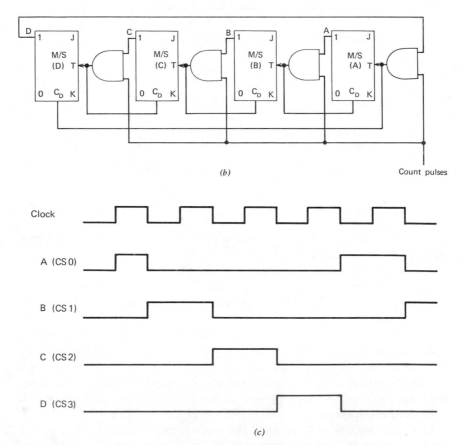

(b)

(c)

Figure 10-5. Count steps generated using ring counter. (*a*) Four-stage ring counter using shift-around register. (*b*) Four-stage ring counter using M/S JK flip-flops. (*c*) Waveforms.

396

set of four timing pulses. Figure 10-5b develops the ring counter operation by toggling consecutive stages and resetting the present stage each clock pulse. Either way the output waveforms of Figure 10-5c result directly from the stage outputs with no gating required.

10-3. Fetch-Execute Cycle

Operation of the control unit depends greatly on the details of the computer—whether it operates in serial or parallel, what type of memory it has, what types of input/output are used, how arithmetic operations are performed, and so on. It also depends on how the computer is programmed. The machine language used in Chapter 3 is for a one-address machine. Two-, three-, and four-address machines have also been built and will be described after some fundamental ideas have been considered. We shall use the one-address machine as our example to make these ideas clear. Recall first that the solution to a problem to be run on a computer requires a listing of computer operations called the program. In its elementary form the program contains machine language statements similar to those described in Chapter 3. Although originally placed on punched card or tape, the program is stored in the computer memory before it is executed. One program step is handled at a time, starting from the first, with the possibility of branch instructions resulting in the elimination of some steps or the repetition of others. With the program instructions stored in memory, the computer must now perform a basic set of steps to operate on these instructions. It must first read the instruction from memory into the control unit (FETCH). In the control unit the parts of the instruction are separated and appropriate control (command and timing) signals are generated to perform the instruction (EXECUTE). The basic FETCH-EXECUTE is then continually repeated until a HALT or STOP instruction is received. As shown in Figure 10-6 some basic parts of the control section are (a) a storage register which holds the address or location of the NEXT instruction to be performed and (b) a storage register which holds the PRESENT instruction being performed including the operation or command and the address of the operand.

During the FETCH operation the word stored at the address of the NEXT address register is read from memory into the INSTRUCTION register. The NEXT address register is also advanced by one count. If the instruction located at address 152 has just been read, the address from which to obtain the next instruction is 153. With the FETCH operation finished, the EXECUTE phase is performed. The operation

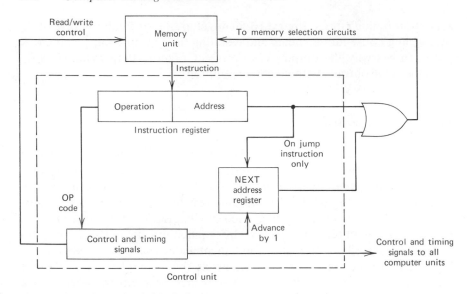

Figure 10-6.   Control unit, block diagram.

part of the word in the instruction register is used to "tell" the control and timing circuits what specific signals are to be generated. If the op code is 10, for example, the decoder circuits will activate the clear-add line and will qualify a number of timing signals to carry out this operation in the various computer units. Then the word stored at the address indicated by the address part of the instruction is read and added to the accumulator of the arithmetic unit after the accumulator has been reset to zero. At the end of the EXECUTE cycle the FETCH cycle begins and, following the example given, the instruction at address 153 is read and is placed in the INSTRUCTION register; the NEXT address register is advanced by 1 to 154.

This procedure is only altered when a branch instruction is performed. If the instruction is an unconditional branch (44), the FETCH operation is still the same and the NEXT address register is advanced by 1. If this instruction is read from location 362, for example, the NEXT instruction register will be advanced to 363. During EXECUTE, however, the operation decoded to mean perform an unconditional branch will cause the address part of the instruction to be dumped or shifted into the NEXT address register. If this address is 325, the stored 362 is replaced by the new 325 address. Since this completes the EXECUTE step, the machine now goes to FETCH, brings the word stored at 325 into the instruction register, and then advances the NEXT address register to 326. As far as the FETCH operation is concerned the machine continues using instructions from consecutive address locations after 325. Had the branch instruction been conditional (45, 46, 47), the operation would have been: Look at the number in the accumulator — if it has polarity specified by the branch (− for 45, + for 46) or, if the value is zero (47), take the address part of the instruction and place it in the NEXT address register; if not, just go on to the next FETCH operation.

The control unit contains decode gates or matrices to select the control lines for the operation code presently in the instruction register. The timing signals are taken from counters and decoding gates that generate a few operating patterns, each of which is wired to perform the specific operation — add, subtract, multiply, divide, and so on.

A computer having a two-address instruction code operates somewhat differently. The instruction code is made up of three parts which may be either (1) op code, operand address, and next instruction address or (2) op code, operand 1 address, and operand 2 address. In the first case it uses the operand address in conjunction with the op code to perform the EXECUTE operation. During the FETCH operation the next instruction address is fed to the memory unit to obtain the next program instruction. No update of instruction address is necessary since each program instruction contains the address of the next instruction. The branch instruction is different in that one of the two address parts of the instruction is used to specify from where to obtain the next instruction. If the branch condition is met or if no condition exists, the next instruction address may be used. If the branch condition is not met, the operand address specifies from where to obtain the next instruction. In the second case the instruction provides the address of both values to be operated on (added, subtracted, etc.) saving an instruction.

With a three-address instruction, two are used to specify where to obtain both operands for an arithmetic operation. For example, an addition instruction will contain the address of word A and the address of word B (where A and B are to be added). The third address might indicate the address or the next instruction or it might be used to indicate where the result of the arithmetic operation is to be placed. A four-address instruction will allow specifying where words A and B are located, where to store the result of that operation, and the address of the next instruction to be performed. Obviously, the more addresses used, the larger the instruction word and the fewer the program steps needed. For a drum memory in which each read operation is cyclical (must wait half a drum revolution on the average), fewer read operations will result in faster overall performance.

Upon decode of a HALT command, the computer will go out of the automatic type of operation just described and into a manual operation during which the machine operator can make changes. With larger computers stoppage after every program would be wasteful, and generally the end of a program only requires a new program to be specified (as with a branch command) to keep the computer operating.

Since the memory may not hold enough different programs to keep the machine operating continuously, the next few program steps might be to read in new cards or tape containing another program and data and then a branch to this new program. When errors occur that the machine is able to determine, it can branch out of calculations on the program in operation and read in another one. In this way larger computer facilities are continuously operating, doing a wide assortment of problems in succession.

10-4.   Operation of a Control Unit

To help clarify how a control unit operates some detail of the circuit logic will be presented. It would be beyond the level of this text to use any real computer control unit in this section. In order to bring out some more basic understanding a much simplified control unit is presented. Although all aspects of the control unit are not covered, we shall discuss how gating, timing, and control operations can be obtained.

Figure 10-7 shows a specific layout of a control unit and memory unit register. In general terms the control unit functions in a two-step FETCH-EXECUTE cycle. A clock signal is used to drive a step counter and decoding circuitry to obtain a sequence of eight count steps. Each time the count step goes from count step 7 (CS7) to count step 0 (CS0) the control unit switches from the FETCH mode to the EXECUTE mode.

During the FETCH mode of operation a word in memory located at an address specified by the program counter is transferred into the control unit. Of the 16 bits of instruction word the proposed computer used 7 bits ($2^7 = 128$ possible address locations) for the ADDRESS with 3 bits for special functions. Within the control unit the op code and address bits are held in two separate registers. In addition, the program counter holds the address of the location from which the instruction was taken. At the end of the FETCH cycle the program counter is incremented by one count so that it now holds the address of the next sequential memory location, which should correspond to the next instruction word.

During the EXECUTE mode of operation the particular function specified in the instruction, which is decoded by the control unit, determines what the computer is to do. In relation to the control unit operation, if the function specified is not a jump or other branch step that is satisfied, the program counter value remains untouched and the count step signals,

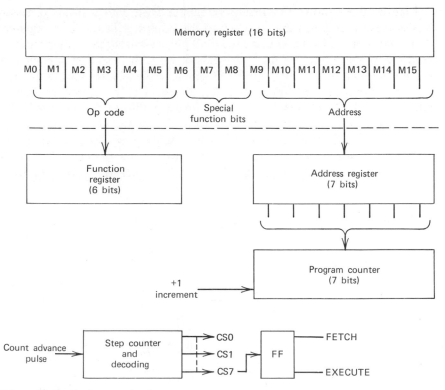

Figure 10-7.   Basic control unit.

along with the decoded function signal, provide signals to operate specific parts of the memory unit, arithmetic unit, or input-output units. If, on the other hand a jump instruction or branch instruction that is satisfied is present, the address in the address register is transferred into the program counter, thereby altering the normal sequence of the program.

The specific details of the step counter operation can be explained by considering a possible logic unit as shown in Figure 10-8a. The four-stage ring counter is made connecting a shift-right register with an inverting shift-around connection so that the pulse pattern shown in the count step table results. Logic gates are used to decode these outputs into eight distinct count steps whose pulse pattern is shown in Figure 10-8b. Notice that when CS7 goes off (and CS0 comes on) a toggle flip-flop is complemented changing mode from FETCH to EXECUTE (and back to FETCH after another eight count steps have occurred). Having established some basic timing pulses we can now see how these timing signals may be used to operate the control unit.

Figure 10-9*a* shows the memory register with data transfer of those bits corresponding to the op code into the control unit function register. At the start of the FETCH cycle the CS0 pulse signals the memory unit to read a new word into the memory register from the location specified in the program counter. During a FETCH cycle the CS1 pulse results in a clear pulse to reset the function register. When a CS3 pulse occurs slightly later in the FETCH cycle the data bits corresponding to the op code in the memory register are dumped (parallel transfer) into the function register.

The logic decoding gates, a few of which are shown as examples, decode the six-bit function register word into a signal on one of the operation output lines. Thus, either CLA, or ADD, or SUB, or STA, or JMP

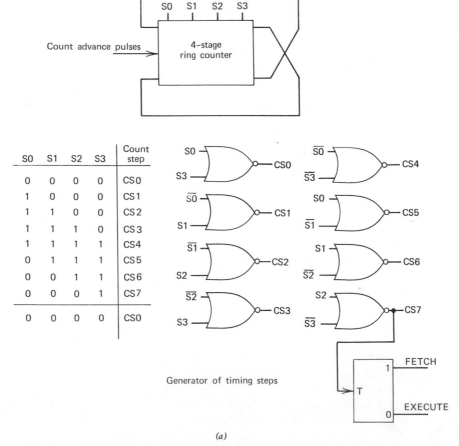

(a)

Figure 10-8.   Step counter and decoding circuits.

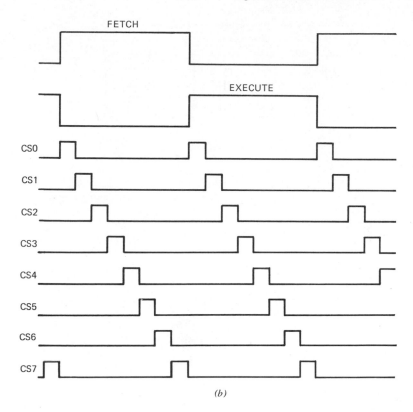

(b)

goes high indicating that the particular operation is to be carried out. This signal is used as a gating signal in such possible locations as the memory unit, arithmetic unit, input or output unit and, along with other timing signals and EXECUTE mode signal, carries out the necessary steps to perform the specified function. For the moment the FETCH cycle has obtained the specified instruction and it is this instruction that will be carried out on the next EXECUTE cycle.

Figure 10-9*b* shows what occurs during this same FETCH cycle in regard to the address register and program counter. On CS1 the address register is cleared. Then CS3 transfers the contents of the address portion of the memory word (bits M9 to M15) into the address register. Recall that a CS0 pulse occurred at the start of the FETCH cycle to load the word at the memory address specified in the program counter into the memory register.

The remainder of the FETCH cycle now takes care of determining what to do to the program counter. Using logic gates we can determine

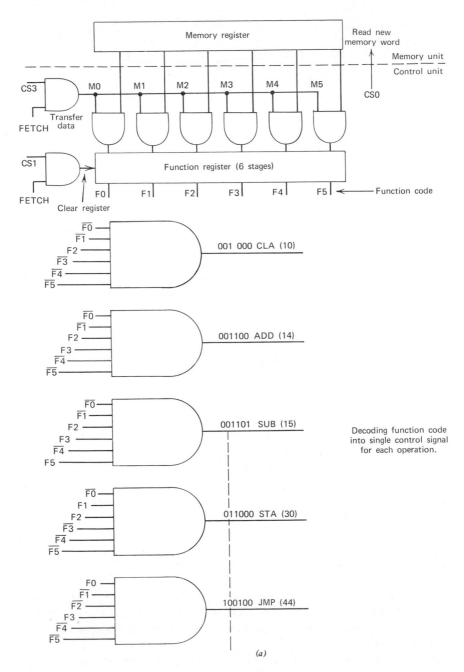

Figure 10-9. Op Code-operand circuits.

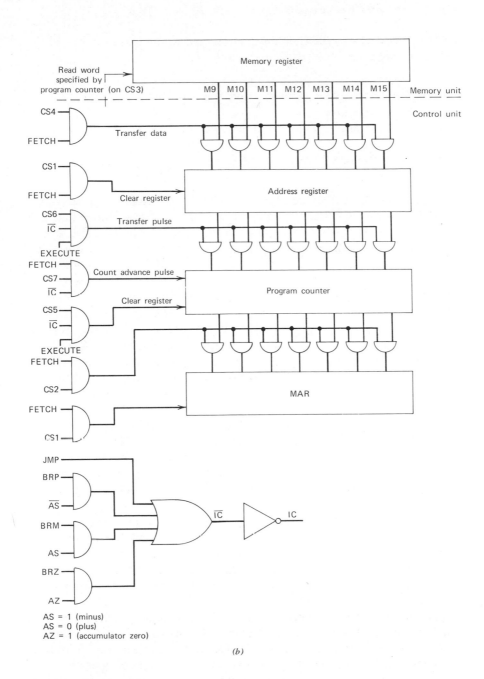

AS = 1 (minus)
AS = 0 (plus)
AZ = 1 (accumulator zero)

(b)

if the op code now in the function register and which results in one of the function logic gates is one of the following.

1. A JMP (unconditional branch).
2. A BRP (branch if positive) and the value of the arithmetic sign (AS) is 0 (positive).
3. A BRM (branch if minus) and the value of the arithmetic sign (AS) is 1 (negative).
4. A BRZ (branch if zero) and the value of the accumulation is zero (AZ $= 1$).

If either of these four conditions occur the increment counter signal (IC) is off (low), and the IC signal is high. That is, the control unit will not increment the program counter at the end of the FETCH cycle. Instead, with IC high on CS4 the program counter is cleared and on CS5 the value in the address register is transferred into the program counter. In effect then, a JMP instruction (or conditioned branch which is satisfied) results in the program counter being changed to correspond to the address specified in the instruction word. The EXECUTE cycle following will do nothing and on the next FETCH cycle the address now in the program counter will be used to obtain the next word of instruction.

If neither of the four conditions specified above is present, then the IC signal is high and on CS7 the program counter is incremented by one count. In this case the program counter now shows that the next sequential location in memory contains the next instruction. The EXECUTE cycle will result in the present instruction in the function register (as decoded by the function logic gates) being carried out. The FETCH cycle after that will use the program counter address to obtain the instruction word. Notice that when the next FETCH cycle occurs the computer circuitry no longer knows whether a sequential memory address or a jumped address location is in the program counter. The control unit merely repeats a FETCH and then EXECUTE cycle over and over. The instructions placed in memory determine the flow of the program. It might be pointed out that in starting a program running the address of the first program instruction is set into the program counter using switches on the control panel of the computer and the run or automatic switch pressed.

This discussion only covers the basic functions of a control unit, and much more is actually done in practice. The present discussion should, however, give the reader some insight into how timing steps and different registers and counters can be used to perform a variety of operations. In practical computers the code is generally 6 or 7 bits allowing up to 64 or 128 different operations. The address part of the word can be anywhere from 12 bits for 4096 memory locations, 13 bits for 8192 locations up to that required for over one million locations in the largest machines. In a smaller word machine using, say, 12 to 16 bits of word length a double word is used to hold a full instruction word so that two read operations of the memory unit are necessary on a FETCH cycle — one to get the op code word, the other the memory address word of the full instruction. The present scheme discussed previously would be modified in this case and the program counter incremented by two steps for the next instruction address location. What should be clear is that each computer type is structured differently and requires somewhat different logic in the control unit. If the basic operation described above is understood, however, any modification of it found in various computers are then easier to understand.

Indirect Addressing.   One additional feature of most computer instruction words is the use of special function bits to provide *indirect addressing* operation. It clouds up the basic discussion to include this feature, but it must be covered to understand how most computers operate. The introduction of indirect addressing basically adds to the normal control unit cycle. Instead of FETCH-EXECUTE the cycle is FETCH-DEFER-EXECUTE, with the added DEFER cycle occurring between FETCH and EXECUTE. In general terms the indirect addressing provides two addresses, the first of which specifies the location in memory where the actual address to be used is stored. That is, an instruction such as ADD *indirectly* 475 means:

add to the arithmetic unit the number stored at the memory location specified by the address stored at location 475. If at location 475 the value is 600 then the instruction effectively performed is ADD 600 meaning add the value stored at location 600.

The indirect feature is that on an indirect instruction the address is not where to find the number to add but where to find the address of where the number to add is located.

For example, consider the following program steps and its resulting operation.

CLA   400   Load value at location 400 into arithmetic unit.
ADD I 500   Add value at address specified at address 500.

location 400   000002
location 500   000600
location 600   012345

Result of instructions is to load the value of 000002 at location 400 into arithmetic unit and add to it the value 012345 stored at address location 600 specified by address value at location 500.

The control unit does nothing during a DEFER cycle in normal operation. If, however, an indirect addressing instruction is encountered, the operation for the above example would be as follows:

1. Normal FETCH-DEFER-EXECUTE cycle (nothing happening on DEFER cycle) for CLA 400 instruction.
2. During next FETCH cycle ADD I 500 is read out of memory and brought into control unit.
3. Address 500 is in arithmetic register.
4. During DEFER cycle memory word in address 500 is read into memory register and address bits are transferred to address register replacing value 500 with 600 in this case.
5. On EXECUTE cycle op code is still ADD and value in address register is 600, so that computer adds value at address 600 to value in arithmetic unit.

Figure 10-10 shows how this operation is carried out. A three-cycle control unit sequence generated by a mod-3 counter and decoding gates provides timing signals for FETCH, DEFER, and EXECUTE cycles. The CS0 to CS7 timing pulses are generated for each of these cycles.

During a FETCH cycle the CS0 pulse (not shown) results in reading the instruction at the address specified by the program counter into the memory register. At CS1 the address register is cleared and at CS3 the memory register address bits are transferred into the control unit address register.

During the following DEFER cycle nothing happens if I = 0 (no indirect addressing specified). If, however, I = 1, then indirect addressing is called for (by the programmer) and the CS0 pulse (not shown) causes the memory unit to read the value at the location specified in the address register into the memory register. Then a CS1 pulse clears the address register and a CS3 pulse transfers a new address value into the address register. The following EXECUTE cycle is then the same as covered previously.

In addition to indirect addressing special function bits are used to indicate short or long instructions and index register use. These two ideas will now be described using somewhat different instruction format than that covered previously in this chapter.

Short-Long Instruction. On some computers having short word length the use of, say, a 16-bit word length with only 8 bits for the address length is too short to specify all locations in a 4096 or 8192 word memory,

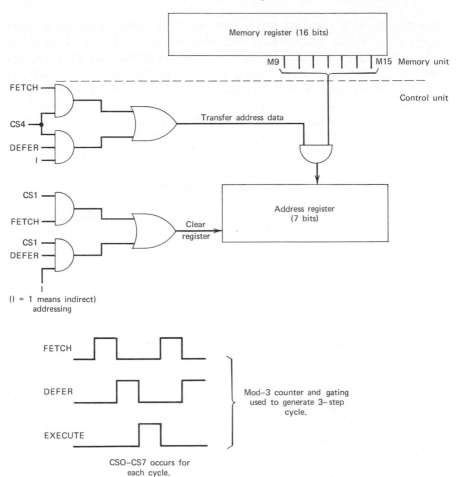

Figure 10-10.   Part of control unit showing indirect address operation.

for example. In this case the short instruction is used to specify a displacement from the present program counter location. Thus, a short instruction such as

location 400   ADD 120

would then mean add the number stored at the location displaced 120 places from the present location—or at location 520 (400 + 120). Using 8 bits the displacement could only be ±128 places—either forward or back by 128 locations. This particular setup is found on the IBM 1130 as example. A long instruction example would be

ADD L 4278

the L indicating the long instruction word (no letter meaning a short instruction word). In this case the address can be greater than ± 128 since more bits are used to specify the address. Where do the extra bits for a long instruction come from? Very simply, two sequential locations in memory are used. The first contains the op code and special function bits. It is one of the special function bits that tells the control unit to look in the next address location for the full address of the instruction — which could be up to 16 bits in this case.

Thus, a short instruction stored in one memory location can only specify a displacement, whereas a long instruction using two sequential memory locations can specify the exact value of any memory location.

Index Register. In addition to special function bits for indirect addressing and short-long instruction format, special function bits may exist for specifying index registers. An index register is generally a hardware register (or registers) that hold a number value that can be used to modify the address part of an instruction.

For example, an instruction such as

ADD L2 4000

is interpreted to mean

Add to the arithmetic unit the value stored at the location specified by the *sum* of address values 4000 and that at index register 2. So, for example, if the number stored at index register 2 is 25, then the computer adds to the arithmetic unit the value stored at location 4025. The index register value modified the address value specified in the instruction. A long instruction was used so that the address value specified could refer to any memory location.

At this point we are perhaps getting too involved in the details of the control unit and although quite important to be aware of, these special function operations are better left to a slightly more advanced text. In particular, the reasons for needing such operations as indirect addressing and index registers is really a function of effective programming techniques, which are studied in a programming language course, not a computer hardware area as is covered in the present text.

10-5.   Encoding and Decoding Matrices

General.   Another means of decoding a binary number into a unique signal for use in a computer is a diode matrix. Some examples for decoding and encoding will be given. A diode matrix for a three-variable decoder is

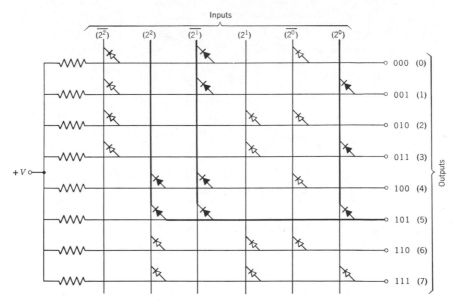

Figure 10-11.   Diode matrix for octal decoding (binary numbers 000 to 111).

shown in Figure 10-11. Since both the TRUE and FALSE of each input is provided, half the inputs will be 1 and half will be 0 at all times. For each input combination (there are 2^3, or 8) a different output line is high. Only one output, however, is high at any time. All other input combinations have at least one diode input at 0 volts. The darkened diodes are those that have high voltage inputs ($+V$) and are back-biased (for the 1 0 1 condition). The low (0-volt) input at (2^2) keeps the top four output lines clamped low, the low input at (2^1) keeps the bottom two output lines clamped low, and the $(\overline{2^0})$ input keeps the 1 0 0 line clamped low. Only the 1 0 1 line, for the example considered, has a high output voltage. Notice that $2^3 \times 3$, or 24 diodes were needed. For 2^n output combinations $2^n \times n$ diodes would be needed. With a six-stage counter (64 counts) this would still require $2^6 \times 6$, or 384, diodes, as with single decoding gates.

An arrangement of "treeing" the inputs will reduce the number of logic elements to 14. The tree connection is named for its physical appearance (see Figure 10-12), as is the diode matrix for its similarity to the ordered arrangement of rows and columns of a mathematical matrix.

To develop the tree connection concept an arrangement of relay switches is used as in Figure 10-13 (Refer back to the relay logic operation described in Section 5-2). There are three relays used — relay A has two contacts, one normally closed (NC) and one normally open (NO); relay B has two contact pairs (four contacts); relay C has four contact pairs

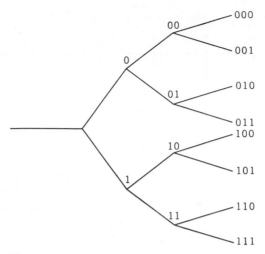

Figure 10-12.   Schematic of tree connection.

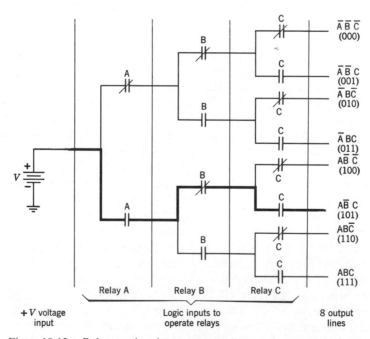

Figure 10-13.   Relay matrix using tree connection to reduce number of elements.

(eight contacts). If relays A and C are selected (relays energized), corresponding to an input of A, *not* B, and C, (logically ABC), the $+V$ voltage will pass through the now closed NO contact of A, the NC contact of B, and the now closed NO contact of C, as shown by the darkened lines in Figure 10-13.

With the given circuit we obtain outputs of open lines (0 volts) on all but one line, the selected line, which is at $+V$ volts. It is thus possible to select one of the eight output lines using only fourteen contacts with the tree arrangement. Extending this idea, for six inputs the tree decoder would require $2^1 + 2^2 + 2^3 + 2^4 + 2^5 + 2^6$ or 126 contacts as compared to 384 contacts for the straight connection matrix.

Diode Matrix.   The diode matrix may be used either to decode a binary code into a single output line or to take a number of single lines and encode that into a unique binary count. As a decode example, consider a digital system that uses excess-three code in arithmetic operations. If the final results are to be displayed on an output light as a decimal number, each excess-three combination (there are 10 for the decimal digits) must light up a different decimal digit. The matrix in Figure 10-14 is fed by a four-stage buffer register. This is a register that holds the binary number while it is being decoded for display and allows the rest of the computer to continue operating. Although the computer is doing other operations or even computing a new number to display, the present value remains in the buffer register. When a new value is to be displayed the excess-three number either is shifted into the buffer register one bit at a time or is dumped (all bits at once), depending on whether the computer operates serially or in parallel on readout.

Since the input to the matrix is from a flip-flop stage, both 1 and 0 signals are available. In Figure 10-14 the decode of decimal eight is shown. Since a straight decode is used, forty diodes are needed. The decimal number chosen to be displayed by the matrix may be operated by a light driver (transistor amplifier) to prevent loading the matrix.

Figure 10-15 shows an encoder matrix for octal numbers. In the circuit arrangement shown an input of 0 volts from one of lines 0 to 7 causes the equivalent binary number to be inserted into the input buffer register. The darkened lines indicate the operation for encoding the octal number 5. Notice that the supply voltage shown back-biases all the diodes so that they have no effect on the register stages. Only an input going low (to 0 volts) will change the number stored in the buffer register.

BCD Decoder.   A popular encoder/decoder matrix involves the BCD (8421) code. Input information that is decimal in nature can be provided

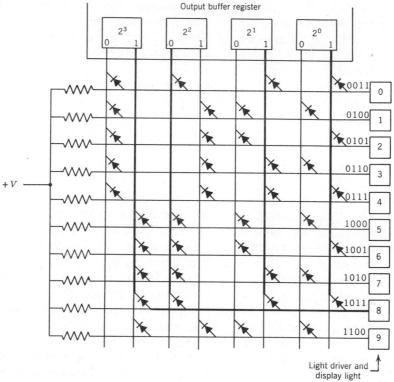

Figure 10-14.   Decoder matrix for excess-three numbers.

on one of ten input lines. Using a decimal to BCD encoder the output of the matrix circuit would be four lines containing BCD code. Figure 10-16*a* shows a block description of the decimal to BCD encoder. The inputs may, for example, be from ten different keyboard keys or switches each labeled in decimal (from 0 to 9). By pressing one key the encoder provides an output on all four lines in BCD code (see Figure 10-16*b*).

A diode matrix operating as an encoder is shown in Figure 10-16*c*. An input of 0 volts (ground) is considered the input when a decimal input line is selected. Input line 3 going low, for example, pulls output lines C and D low (through diodes), leaving lines A and B high so that the code 0011 results on the BCD lines. If no keys are pressed, the output lines are all high, which is not a BCD code character and therefore can be ignored.

BCD Encoder.   Another very common application takes a BCD code character from a digital circuit and decodes it into one of ten decimal lines used to drive one of ten separate segments of a Nixie display tube. Thus,

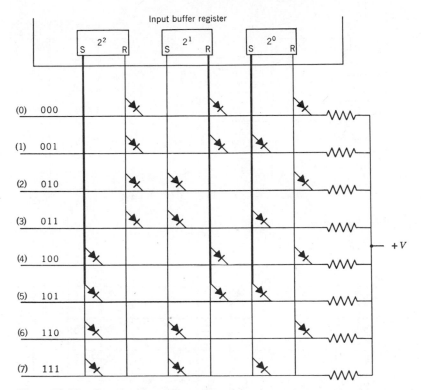

Figure 10-15.   Encoder matrix for octal numbers.

for a four-bit BCD code character the Nixie tube displays the equivalent decimal character. Figure 10-17 shows the diode decoder matrix. The input BCD code (four input bits and their negation) selects one of the output lines (by disqualifying the other nine lines) so that only one has an output of $+V$ and all others 0 volts. The Nixie segment driven with $+V$ volts provides the necessary voltage to excite that Nixie segment which then visually displays the decimal equivalent character.

Display on Seven-Segment Light. Another popular display device is a seven-segment display as shown in Figure 10-18. The basic display light has seven segments in Figure 10-18a. By selecting different combinations of these segments the decimal characters from 0 to 9 can be observed as demonstrated in Figure 10-18b.

A decoder circuit taking BCD code and providing outputs on seven lines would be required to operate such a display device. Figure 10-19a shows the basic connection to a BCD to seven-segment decoder matrix.

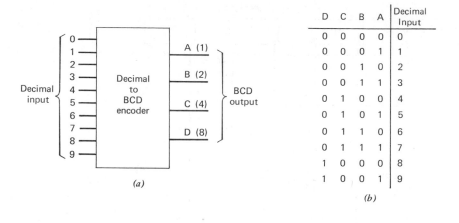

D	C	B	A	Decimal Input
0	0	0	0	0
0	0	0	1	1
0	0	1	0	2
0	0	1	1	3
0	1	0	0	4
0	1	0	1	5
0	1	1	0	6
0	1	1	1	7
1	0	0	0	8
1	0	0	1	9

(b)

(a)

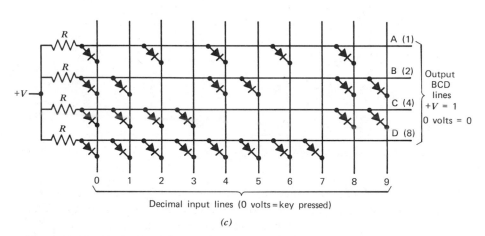

(c)

Figure 10-16.   Decimal to BCD encoder.

In setting up the matrix a code table such as that in Figure 10-19*b* is needed. The table shows the input BCD code for each decimal character (0 to 9) and the necessary segments that must be turned on (logical-1) to form that character using the segment numbering of Figure 10-18*a* as reference.

To provide the necessary decoding of all seven segments a possible scheme is shown in Figure 10-20*a* to convert the BCD code into one of ten decimal lines and then to decode further into various combinations of the seven segments, as specified in the table of Figure 10-19*b*.

Figure 10-20*b* shows the part of the decoder that converts the ten-line decimal selection (0 volts for the selected line in this case) into voltages

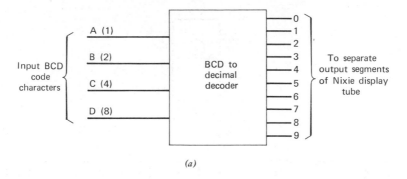

(a)

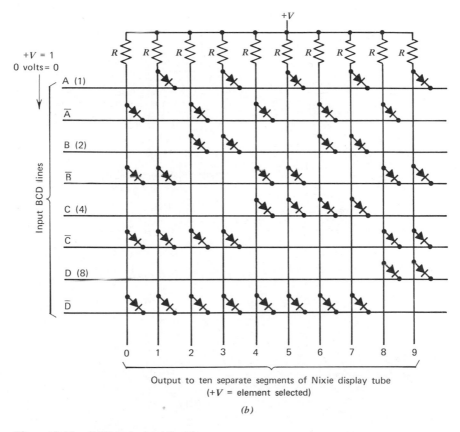

Output to ten separate segments of Nixie display tube
(+*V* = element selected)

(b)

Figure 10-17.   BCD to decimal decoder.

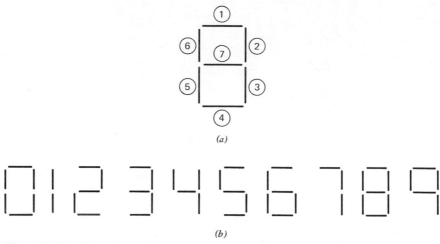

(a)

(b)

Figure 10-18.   Seven-segment display.

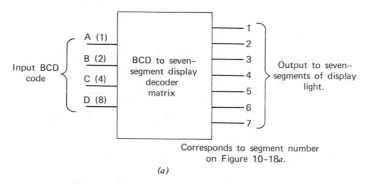

Output to seven—
segments of display
light.

Corresponds to segment number
on Figure 10-18*a*.

(a)

D	C	B	A	Decimal Character	7	6	5	4	3	2	1
0	0	0	0	0	0	1	1	1	1	1	1
0	0	0	1	1	0	0	0	0	1	1	0
0	0	1	0	2	1	0	1	1	0	1	1
0	0	1	1	3	1	0	0	1	1	1	1
0	1	0	0	4	1	1	0	0	1	1	0
0	1	0	1	5	1	1	0	1	1	0	1
0	1	1	0	6	1	1	1	1	1	0	1
0	1	1	1	7	0	0	0	0	1	1	1
1	0	0	0	8	1	1	1	1	1	1	1
1	0	0	1	9	1	1	0	0	1	1	1

(b)

Figure 10-19.   BCD to seven-segment decoder matrix.

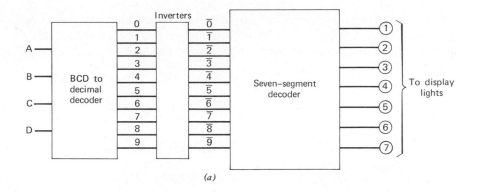

(a)

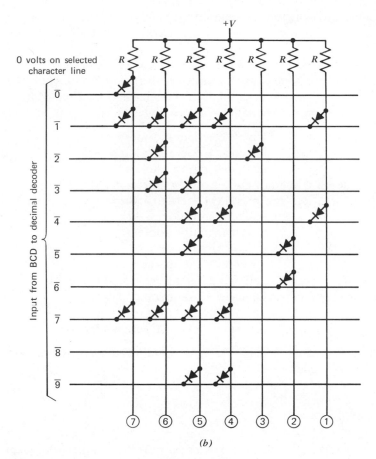

(b)

Figure 10-20.   BCD to seven segment decoder.

419

on all seven lines as required to display the selected decimal character. Although the scheme shown here requires more decoding than the Nixie display alone, the seven-segment display may be desired because of its appearance.

Summary

Some of the basic parts of the control unit were discussed. These included counters with decoder gates, ring counters, and diode matrices. Sequential pulses are generated for timing operations controlling the order in which operations occur.

Diode matrices may be used to encode signals — take a number of input lines and convert a signal on any one into a binary count; or, to decode signals by taking a binary count and converting each count into an output on a different line.

A basic machine cycle is the FETCH-EXECUTE. During FETCH the computer calls for a new instruction to perform. In EXECUTE the operation is carried out. Because there are single- and multiple-address machines, the following summary of their meaning is given.

1	address instruction	Op code + operand address
2	address instruction	Op code + operand address + next instruction address
	or, Op code + 1st operand address + 2nd operand address	
3	address instruction	Op code + operand address + 2nd operand address + next instruction address
		or
		Op code + 1st operand address + 2nd operand address + result address
4	address instruction	Op code + 1st operand address + 2nd operand address + result address + next instruction address

The main difference between these is whether a next instruction address register is needed.

PROBLEMS

§**10-2**   **1.** Using OR and AND gates only prepare the interconnection diagram to decode all combinations of a three-stage counter.

2. Using only NAND gates prepare the decoder gating interconnection diagram for a two-stage counter.

§10-4   **3.** A very simple model of the control part of a computer is shown in Figure 10-21. The instruction register is two bits and address register

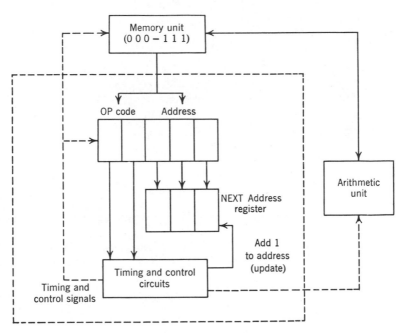

Figure 10-21.   Simple control unit for Problem 3.

three bits. For two bits only four commands are possible. Use the following for this example:

0 0 — Add
0 1 = Subtract
1 0 = Branch if minus
1 1 = Store in memory

With only three bits there are eight different memory cells that can be specified. For this simple system prepare a detailed description of what occurs during the FETCH and during the EXECUTE part of the cycle for each step of the following program. Only binary numbers are used in this simple setup. Instead of adding more bits to allow more operation codes, halt will be indicated by the word HALT in place of any real instruction. The program should be started at location 0 0 0, and the accumulator is assumed here to be clear.

Instruction

Location	Operation	Address
0 0 0	0 0	1 0 1
0 0 1	0 1	1 1 0
0 1 0	1 0	1 1 1
0 1 1	1 1	1 1 0
1 0 0	HALT	
1 0 1	0 1	1 1 1
1 1 0	1 1	1 1 1
1 1 1	HALT	

4. Repeat Problem 3 for the following program. Again assume the accumulator is clear when the program starts at 0 0 0.

Location	Operation	Address
0 0 0	0 0	0 0 0
0 0 1	0 0	1 0 0
0 1 0	1 1	0 0 0
0 1 1	HALT	
1 0 0	0 0	0 0 1

§10-5   **5.** Draw the circuit diagram of a diode matrix to decode the three counts of a mod-3 counter.

6. Draw the circuit diagram of a diode matrix to encode four input lines of BCD information into the binary count of a four-stage register.

1011

Computer memory

11-1. General Memory Description

A computer memory plays a very important part in how effective a computer operates. A fast memory allows for quicker operation providing more solutions. Large memory capacity allows handling more data and doing more complex operations. Low memory cost allows the computer to be a practical reality. These three factors — speed, size or capacity, and cost — vary considerably for the different types of memories used and are important criteria in the selection of a suitable memory.

A digital memory is an element that can maintain either of two stable states indefinitely (as long as power is not shut off). A flip-flop falls under this definition. Because of the large capacity required of even a small computer memory system and because of the size and cost of a flip-flop circuit, flip-flop circuits have not been used for large-scale memory storage. They have become more popular in IC large-scale integrated units and are being used in some newer computers. Flip-flop registers are also used as intermediate or buffer memories between sections of a computer handling a few words of information at a time. A memory system may handle thousands to millions of words (a fixed number of bits define a word). A word may be a few bits long or as many as 36, 48, or 64 bits for some computers. For discussion in this book consider a word to be ten bits unless otherwise stated. Two very popular memory devices are magnetic cores and magnetic drums. Although such devices as mag-magnetic tape, paper tape, and punched card, are also memory devices, their use is primarily that of providing data into the computer and saving data from the computer. They are best classed as input/output equipment. This distinction comes about from considering whether the memory unit is used directly by the arithmetic unit. Those used directly will be called

423

computer memories. Those storing data which is fed into the internal computer memory or taking data from the internal computer memory are considered input or output equipment. These latter units are discussed in Chapter 13. Other less popular internal computer memories exist, such as optical, tunnel diode, multiaperture core or transfluxor, twistor, cryogenic, thin-film, ferrite, and so on. Some of these will be discussed briefly. They are basically faster or smaller, are generally more costly, and are presently under research or in limited practical use. Awareness of these memory types is important, for they may someday gain prime importance. The present popularity of the magnetic core to a lesser extent, of the magnetic drum, and also IC storage registers requires more detailed consideration of their usage. In addition, these three types are organized differently and will provide for a discussion of the types of memory organization, an important factor in their usage.

A number of different expressions are used in connection with memory operation. *Bit serial* means that each bit is taken sequentially, or one at a time. *Word serial* indicates that each word is read out sequentially, or one word at a time. *Bit parallel* would mean that a group of bits are read out at one time and *word parallel* that a group of words are read simultaneously. *Access* is the operation of getting a word or bit out of memory. Time of access or *access time* is a very important factor in the speed of a memory unit and indicates the amount of time involved in getting data from the memory. For example, finding page 459 in a book takes a certain amount of looking time. With the book closed after each look the amount of time to find a certain page will vary. If you have to advance one page at a time, getting to page 625 will take much longer than getting to page 27. Advancing in this prescribed manner is considered a *sequential access*. As opposed to this, the pages could be indexed and you might be able to turn directly to the page asked for. In such a case, the time to find one page is the same as to find another. Such a memory operation is called *random access*. Obviously the random access is much faster than the sequential access memory. Since there is a trade off between between speed and economy in operating these memory types, different combination, of bit or word and sequential or random access operation are chosen to best fit the particular problem.

11-2. Magnetic Core Operation

Because the magnetic core memory is at present the most popular computer memory element, it will be the first one considered. Before discussing the organization of such a memory and its properties, the memory characteristic of a magnetic core must be considered. The magnetic core is generally a round toroid very much like a doughnut in shape. It is so small that many thousands can be held in a sewing thimble. The core is made of ferromagnetic material of specified characteristic. A few turns of wire wound around a magnetic core carrying a current will produce a magnetic flux. If the current is passed in one direction through the wire, the flux direction (north-south poles) can be determined by the right-hand rule. A typical configuration showing flux, current, and direction is that of Figure 11-1.

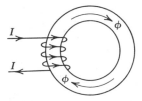

Figure 11-1.   Flux flow in magnetic core.

As the current is increased the flux first increases linearly (equal flux change for a fixed current change), then changes less and less for each current interval, and finally there is no flux change for an increase in current. At this point the core is *saturated* and will allow no further increase in flux as current is increased. Actually, there is always a very slight increase in flux, but for our purposes the core is fully saturated. Thus, the core will "store" or "remember" the signal applied long after it has been removed. There, of course, must be two distinct states if it is to be used as a binary memory element.

We can reverse the current direction in the winding of the core, causing the magnetic flux to be reduced even further until it goes to zero and then becomes negative. "Negative" means that the north-south poles of the core are reversed and that the flux flows in the opposite direction. Flux is usually considered as flowing from a north pole to a south pole. The flux fully saturates in the opposite or negative direction. If the current is now decreased, the amount of flux decreases until the current is completely removed and until residual flux is flowing in the opposite direction.

An important consideration in using the magnetic core is how to "read out" the state of the core. We know that it is magnetized and flux is flowing in one of two directions—one being arbitrarily designated binary ZERO, the other binary ONE. Which way is it magnetized? Since there is a constant flux flowing, it is difficult to know which way. The flux must be made to change to "sense" the direction. Only a change in flux can induce a voltage in a stationary element. However, in causing it to change it is no longer magnetized as before. In order to read the stored information it is necessary to "destroy" it. This is referred to as *destructive read-out*. To make it possible to use the same information a number of times, additional operations must be added to *rewrite* the data to "save" it. With these general ideas in mind let us now go back and look more closely at how the magnetic core operates and is organized in a memory system.

A ferrite core used in a computer memory has a "square" loop characteristic as shown in Figure 11-2. Points *a* and *b* show the amount of flux

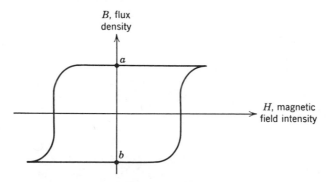

Figure 11-2.   B-H curve of magnetic core for storage use.

remaining after the drive signal is removed. Consider point *a* as the ONE state and *b* as the ZERO state for memory use. To "switch" the core from one binary state to the other requires a driving signal of correct polarity and intensity. A core and drive winding are shown in Figure 11-3*a*. The wire is wrapped around the core, and by the right-hand rule the magnetization direction may be obtained. For a fixed number of turns of wire the

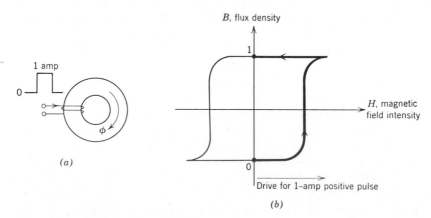

Figure 11-3.   Positive drive (from 0 to 1).

current is directly proportional to H, where H is the driving magneto-motive force determined by the number of winding turns and the amount of the drive current. Figure 11-3*b* shows how the core is magnetized for the given signal input. After the drive signal goes back to zero the core remains at binary ONE. Applying a pulse to the same core in the negative direction will bring the core back to binary ZERO. See Figure 11-4.

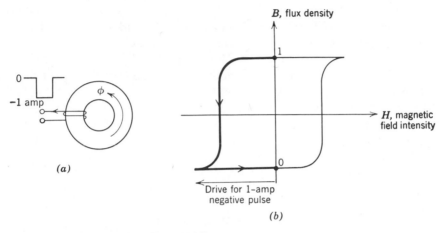

Figure 11-4.   Negative drive (from 1 to 0).

When the core is pulsed it takes a certain amount of time to switch states, depending on the intensity of the driving pulse and its rate of change. Fast cores are operated in less than one-millionth of a second, or 1 μsec. Slow operation is around 5 μsec. Thus, access time for magnetic cores is from 1 to 5 μsec. Let us use 1 μsec as the switching time for this discussion. When a magnetic core is used in a memory, it can be set to the ONE state or reset to the ZERO state by pulsing it with a correct polarity current signal. Since the core element is made as small as possible, it is wound with only one turn, with the wire generally being as fine as human hair. It is desirable to operate the core with as few wires as possible to obtain the smallest unit.

When a core is read it may not maintain state after the read operation. If the core changes state, as sensed by a pickup wire, the core is considered to have been in the ONE state. If it does not change state, it is considered to have been in the ZERO state. The change of flux when going from ONE to ZERO induces a voltage in a pickup wire or *sense wire* indicating the storage of a ONE in the sensed memory element. No pickup voltage indicates that a ZERO was stored. In either case the core is at ZERO *after* a read time. This type of readout is *destructive* since it destroys the stored information. A ONE stored in the core can only be read once. If the core is read again it will read ZERO. In comparison, a flip-flop output can be gated with an AND gate, which allows a read pulse through if the TRUE side is at ONE. In reading, the flip-flop state is unchanged. Unfortunately, magnetic core readout is destructive. To provide a more permanent storage operation the data must be written back into the core after each read operation. This means that the basic operation of the core memory requires a read-write cycle. Every time a core is read, the data is written back in. When a ONE is read, a ONE is written back in. When a ZERO is read, the core is left alone. Resetting the core requires only a read pulse to insure that it is in the ZERO state.

A major consideration in organizing the core memory is to keep track of where data is stored. One method requires labeling each individual core, so that any specific core may be read. This is a *bit-organized* core memory. To reduce the amount of selection needed the cores may be arranged into words (ten bits per word, for example) and each word may then be separately selected. In this case ten times less specification is needed and the data is read out, or written in, a word at a time. This is a *word-organized* core memory.

Read.   A single core may have as many as four wires as shown in Figure 11-5. We will later consider how cores are organized in a large memory

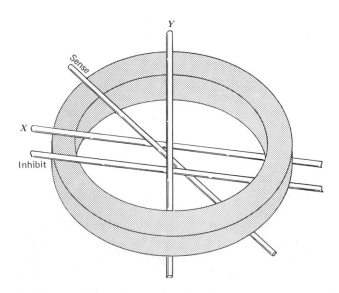

Figure 11-5.   Ferrite core memory element.

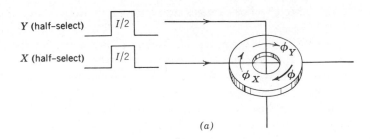

(a)

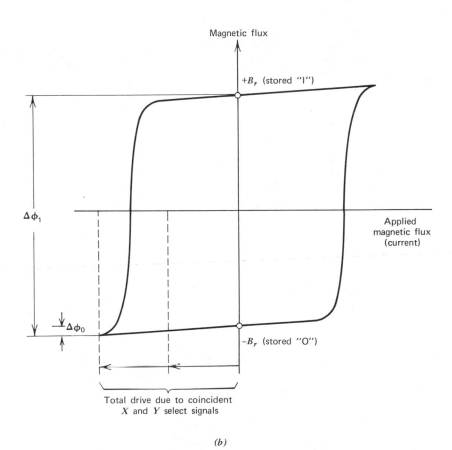

(b)

Figure 11-6.   Reading a core using coincident-current pulses.

system. For the present we will consider how an individual core may be operated. Basically the X and Y wires provide *half-select* pulses to read the stored information in the magnetic core. The change in magnetic flux caused by the read pulses causes a voltage to be induced in the sense wire.

In order to read from a core, the half-select pulses must be present at the same time for the two selection wires threading the core. Only one core on a plane receives such coincident signals as will be discussed later. For the core receiving two coincident half-select current pulses the resulting drive signal (or applied magnetic field) is the algebraic sum of the drive due to the current pulse in each wire. Figure 11-6a shows two coincident read pulses applied to the two selection lines of a core. If these pulses are of a current direction to provide a net negative drive as shown in Figure 11-6b then a "large" change in flux, $\Delta\phi_1$, from a stored 1 condition, or a "small" change in flux, $\Delta\phi_0$, from a stored 0 condition, occurs. The sense wire has much larger voltage induced in it due to a $\Delta\phi_1$ flux change than from the smaller $\Delta\phi_0$ flux change.

Thus, the induced voltage in the sense wires when the read pulses occur indicates a stored logical-1, whereas a very small voltage induced in the sense wire at the read time indicates that a logical-0 was stored. We will see later how this data bit is used by the outside circuitry. The act of reading causes the core to go to the 0 flux condition. Whether the stored logical condition was 1 or 0, after a read operation the core is at the flux condition of logical-0. Thus, the information stored in the core had to be destroyed in order to read it. It is not, however, lost since core operating circuitry include storing the data read in a flip-flop register and then writing the same data read back into the core.

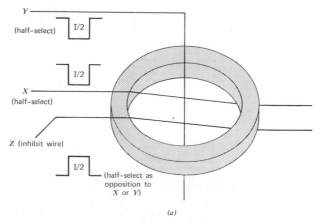

(a)

Figure 11-7.   Writing into a core using coincident current and inhibit pulses. (a) Use of inhibit wire. (b) Writing a ONE. (c) Writing a ZERO .

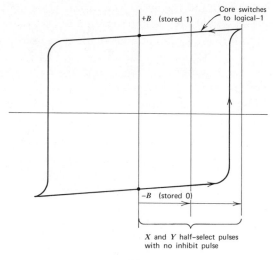

+B (stored 1)   Core switches to logical–1

–B (stored 0)

X and Y half–select pulses
with no inhibit pulse

(b)

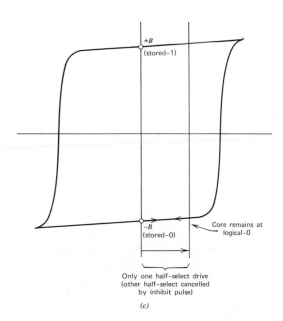

+B
(stored–1)

–B
(stored–0)   Core remains at
logical–0

Only one half–select drive
(other half–select cancelled
by inhibit pulse)

(c)

Write.   To understand the write operation we must keep in mind that a read operation will always occur before a write operation so that the core being written into is always logical-0 when the write takes place. In this regard the use of the inhibit wire as shown in Figure 11-7a is to provide an inhibit pulse of polarity to cancel out one half-select drive on the X or Y wire thereby preventing the core from switching from the logical-0 state. On a write operation the X and Y half-select pulses are of polarity to switch the core to the 1 state.

Writing a 1:   No inhibit pulse occurs; X and Y half-select pulses switch core to logical-1 state as shown in Figure 11-7b.

Writing a 0:   Inhibit pulse occurs to cancel out one half-select pulse and block core from changing *from* logical-0 state (see Figure 11-7c).

Read/Write Cycle.   The operation of the memory requires a complete read/write cycle. This cycle is necessary to provide for overall nondestructive readout of data. Since we must always do a write *after* each read, we must also always do a read *before* each write operation. A read operation always results in resetting all cores of the word read to ZERO. Thus, before each write we are assured that the cores to be considered are all in the ZERO state. With this in mind we can now see how the inhibit properly provides for writing in a desired bit. If no signal is applied to the inhibit winding, the X and Y select pulses will cause the flux of the selected core to go clockwise, thereby storing a ONE. Figure 11-8a shows the read/write cycle when a ONE is stored.

If the inhibit winding (Z winding) has a negative pulse present at write time (see Figure 11-8b), it will oppose the flux of one half-select signal, thereby maintaining the core as it was, *which was a* ZERO *because*

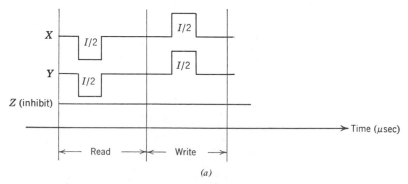

(a)

Figure 11-8.   Read/write cycle. (a) Read/write cycle for storage of a ONE. (b) Read/write cycle for storage of a ZERO.

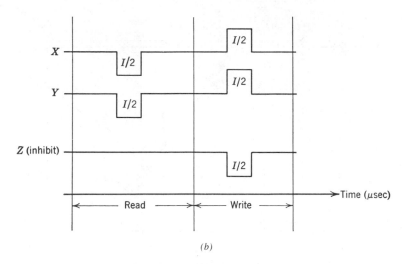

(b)

of the preceding read operation. By inhibiting any change the Z winding causes a ZERO to remain stored in the core. A complete memory cycle, consisting of a separate read and write operation, takes in the order of a microsecond in most present-day computers.

11-3. Magnetic Core Organization

Two main problems in organizing the data of a core memory are the large number of wires needed for exclusive read, write, and sense of data, and the large amount of selection circuitry needed to provide the control and operation of the memory. A single core could require separate read, write, and sense wires. A 1024-word memory (memory capacity is usually numbered in binary powers — 2^{10} being 1024) might then require over 3000 wires. Even with small sized cores, 3000 wires take up considerable space. A number of cleaver techniques using some form of coincident current selection as discussed in Section 11-2 has been adopted.

For example, an array of 100 cores using separate read, write, and sense wires would need 300 wires. Organizing these 100 cores in a coincident selection array as in Figure 11-9 requires only ten x-lines, ten y-lines and one *sense*-line for a total of 21 wires. To pick out core 12, for example, requires selecting both x_1 and y_2. Either alone is not sufficient. Only core 12 is then selected, since no other core receives two half-selection signals.

Requiring only 21 wires instead of 300 wires is a savings of roughly 93 percent. A 1024-core memory would need only 32 x-wires, 32 y-wires,

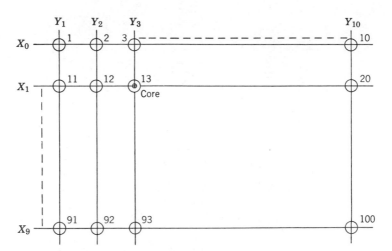

Figure 11-9.   General core array using X-Y selection.

and one *sense* wire, a total of 65 wires compared to 3072 separate read, write, and sense wires. It should be clear then, that some means of coincident current selection is necessary (and desirable) to hold down the total number of wires needed to operate the cores.

Generally, core memories can be classified as one of three different types of organization schemes: 2D (linear select), $2\frac{1}{2}$D, 3D (coincident current). These designations refer to the number of logical dimensions of control or addressing used in reading and writing information in the core memory array.

2D Memory Selection.   Probably the simplest organization scheme to consider is the 2D or linear select system. Figure 11-10 shows a basic block diagram of how 2D core organization is achieved. The cores are arranged in a two-dimensional array. In general we can specify the array as having

$$N \text{ bits per word and}$$
$$M \text{ words}$$

for a total of $N \times M$ bits in the array. For example, a 4096-word memory having 16 bits per word would then have

$$N = 16 \text{ and}$$
$$M = 4096 \ (= 2^{12})$$

The *address register* receives address information from the control unit. Each address value is *decoded* so that a particular *word driver* and thus

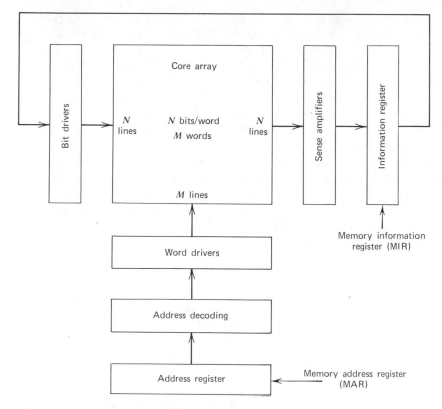

Figure 11-10.   Block diagram of 2D memory.

a particular word of memory is selected. In this case the number of word drivers is quite large since one is required for every word of memory. Using 4096 words, for example, 4096 driver (current switches) circuits are required. Corresponding to the word line selected by the address register and decoding circuits, 16 cores are pulsed corresponding in this example to the 16-bit positions of the selected word. Using a single sense line for each bit position—a total of 16 sense lines in this example (N lines, in general)—provides simultaneous output to 16 sense amplifiers. Data read from the core memory is then dumped (parallel transferred) into a flip-flop register called the memory information register (MIR). From the MIR the data read is available to the rest of the computer units.

Since readout of a core is destructive, the basic operating cycle is a read/write cycle. Using 16 lines in this example from the memory data register provides gating for bit driver circuits on the write cycle operation. Although in this memory organization the read was accomplished by using full switching level current pulses with no attendant savings in core wires, the write operation is carried out using coincident current. At the write time a half-select current (I/2) is generated on the word wire selected by the address register and decode gating. For those bits for which a 1 is to be written back an additional half-select pulse (I/2) is generated on the bit wire. For those bits that are 0 no I/2 select current results and the particular cores remain in the 0 state (which resulted on the read operation).

Although the 2D organization is relatively straightforward, it is obviously quite a poor choice since the number of word lines required is exactly the same as the number of words — which is generally quite large. It is possible to use a matrix arrangement that allows the number of word drivers to be reduced from M to $2\sqrt{M}$. In this example the word drivers could be reduced to $2\sqrt{M} = 2\sqrt{4096} = 2(64) = 128$ drivers, which is quite a savings. The price for this reduction would be the addition of $2M$ diodes (8192 in this example) to build the matrix.

Since the 2D scheme does not prove to be the most popular we will leave it as academic discussion of concepts that will prove useful later. It actually could be considered useful for very small memory sizes where speed is important and it has had some application in this regard. However, the 3D and to a growing extent, the $2\frac{1}{2}$D memory organizations are by far the most used and will thus be covered in even more detail.

3D Memory Selection.   A 3D or coincident current organization is presently the most popular. As was shown in Figure 11-5 a single core used in a 3D system has four wires threaded through it. The X and Y selection wires provide coincident current pulses on both read and write cycles. To read a core it is necessary to cause the core to switch to 0, the change of flux inducing a voltage in the sense wire. After a read operation the core is in the 0 state. A write operation provides X-and Y select pulses of opposite current direction in the X and Y wires than during the read operation. The X and Y currents are sufficient to write a 1 in the core. However, the inhibit line may have an additional current pulse. If an inhibit pulse is present the total flux drive is insufficient to switch the core and it remains in the 0 state. With no inhibit pulse the X and Y line pulses switch the core to the 1-state. Refer back to Figure 11-8 for the waveforms in a read/ write cycle for both 1 and 0 conditions.

Figure 11-11 shows how a number of cores are arranged into an array with X, Y, sense, and inhibit wires — 4 in each core. Also included are the positive current flow directions and voltage polarity in sense line. There are 8×8 or 64 cores in the core plane shown. To provide both read

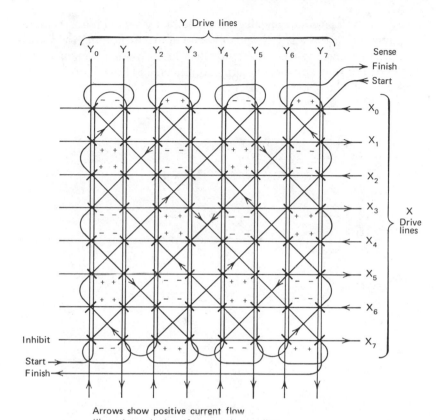

Arrows show positive current flow
Signs show phasing of core and sense line
relative to drive lines

Figure 11-11.   Organization of a core memory plane.

and write capability there are

> 8 X-lines
> 8 Y-lines
> 1 *sense*-line
> 1 *inhibit*-line

for a total of 18 lines to operate 64 cores.

The sense wire is threaded in a special way to provide some cancellation of the slight voltages induced in the sense wires by those cores which, although not switching state on read, do provide a slight flux change and thereby a slight voltage in the sense wire. If the core contains many thousands of cores the individual small voltages could add up to a large voltage if the sense wire was not looped through the cores as shown in

Figure 11-11*b* to provide cancellation of the many small induced voltages. The inhibit wire is threaded up and down on alternate columns as shown.

A real core plane is shown in Figure 11-12 to provide a somewhat more realistic idea of how small each core actually is, and how many cores may be wired in a single plane.

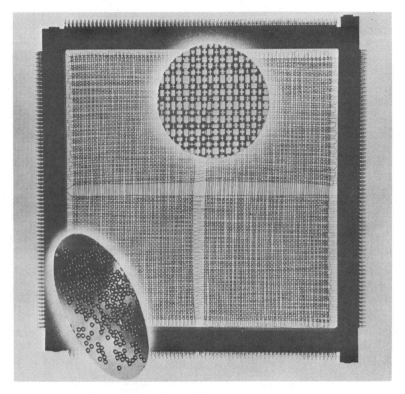

Figure 11-12.   Magnetic core plane.

Let us first consider how the 3D core system is organized and later go into the details of the parts of the system. Figure 11-13 shows a full block diagram of a 3D core organization. Notice that a three-dimensional core stack is shown. As we shall shortly see there are many cores planes, each the same, similar to a plane of cores as shown in Figures 11-11 or 11-12. For example, consider a core memory, organized in a 3D scheme having 4096 words (M) with 16 bits per word (N). There are $\sqrt{M}$ ($\sqrt{4096} = \sqrt{2^{12}} = 2^{6} = 64$) lines of X-select and the same number of Y-select lines. In our example there would be 64 X- and 64 Y-select lines or 128 lines in

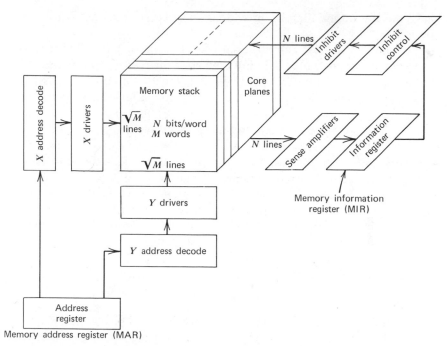

Figure 11-13.   3D core memory organization.

total. Corresponding to an address set into the *memory address register* (MAR), a part of the address is fed to the X-address decode circuitry and a part to the Y-address decode circuitry. This results in one of the 64 X-select drivers being pulsed. The pulses select a single core on each plane, there being N planes or as many core planes as bits per word. If, in the given example, word 52 is specified by the address, then core 52 on plane 1, core 52 on plane 2, up through core 52 on plane 16 are all pulsed by a read pulse. A separate sense wire on each of the 16 planes has a logical-0 or logical-1 voltage induced depending on the bit stored in the core of that plane.

Since the induced voltages appear on the various sense lines only at the time the read pulse occurs, the data from the sense amplifiers is strobed (gated) into a memory information register (MIR) which is a flip-flop register that will now hold the 16 bits of data of one word until the next read operation. Following the read operation is a write operation in which the data just read is used to gate the inhibit control and driver circuits so that inhibit pulses can be generated (or not) on each of the 16 lines (one per plane). The X and Y select lines are pulsed by a write pulse, which, with the inhibit pulse (if present), cause the data in the MIR to be written back into the cores, thereby providing an effective nondestructive read operation.

The data in the MIR can be serially shifted out or parallel transferred out to any other computer unit any time after the read operation or before another read operation takes place. If, as is most common, the MIR data is transferred in parallel, it can be taken any time after a read operation is completed, even during a write operation since the data is a logical signal that can be fed to more than one circuit as a data signal.

The basic 3D memory requires $\sqrt{M}\,X$ drivers and the same number of Y drivers, plus N inhibit drivers. It is possible to use a diode matrix to reduce the number of drivers required from $2\sqrt{M}$ to $4[M]^{1/4}$ at a cost of $4\sqrt{M}$ diodes. For $M = 2^{12}$ and $N = 16$, the number of drivers required was $2^6 = 64\,X$ drivers, $64\,Y$ drivers, and $N = 16$ inhibit drivers, or 144 drivers in total. Using a set of $4\sqrt{2^{12}} = 4 \times 64 = 256$ diodes in a matrix connection the number of drivers required can be reduced to $4[2^{12}]^{1/4} = 4(2^3) = 32\,X$ drivers $+ 32\,Y$ drivers and 16 inhibit drivers, a total of 80 drivers instead of 144 drivers. Since a core driver is a sophisticated amplifier current switching device it is far more economical to replace 64 drivers by 256 diodes.

The details of the parts of the 3D core system will be covered in a later section. At present we can continue with the general organization of a 3D core memory for a few examples.

Example 11-1.   How many cores per plane and planes are required for a 16K memory of 12 bits per word, for 3D core organization.

Solution: From the description above

$$M \cong 16\,\text{K or } 2^{14} = 16{,}384 \text{ exactly}$$
$$N = 12 \text{ bits per word}$$

There are then M cores in each plane, or

$$M = 16{,}384 \text{ cores per plane and } N = 12 \text{ planes}$$

Example 11-2.   How many X and Y lines are required in the 3D core memory of Example 11-1? How many total wires per plane?

Solution: There are $\sqrt{M} = \sqrt{2^{14}} = 2^7$ lines of X and 2^7 lines of Y select.

$$\text{Number of } X \text{ select lines} = 2^7 = 128$$
$$\text{Number of } Y \text{ select lines} = 128$$

The total number of lines in a plane are then

$$128 + 128 + 1 + 1 = 258 \text{ lines}$$

where only a single sense and single inhibit line are required for a plane. Thus, only 258 lines are required to operate a core plane of 16,384 cores.

Example 11-3. In the 3D core plane of Examples 11-1 and 11-2, how many total cores, sense amplifiers, and inhibit drivers are required?

Solution: The total number of cores is

$$M \times N = (2^{14})(12) = (16,384)(12)$$
$$= 196,608 \, (\cong 200,000 \text{ cores})$$

For the 12 planes there are 12 sense amplifiers and 12 inhibit drivers.

2 1/2D Core Organization.   The $2\frac{1}{2}$D core organization has recently become quite popular. It requires only 3 wires per core (compared to 4 wires for the 3D organization) and provides fast operation with quite large memory sizes. In addition the $2\frac{1}{2}$D memory plane is not organized square (same number of X and Y lines) as is often found in the 3D system.

Figure 11-14 shows the organization of a $2\frac{1}{2}$D core memory. An address in the memory address register (MAR) is divided up so that the X bits after decoding selects one of the X drivers. A half-select pulse is then provided by the one driver selected to an X line on each plane. As in the 3D system, there are as many planes as bits per word (N). The Y address bits are decoded to select one of the Y drivers. A full set of Y drivers is provided for each plane so that there are N sets of Y drivers. This is the difference between $2\frac{1}{2}$D and 3D—the 3D requires only one set of Y drivers.

Reading in the $2\frac{1}{2}$D system is accomplished as follows. One core on each plane is selected by a half-select read pulse on an X wire and another half-select pulse on a Y wire. A single sense wire threads all the cores of one plane so that there are N sense wires brought out and N sense amplifiers to provide the N data bits of the word read for storage in the memory information register (MIR). Even though a separate Y driver is required for each plane (as compared to one driver to handle all the same Y lines of all planes in a 3D system), the read operation described in $2\frac{1}{2}$D is effectively the same as in 3D.

The difference between the systems is seen in the write operation for which a $2\frac{1}{2}$D plane has no inhibit wire (a savings of one wire through a core making wiring of the core plane simpler and cheaper). After a read operation, with all cores of the word just read now at the logical-0 state, a write operation commences. A half-select write pulse is provided on the X wire selected by the X address bits and decoding circuitry. In addition, a Y line half-select pulse may be provided to the Y line selected by the Y

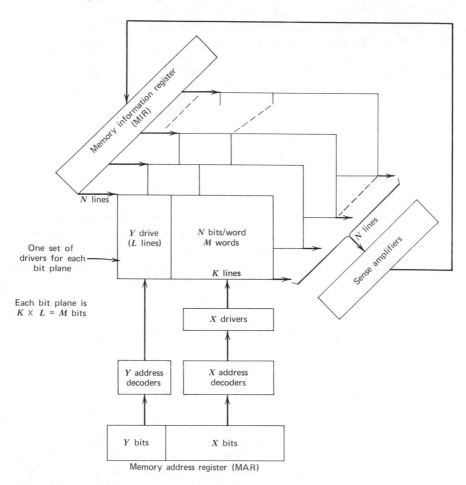

Figure 11-14. $2\frac{1}{2}$D core memory organization.

address bits. If a 1 is to be written, then those Y drivers are gated to provide a half-select Y line pulse. The Y drivers of those planes whose bit to be written as a 0 are gated so that no Y pulse occurs and the cores on those planes remain logical-0, as desired. A specific example should help clarify these details.

Example 11-4.   A core memory is organized in $2\frac{1}{2}$D and has 16 bits per word (N) for 4096 words (M). How many core planes and address bits are required?

Solution: In either 3D or $2\frac{1}{2}$D there are N core planes, 16 planes in this example. Also in either organization there would be for $2^{12} = 4096$ words, 12 bits of address.

Example 11-5.   If the 12-bit address is divided in a $2\frac{1}{2}$D organization so that 4 bits are Y select and 8 bits are X select, how many X drivers and Y drivers are required?

Solution: For 8 X address bits the, X decoders can select one of $2^8 = 256$ drivers ($K = 256$). There are then 256 X drivers and 256 X wires in a plane. However, although each plane has 256 wires, only one set of 256 X drivers is needed.

For 4 Y address bits the Y decoders can select one of $2^4 = 16$ drivers ($L = 16$). There are then 16 Y drivers and 16 Y wires in a plane. There are, however, a set 16 Y drivers for *each* plane so that in this case there are 16 planes of 16 drivers or

$$16 \times 16 = 256 \text{ } Y \text{ drivers in total}$$

The driver electronics required for the core memory under consideration is then

$$256 + 256 = 512 \text{ driver circuits, total}$$

Example 11-6.   How many wires per core, wires per plane, and number of stages of MIR are there in the present example $2\frac{1}{2}$D core organization?

Solution: There are only 3 wires per core for $2\frac{1}{2}$D core organization. For each plane in the present example there are 256 X wires, 16 Y wires, and one sense wire for a total of 273 wires per plane. The MIR has 16 stages corresponding to the number of planes.

Notice in Example 11-5 that there are 256 X lines and only 16 Y lines. The ratio of X/Y lines is 16:1 in this case. Typically it is 8:1 or 16:1. The $2\frac{1}{2}$D organization is not square (same number of X and Y lines). In either $2\frac{1}{2}$D or 3D, however, the drivers can be arranged in a matrix form using diodes to reduce the total number of driver circuits required.

There are a number of advantages to the $2\frac{1}{2}$D core organization. The elimination of the fourth wire provides a simpler core wiring. In addition, the electronic drivers used can be simpler and cheaper due to the reduced load by the core stack. Shorter delays, faster recovery from current pulses as well as inherently lower noise from the read operation result in 2D organization. Consequently, a $2\frac{1}{2}$D core memory is somewhat faster than a 3D memory (using the same sized core). A $2\frac{1}{2}$D memory cycle time (full read and write operations) of about 350 nsec is commercially available, whereas 3D core memories are more typically about 1 μsec cycle time.

The $2\frac{1}{2}$D organization has also been used for building very low-cost, high-capacity memory (referred to as bulk core or mass core storage). In this particular application the third (sense) wire is eliminated leaving only two wires per core. The readout signal is sensed on the N sets of X drive wires, which imposes some rather stringent requirements on the sensing electronics, increasing their cost. However, the savings in eliminating the long continuous sense wire compensates for this increased cost. Mass memories of 2^{18} words of 72 bits per word have been built and larger ones will certainly be quite in demand. Even the basic core memory size has substantially increased so that a few hundred thousand word to a few million word memory is becoming common.

The disadvantage of a $2\frac{1}{2}$D memory is basically in the increased number of core driver electronic circuits, but as discussed above many advantages more than make up for this.

11-4.   Details of Core Memory Units

With the background of organizing 2D, $2\frac{1}{2}$D, and 3D core memory systems we can look at different parts of these memory systems in some detail. We shall consider such parts as the memory address register, decoding circuits, driver circuits, sense amplifiers, inhibit drivers, and the timing chain to provide a read/write operating cycle.

Address Decoding.   The address of a word to be read (or written) in a core memory is provided as a binary number that is placed into the memory address register (MAR). For example, Figure 11-15 shows a 12-stage address register. When a new address is to be transferred the MAR is first cleared and then a transfer pulse dumps a new memory address value into the MAR. This address is taken from the control unit and represents either a next word of instruction in a Fetch cycle or a next data value in an EXECUTE cycle. In either case the address specifies which of the 4096 words of memory ($2^{12} = 4096$) is to be read from the memory. It also could represent the address location of a new word to be stored in the core memory on an EXECUTE cycle of a store or input instruction. Regardless of the action required, the operation of the circuitry shown in Figure 11-15 is only to select the X line and one Y line to select only the word specified by the MAR address value.

The address value is a single 12-bit number with each register stage providing two outputs as shown in Figure 11-15. The X and Y bits for a 3D system would be equal, so the present example shows that 6 bits specify the X address and 6 bits the Y address. Using 6 bits allows 2^6 or

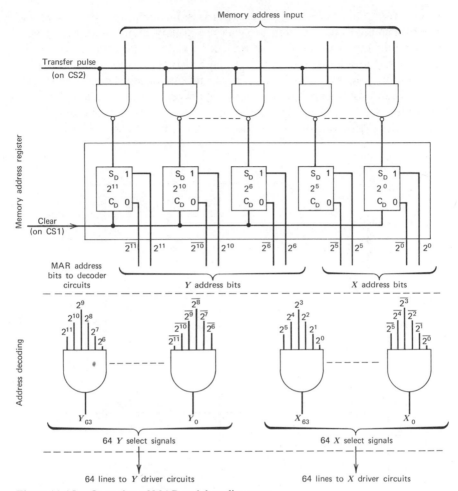

Figure 11-15.   Operation of MAR and decoding gates.

64 different values. Thus, the X address bits can specify one of 64 possible X lines and the Y address bits can specify one of 64 possible Y lines. This decoding of X and Y address is done basically by 64 X and 64 Y decoding gates. There are 6 inputs to each of the decoding gates so that any address value selects only one of the 64 X lines and only one of the 64 Y lines.

Core Drive and Sink Circuits.   Recall that although two of 128 lines are selected the coincident current wiring scheme results in only one of 4096 cores in a plane ($64 \times 64 = 4096$) being selected. Operation of the driver circuits are shown in Figure 11-16. A basic approach is shown for ease of explanation, although, as was previously mentioned, the drivers could be arranged using a diode matrix to reduce the number of driver circuits. As shown there are 64 X and 64 Y driver circuits. Corresponding to a memory address value, one of the X and one of the Y decoding signals is high so that only one X and only one Y driver gate is qualified (gated) at this time. A read pulse then results in a current pulse along one X and one Y wire, with the one core (out of 4096) being selected by the co-

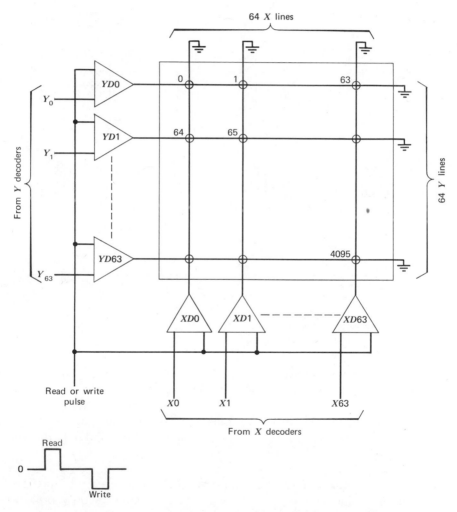

Figure 11-16.   Possible operation of driver units for read/write operations.

incident current pulses. If $XD0$ and $YD0$ are selected, then core 0 is read. Decoder signals $YD1$ and $XD0$ would select core 64, and so on.

The write operation would require that a current pulse be provided that is of opposite polarity to that shown in Figure 11-16. This would require an electronic driver gate that is bilateral or that can provide either a current pulse flowing into the line or draw current from the line. Such a complementary driver is a complex electronic circuit providing action as a current source on read and current sink on write operation as indicated by the read/write pulses shown in Figure 11-16. As was mentioned, a matrix arrangement is possible using diodes to reduce the number or complexity of the driver circuits.

To see how a diode array arrangement of the drivers can be applied, an example of a 16-bit core plane requiring only 4 address bits is shown in Figure 11-17. To simplify the figure only the X driver and diode matrix is shown, the Y circuitry being exactly the same. Two of the four address bits are decoded into four lines marked $X0$ to $X3$ on Figure 11-17. Only one of the $X0$ to $X3$ lines is high at any time. This gates one of the four read drivers ($RD0$ to $RD3$) and also one of the write drivers ($WD0$ to $WD3$). During read cycle the read signal is high (and write signal is low) so that the read sink (RS) driver is on. When a read pulse occurs it pulses all four read drivers, but only the driver selected by the $X0$ to $X3$ signals turns on, driving current through the line from top to bottom, as shown in Figure 11-17, with the current flowing through the read sink circuit into ground. If, for example, word 9 were to be read, then $RD1$ would be gated by the $X1$ signal and a half-select pulse would be fed to cores 1, 5, 9, and 13. The Y select would provide the other half-select pulse to pulse cores 8, 9, 10, and 11 with only core 9 being read. This would correspond to one bit of word 9, the other bits being obtained from each of the other core planes having exactly the same setup. In fact, the electronics shown drives all the core planes.

On a write operation the X-select signal, $X1$ in the present example, is still the same. The write signal goes high (and read goes low) so that the write sink (WS) circuit is turned on and a write pulse is fed to all write drivers. Only write driver $WD1$ would be operated in the present example, causing a half-select signal to again drive core 9, but the current pulse goes up the line in an opposite direction than on the read operation.

The circuit of Figure 11-17 allowed separate driver and sink circuits whereas the scheme of Figure 11-16 required a more complex complementary driver sink switch.

Figure 11-18 shows how read/write control and read and write pulses might occur within each operation. These pulses will continually occur in a computer with a read/write cycle which repeats constantly.

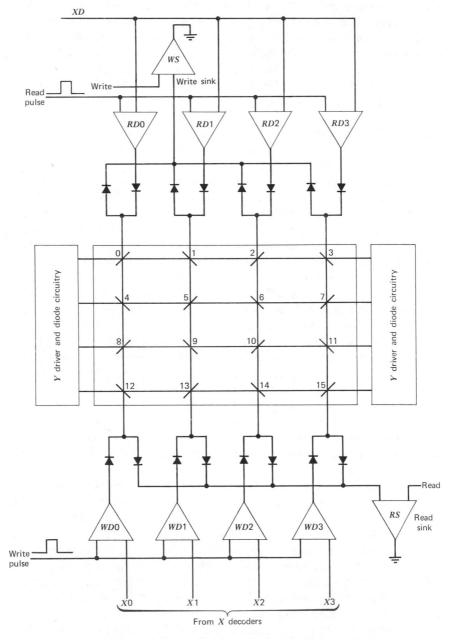

Figure 11-17.　Possible connection for X-driver only showing diode matrix arrangement.

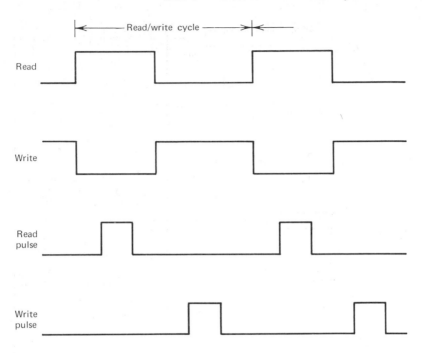

Figure 11-18.   Read/write cycle pulses for circuit of Figure 11-17.

Sense Amplifiers.   The output of each plane is obtained on a single sense line. There are then N sense lines followed by N sense amplifiers as shown in Figure 11-19. The two ends of the sense wire are brought to the sense amplifier. On a read operation a voltage induced in the sense line corresponds to a 1 bit read from the core. This voltage, generally millivolts of signal, is amplified to provide a logic level voltage to operate a logic gate. At a set time after the read is initiated, a strobe pulse (narrow pulse) is used to gate the data bits read into the stages of the memory information register (which had been cleared at the start of the read operation). The strobe pulse is necessary to transfer the output of the sense amplifiers only during the time after a read pulse occurs when the core, in switching, induces a voltage on the sense line.

Figure 11-20 shows how the clear and strobe pulses might occur in the read part of a read/write cycle. The READ signal going high results in a short clear pulse occurring to clear all register stages to the 0 state. After the clear pulse is completed the read pulse occurs causing selected core to be pulsed. A fixed time after the read is initiated a strobe pulse transfers the data of the sense amplifiers into the MIR.

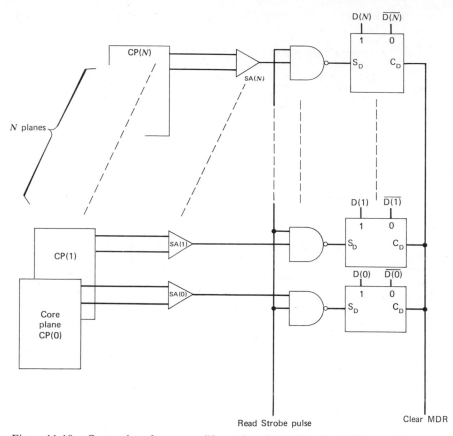

Figure 11-19. Connection of sense amplifier and strobing of data into MIR.

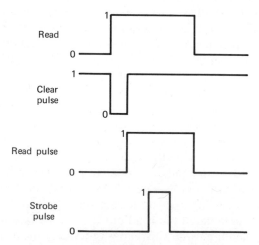

Figure 11-20.   Timing pulses during READ operation part of read/write cycle.

450

Write and Inhibit Operation.   The data read into the MIR must be written back into the cores to restore the data so that an effective nondestructive read operation results. Figure 11-21 shows the operation during the write

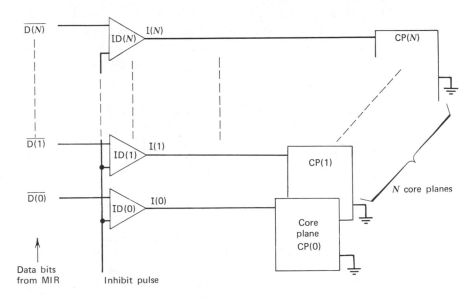

Figure 11-21.   Circuitry for **WRITE** operation.

cycle. The data bits $D(0)$ to $D(N)$ from the N stages to the MIR gate the N inhibit drivers, $ID(0)$ to $ID(N)$. If the data bit is a 0, then the inhibit pulse is gated to operate the particular inhibit line. Data bits of 1 result in disabling the particular inhibit driver so that no inhibit pulse occurs on

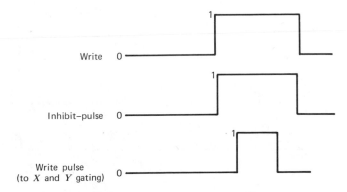

Figure 11-22.   Timing pulses during write operation.

that line. Recall that during a write operation X and Y write pulses occur for each core of the selected word. The inhibit drive signal then blocks the core from switching to write a 0 or it allows the core to switch to write a 1.

Figure 11-22 shows the timing signals during the write part of the read/write cycle. A write line goes high as well as the inhibit pulse. The write pulse (used by X and Y drivers) then occurs causing the selected cores to be switched (to write a 1), or not, depending on the inhibit signal to each plane.

Read and Write Operations.   The basic timing signals for a read/write cycle constantly repeat. If the overall operation required is a READ the data is read into the MIR as specified by the address in the MAR. A write operation automatically occurs during the write part of the cycle even though the operation called for is a READ.

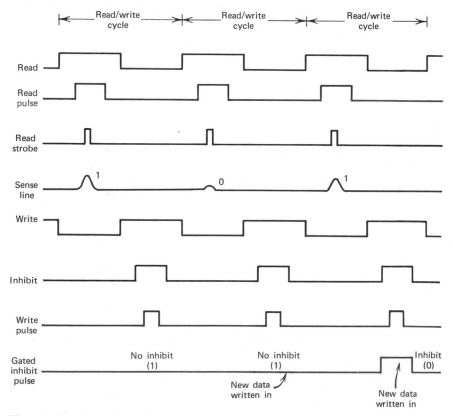

Figure 11-23.   Some timing and data signals during read/write cycles.

When a WRITE operation is called for (by the instruction in the control unit) the read part of the cycle occurs as always. What changes the effective operation is that the data read is not strobed into the MIR so that it holds the data transferred in at the start of the write operation. Since the cores are read they are cleared to the 0 state as expected. During the write part of the cycle the new data in the MIR is then written into the word of core memory specified by the address in the MAR.

Thus, in the case of either a READ or WRITE operation a full read/ write cycle still occurs. Figure 11-23 shows some timing and data signals for a few read/write cycles as example. During the read part of the cycle a read pulse causes the selected core lines to be read. The example shows a 1 bit read (and then a 0 and 1 bit on later read cycles). The sense line has an induced voltage that may be strobed into the MIR.

On the write part of the cycle an inhibit signal and write pulse occur. When a 1 is to be written back into the core no gated inhibit pulse (inhibit signal gated with data bit) occurs and a 1 is written into the selected core. When a 0 is to be written into the core a gated inhibit pulse occurs and a 0 is left in the selected core. Although the core is read, it is not strobed into the MIR if a write operation is to be done.

Figure 11-23 shows reading and writing a 1 on a READ operation and then reading a 0 + 1 and writing a 1 and 0 on a WRITE operation.

11-5. Magnetic Film Memories

A technique that is newer and only beginning to be used is magnetic film or thin film. The basic magnetic storage element is a very thin, flat layer of nickel iron alloy, which has a property that along one geometrical axis it is easy to magnetize but along another it is quite hard. Figure 11-24 shows hysteresis loops for a film along the two axis that provide "easy" and "hard" magnetization. Along the easy axis of operation the core remains magnetized even after the drive pulse is removed, whereas along the hard axis of operation almost no magnetic flux remains after the drive pulse goes to zero.

If a magnetic film is subjected to a magnetic field along its hard axis, the internal magnetic property of the film will rotate very rapidly so that it aligns with the applied field. (This is somewhat analogous with a compass needle following the field of a magnet brought near it). When this is done the magnetization along the easy axis reduces to zero. A net flux change results. If the change is negative a 1 was stored and if positive a 0 was stored, sensed as a negative or positive voltage pulse.

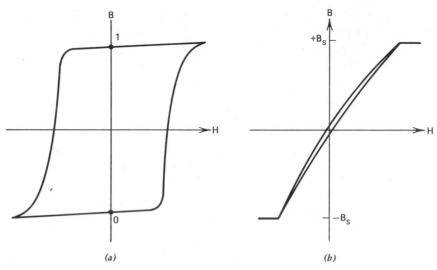

Figure 11-24.   Magnetic film hysteresis loops. (*a*) Easy axis. (*b*) Hard axis.

The small thin spot acts as a storage element so that it holds either the 0 or 1 easy state as shown in Figure 11-24*a* (shown on a single storage spot in Figures 11-25*a* and 11-25*b*). The flux can remain in either state and is equivalent to storing a 0 or 1 as opposite flux conditions in a single core. A difference can be seen when the thin film spot is caused to switch to the hard state (which does not exist for a magnetic core, and is due to

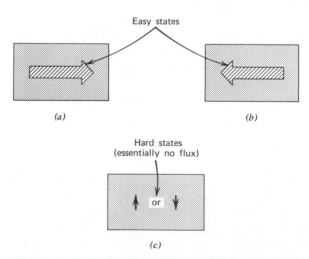

Figure 11-25.   Flux states of thin film spot. (*a*) Internal flux for stored 0 state. (*b*) Internal flux for stored 1 state. (*c*) Internal flux in hard state.

the very thin layer of magnetic material deposited to make the storage spot or element). Figure 11-25*c* shows that in the hard state shown to be along the smaller width of the spot the flux remaining is quite small as shown also in the hysteresis curve of Figure 11-24*b*.

In effect, then, a thin film storage spot can store either a 0 or 1. In reading the core information, however, it will be noted that the internal flux of the core must be switched (caused to change) in order to sense the stored information, as was also necessary in a magnetic core. The switching action required in a thin film spot is from either the 1 or 0 state to the hard state (essentially no flux), which is a destructive readout process. Figure 11-26 shows a sense line used to pick up an induced voltage when

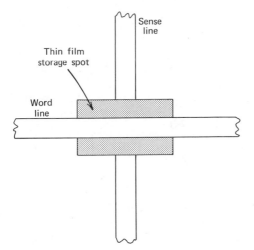

Figure 11-26.   Single thin film storage spot showing driver word line and pickup sense line.

the spot read switches flux state. A current fed into the word line (it passes across additional elements as will be shown) will cause the core to switch to the hard state, the flux change inducing a voltage in the sense line. Notice that the thin film spot is a solid element with a wire running below it (sense line) and another wire (along the easy axis) running above it (word line).

Figure 11-27 shows the action of reading a stored 1 from a thin film storage element. Initially a stored 1 is a large internal flux along the easy axis. A current in the word line as shown will result in a flux in the thin film element under the wire in the indicated direction. The resulting action is to switch the net flux to move clockwise and the flux switches from the easy state to the hard state leaving little internal flux after the read current is removed, as shown in Figure 11-27*b*. The flux, in switching,

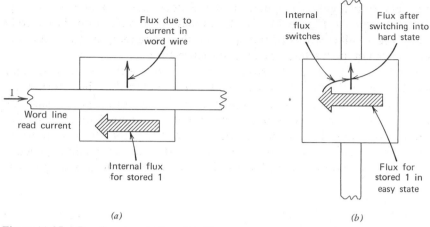

Figure 11-27.   Reading stored 1 from thin film.

cuts the sense line inducing a voltage in the line, the induced voltage polarity indicating a 1 was read.

Figure 11-28*a* shows the action of reading a stored 0 from a thin film element. The initial stored 0 flux is shown along the easy axis. The read current along the word line causes a flux as shown in Figure 11-28*a*, this time resulting in the flux switching counterclockwise to the elements hard state as shown in Figure 11-28*b*. This time the flux changing cuts the sense line in a counterclockwise direction inducing a voltage, opposite in polarity to that when reading a 1.

A voltage polarity sensitive amplifier, called a differential amplifier,

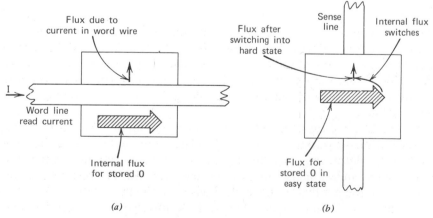

Figure 11-28.   Reading stored 0 from thin film.

is used to feed the signal on the sense line for transfer into the memory information register (MIR) for storage.

The result of reading either a 0 or 1 is to leave the thin film element in the hard state. Writing then consists of either switching the internal flux to the easy state of the 1 or 0 flux condition. To provide writing operation, an additional wire, the information line, is used as shown in Figure 11-29. Currents in the information line and word line as shown in Figure 11-29a result in a flux that will cause the thin film flux to switch to the easy state stored-1 condition. When the writing currents are removed the element remains in the stored-1 state. Similarly, currents in the word line and information line (opposite than for writing a 1) result in a net drive flux to switch the element to the stored-0 state, as shown in Figure 11-29b.

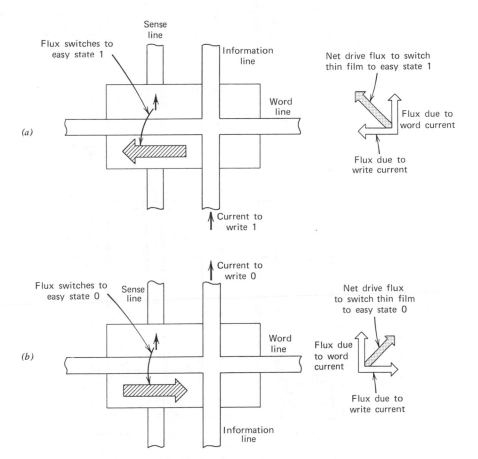

Figure 11-29.   Writing 1 or 0 in thin film element.

The thin film elements are organized in an array that is essentially a 2D selection scheme. Figure 11-30 shows for example, an eight-word, five bit per word thin film memory plane. A memory address register (MAR) and decoding logic select one of the eight memory words, providing a drive pulse on the selected word line. All five bits of the selected

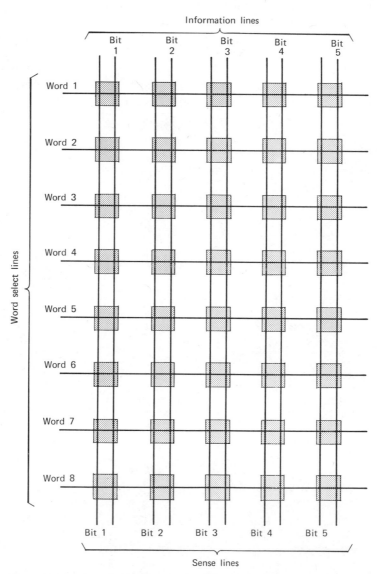

Figure 11-30.   Sample thin film plane for eight-word, five bits per word memory.

word are read out on the five sense lines. The information from the sense line is available after sense amplifiers for transfer into a memory information register (**MIR**).

On the read operation the cores read are all switched to the logical-0 state. A following write operation uses the information read into the **MIR** to provide inhibit signals on the bit information lines so that a drive pulse on the selected word line causes switching for those cores that should be logical-1. Figure 11-31 shows the organization of the registers and other circuitry to operate a thin film memory core plane, as discussed above.

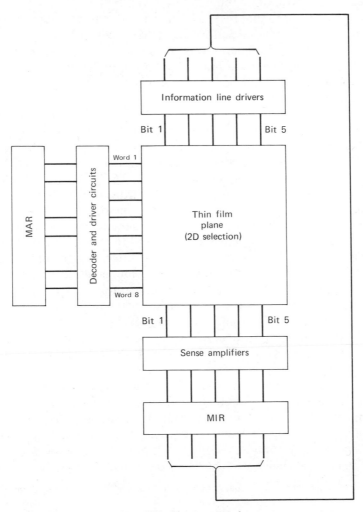

Figure 11-31.   Operation of thin film memory plane.

Superconductive Magnetic Memory.   Another storage device that is being investigated is a superconductive memory element, which provides extremely high packing densities. Presently about 15,000 cells per square inch is possible, much more than only a few tens of cells using magnetic cores or a few thousand using IC techniques.

The basic principle of a superconductive memory cell is based on the fact that some metals when placed at a very low temperature drop to a resistance of exactly zero. It is startling to note that the resistance of a superconductive drops to exactly zero when its temperature is decreased below a transition temperature level. It is not a very small resistance but exactly zero that results in the superconductive region of operation. An experiment was performed at MIT beginning in March 1954 when a few hundred amperes was induced in a lead ring immersed in liquid helium. The current continued to flow until the experiment was voluntarily ended in September 1956, with no noticeable decrease in the magnitude of the current.

Typical transition temperatures range from near $4°K$ (Kelvin[1]) to near $8°K$ for some twenty-odd possible superconductive elements which have been found so far. When a superconductive element is in its superconductive state, a magnetic field of sufficient strength will destroy the zero resistance action in the area of the magnetic field, causing normal resistance to be present. The time required for transition between superconductive and conductive states is only about 1 nanosecond.

The superconductive property with magnetic field switching from superconductive to conductive state is used to make a memory element called a *cryotron*[2]. Tin is used as the basic storage element and lead for the drive line. The memory elements must be immersed in a bath of liquid helium to provide the required very low temperature.

The manufacturing techniques for making thin film cryotrons is similar to those used for IC and magnetic thin film devices. A storage loop is made by depositing a thin layer of tin. Above that a thin layer of insulating silicon monoxide is deposited to form lead drive lines as shown in Figure 11-32.

The cryotron stores a data bit as a circulating current in the storage loop. One can consider a circulating current as storage of a logic-1 and no current as storage of a logic-0. To read the stored data in a loop requires switching off the loop current (thereby destroying the stored data as in the magnetic memory devices already considered). A coincident current selection provides half-select currents to the X and Y drive lines, the total

[1]The Kelvin temperature scale starts at absolute zero ($-273.18°C$), at which no motion of any kind occurs.
[2]The name *cryotron* is derived from the Greek word *kryos*, meaning "icy cold."

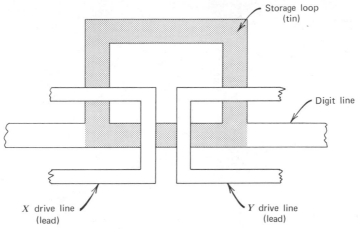

Figure 11-32.   Basic form of cryogenic thin film storage element.

resulting magnetic field being sufficient to switch the loop from the super-conductive to conductive state, thereby causing a loop resistance to result and loop current to decay. The momentary voltage resulting when the loop current flows through the conductive resistance before it decays is read across the ends of the digit line. If no current had been circulating, no voltage would have resulted.

Since the readout is basically destructive a write operation must follow to write back the data read. A current applied along the digit line will result in a circulating current again flowing in the loop *if* no magnetic field is locally present due to X and Y drive currents.

The main disadvantage of the need of a very low temperature container to hold the cryogenic memory plane should be overcome by the advantages of extremely fast switching speeds and extremely high storage element density so that more of this type memory device can be expected.

Plated-Wire Memory.   Another magnetic memory technique presently being used is a plated-wire element similar in operation to the thin film previously described. Figure 11-33 shows a plated-wire memory element. The easy magnetization direction around the wire circumference and hard magnetization axis axially along the wire is indicated in the diagram. Word lines are formed by flat strips of wire. Operation of this form of magnetic storage element in a 2D scheme is essentially the same as that covered in the discussion of a thin-film element.

A bit is stored at each intersection of a word strap and wire in the form of a directional magnetic field (opposite magnetic field directions for binary 1 and 0).

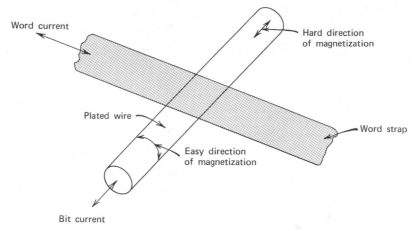

Figure 11-33.   Plated-wire memory element.

11-6.   Magnetic Drum Memory

A drum memory is quite different from a core memory. The core is very fast while the drum is slow; the core can be operated random access, the drum cyclically; the core is made of individual bit storage cells, the drum of a large storage surface; cost of core memory is high, for the same storage capacity the drum is cheaper; the core size is relatively small, the drum unit much larger. The drum memory is made of a cylinder whose surface is coated with a magnetic material. Data can be stored in rows around the circumference of the drum unit as in Figure 11-34. A special "head" is used to write or read information on the drum, the information being small magnetized areas as indicated. The drum is rotated at a fixed speed so that a drum revolution takes a specified time interval. A rotational speed of 12,000 revolutions per minute, for example, would produce a single cycle of rotation in

$$T = \frac{1}{\text{speed}} = \frac{1}{12,000} \frac{\text{min}}{\text{rev}} \times 60 \frac{\text{sec}}{\text{min}} = \frac{1}{200} \frac{\text{sec}}{\text{rev}}$$

$$T = 5 \frac{\text{msec}}{\text{rev}}$$

This is a realistic time for drum memories. Compare this to 5 μsec for a core memory and you will see that there is a difference of a factor of 1000. This is an appreciably great difference. Actually, the data coming by the read head may appear immediately after it is desired or as long as 5 msec later. On the average it may take 2.5 msec using half a cycle as the

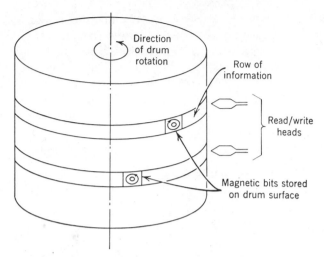

Figure 11-34.   Magnetic drum memory, simple sketch.

average. This still is considerably different from the core access time. A computer using drum memory is therefore a slower-operating machine. This does not mean that the circuitry works at a slower clock rate. The bits may be coming off the drum at the rate of 1 million per second, but until the desired data comes by the read head may be milliseconds later. With a 5-msec cycle time, storing 5000 bits on a row or track would mean that 5000 bits pass by every 5 msec, or $5000/5 \times 10^{-3} = 1 \times 10^6$, or 1 million bits per second, as was previously indicated.

Drum rotational speed is limited by the mechanical drive system and the size and weight of the memory drum. Practical limits presently keep the cycle time to about 0.5 msec. In order to get a reasonable amount of data on the drum surface, the diameter must be fairly large. A 12-in. diameter might be considered average. Because the drum is useful for large memory storage, the cylinder height is about 8 in. to accommodate the large number of tracks desired. Figures of 20 tracks per inch and 200 bits per track inch (circumferential distance) are typical. A 100,000-bit drum memory is an average capacity. Compare this to the complexity of 100,000 cores in many planes with all the operating circuitry. The drum requires only one read/write head per track, so that a few thousand bits need only one drive or pickup circuit. The selector gating need only pick the one track out of a few dozen. Simplicity of operation leading to a cost per bit much lower than that of the core system is a prime asset of the drum system. Large capacity and low cost then are the main assets of the drum system, and these are the main points to consider. Slow speed, although undesirable, is acceptable when capacity and cost are the main considerations. When speed is too important to lose, the core must be used. There are, as would be expected, some special systems using both drum memory for large storage and small "scratch pad" core memories for high operating speed. The two work together, so that the computer is always operating at its highest speed and the core and drum aid each other.

A simplified picture of the read/write function is shown in Figure 11-35. The read and write operation can be considered separately. To

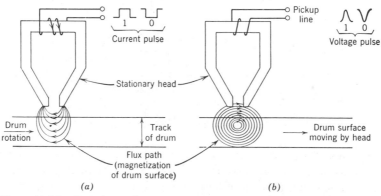

Figure 11-35.   Write/read function on magnetic drum. (*a*) Write. (*b*) Read.

To write a ONE or ZERO requires magnetizing a small segment of the track as it moves by. By controlling the current polarity in the write head, the flux direction is fixed. Clockwise could be a ONE and counter-clockwise flux a ZERO. The amount of flux induced on the drum depends on the strength of the current pulse (and fixed factors such as number of turns, core reluctance, surface-to-head spacing, and so on). The amount of voltage pickup depends on the strength of the magnetic field produced by the stored bit on the drum surface (and the fixed factors or rotating speed, air-gap, number of turns, head-surface spacing, and so on). The spacing (distance) of pickup or write head from the surface is very important. Distances of less than 5 mils (5/1000ths of an inch) are typical. Some high-speed machines use a technique of "floating heads" to try to achieve the minimum spacing. The heads are held off the surface by air pressure. As the surface expands from heating, the head spacing is kept constant by the air pressure. If the head were rigidly fixed 1 mil away and the surface expanded by a mil from heating, the two would touch, destroying that part of the drum. Floating heads provide improvement but also add mechanical complexity and cost.

Data is stored sequentially around the track and passes by the read/write head each cycle. To provide for simple addressing of the data, the information is laid out from a fixed starting point. Each word does not need an address number stored with it on the drum. Knowing that it is word 27 of track 6 is sufficient to allow reading it out. The outside circuitry must count the number of words coming by on the desired track and provide a start read command (and stop read command) at the correct time. Information is generally arranged bit serial, ten bits in a row representing a given word, for example. Since the tracks may be read out simultaneously, the data may be handled word parallel for expediency. Although a single head is able to read all the information by shifting it from track to track, such action further slows down operating speeds and provides poorer track resolution since mechanical accuracy will be reduced. It is usual to have a fixed head for each track.

Magnetic Drum Organization.   A number of ways of organizing data on a drum are possible. Data could be stored in bit-serial format with words stored circumferentially in one track. For example, consider a drum containing 32 tracks of 4096 bits per track. For a bit-serial machine (Figure 11-36) with 32 bits per word, each track will contain 128 words:

$$4096 \frac{\text{bits}}{\text{track}} \div 32 \frac{\text{bits}}{\text{word}} = 128 \frac{\text{words}}{\text{track}}$$

Track 1 will contain words 0 to 127, track 2 will contain words 128 to 255, and so on. Since each track will have its own read/write head, access time for a word of any track will be the same. Once the beginning of the desired word appears under the fixed head of that track, it will take 32 bit-times to read out the full word. If the drum rotational speed is 3600 revolutions per minute (60 revolutions per second) the transfer rate to (to or from the drum) will be

$$128 \frac{\text{words}}{\text{rev}} \times 60 \frac{\text{rev}}{\text{sec}} = 7680 \frac{\text{words}}{\text{sec}}$$

A second organization of the drum information would be *bit-parallel* (or word-serial). In this case the 32 bits of a single word are read at the same time (Figure 11-36), each bit coming out of a different track head. Access is still sequential but the word appears at one bit time. The word transfer rate for this case will be

$$4096 \frac{\text{words}}{\text{rev}} \times 60 \frac{\text{rev}}{\text{sec}} = 245,760 \frac{\text{words}}{\text{sec}}$$

This is much higher rate than the bit-serial operations and might be desirable in some applications.

Somewhere between the two extremes, bit-serial and bit-parallel, is

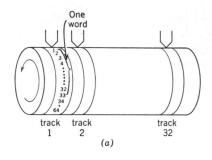

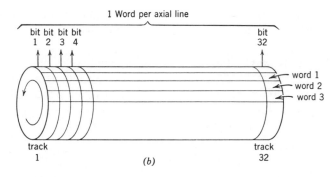

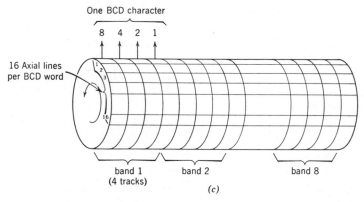

Figure 11-36.   Organization of data on a magnetic drum memory. (*a*) Bit-serial organized memory. (*b*) Bit-parallel organized memory. (*c*) Bit-serial-parallel organized memory.

bit-serial-parallel (Figure 11-36). This organization may be required for special coded forms of data. For example, in using binary-coded decimal (BCD) data, four binary digits are needed to store a BCD character. From this consideration the data might be organized in 8 bands, 4 tracks to a band. A character would be 4 bits of BCD. If a word contained 16 characters, each band would contain 256 words for a transfer rate of 15,360 words per second. In all cases, the bit rate of any track would be

$$4096 \frac{\text{bits}}{\text{rev}} \times 60 \frac{\text{rev}}{\text{sec}} = 245,760 \frac{\text{bits}}{\text{sec}}$$

requiring circuitry to operate at a clock rate of about 250 kHz.

Maximum access time would be 1 revolution or about 16 msec (1/60 sec per revolution). Average access would then be 8 msec. Although it takes a relatively long time to get to the information desired, the data comes off the drum at a high rate. Both the initial access time and the data transfer rate (bits per second) are necessary to describe a magnetic drum memory system.

Recording on Magnetic Surface.   Having considered the general organization of a magnetic drum memory, it might be well to look into some details of how data is stored on the magnetic drum surface and how it is read back. Recording methods fall into two classes, *return-to-zero* (more generally return-to-reference) and *nonreturn-to-zero*. In return-to-zero (RZ) recording the flux on the magnetic surface within defined track always returns to a reference value between adjacent bits of stored information. This reference value may be zero. For the zero-flux reference value, binary storage might be flux saturation in one direction or the other. Figure 11-37 shows the input recording data of an arbitrary group of bits for

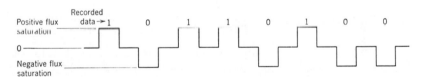

Figure 11-37.   Return-to-zero (RZ) recorded data.

RZ operation. Saturating the surface area where a bit is stored helps decrease voltage pickup variation produced by variations in the write current. The recording head used for RZ recording might be that of Figure 11-38 where recordings of a ONE and of a ZERO are shown

Circumferentially, the packing density depends on the head-to surface spacing, on the width of flux that penetrates the surface, and so on. It is also related to the recording method. In RZ a guard position of zero flux exists between adjacent bits. Furthermore, the negative voltage slope need not be considered when reading back the data. Figure 11-39 shows a few arbitrary data pulses, a clock signal which is used as a strobe (used to set specific times when data is read), and the output data.

Notice that the same output would result if the negative data pulses

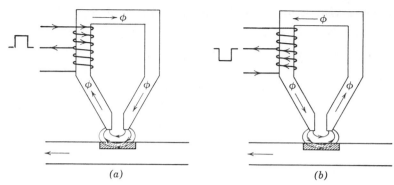

Figure 11-38.   Magnetic recording using RZ method.

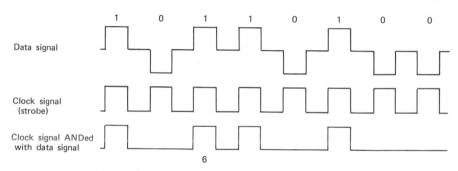

Figure 11-39.   Data read from RZ recording.

were not present, since an output from an AND gate occurs only when both inputs are present. This leads us to believe that more data could be stored in the same space. Before considering this increased density recording method, it should be pointed out that return-to-bias or reference recording, although providing the same recording density as RZ, does have an important advantage. If the bias level chosen is opposite saturation to that of the recorded ONE bit, the recovered signal is roughly twice that for RZ, and bipolar signals need not be handled by the read amplifiers. Figure 11-40 shows the data read with a return-to-bias method.

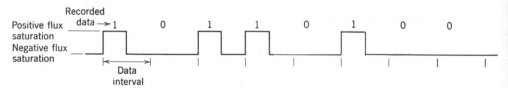

Figure 11-40.   Return-to-bias recorded data.

A method of recording data at a higher density than that recorded by RZ is called nonreturn-to-zero (NRZ). Figure 11-41 shows the same recorded data as in Figures 11-37 and 11-40 for RZ and return-to-bias recording. Compare the three figures carefully to see the difference between

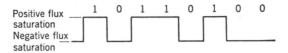

Figure 11-41.   Recorded data using nonreturn-to-zero (NRZ) recording.

them. Notice especially the difference between nonreturn-to-zero and return-to-reference recordings; these two appear the same to a casual glance but are quite different when observed carefully. In nonreturn-to-zero recording the binary digit is represented by a flux level (saturation level preferable). If groups of similar digits are recorded in NRZ, the flux remains unchanged. In RZ or return-to-bias the flux always changes between adjacent bits, even if they are the same binary value. The largest number of flux changes in NRZ recording occurs when alternate ONE and ZEROs are recorded, and even here the number of flux changes in half that of RZ recording. By using NRZ recording, twice the packing density of RZ recording is obtainable. In reading NRZ data, some means must be incorporated to indicate what the data read is when adjacent bits are the same, since the flux change occurs only when there is a data change and none occurs when bits are the same. Figure 11-42

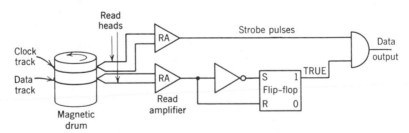

Figure 11-42.   Circuit for reading NRZ recorded data.

shows how a simple flip-flop circuit may be used to read data stored as NRZ. The waveforms of the signals throughout the read circuitry are shown in Figure 11-43.

The flux waveform of the NRZ recorded data clearly shows the information stored. Since only flux changes can be sensed, the constant-flux level of repeated ONEs and ZEROs is not directly evident in the amplifier

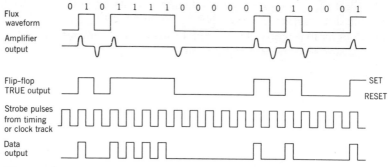

Figure 11-43.   Waveforms of signals for reading NRZ recorded data.

output waveform. If this output is used to SET and RESET a flip-flop, however, the recorded bits are clearly evident. In the circuit shown the negative-going pulse triggers the flip-flop inputs. By using strobe or timing pulses taken from a clock track on the drum, the data output is produced, providing bit-serial data that may be read into a buffer or storage register for use outside the memory unit.

Another NRZ recording method records only one of the binary signals. Called NRZI (I meaning invert), the recording considers only, say, binary ONEs and records them as a single flux change (see Figure 11-44).

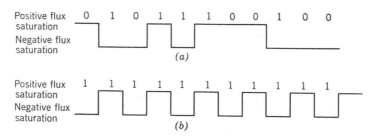

Figure 11-44.   Two binary digit waveforms using NRZI recording.

Because of this the ONE digit is sometimes a positive recorded signal and sometimes a negative recorded signal. Any flux change is indicative of a ONE being stored and no flux change of a ZERO. Figure 11-44 shows that the pattern for successive ONEs have a flux change for every ONE recorded. Reading data is similar to that just described.

A third method of NRZ recording is called "phase recording" (or "Ferranti" or "Manchester"). Figure 11-45 shows two waveforms using this method. In recording a ONE, for example, the bit is recorded as a positive flux followed by a negative flux. A recorded ZERO would then

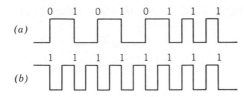

(a)

(b)   Figure 11-45.   Phase recording of data
(an NRZ method).

be a negative followed by a positive flux. What is most important about this method is that from the highest frequency recording (all ONEs or all ZEROs) to the lowest, the frequency change is one-half. If the highest frequency the signal changes at is 200 KHz, the lowest is only 100 KHz. The lowest frequency occurs for alternating ONEs and ZEROs. With the two other NRZ recording methods the recording of a large number of ONEs and ZEROs would appear as a steady or quiescent level approaching dc operation. This is a restriction on the read-write amplifiers used since they must operate from direct current up to maximum frequency. With the phase-recording method indicated, the frequency range is quite limited and transformer-coupled amplifiers can be used. Reading the stored information is substantially that indicated in the first NRZ recording considered and need not be elaborated on here. It need only be noted that recording and reading of data must be carefully timed with this method, as with all others.

Read Start and Gating.   Having considered how data is both stored on a magnetic drum and organized on the drum, let us look at how the overall drum read and write operation is controlled. An *origin* (start) track containing only a single bit at the proper starting place circumferentially is provided. Another track called the *clock track* is also present for synchronizing purposes. This track contains alternate ONEs and ZEROs to provide an output clock whose frequency is fixed by the drum rotational speed (and bits per inch). Because this speed may vary, and because an external clock may not occur at the recorded time of a bit passing under the head or may drift, this drum-controlled clock is the best for synchronization of read/write operation. The external controller contains a bit or word counter which uses the track clock pulses and resets or starts over at the occurrence of the single origin pulse. In this way the data is always timed according to the track layout. Where the mechanical construction causes small alignment errors between tracks, the data is *strobed* or read out at a single favorable time for each bit. Details of timing and strobing are found in many books on drum memory design. What is important here is that drum memory data must be handled cyclically and that external circuitry in conjunction with origin and clock tracks on the drum are used to operate the memory. Figure 11-46 shows the block diagram for cyclical readout.

The word buffer register is the link between the computer and the memory, just as the A register was the connecting register for the arith-

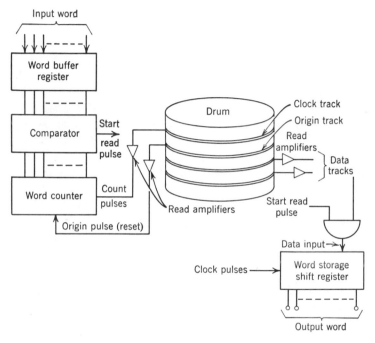

Figure 11-46.   Cyclical readout gating.

metic section. A word command tells the memory which word is desired. At the start of the data, as indicated by the origin track pulse, the counter is reset to zero and pulses from the drum clock track are counted. When the comparator "sees" the same number in the two registers, it puts out a start read pulse. This allows the data coming out of the read amplifiers to feed into a storage shift register. The clock pulses are used as shift pulses, since they are synchronized with the data. After the readout of ten pulses (word length for this case), the read operation is ended and the data is available for use in other computer circuits. Actually, the buffer register may have been used instead of another register, for the command word is not needed once read begins, and after shifting data into the buffer register it may be read in parallel (or serially) to another computer section.

11-7.   Other Memory Devices

The two main memory types considered so far have erasable memory. That is, data can be erased and new data written in during operation. Some other memory devices do not have this desirable erasable feature. An optical memory is an example of a nonerasable memory. A drum made of optically clear material is coated with a photographic emulsion and exposed to a fixed code or data pattern. Once the data is imprinted on the drum it is permanent. Certain types of data are immediately useful with this type of memory. Tables of any kind that are referred to by the computer may be stored on such a memory. Being a drum memory, the access time is similarly restricted by mechanical speed considerations and access times of 1 msec are good. Two main features of an optical memory are its large storage capacity and the fact that it costs less than the magnetic drum memory. The data is read by illuminating the track of data with a light source and using photo detectors to sense light. A ONE may be the absence of any coating on the optical drum so that light is received by the photo sensor, and a ZERO may be no light received because there is an opaque coating. Data is stored in tracks and read sequentially, as in the magnetic drum. Timing tracks are printed on the drum surface for readout synchronization.

IC Memory.   We must recall that a device should have a number of basic properties for consideration as a memory cell — small size, low cost per bit, and very fast access (typically low μseconds). Development of integrated circuit technology has advanced so that all three desirable features can be found in an IC flip-flop storage cell. In particular, the use of MOSFET devices has provided the smallest size and lowest cost of all IC types.

A single chip providing a large capacity memory plane made of IC circuits is generally referred to as large-scale integration (LSI), meaning that a considerable amount of circuitry is provided within one single package. For example, a Fairchild 3530 unit is listed as a 64-bit static random access memory and is also referred to an MOS/LSI integrated circuit. This later designation states that it is made using metal oxide semiconductor FETs and the amount of circuitry on the single chip classifies it as a large scale integration unit. Figure 11-47 shows the connections available with the single chip. The unit shown is essentially a 64 word by 1 bit nondestructive read-out (NDRO) static random access memory. A 6-bit address input selects one of the 64 words. On a write operation the write enable (WE) signal is present along with the data in to be stored. On a read-out operation the read enable (RE) signal results

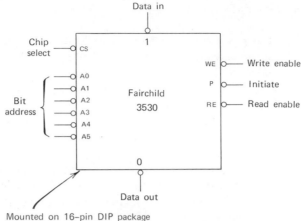

Figure 11-47.   MOS/LSI 64-word, 1-bit memory unit.

in the bit stored at the specified address to be brought to the data out terminal. Memory speed around 1 μsec is typical.

For a 64-word, 16-bit memory, 16 such chips would be required. Notice that word decoding, selection, and driver operating circuitry is already part of the chip. A 1024-word, 16-bit core memory would require 256 units. For low capacity memory size, such as a scratch pad memory, special device memory such as in-line printer, card reader, magnetic tape, or magnetic disk interface the choice of MOS/LSI is becoming quite popular. Large size memories such as the main computer memory are presently magnetic core units.

Read Only Memory (ROM). Another approach using IC devices as a memory provides a permanent (fixed) memory data allowing only read-out. This read only memory (ROM) facility has gained considerable popularity and there are many applications where such operation is quite useful. A ROM is a digital storage device whose information cannot be altered during the normal operating sequence. Information is stored during the manufacturing process and cannot be electrically altered. The storage pattern is inserted as a final step in the processing sequence corresponding to the specifications of the user.

A large number of applications using ROM units have developed. These include code translation for a great variety of popular codes, and instruction sequencing to allow altering the machine code structure of a computer by interchanging ROM cards. This latter application allows running one computer machine language program on another type computer. Another use is to provide fixed data tables. Applications then, such as microprogramming, code conversion, table lookup, and control logic, make ROM devices quite useful, especially if the same is provided by a low-cost, small-size unit containing the necessary selection and driver circuitry.

For example, the National Semiconductor MM521 is a 1024-bit element (256×4) ROM unit packaged in a 16-pin dual in-line case. The basic elements are MOS devices operating typically around 500 nanoseconds.

Delay Line (Using MOS Shift Registers).   Another approach to storage using MOS IC technology is a delay line made as a shift register. Essentially, a number of shift register stages are used with access to the input stage and output stage. For example, the Fairchild 3304 is a dual 16-bit static shift register that can operate as a delay line memory. Sixteen bits can be stored in one unit. If a shift-around operation is kept operating by constantly circulating the data, the device is effectively a delay line in which a data bit appears at the output after a delay of 16 steps from the time it was applied as input.

Also, a dual 25-bit dynamic shift register could be used to provide a 2-bit, 25-word delay line operation where data is circulated and read out when the desired word bits arrive at the delay line output terminals. A number of such IC units could be used to build, say, a 16-bit, 25-word delay line memory for use by some special device such as a data terminal receiving or sending serial data over telephone lines.

Summary

A computer memory, as distinguished from input or output storage, must be small and relatively inexpensive, if possible, but most of all it must be very fast: The magnetic core memory is presently the most popular although IC memories are quickly gaining in importance. Magnetic core memories have continued to become smaller, faster, and are used in larger and larger memory capacities. Memory capacities in the tens to hundreds of thousands are becoming quite popular. Access time (time to read a word from the memory) are now in the tenths of microseconds.

The core memory is organized as coincident-current random access. Coincident-current methods reduce the overall number of wires considered. Random access indicates that calling for a word from one memory location takes as little time as from any other. Although the actual read operation with a core is destructive, use of a read/write cycle makes it possible to save the data stored when read. New data may, of course, be placed in a desired memory location during a write operation.

Magnetic drum memory is no longer used as the main computer memory. It is used as auxiliary memory especially in time-shared systems.

A number of methods are used in recording data on a magnetic surface. These include return-to-zero (RZ) or return-to-bias method, nonreturn-to-zero (NRZ), and phase recording. Phase recording is different in that the lowest data frequency is one-half the highest and allows using ac transformers and amplifiers for read/write operation.

The organization of a magnetic drum can be bit-serial, bit-parallel, and so on. In all cases the drum contains a clock track for timing operations with the drum and an origin track with a single pulse indicating when to start counting data bits on the track.

Integrated circuits manufactured as large-scale integrated (LSI) memory units are becoming quite popular. Thin film memories with potentially faster operation than core memories are also gaining significantly in importance.

PROBLEMS

§11-3   **1.** How many cores per plane and planes are required for an 8K memory of 16 bits per word, for 3D core organization?

2. How many X and Y lines are required in the 3D core memory of Problem 1? How many total wires per core and wires per plane?

3. How many total cores, sense amplifiers, and inhibit drivers are required in the core memory of Problem 1?

4. An 8 K $2\frac{1}{2}$D core memory has 12 bits per word. How many core planes and address bits are required?

5. How many stages of storage are needed for the row address register (X), column address register (Y), and word register (Z) of a 10,240-word core memory having a word length of twenty bits?

6. How many stages are needed for the X, Y, and Z registers (as in Problem 5) for a 20,480-word core memory having ten bits per word?

§11-6   **7.** (a) What is the average access time of a drum memory rotating at 18,000 revolutions per minute?

(b) What is the bit transfer rate (bits/second) if there are 1024 bits around a track of the drum?

(c) What is the time interval during which a single bit may be read?

8. A magnetic drum has 16 tracks of 2048 bits per track. If the drum is run at 12,000 revolutions per minute, what is its average access time?

9. (a) If the drum in Problem 8 is organized bit-serial, what is the data transfer rate (bits/second)?

(b) If the drum in Problem 8 is organized bit-parallel, what is the data transfer rate?

10. Show two ways the drum of Problem 8 may be organized for BCD characters.

11. Draw the flux waveform for return-to-zero recording of the following data:

(a) 1101101110110   (b) 1010110011000.

12. (a) Draw the flux waveforms for nonteturn-to-zero recording for the data given in Problem 11.

(b) Repeat using NRZI recording.

13. Draw the flux waveforms for phase recording of the data of Problem 11.

1100

Arithmetic operations

12-1. General Arithmetic Section Operation

The arithmetic unit of a digital computer contains the logic circuitry for performing additions, subtractions, multiplications, and divisions. Information to be processed by the computer is generally placed in memory first and taken into the arithmetic unit at some later time. Answers from the arithmetic section are returned to the memory unit. Because of the high speed of arithmetic operations (a clock rate of 1 to 10 MHz is typical) and the lower speed of taking data into the computer (anywhere from a few cycles per second to around 10,000 cps), the function of the memory as a speed buffer is essential. In fact, the high speed of the arithmetic section often necessitates a special high-speed memory—called a "scratchpad memory"—for use solely with the arithmetic unit. A separate, larger-capacity, slower-speed memory is also used for overall computing functions and program storage.

Since multiplication and division in a general-purpose digital machine is done by repeated additions and repeated subtractions, respectively, the arithmetic operations performed need only be those of addition and subtraction. However, a large amount of additional logic and data-handling circuitry is required for these operations. Other more complex functions such as square root and trigonometric functions are either obtained from stored tables (requiring large data storage) or calculated from iterative formula under control of a stored program. These iterative operations only require using the four basic arithmetic functions so that with the use of logic gating, timing control, and stored program the add and subtract operation provides the computer with all essential mathematical operations.

479

In Chapter 2 the addition operation was considered for the straight binary code as well as for a few other codes. Subtraction was also considered using ONE's or TWO's complement. Neither topic considered the addition and subtraction of numbers with sign included. Only the absolute value of a number was operated on. This additional, but very real factor, will be examined in the present chapter, as will the details of multiplication and division as handled by a computer.

12-2.   Adder Unit–Serial and Parallel Operation

The heart of an arithmetic unit is the operation of the adder section. Two basic ways for carrying out the addition are *serial* and *parallel*. Serial addition is carried out bit by bit using a single full-adder circuit and is slow. Parallel addition provides addition of all bits at the "same" time, which is very fast but at the cost of a full-adder circuit for each bit position. We will cover both starting with the simpler serial addition operation. It should be noted, however, that most computers use parallel addition since speed is so essential to the overall action of the computer.

Serial Adder.   A picture of the operation of a serial adder unit can be obtained from the simplified block diagram of Figure 12-1. In this simpli-

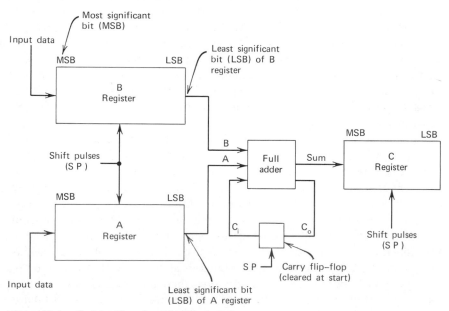

Figure 12-1.   Serial adder, simplified block diagram.

fied presentation we make no connection between arithmetic and memory unit. Input data in the form of two binary numbers are brought into the A and B storage registers. This data can be shifted into the two registers by the shift pulses shown to operate both registers at the same time. If, for example, registers A, B, and C were each 16 stages (16-bit capacity), exactly 16 shift pulses would be used for operating these stages.

Notice that the data stored in the A and B registers goes into the adder circuit, least significant bit (LSB) first; that is, the addition takes place from the low-order end of the number as would be expected. At the start the low-order bit of each number is connected as A and B inputs to a full-adder logic circuit. A carry flip, which is cleared (logical-0) at the start is used to provide the carry bit resulting in the binary addition as input to the full-adder. The sum of input bits A, B, and carry-in (C_i) is the adder output provided as input to a C register which will have the full sum after a 16-step serial add cycle.

The carry-out (C_o) bit resulting from adding bits A, B, and C_i is provided as input to the one stage carry flip-flop. This carry-out bit will be shifted into the flip-flop stage when the next A and B bits are shifted down their respective registers so that the next higher order bits appear as adder inputs. Thus, the carry-out bit is provided as carry-in bit with the next higher position bits as required. Each shift pulse moves the A and B number bits down (to the right) to the adder circuit so that next higher bits and the carry bit from previous position bit addition are then inputs to the adder circuit. The resulting sum for each bit position addition (including carry) is shifted into the C register which will have the full sum of the 16 bit numbers in A and B after 16 pulse steps have occured.

To help you see what occurs the first two steps of operation for sample 16-bit numbers are shown in Figure 12-2. At the start, before any shift pulses are applied the bits in the LSB position of A and B registers are inputs to the adder as is the initially 0 carry-in bit. The adder logic circuit will output a sum bit of 1 and carry-out bit of 0 at this time. Notice that although the sum bit is already 1 it will not be stored by the C register until a shift pulse occurs.

After one shift pulse occurs the date appears as shown in Figure 12-2*b*. The A and B data have moved one bit to the lower order position and inputs from A and B are both 1 at this time. The carry-in is 0 so that the sum of 0 and carry-out of 1 result. Notice that only the bits in the LSB positions of the A and B registers will be added at this shift step. The MSB position is not shown to contain any specific data. (Actually when the data is shifted to the right logical-0 might be shifted in to fill up the MSB stage position). The carry-out is shown to be logical-1. This is to be used as carry-in on the *next* high position bit addition and will not

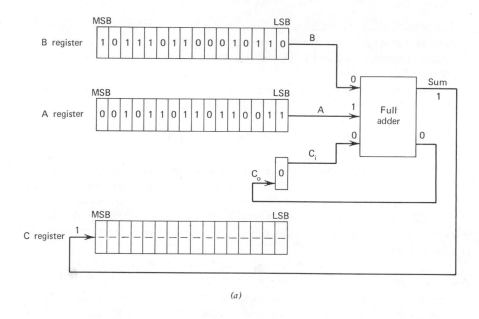

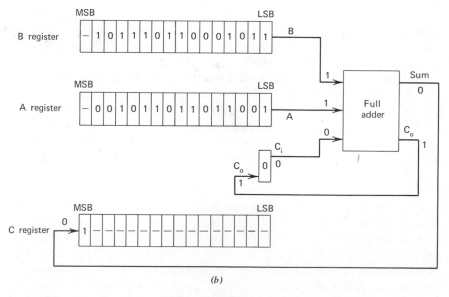

Figure 12-2. Details of serial adder for two steps of operation. (a) Data at start. (b) After first shift pulse.

move into the carry stage until the next shift pulse occurs. It will then be the C_i bit with the next higher position bits. This operation will continue for 16 shift steps after which time the C register would contain the 16-bit sum of the original values in registers A and B.

We might at this time consider something about the range of the numbers added. If, as would be true, the memory word and arithmetic register size are the same, then, using the present example, the numbers to be added are both 16 bits and the resulting sum is also 16 bits. If the numbers added were "too large" as for example if initially the MSB values were both 1 then the resulting sum would need 17 bits of storage — with only 16 stages available (to agree with memory word capacity). Thus, it is possible when adding two numbers to get an answer that is too large for the fixed capacity of the register and memory word. How this problem is taken care of will be considered later in the chapter. Our discussion at present is to introduce the concept of *overflow*. A resulting carry bit of logical 1 at the end of the add operation (all 16 bits added) is indication that the numbers added resulted in too large a sum. Thus, a carry bit of logical 1 *after* addition has been completed is indication of an overflow condition. This means that the 16-bit sum value cannot be stored as a correct sum value. The computer can be instructed to check the carry flip-flop output after addition has ended to determine whether overflow has occurred, and appropriate action could then be called for. Overflow occurs in fixed word capacity adders and the overflow is signaled by a logical-1 bit in the carry flip-flop *after* an addition operation is completed.

A second example of serial addition operation is shown in the block diagram of Figure 12-3. In this example we make some connection between memory unit and arithmetic unit — but presently only on a simplified scale. The operation of this adder unit is also different from that shown in Figure 12-1 with the present unit operating as an *accumulator*. This means, essentially, that each number added is summed with the previously resulting sum so that numbers can be added with the accumulated sum being held by the arithmetic unit.

Numbers in the input register and accumulator are shifted through the one full-adder circuit, the result of the serial addition being shifted into the accumulator register. Thus, the sum of input number to be added to accumulator value ends up in the accumulator. This action is like that of a mechanical (or electrical) calculator adder where an input number is added to the present displayed value, the resulting (accumulated) sum then being displayed.

We might now consider how the numbers stored in the memory are brought to the arithmetic unit for addition and the results placed back in the memory unit. To simplify connections input data is brought only to

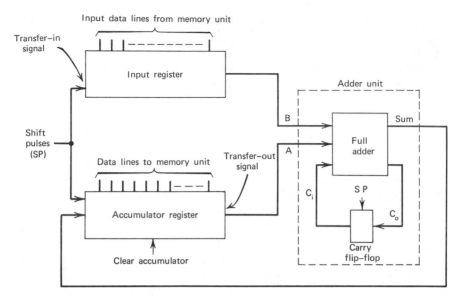

Figure 12-3.   Serial accumulator, simplified block diagram.

the input register and output data is taken only from the accumulator register. Parallel transfer to and from the memory unit is shown although serial transfer could have been used.

To load a binary number from the memory unit into the arithmetic unit as instructed by a clear-add (CLA) instruction requires an add cycle as follows. A clear-accumulator pulse resets the accumulator value to zero. Then a transfer-in pulse parallel transfers the word read out of the memory (and held in the MIR) into the input register. A sequence of shift pulses then adds the accumulator value (of zero) to the input value, the resulting sum being shifted into the accumulator. We now have the accumulator loaded with the first number to be added.

An add instruction (ADD) will now cause the memory word value to be added to the accumulator value, the accumulator holding the result after addition is complete. In the add cycle an input number is first transferred into the input register. Then a sequence of shift pulses causes the input value to be added to the present accumulator value, the resulting sum going into the accumulator.

If the sum value is then to be stored in the memory unit, a transfer-out pulse will parallel transfer the accumulator value to the MIR of the memory unit.

The operation discussed for the accumulator can be now considered in a little more detail using signals from the control unit as covered in Chapter 10 and the MIR unit as discussed in Chapter 11. In particular, refer to the clock step signals of Figure 10-8 and operation decoded signal of Figure 10-9.

We shall consider some details of operation for clear-add, add, and store instructions. On a CLA instruction decoded by the control unit during an execute cycle, the occurrence of CS1 is used to clear the accumulator register as shown in Figure 12-4. If we assume that during

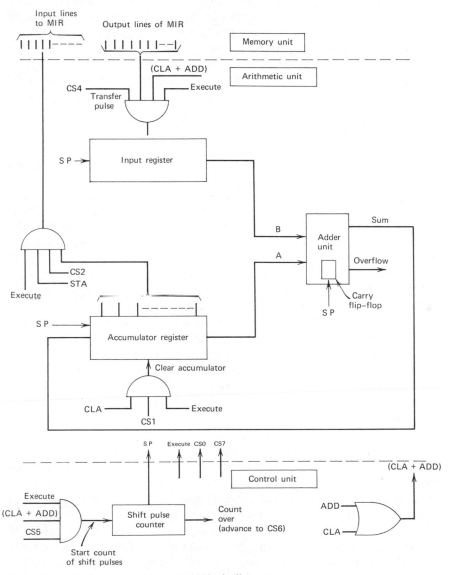

Figure 12-4.   Serial accumulator, detailed logic diagram.

CS2 and CS3 the number to be clear-added is read by the memory unit into the MIR location, then on CS4 the number in the MIR is parallel-transferred to the arithmetic input register. The partial logic circuitry shown to be in the control unit then initiates a sequence of shift pulses when CS5 occurs. A shift pulse counter provides the exact number of shift pulses required (same as the number of bits per word of memory and stages of register in arithmetic unit). The shift pulses cause the zero value in the accumulator and number in the arithmetic input register to be added serially with the sum going into the accumulator. The net effect is to load the accumulator with the number read from memory as specified by the machine instruction fetched by the control unit.

Notice that the operation shown in the control unit has the shift pulse counter provide an advance pulse to the step counter circuit to advance to step CS6 after the full number of shift pulses have occurred. Also, since shift pulses are needed on both CLA and ADD instructions (as well as subtract and other instructions not covered at this time), a combined signal (CLA + ADD) is formed by ORing two of the signals available in the control unit.

The control unit completes the execute cycle and another fetch then occurs. If an ADD instruction is then present, the execute cycle will be the following. During CS1 to CS3 the number to be added is read into the MIR location. On CS4 the data read is transferred into the arithmetic input register. During CS5 the shift pulses cause input value and accumulator value to be serially added with the result being placed into accumulator. This essentially completes an add operation with sum in accumulator and overflow indication available as carry flip-flop output.

On a store (STA) instruction the data in the accumulator register is parallel transferred to the MIR of the memory unit on CS2. The control unit will then cause the MIR value to be written into core at the location indicated in the instruction. Although more detail on the arithmetic operation is yet to be considered, some basic interaction between the arithmetic, memory, and control units (which make up the CPU) are becoming apparent.

Parallel-Adder.   An example of a parallel adder is shown in Figure 12-5. The logic circuitry is simpler since only an add signal is required to obtain parallel addition. On the other hand, a full-adder (FA) circuit is required for each bit position (although lowest order stage could be a half-adder since no carry input is present for that position).

On an add (ADD) instruction the data read into the MIR is added to that in the accumulator on CS5, the resulting sum being transferred into the AR. The bits of the same position are added at the same time (CS5).

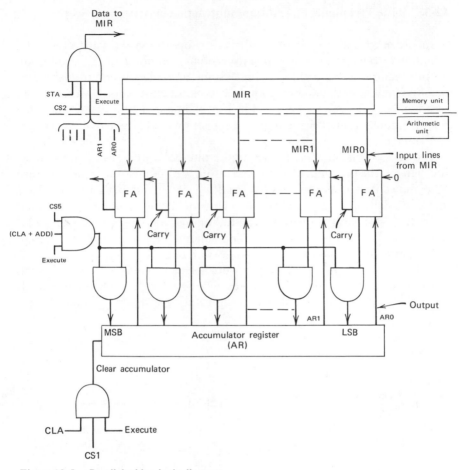

Figure 12-5.   Parallel adder, logic diagram.

It is necessary to allow carries from the low-order stages to propogate (or ripple) to the highest order stage (if such carry results). Greater detail of a parallel adder will be covered later in this chapter.

On a store (STA) instruction the data in the AR is transferred to the MIR on CS2 (and then written into core). When the carry is allowed to ripple down to the higher order stages the add time is slowed down. To obtain faster operation, logic gating is sometimes used to perform fast adder operation. Since the addition operation is so basic to the computer arithmetic functions, the fastest possible adder is usually desired.

12-3.   Basic Techniques of Addition/Subtraction in Arithmetic Section

In order to understand the subtraction operation we must cover the handling of both positive and negative binary numbers in either addition or subtraction in the arithmetic unit. Since a number is either positive or negative and stored data in a computer contain either 0 or 1 bits, the sign of a number is stored as a 0 or 1 bit. For example, a 0 bit could indicate a positive number and a 1 bit in the sign position could then indicate a negative number.

Using a 16-bit number, for example, one bit would always be read as the sign bit, the remaining 15 bits indicating the number magnitude. Figure 12-6 shows two basic schemes for handling signed numbers. Figure 12-6*a* shows a sign bit and the absolute value of the magnitude. This would seem to be the straightforward way to handle numbers but it causes difficulties in circuit implementation. The scheme indicated in Figure 12-6*b* uses complement notation and we shall soon see why it is preferred.

If the sign-magnitude technique were used, it would be necessary on addition to compare signs first to see whether they are like or unlike. If like, the magnitudes are added and the same sign used. If unlike, it may

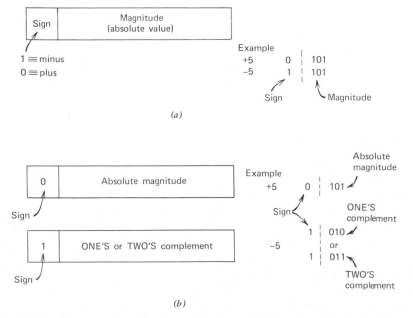

Figure 12-6.   Representations for sign and value. (*a*) Sign and magnitude. (*b*) Sign and complement notation.

be necessary to form both A − B and B − A to see which is positive thereby determining the sign of the resulting answer. Since such a method would prove not to be the simplest it will not be further covered to avoid confusing the issue.

The method using complement notation will be covered, mostly using 1's complement for simplicity of discussion although 2's complement is frequently used in practical systems for speed of operation.

Complement Technique.   A simple procedure for mechanizing addition and subtraction with sign is described next. Utilizing the 1 or 0 bit to specify the plus or minus sign, this procedure *specifically requires* using 1 for negative sign and 0 for positive sign. Positive numbers are written with the 0 sign in the most significant position with the positive absolute value, and negative numbers are written with the 1 sign in the most significant position and the ONE's complement form of the number. Both numbers should be written with equal digits and of sufficient number to include the sum number without mixing up the sign with the number part. All this can be more easily seen in the following examples. It should be pointed out, though, that these are rules for procedure and do not complicate the mechanization. As we shall see, the whole procedure only requires using the specified format and adding the two numbers and their signs — all as if they were number digits. This being true, the mechanization is no more complicated than that of adding two binary numbers together — without considering sign. In doing problems on paper the correct format must be assured. Once set up, however, the operation is carried out mechanically as if no sign were present. The answer read is in the prescribed format.

Example 12-1.   Write the following numbers in signed form

    (a) +7   (b) +12   (c) −3   (d) −9   (e) −20

Solution:

Number	Absolute Magnitude	Signed (1's Complement)	Signed (2's Complement)
		sign ↓	sign ↓
(a) +7	000111	0 000111	0 000111
(b) +12	001100	0 001100	0 001100
(c) −3	000011	1 111100	1 111101
(d) −9	001001	1 110110	1 110111
(e) −20	010100	1 101011	1 101100

As shown in Example 12-1 the signed number is written as 0 sign and absolute magnitude for positive numbers and as 1 sign and 1's (or 2's) complement for negative numbers.

This notational scheme allows addition and subtraction to be carried out automatically without the need for the computer logic to check which number added or subtracted is larger or what the sign of the answer should be. This comes out automatically if the notational scheme being discussed is used. In any actual arithmetic unit the size of each number being added is the same (same number of bits). Also the numbers added cannot overflow in the answer for proper operation. With this in mind we can see how addition of signed numbers works out.

Example 12-2.   Add the following two positive numbers.

    (a) $+6, +1$ (b) $+9, +4$ (c) $+2, +8$ (d) $+8, +9$

Solution: (a) $+6$ 0 110
                      $+1$ 0 001
                      $+7$ 0 111   Answer: $+7$

            (b) $+9$ 0 1001
                    $+4$ 0 0100
                    $+13$ 0 1101   Answer: $+13$

            (c) $+2$ 0 0010
                    $+8$ 0 1000
                    $+10$ 0 1010   Answer: $+10$

            (d) $+8 = 0$ 1000
                    $+9 = 0$ 1001

However, because the answer will require five bits, the numbers should be written using five bits (the fifth and most significant bit for each is zero, which is trivial for this case but more important when the complement is taken with negative numbers).

                $+8$ 0 01000
                $+9$ 0 01001
                $+17$ 0 10001   Answer: $+17$

Notice that although you have to be careful in setting up the problem, when an adder circuit is used it has fixed number of places and automatically handles the data properly. For example, with a ten-bit adder register, one bit is for sign, and nine bits are for the numbers to be summed. The largest answer is limited by the nine magnitude bits.

Example 12-3.   Add the following two numbers where the larger magnitude is positive (1's complement scheme is used):

      (a) $+6, -3$ (b) $+8, -4$ (c) $+9, -6$ (d) $+8, -5$

Solution: (a) $+6$ 0 0110
             -3 1 1100   (where 3 is 0011)
            $\overline{+3}$ $\overline{10\ 0010}$
                       $\longrightarrow 1$ (end-around carry)
                $\overline{0\ \underbrace{0011}}$
                   3   Answer: $+3$
               $+$ sign

     (b) $+8$ 0 1000
             -4 1 1011   (where 4 is 0100)
            $\overline{+4}$ $\overline{10\ 0011}$
                      $\longrightarrow 1$ (end-around carry)
               $\overline{0\ \underbrace{0100}}$
                  4
              $+$ sign   Answer: $+4$

     (c) $+9$ 0 1001
             -6 1 1001   (where 6 is 0110)
            $\overline{+3}$ $\overline{10\ 0010}$
                      $\longrightarrow 1$ (end-around carry)
               $\overline{0\ \underbrace{0011}}$
                  3
              $+$ sign   Answer: $+3$

     (d) $+8$ 0 1000
             -5 1 1010   (where 5 is 0101)
            $\overline{+3}$ $\overline{10\ 0010}$
                      $\longrightarrow 1$ (end-around carry)
               $\overline{0\ \underbrace{0011}}$
                  3
              $+$ sign   Answer: $+3$

Example 12-4.   Add the following two numbers where the larger magnitude number is negative.

      (a) $+9, -12$ (b) $+6, -7$ (c) $+15, -18$ (d) $+2, -4$

Solution: (a)   +9   0 1001
               −12   1 0011   (where 12 is 1100)
               ───   ───────
               −3   1 1100
                             ︸
                           1's complement
                              of 3
                           sign   Answer: −3

               (b)   +6   0 110
                      −7   1 000   (where 7 is 111)
                      ──   ─────
                      −1   1 110
                                    ︸
                                  1's complement
                                     of 1
                                  sign   Answer: −1

               (c)   +15   0 01111
                      −18   1 01101   (where 18 is 10010)
                      ───   ───────
                      −3   1 11100
                                     ︸
                                  1's complement
                                     of 3
                                  sign   Answer: −3

               (d)   +2   0 010
                      −4   1 011   (where 4 is 100)
                      ──   ─────
                      −2   1 101
                                    ︸
                                  1's complement
                                     of 2
                                  sign   Answer: −2

Example 12-5.   Add the following two negative numbers.

(a) −3, −4   (b) −9, −6   (c) −12, −10   (d) −8, −14   (e) −13, −16

Solution: (a)   −3   1 100
                     −4   1 011
                     ──   ──────
                     −7   10 111
                                └───→1   (end-around carry)
                                ───────
                                 1 000
                                   ︸
                                 1's complement
                                    of 7
                                 sign   Answer: −7

(b) -9 1 0110
     $\underline{-6}$ $\underline{1\ 1001}$
     -15 10 1111
              $\llcorner\!\!\longrightarrow 1$ (end-around carry)
              $\overline{1\ \underbrace{0000}}$
                    $\uparrow$
                    1's complement
                       of 15
              $\llcorner$ sign   Answer: -15

(c) -12 1 10011
     $\underline{-10}$ $\underline{1\ 10101}$
     -22 11 01000
              $\llcorner\!\!\longrightarrow 1$ (end-around carry)
              $\overline{1\ \underbrace{01001}}$
                    $\uparrow$
                    1's complement
                       of 22
              $\llcorner$ sign   Answer: -22

Notice that 12 and 10 were written using five digits, since the answer required five.

(d) -8 1 10111
     $\underline{-14}$ $\underline{1\ 10001}$
     -22 11 01000
              $\llcorner\!\!\longrightarrow 1$ (end-around carry)
              $\overline{1\ \underbrace{01001}}$
                    $\uparrow$
                    1's complement
                       of 22
              $\llcorner$ sign   Answer: -22

(e) -13 1 10010
     $\underline{-16}$ $\underline{1\ 01111}$
     -29 11 00001
              $\llcorner\!\!\longrightarrow 1$ (end-around carry)
              $\overline{1\ \underbrace{00010}}$
                    $\uparrow$
                    1's complement
                       of 29
              $\llcorner$ sign   Answer: -29

These examples should have shown that adding the sign digit *as if it were a number digit* leads to the correct answer for *all* possible combinations of sign and magnitude when the prescribed rules of operation are used.

Exercise 12-1. Write the binary forms of the following numbers as in Example 12-1.

(a) $+3$ (b) -11 (c) -17 (d) $+26$ (e) -19 (f) $+17$

Exercise 12-2. Add the following two numbers using the method of Examples 12-2 through 12-5.

(a) $+6, +12$ (b) $+8, -6$ (c) $+6, -8$ (d) $+13, -13$
(e) $+9, -12$ (f) $-8, -12$ (g) $-2, +4$ (h) $-16, +13$
(i) $-10, -12$ (j) $-21, +25$

Subtraction. Doing subtraction by the method just indicated is valid but slightly more confusing. Rather than go into any detail, an example of each of the four types is given. No new understanding of the technique is considered. Subtraction is performed by *adding* the 1's complement in these examples.

Example 12-6. Subtract the following two positive numbers:

(a) $+6$ minus $+4$ (b) $+4$ minus $+6$

Solution: (a)

```
      +6              0 0110              00110
(−)  +4    →    (−)  0 0100    →   (+)  11011
    ─────         ─────────           ────────
      +2                              100001
                                        └──→1
                                       ─────
                                       00010    Answer: +2
```

(b)

```
      +4              0 0100              00100
(−)  +6    →    (−)  0 0110    →   (+)  11001
    ─────         ─────────           ────────
      −2                              11101    Answer: −2
```

Example 12-7. Subtract the following two numbers:

(a) $+6$ minus -2 (b) $+2$ minus -6

Solution: (a)

```
      +6              0 0110              00110
(−)  −2    →    (−)  1 1101    →   (+)  00010
    ─────         ─────────           ────────
      +8                              01000    Answer: +8
```

(b)

```
      +2              0 0010              00010
(−)  −6    →    (−)  1 1001    →   (+)  00110
    ─────         ─────────           ────────
      +8                              01000    Answer: +8
```

Example 12-8. Subtract the following two numbers:

(a) -4 minus -6 (b) -3 minus -2

Solution: (a) $\begin{array}{r} -4 \\ (-)\ \underline{-6} \\ +2 \end{array}$ $\rightarrow$ $\begin{array}{r} 1\ 1011 \\ (-)\ \underline{1\ 1001} \end{array}$ $\rightarrow$ $\begin{array}{r} 11011 \\ (+)\ \underline{00110} \\ 100001 \\ \llcorner\!\!\longrightarrow\!1 \\ \hline 00010 \end{array}$ Answer: $+2$

(b) $\begin{array}{r} -3 \\ (-)\ \underline{-2} \\ -1 \end{array}$ $\rightarrow$ $\begin{array}{r} 1\ 1100 \\ (-)\ \underline{1\ 1101} \end{array}$ $\rightarrow$ $\begin{array}{r} 11100 \\ (+)\ \underline{00010} \\ \hline 11110 \end{array}$ Answer: -1

Example 12-9.   Subtract the following two numbers:

(a) -6 minus $+2$ (b) -2 minus $+6$

Solution: (a) $\begin{array}{r} -6 \\ (-)\ \underline{+2} \\ -8 \end{array}$ $\begin{array}{r} 1\ 1001 \\ (-)\ \underline{0\ 0010} \end{array}$ $\rightarrow$ $\begin{array}{r} 11001 \\ (+)\ \underline{11101} \\ 110110 \\ \llcorner\!\!\longrightarrow\!1 \\ \hline 10111 \end{array}$ Answer: -8

(b) $\begin{array}{r} -2 \\ (-)\ \underline{+6} \\ -8 \end{array}$ $\rightarrow$ $\begin{array}{r} 1\ 1101 \\ (-)\ \underline{0\ 0110} \end{array}$ $\rightarrow$ $\begin{array}{r} 11101 \\ (+)\ \underline{11001} \\ 110110 \\ \llcorner\!\!\longrightarrow\!1 \\ \hline 10111 \end{array}$ Answer: -8

As extra practice try the following problem for subtraction.

Exercise 12-3.   Using the method shown in Examples 12-6 to 12-9, subtract the following numbers.

(a) $+7$ minus $+3$ (b) -8 minus $+4$ (c) -5 minus -6
(d) $+9$ minus $+12$ (e) -4 minus -2 (f) -6 minus $+9$
(g) $+12$ minus -8 (h) $+15$ minus -17

12-4.   Adder and Subtractor Circuitry for Signed Numbers

Having presented a useful technique for adding or subtracting signed numbers, we can go into detail on the circuitry used to implement such a scheme. This detail will include circuitry to convert a number to 1's or 2's complement form, provide overflow logic, and allow for both addition or subtraction operations.

The circuit of Figure 12-7 is used to show how complement logic control can be obtained for 1's complement operation. The circuit shown

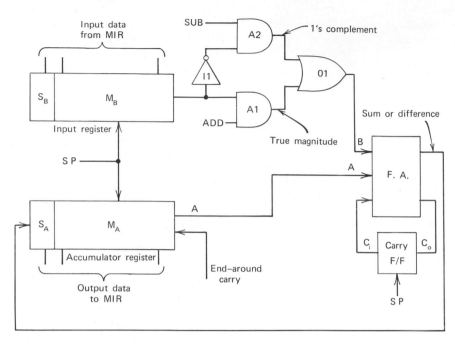

Figure 12-7.   Adder/subtractor using 1's complement scheme, simplified circuit.

can function as either an adder *or* a subtractor. Compare the circuit to the adder of Figure 12-3. If only the ADD operation is specified (ADD = 1, SUB = 0), then the B register (input register) data is the B input data to the full adder. The SUB signal being logical 0 blocks AND gate A2 from operating so that it has no effect at this time. The sequence of bringing an input number from the MIR, a series of shift pulses to move the A and B data serially through the full adder and shifting the resulting sum into the accumulator is almost the same as has previously been considered. The present adder using signed numbers must also provide the end-around carry operation as covered in Section 12-3. For the present we shall ignore how an end-around carry signal is developed and gated to operate the accumulator. We can assume the accumulator is also a counter that can be incremented by one when an end-around carry occurs. More specific consideration will be covered later.

If the instruction specified is a subtraction (SUB = 1, ADD = 0), then the inverted B data (1's complement of B data) is applied as the full adder B input. Effectively then, for a subtraction instruction the resulting operation is the addition of A and the 1's complement of the B data giving effectively $A + (-B)$ or $A - B$. Thus, the accumulator value (A) minus input value (B) is the desired subtraction operation. From Section 12-3 we learned that by merely adding the complement of the number to be subtracted, including the sign bit in the addition (and including end-around carry) the addition operation effectively was a subtraction of $A - B$. The answer resulting is in absolute magnitude form if the resulting sign is 0 and is in 1's complement form if the resulting sign is 1.

We now can consider why 1's complement operation can be more troublesome to mechanize that 2's complement. The necessity of adding the end-around-carry requires that either an extra cycle of serial addition is used to add one to the accumulator value or that the accumulator be a shift register and counter with logic to gate the counter operation when the end-around-carry results.

Figure 12-8 shows how simple the mechanization is using 2's complement operation. Instead of the simple inverter action to get the 1's com-

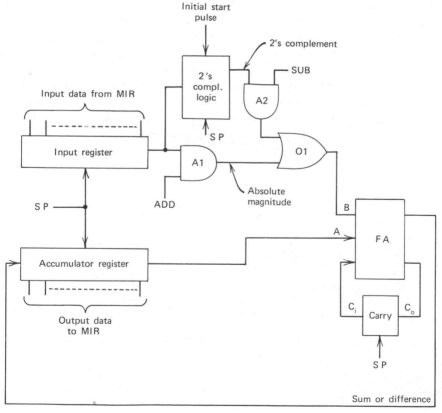

Figure 12-8.   Adder/subtractor using 2's complement scheme.

plement of B, a logic circuit is required to obtain the 2's complement of B. But now, *no* end-around-carry is necessary and the value in the accumulator is the correct answer. Including a 2's complement logic circuit is far simpler than requiring a two-cycle add operation or a shift/counter register for the accumulator.

It should be pointed out that we have assumed that numeric values obtained from memory are already in complement form (if negative). This is a valid assumption. If the number read was the result of a previous arithmetic operation it would be in complement form (if negative). Numbers read from an input unit must be stored in the prescribed complement scheme form.

2's Complement Logic.   Since the mechanization of a 2's complement scheme is far easier, it only remains for us to see how a logic circuit can convert an absolute magnitude value to 2's complement form. We wish, then, to consider the details of the logic in the box labelled 2's complement logic in Figure 12-8. One possible serial 2's complementing circuit is shown in Figure 12-9. In order to understand how the circuit operates we first consider how a 2's complement can be obtained. A simple rule is the following:

Operating serially on an absolute magnitude number complement every bit after *the first 1 has passed, starting with the least significant bit.*

A few examples using this rule are shown below.

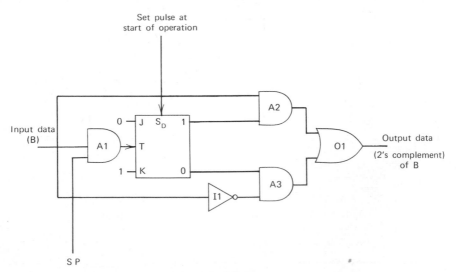

Figure 12-9.   Serial 2's complementing circuit.

Example 12-10.   Operate on the following binary numbers using the rule stated above to convert to 2's complement.

(a) 01101   (b) 101100   (c) 1010

Solution:

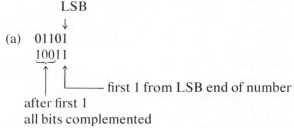

Result is that 2's complement of 01101 is 10011 (check by obtaining 1's complement plus 1)

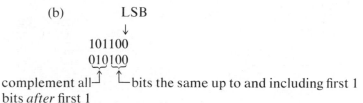

∴ 2's complement of 101100 is 010100.

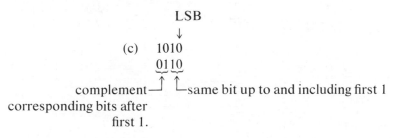

The circuit of Figure 12-9 operates as follows:

1. At the start of an arithmetic operation the complementing flip-flop is initially SET.
2. With the complementing flip-flop SET, gate A3 is disabled and gate A2 is enabled so that the input data appears at the output.
3. When the first input data bit of 1 appears, the shift pulse then occurring will trigger the complementing flip-flop stage, which is biased by the JK inputs, to CLEAR when triggered. Thus, *after* the first 1 bit appears the complementing flip-flop is RESET so that gate A2 is

then disabled and gate A3 enabled so that the inverted input data appears at the output from then on. Any further triggering of the flip-flop will only leave it RESET.

The circuit then passes the input data as received until after the first 1 appears, then it complements all following data bits.

We can include the gating to provide either the absolute magnitude or 2's complement of input data as B input to full adder in the complementing

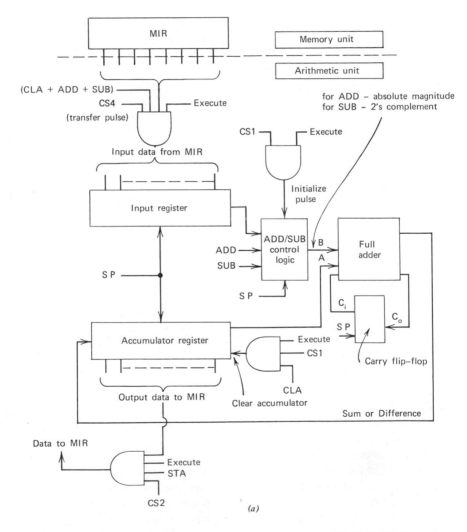

Figure 12-10.   (a) Adder/subtractor using 2's complement scheme. (b) Add/subtract logic control circuit.

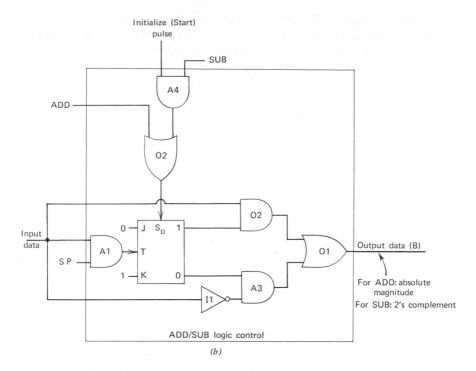

(b)

logic control circuitry. Figure 12-10 shows a workable adder/subtractor unit including complementing logic for 2's complement operation.

An initialize pulse (say, CS1) is applied to the complement control circuitry. If the instruction is ADD, then the B data to the full adder appears as received by the input register from the MIR (say, on CS4). If the instruction is SUB, then the 2's complement of the data in the input register is applied as B data to the adder. Since this uses the 2's complement scheme *no* end-around-carry is required and the resulting value in the accumulator is correct.

The highest order bit of the data bits is the sign bit. Notice that no special concern for sign bit had to be taken in adding or subtracting and it was treated as another bit to be added in the full adder. The sign bit then is considered only in *interpreting* the value of the number.

The circuit shown in Figure 12-10 then provides add/subtract capability with signed numbers just as the circuit of Figure 12-4 provided only add ability with only absolute magnitude numbers (no sign). In the circuit of Figure 12-4 a carry of 1 at the end of the serial addition cycle indicates an overflow. We shall next consider what must be done to indicate an overflow condition for either addition or subtraction using signed numbers as in the circuit of Figure 12-10.

Overflow Detection in Serial Adder/Subtractor Circuit. We will consider the conditions for overflow for both addition and subtraction. For addition an overflow *may* occur only if the signs of the numbers added are initially the same. The overflow condition is indicated if the resulting sign is different. Consider the following examples.

Example 12-11. Show the overflow condition on addition of positive and of negative numbers for

$$\text{(a) } +12, +7 \qquad \text{(b) } -12, -7$$

Solution: (a) $+12 = 0\ 1100$ (MSB is sign bit)

$$\frac{+7\ = 0\ 0111}{1\ 0011}$$

$$\uparrow$$

sign indicating negative number

The sign of the sum is different from the like signs of the two numbers added thereby indicating an overflow condition.

(b) $-12 = 1\ 0100$ (2's complement form)

$$\frac{-7\ = 1\ 1001}{\cancel{1}0\ 1101}\quad \text{(2's complement form)}$$

$$\uparrow$$

(carry ignored)   └─sign indicating positive number

Again the sum sign is different from the like signs of the numbers added thereby indicating an overflow condition.

The rule for determining an overflow condition in addition of signed numbers is then

Overflow condition occurred if sum sign was different than like signs of numbers added.

Expressed in Boolean terms

$$\text{(Overflow)}_{\text{addition}} = \text{OA} = C_S \bar{A}_S \bar{B}_S + \bar{C}_S A_S B_S$$

where, $C_S \equiv$ sign of sum bit after addition

$A_S \equiv$ original sign of A number

$B_S \equiv$ original sign of B number

It should be clear that adding opposite sign numbers will not cause an overflow since the sum must be less than either number added.

In subtraction the situation of subtracting like signed numbers will not cause an overflow. An overflow *may* only result when subtracting unlike sign numbers. If an overflow does happen, it can be determined by the sum sign as the following examples indicate.

Example 12-12.   Show the overflow condition on subtraction of positive and negative numbers for

$$\text{(a)} -12, +7 \qquad \text{(b)} +12, -7$$

Solution: (a)

$$
\begin{array}{rll}
-12 = & 1\ 0100 & \qquad 10100 \\
(-)\ \underline{+7} = (-)\ \underline{0\ 0111} & \rightarrow & (+)\ \underline{11001} \\
& & \cancel{1}01101 \\
& & \quad\uparrow
\end{array}
$$

(carry ignored)   sign different than in numbers above (∴ overflow)

(b)

$$
\begin{array}{rll}
+12 = 0\ 1100 & \qquad & 0\ 1100 \\
(-)\ \underline{-\ 7} = \underline{1\ 1001} & \rightarrow & (+)\ \underline{0\ 0111} \\
& & 1\ 0011 \\
& & \uparrow
\end{array}
$$

sign different than in numbers above (∴ overflow)

The examples given show that after the number to be subtracted has been complemented the overflow indication is the same as for addition. To tie this all together the extra circuitry necessary for overflow detection is shown in Figure 12-11. Figure 12-11*a* includes the circuit of Figure 12-10 modified by the following.

1. Input register data after complement logic is shifted around to provide sign bit of B value added to A.
2. Initial sign of accumulator register (AR) number is saved in separate storage stage (at CS1) since sign of AR after arithmetic operation is that of sum (or difference) value.
3. Overflow logic circuit is detailed in Figure 12-11*b*. Add/subtract control logic block is the same as in Figure 12-10*b*.

The condition of an overflow determined after the arithmetic add or subtract operation is over is tested at CS6. If an overflow did occur, the overflow alarm is turned on (OA = 1) to provide indication that the accumulator register value is not arithmetically valid. On most computers an instruction for testing whether the OA line is 1 is provided so that action can be prescribed by the program instructions.

Parallel Add/Subtract with Signed Numbers.   Using the complement scheme for signed numbers we will next see how both addition and subtraction operations can be obtained in parallel operation. Both 1's and 2's complement schemes will be shown to compare their mechanization for parallel operation.

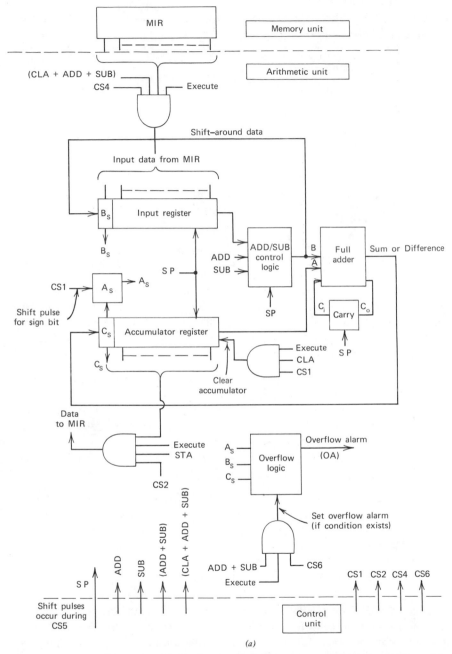

Figure 12-11. Adder/subtractor for signed numbers with overflow logic. (a) Complete logic diagram. (b) Overflow logic circuit.

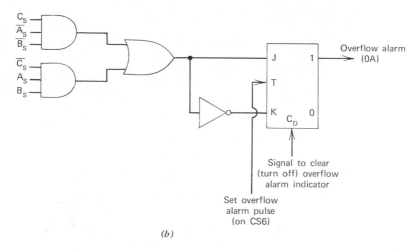

(b)

2's Complement Scheme for Addition/Subtraction. A procedure for carrying out either addition or subtraction of signed numbers using the 2's complement scheme is shown in Figure 12-12. If an add instruction is done the operation is simply that of adding the bits from each position in the respective full adder. Allowing time for any carries resulting to propagate, the resulting sum is then transferred into the accumulator on CS6.

If the instruction is clear-add (CLA) then with the accumulator cleared at CS1 and memory data read into the MIR on CS3, the input register is loaded at CS4. Then an add operation (adding input value to zero in accumulator) is carried out on CS6 thereby resulting in loading accumulator with data read from memory.

The subtraction instruction is accomplished by complementing each bit in the input register stage (on CS5) so that a 1's complement is then added to the accumulator value. The resulting operation is then a subtraction of the input register value from the accumulator value. The 2's complement operation is obtained by setting the carry into the lowest order stage (2^0 stage) to a 1 (SUB signal is 0 only during subtraction instruction). This results in an extra 1 being added thereby giving the correct answer—in 2's complement form, if negative and in absolute magnitude form, if positive.

On a store (STA) instruction the value in the accumulator stages is transferred to the MIR on CS2 (and stored in core on CS3).

1's Complement Scheme for Parallel Addition/Subtraction. Parallel addition/subtraction using a 1's complement scheme can be quite straight-

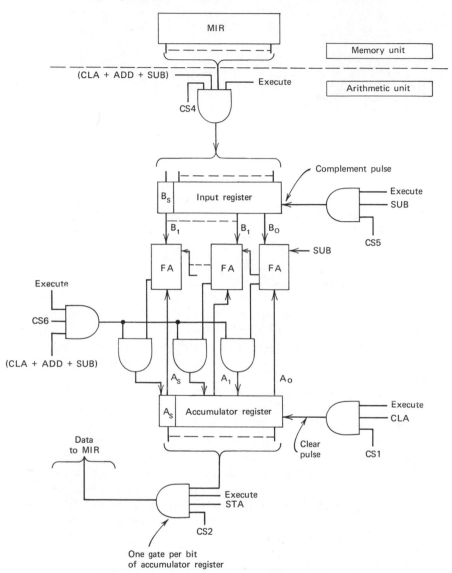

Figure 12-12.   Parallel adder/subtractor using 2's complement scheme.

forward. Even the end-around-carry is simply mechanized connecting the end carry to the low order stage carry input. Figure 12-13 shows the logic circuit for the addition/subtraction operation. The circuit operates essentially the same as the 2's complement circuit of Figure 12-12 except in the connection of end-around-carry. In the present circuit a resulting

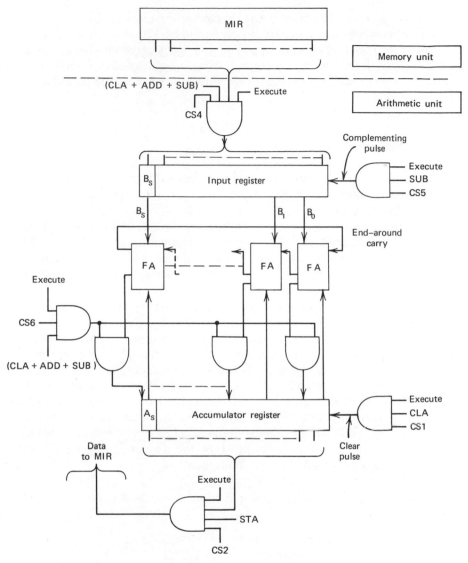

Figure 12-13.   Parallel adder/subtractor using 1's complement scheme.

carry from the highest order stage (sign stage) is applied as carry input to the lowest order state (2^0 stage) adding one count. The speed of this adder is limited basically by the time taken by the resulting carry signals to propagate around the adder units. At worst, the carries propagate the amount of delay in all the adder stages. For a 16-bit number the worst (slowest) case would occur with 16 carries resulting, which at, say, 20 nanoseconds delay per adder circuit would be 320 nanoseconds. After this time the sum bits are correct and may be transferred into the accumulator register. In effect then, enough time must be allowed on CS5 for any resulting carries to ripple around the adder units before the sum data is transferred.

12-5. Computer Multiplication

So far we have seen how both addition and subtraction were possible using only an adder unit. Now we shall see how the adder can be used to achieve binary multiplication.

Operating as fast as it does, the computer is capable of doing multiplication by repeated additions. Although with decimal numbers this may be quite lengthy, it is not so with binary. For example, 74×86 would require adding 74 six times and then 74 eight times, one digit position higher. In binary, since the digit can only be zero or one, the maximum number of additions for each position is one and a ten-bit number would require only ten addition steps. At 1 μsec per step this would be 10 μsec total, or a rate of 100,000 multiplications per second. Since other considerations must be made — timing, data shifting, and so on — fewer multiplications are performed, but the rate is still so high and the implementation so easy that the method is readily used by general-purpose computers. To distinguish between the method people use and the method the machine uses, the first will be called "pencil multiplication" and the latter "machine multiplication." An example of each, using the same numbers, will be given to show the difference and to point out how the machine implements this operation. First, consider a "pencil multiplication."

Example 12-13.   Do a pencil multiplication of the binary numbers 1011 and 1001.

Solution:

```
     1011    multiplicand
     1001    multiplier
     ────
     1011  ⎫
     0000  ⎪   partial
     0000  ⎬   products
    1011   ⎭
  ───────
  1100011    product
```

Notice in the above example that either the multiplicand is to be added as a partial product or zero is to be added, depending on the multiplier digit. As a rule then, multiplication can be carried out as a repeated addition, adding the multiplicand only when the multiplier bit is 1 and adding the multiplicand one position over each time the multiplier digit in the next position is used.

The multiplication can be carried out using essentially one adder unit for serial addition. It is necessary to repeat the addition a number of times equivalent to the bit positions in the multiplier (same as multiplicand). A basic cycle of adding multiplicand and accumulator values and then shifting multiplier and accumulator values one position over is then repeated for all multiplier positions to effect the multiplication. Notice in Example 12-13 that although the multiplier and multiplicand were each four bits, the product was seven bits (up to eight bits long in general). To provide for a product that can be up to twice the number of bit positions an additional register of the size of the accumulator, called the accumulator extension register, is required.

A logic diagram of a possible multiplication circuit is shown in Figure 12-14. The input register and accumulator register are basically the same

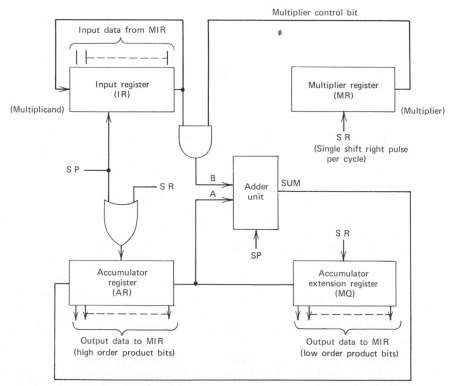

Figure 12-14.   Logic circuit for multiply operation.

as used in performing only addition. Two additional registers are shown, one being an extension of the accumulator register, which will be abbreviated MQ, the other a multiplier register (MR). Essentially a number in the accumulator is multiplied by a second number brought from memory to the input register, the resulting product having lowest order product bits in the MQ and highest order product bits in the AR. Before going into the operation consider the following machine multiplication using the same numbers as in Example 12-13.

Example 12-14.   Show a machine multiplication of the same two numbers as in Example 12-13.

Solution:

1.	101 1	
2.	100 1	multiplier bits moved right each shift step
3.	1011	add (since multiplier bit is 1) to initial zero value
4.	101 1	shift data and multiplier right (1 place)
5.	0000 ↓	add 4 and 5
6.	0101 1	sum in registers AR and MQ
7.	010 11	shift right (1 place)
8.	0000 ↓↓	add 7 and 8
9.	0010 11	sum in registers AR and MQ
10.	0001 011	shift right (place)
11.	1011 ↓↓↓	add 10 and 11
12.	1100 011	
13.	0110 0011	shift right (1 place) -product in AR and MQ

most significant   least significant
part in AR   part in MQ

Answer: 01100011

The example shows how a repetition of add/shift-right for four cycles results in the product in AR and MQ. This procedure will now be shown in the circuit of Figure 12-14. Recall that a multiply operation is programmed by loading a number into the accumulator register and then multiplying it by a number from memory. Starting with one number in the AR and the other in the IR an initializing step must be performed to transfer the AR and the other in the IR an initialitzing step must be performed to transfer the AR data into the multiplier register (MR) The binary number now loaded into the multiplier register will act as the multiplier value and input register value as multiplicand value with product formed by repeated addition being placed into the AR and MQ as product form.

The basic cycle carried out by the circuit is the following:

1. Add accumulator register and input register values placing sum into accumulator register under control — multiplicand value added to accumulator value *if* multiplier control bit is presently 1; zero added to accumulator value *if* multiplier control bit is presently 0.
2. Shift AR, MR, and MQ right one position (using single shift right pulse (SR).
3. Increment cycle count — stop *if* add/shift-right cycles completed; repeat steps (1) to (3) until all add/shift-right cycles completed (four in the present example).

During the add part of a cycle the accumulator register value is added to the input register data gated with the lowest order bit of the multiplier register. If the multiplier bit (which does not change during add part of cycle) is 1, then the multiplicand value is added; if multiplier bit is 0, then AND gate output remains zero for add part of cycle. Next, a single shift-right pulse moves the multiplier register data one position to the right thereby bringing the next multiplier bit into the control position. Also, the accumulator and accumulator extension data (in MQ) are moved right one place (as in step 4 of Example 12-14). The cycle counter (not shown here) is stepped and if four cycles (in this example) have not been done, then another add/shift-right cycle is performed.

Notice that the input register data is shifted around each add cycle so that the original multiplicand value is kept in the IR for the repeated cycles of the multiplication. One other point is worth mentioning here — the resulting product in AR and MQ has twice the number of bits of a memory word and a full product can be stored only in two separate memory locations. As a compromise one word of, say, highest order bits could be stored, dropping lowest order bits from the answer. This problem is one for the programmer but we should realize that both AR and MQ words may require storage in memory as provided for in the logic circuit of Figure 12-14.

Some consideration of the data in the MQ during the multiply cycles will show that as only one new bit of data is shifted into the MQ per cycle it is possible to use the MQ to hold the multiplier data, thereby eliminating need for a multiplier register. As single bits of data are shifted into the MQ, the multiplier word is shifted right one place and no conflict occurs. Figure 12-15 shows this modified circuit using only three arithmetic registers. The initialization step of transferring the accumulator number into the MQ occurs, after which the cycles of add/shift-right repeat as previously discussed.

It is possible to multiply signed numbers by first determining the

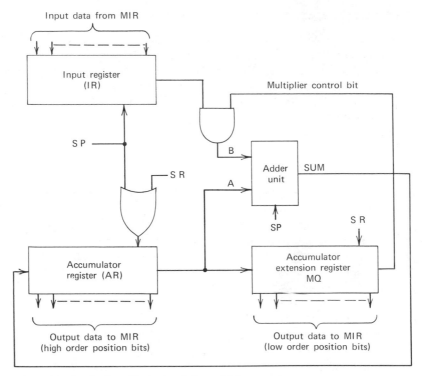

Input data from MIR

Input register
(IR)

Multiplier control bit

S P

S R

B

A

Adder
unit

SUM

SP

S R

Accumulator
register (AR)

Accumulator
extension register
MQ

Output data to MIR
(high order position bits)

Output data to MIR
(low order position bits)

Figure 12-15.   Reduced logic circuit for multiply operation.

product sign, then putting both numbers multiplied in absolute magnitude
form.

As the previous examples showed, the machine method is a repeated
addition and shift right. In terms of the registers shown in Figure 12-15,
the MQ holds the multiplier number and the IR holds the multiplicand.
On the first addition (with AR cleared) the multiplicand is added to the
value in the AR (zero at first) and the sum obtained is placed back into
the AR. All registers are now shifted right so that the AR and MQ
registers are shifted one extra place to the right. With the extra shift in
the AR and MQ the data is moved one place over so that the next sum is
added in at a higher order position. Moreover, by shifting the MQ one
extra place, the next multiplier bit (0 in this case) is used to qualify adding
the multiplicand or not on the next add time. This procedure is repeated
as many times as the number of bits per register or word. Here it was
repeated four times. Follow the next two examples and then try a few
problems yourself.

Example 12-15. Show the machine multiplication of 10101 × 10110. Do the pencil multiplication as a check.

Solution:

10101		multiplicand
10110		multiplier
00000		add zero to AR
0000	0	shift right
10101		add multiplicand to AR
10101	0	
1010	10	shift right
10101		add multiplicand to AR
11111	10	
1111	110	shift right
00000		add zero to AR
01111	110	
0111	1110	shift right
10101		add multiplicand to AR
11100	1110	
01110	01110	product

in AR in MQ   *Answer:* 01110 01110

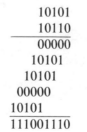

Check:

```
        10101
        10110
        00000
       10101
      10101
     00000
    10101
    111001110      Answer
```

Example 12-16. Show a machine multiplication of 101×11. Check using pencil multiplication.

Solution:

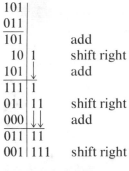

101		
011		
101		add
10	1	shift right
101		add
111	1	
011	11	shift right
000		add
011	11	
001	111	shift right

Answer: 001111

Check:

$$
\begin{array}{r}
101 \\
011 \\
\hline
101 \\
101 \\
\hline
1111
\end{array}
$$

Exercise 12-4. Show a machine multiplication of the following numbers (check each using pencil multiplication).

(a)   110   (b)   1011   (c)   11010
     $\times$ 10 $\times$ 1011 $\times$ 10010

12-6.   Computer Division

Division can be accomplished in a manner similar to multiplication in that a repeated *subtraction* and *shift left* is used. For this operation only three registers are needed with the answer (quotient) having one word capacity. Whereas multiplication of two ten-bit numbers gave a twenty-bit answer, the division of two ten-bit numbers will give, at most, a ten-bit answer (with restriction that division is of smaller value by larger value). Using the same three registers as in Figure 12-15 the logic control for division is shown in Figure 12-16. Discussion of this divider circuitry will show how the basic pattern of subtraction and shift left is carried out. The arithmetic unit shown as a subtractor would actually still be the

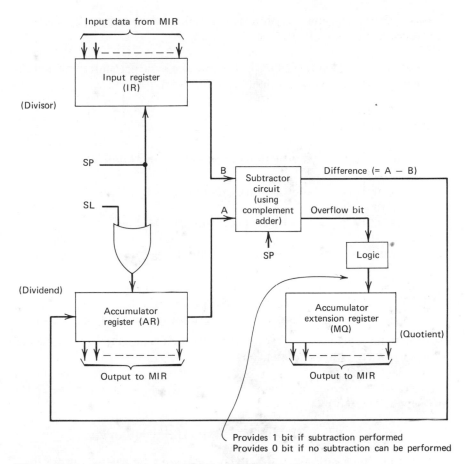

Figure 12-16.   Simplified logic circuitry for division operation.

same full adder unit used in addition, subtraction, or multiplication with complement addition being used to effect the indicated subtraction. To simplify the logic circuitry presented as much as possible so that the division operation is shown most clearly we shall refer to the complementary adder unit as a subtractor unit in the present discussion of division.

The program instructions to provide for division are: first load a number (dividend) into the accumulator register; then, instruct the computer to divide by a number brought into the input register (divisor). As we shall soon see the answer (quotient) will be placed into the MQ register (MQ now can be seen to stand for multiplier-quotient for the data held by it in these two arithmetic operations).

First, let us see how division can be effected by repeated cycles of subtraction and shift left (1 place).

Example 12-17.   Divide 328 by 8 showing the subtract/shift cycle operation and determination of quotient bits (MQ bits).

```
              101001
1000)  101001000
     − 1000
        00100          subtraction performed (∴ MQ bit is 1)
      −  1000
         001001        subtraction cannot be done (∴ MQ bit is 0)
       −   1000
          0000010      subtraction performed (∴ MQ bit is 1)
        −   1000
           00000100    no subtraction (∴ MQ bit = 0)
         −    1000
            000001000  no subtraction (∴ MQ bit = 0)
          −      1000  subtraction performed (∴ MQ bit = 1)
             000000000 remainder (only zero for this made up example)
```

Subtract/shift cycle stops after being performed same number of times as bits per word (or stages per register).

Exercise 12-5.   Show a machine division of the following numbers. Check using pencil method.

$$\text{(a) } 101\overline{)11001} \qquad \text{(b) } 111\overline{)110001}$$

In actual divider circuitry the division can only be carried out for division of a larger number by a smaller number with the answer a fractional value. Actually, numbers are considered to be only fractional values in the internal operation of the either multiply or divide circuitry even though they are scaled by the program to be of "any" magnitude desired.

12-7.   Floating Point and Decimal Arithmetic Operation

A brief mention should be made about the various circuitry that may be provided in a computer arithmetic unit. Usually, numbers stored in the computer memory are "straight" binary numbers. It is necessary to represent decimal numbers as binary-coded numbers for input/output operations so that external to the computer CPU the numbers seen are decimal. It is then necessary to provide for conversion of the decimal number (stored in binary-coded form) to a straight binary number so that arithmetic operations can be simply performed. This conversion to and from binary can be carried out by either a set of computer instructions as a stored program or, as would concern us here, by computer hardware in the arithmetic section of the computer. In effect, then, the conversion can be carried out by software or by hardware.

Software conversion costs no money but requires a program stored in the computer memory and the lengthy time of executing a many-step operation. Hardware conversion requires that circuitry be provided, at a greater cost, but has the advantage that the conversion is performed quickly and with no effort required by the programmer. In the case of the IBM 360, for example, the user has the option of using available conversion software or paying extra to have decimal arithmetic hardware added to the arithmetic section of the computer.

Similarly, there is a choice of software or hardware for handling floating point numbers. A number having a decimal value and an exponent part which indicates decimal point location is necessary in scientific calculations where numbers can range over considerable limits. Software programming, which then takes many steps to perform, can provide floating point operation. Floating point arithmetic hardware will do the same operation much faster. The details of hardware circuitry to operate on decimal numbers or floating point numbers is beyond our basic considerations, but we should be aware that such circuitry can exist in computer arithmetic units.

Summary

The arithmetic unit contains circuitry to carry out addition, subtraction, multiplication, and division. Some circuits were shown to carry out these operations, although many others exist in practice.

In addition (or subtraction) the two numbers to be added (subtracted) are applied to adder (subtraction) circuits for parallel operation with the sum (difference) then transferred to an output register. In serial operation the numbers are shifted bit by bit until the full binary answer is obtained. In multiplication (division) the two numbers are processed by addition (subtraction) and shift-right (shift-left) operations in a repeated cycle.

The addition or subtraction of two numbers including sign can be easily implemented using a 0 or 1 to represent the sign in the most significant digit and performing the operation as if the sign bit were part of the number.

PROBLEMS

§**12-3**   **1.** Write the binary form (as in Example 12-1) of (a) + 27, (b) − 36.
      2. Write the binary form (as in Example 12-1) of (a) + 72, (b) − 56.
      3. Add the following two numbers, using the method of Examples 12-2 to 12-5: (a) + 22, + 16, (b) + 25, − 15.
      4. Repeat Problem 12-3 for (a) − 19, − 33, (b) − 18, + 15.
      5. Subtract the following numbers using the method of Examples 12-6 to 12-9: (a) + 18 minus + 8, (b) + 25 minus − 16.
      6. Repeat Problem 12-5 for (a) − 36 minus + 14, (b) − 24 minus − 12.

§**12-5**   **7.** Show a machine multiplication of 1001×11.
      8. Show a machine multiplication of 11010×101.

§**12-6**   **9.** Show a machine division of $1010\overline{)1100100}$ and check using pencil method.
      10. Repeat Problem 12-9 for $10\overline{)1010}$.

1101

Input/output equipment

13-1. General Input/Output Techniques

Since most pieces of equipment used with computers are capable of providing data to the computer and also of reading it from the computer, input/output equipment will be considered as one topic (See Figure 13-1). For the computer user the input/output pieces of equipment are the most important. They enable him to handle his data in the most efficient and expeditious manner. The computer proper is merely a high-speed calculator performing many solutions per second. It is the input/output equipment that is usually of most concern to the user. In the simplest terms, input equipment consists of pieces that provide binary or binary-coded data for use in the computer, and output equipment consists of those that accept binary (or binary-coded data) from the computer for outside handling or storage. The best-known units, such as punched card, magnetic tape, magnetic disk, paper tape, or high-speed printer, are used with general-purpose computers in varying types and combinations. Special-purpose computers use standard but less familiar equipment for analog-to-digital or digital-to-analog conversion operations. These will be discussed separately because they present different ideas and techniques.

Control of the input/output equipment may be in the central computer itself, in the specific piece of equipment, or in both. When only one or two units are operated, the central computer will provide timing signals that determine when to start feeding data, what data to use, and when to stop. Where larger numbers of units are controlled, the computer may send only a timing signal telling the specific outside unit to start, letting all other control be handled by the peripheral equipment. Since the input/output units are the slowest-operating of a computer system, the integration of many different pieces of equipment is necessary to provide the

Courtesy of IBM

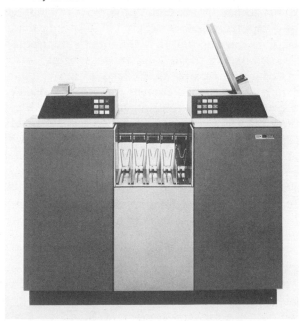

Courtesy of IBM

Figure 13-1.   Typical input/output units.

520

Courtesy of IBM

Courtesy of IBM

computer arithmetic unit with sufficient data to operate continuously. It is possible for one central computer unit to have a dozen magnetic tape and magnetic disk units providing input data to it while feeding data out to other magnetic tape disk and high-speed printer units. In fact, the problem of getting data fast enough and feeding it out to visual display equipment has required constant improvement in the fields of type printing, graphical presentation, visual oscilloscope, or cathode-ray display to provide the large amount of data processed to be presented in usable form for the operator.

Analog-to-digital (A/D), and digital-to-analog (D/A) equipment, on the other hand, generally provides data quickly enough to the computer but requires continued improvement in conversion accuracy. Direct current, alternating current, and rotation of mechanical shaft are examples of analog signals that must be converted into an equivalent digital form for use in the computer. For example, the dc voltage from 0 to + 10 volts can be broken up into steps of 0.5 volt and represented for each 0.5-volt step by the binary numbers from 0 to 20. Two dc voltages can be added together in the computer by adding the binary numbers of these quantized voltages (remember that the computer proper can operate only with binary numbers) and the resultant number converted back to a voltage, if that is desired. Obviously, this procedure will not be necessary for such a simple operation. However, when many operations at high speed and high accuracy are desired, the computer becomes important. Specific conversions of present importance, such as dc voltage to digital (and digital to dc voltage) and shaft position A/D and D/A, are considered in some detail.

13-2. Punched Card

Punched card data processing provides a widely used method of feeding digital information to a computer. The card has a fixed layout and stores binary data in the form of punched-out holes or none for 1 and 0, respectively. The data storage is, of course, permanent. However, for many operations this is a very desirable feature. A card can hold a small amount of data, usually on a specific item. Its direct relationship with one item (it could be an individual student in a school or a specific item of manufacture — such as a part for a car) is very useful when the ability to handle each card or each item separately is desirable, if not necessary. When items of data are stored on one card the cards can be separated by item using a card-sorting machine. For a set of cards representing each student in the school, the cards can be sorted by class section, degree program, or any other desirable breakdown for record purposes.

A standard card contains eighty columns and twelve rows (see Figure 13-2). Each column can be used to represent a character. The data is coded using a simple (not efficient) code so that the cards are easily read by an operator. Table 13-1 lists this code, and you will see that it can be applied and recognized quite easily and quickly. Refer to Table 13-1 and the card of Figure 13-3. The numerics are coded using the number of that row only. There are rows numbered 0 to 9, which then represent the decimal numbers 0 to 9 when a hole is punched there. Only one hole of twelve rows is punched for a number. To define a letter rows 12, 11, or 0 (called zones) are punched out in addition to a numerical row (1 to 9). For example, a hole in row 12 and row 1 *in the same column* represents the letter A, row 11 and row 2 the letter K, and row 0 and row 9 the letter Z (see Figure 13-3).

Table 13-1.   *Punched Card Code*

Numerical Row Only	Zone 12 Plus Numerical Row Below	Zone 11 Plus Numerical Row Below	Zone 0 Plus Numerical Row Below
0 = 0			
1 = 1	1 = A	1 = J	
2 = 2	2 = B	2 = K	2 = S
3 = 3	3 = C	3 = L	3 = T
4 = 4	4 = D	4 = M	4 = U
5 = 5	5 = E	5 = N	5 = V
6 = 6	6 = F	6 = O	6 = W
7 = 7	7 = G	7 = P	7 = X
8 = 8	8 = H	8 = Q	8 = Y
9 = 9	9 = I	9 = R	9 = Z

Punched cards are handled surprisingly fast. Reading rates of over 1000 cards per minute are currently available. Punching rates vary from 120 cards per minute (2 per second) to 250 per minute. There are two popular types of card-reader units. The slower method uses wire brush sensors. If the brush goes over a hole it makes contact with a metal plate below and passes this on as a signal of a binary 1 being read. The brush-type readers only operate up to rates of about 200 cards per minute. The faster card-reading rates mentioned previously are obtained using optical readers. A light source on one side of the card will activate a photodetector (photodiode, photocell, and so on) if there is a hole to pass through (a binary 1) and does not activate the detector when the card face is present. Since the optical cell responds quickly, the reading rate

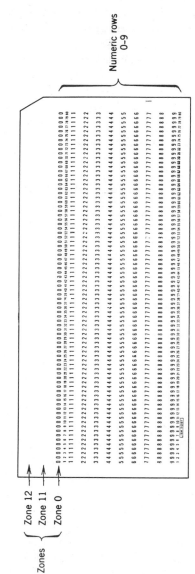

Figure 13-2. Standard 80-column card.

524

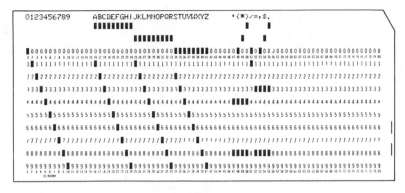

Figure 13-3. Punched card showing alphameric code.

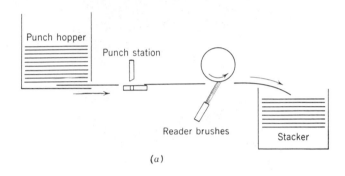

(a)

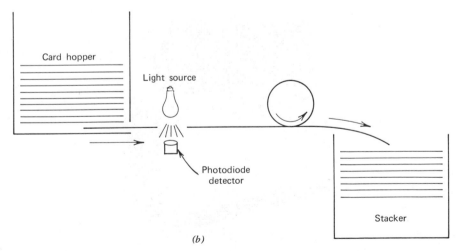

(b)

Figure 13-4. Card read and punch techniques. (a) Wire brush punch and reader. (b) Optical reader.

525

can be increased considerably. Figure 13-4 shows a wire brush punch and reader, and an optical reader.

Control of the card reader or card punch is generally within the external unit; the computer only controls when to start reading. The data stored on many cards might be used to fill up part of the core memory. Once filled, the computer operates at high speed from the internal memory.

Courtesy of IBM

Courtesy of IBM

Figure 13-5.   High-speed card reader and punch units. (*a*) IBM 3505 Card reader. (*b*) IBM 3525 Card punch.

Punched cards may hold both program material and data for use in the computer. Recalling that the hardest part of the job may often be to provide data fast enough to keep the computer arithmetic section busy, you may find such combinations as punched cards feeding magnetic-tape units which are then used to fill up the core memory. Punched cards were necessary for easy handling of data on company products, magnetic tape for arranging the data in larger blocks of information (with faster reading rate into the computer), and magnetic cores for handling smaller pieces of the large amount of data but handling it as fast as the computer can use it. Figure 13-5 shows a high-speed card reader and a high-speed card punch unit.

13-3. Punched Paper Tape

Filling another practical need is the punched paper tape input/output unit. Data is again stored in the form of punched holes (or none) and is permanent. The main advantages of punched tape are the ability to store small amounts of data in a more compact form than card, the ability to see what data is on the tape (not so with magnetic tape), the ease of handling these small amounts of information, and the low price of paper tape units. The use of teletype (TTY) terminals having paper tape I/O capability is quite popular because of low price and simplicity. A magnetic tape can only be handled in fairly large reels and is poorly set up to handle only a small amount of information. (Newer cassette type magnetic reels, however, are becoming popular.) When the individual piece requirement of punched cards is unnecessary, punched tape is a cheaper, more efficient method of handling the data. For example, a program routine may be stored on punched tape. One program may be 5 feet of tape long, another 6 inches. In either case each program can be separately stored and put into the machine when needed. Large tape drive units are not necessary and the tape may be easily put on the machine, taken off, held in your hand, looked over, pocketed, and so on. This ease of handling is a distinct advantage over magnetic tape. Of course, when large amounts of information are being processed, the speed and storage capacity of magnetic tapes are necessary, and this storage method does find the largest overall use. Probably the most popular use of paper tape occurs with small computers or time-shared terminals using teletype with paper tape reader-punch operation. The point here is that each of the three types considered have distinct operational advantages and find use in industry.

Paper tape readers (see Figure 13-6) operate around 100 characters per second for mechanical readers and 1000 for optical. Tape punch units

(a)

Courtesy of IBM

(b)

Courtesy of IBM

Figure 13-6. Paper tape punch units. (a) IBM 1017 paper tape reader. (b) IBM 1018 paper tape punch.

528

can punch as many as 10 characters per inch at rates of 50 characters per second. Generally there are 8 rows of binary-coded information plus a small sprocket hole that serves to advance the tape through the machine (see Figure 13-7). The 8 rows provide an 8-bit code, each column storing a character. The tape can be as long as any program desired, or as short. In reading the tape the reader unit drives the tape via the sprocket holes and wire brush pins, or optical readers are used (see Figure 13-7c).

The data is punched as one character per column. Generally, three

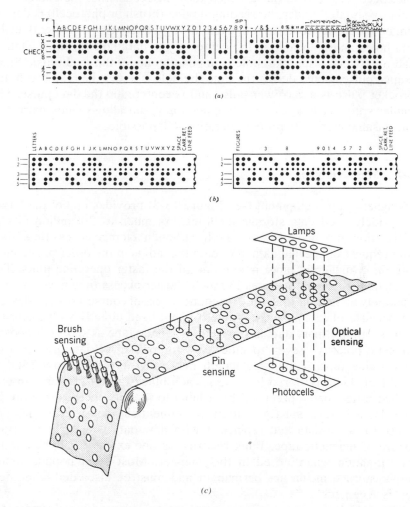

(a)

(b)

(c)

Figure 13-7.   Paper tape showing (a) eight-channel code, (b) five-channel code, (c) methods of reading punched tape.

rows are on one side of the sprocket holes, and the rest are on the other. These three are often the 1, 2, and 4-weighted positions as shown in Figure 13-7a. The next row (after the sprocket hole) is the 8-weighted position. The check bit position contains a parity bit (usually odd parity, as discussed in Chapter 4) to provide a validity test when reading in data. The sprocket holes on the tape serve two important purposes. First, it is used in the movement of the tape through the reader. The mechanical advance mechanism moves the tape a character at a time via the sprocket hole. Second, the read pulse which tells the reader that the character is properly situated under the reading device (brush or photocell) is dependent on the sprocket hole. Notice that the sprocket hole is smaller than the data holes and is located in the center of the data hole position. Data is read only when a sprocket hole is in position under the read brush. Since a signal pulse occurs during the time the hole is under the read brush, the sprocket pulse is a narrower pulse and is centered in the data pulse. The smaller sprocket hole aids reading accuracy and allows some margin of hole misalignment with proper operation still possible.

13-4.   Magnetic Tape

Magnetic tape equipment (see Figure 13-8) provides one of the larger and widely used data storage facilities. As much as 20 million bits of information may be stored on a reel. Although average access time (time from request of specific data until data is read) is in the order of seconds, *mag tape* (magnetic tape) is still one of the faster operating units. The magnetic disk which operates in much shorter access time is considered separately in Section 13-5. The magnetic tape is of course a storage device, but because of its long access time it is not used directly with the arithmetic section. Binary data is stored on magnetic tape as spots of opposite magnetic polarity. Seven to nine rows (or tracks) of data are usual on 1-inch-wide tape. Total tape length may range typically from 1800 to 2400 feet. Data is stored in blocks, each block (group of words in prescribed order) being preceded by a label to identify the position on the tape. Data is read out (or written in) sequentially and is erasable. The ability to erase data and replace it with new data is a very important feature of magnetic tape. Bank records, as one example, can be continually updated when stored in this manner. Most other popular input/output storage media are permanent and must be discarded when new data is accepted.

Figure 13-9 shows a magnetic tape section with read/write heads. It is similar to that used for home tape recording but has more tracks and stores

(a)

(b)

Courtesy of Honeywell   Courtesy of Burroughs Corp.

Figure 13-8.   Magnetic tape units. (a) Honeywell Corporation. (b) Burroughs Corporation.

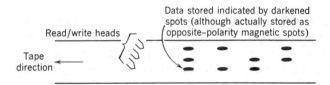

Figure 13-9.   Magnetic tape data storage.

the data in simple magnetized spots rather than complex wave patterns as for music and voice. Figure 13-10 shows a piece of magnetic tape whose characters are stored as a seven-bit alphameric (alphabetic and numeric) code. Although the bits are written as magnetized spots of clockwise or counterclockwise polarity, they are shown here as the presence or absence of a magnetized spot for clarity. It should also be clear that although data may be erased, it is considered permanent in the sense that it can be retained indefinitely (with proper handling and storage of reel). Magnetic tape storage is nonvolatile in that the data will remain stored even if power to operate the unit is turned off. The magnetic tape unit functions as both an input and output device.

In the tape code shown (Figure 13-10) data is recorded in seven parallel channels or tracks, and each column (the width of the tape) contains a

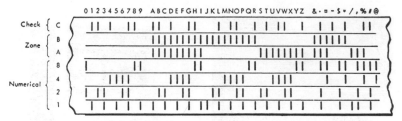

Figure 13-10.   Spots on magnetic tape showing alphameric code.

single character. The spacing between rows is fixed by the head spacing, and the spacing between characters is automatically established by the magnetic tape unit. Character density is 800 to 1600 characters per inch. The tape characters are stored with a check bit for even parity. In addition to this character parity check a track parity check may also be made on each record. At the time the data is recorded, the bits for each track are added and a check character is recorded at the end of the block. For each track with an odd bit count a check bit is recorded. Thus, when the record is read it should provide a satisfactory even parity check of each character and of the check word. Since all this data checking is being done by the magnetic tape unit, the computer need not be involved because the check character is not included as part of the record when it is passed on to the computer.

The magnetic tape drive mechanism (Figure 13-11) is more advanced than that used in a home recorder since high operating speed, fast start and stop, and greater reading and writing alignments are necessary. Drive motors are often kept running continuously, the capstan or pressure roller being controlled to move tape or not. This allows for faster response since the tape immediately takes off at high speed instead of being slowly accelerated as the motor speeds up. When the tape is to be moved, the drive capstan makes contact with the tape. When the tape is to be stopped, the drive capstan is removed and the stop capstan is immediately engaged to halt the tape fast. To allow for such high-speed start and stop operations without breaking the tape, a loop of tape may be held in a vacuum column, one for each reel. Since data may occur anywhere on the tape, the drive mechanism can backspace the tape or rewind it to the beginning of the reel. The reel is then driven until it reaches the desired place on the tape. On some tape drive units the tapes may even be read backward (opposite to the direction when data was written).

As the tape moves by the write head, pulses of flux magnetize spots on the surface of the tape. The seven read/write heads are operated simultaneously. Although the tape is moving by the heads at speeds in the order of 150 inches per second or higher, the write time is so short

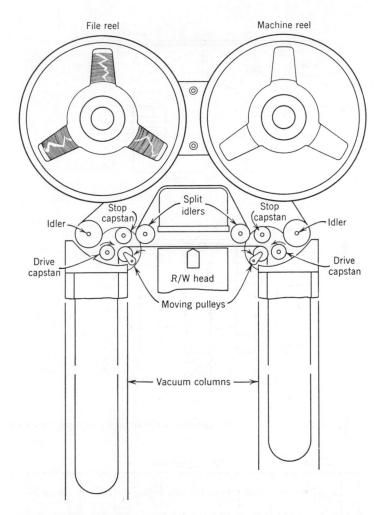

Figure 13-11.   Tape drive mechanism.

that the tape appears to be virtually stationary. Two popular types of heads are the one-gap and two-gap heads. The one-gap head (Figure 13-12*a*) can be used for either read or write but only one at any time. The two-gap head (Figure 13-12*b*) can write a bit and read it back while the bit is still positioned under the head. This is convenient for use with the tape-validity checking operations discussed.

The size of a record is generally not limited. It may be only a few characters or a few thousand. However, each record is preceded by a gap (about 3/4 inch) that allows for stopping and positioning of the tape

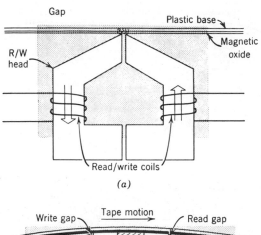

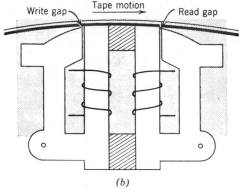

Figure 13-12. (a) One-gap read/write head. (b) Two-gap read/write head.

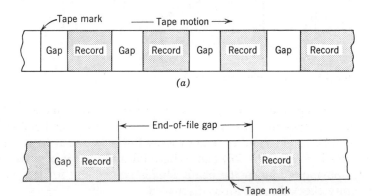

Figure 13-13. Interrecord gap on magnetic tape. (a) Tape mark at end of file. (b) End-of-file gap.

before the desired data is read (see Figure 13-13). During the write operation a fixed gap is left between or after every record recorded. In this way every record is preceded and followed by an interrecord gap. This blank section also allows for starting and stopping the tape between records.

As a summary, the magnetic tape can store from 800 to 1600 characters per inch, or tens of millions of characters on a 2400-foot reel of tape. Storage is sequential, in blocks or records, and is erasable. It is cheap storage per bit but expensive for millions of characters. The magnetic tape unit has large storage capacity but long access time.

12-5. Magnetic Disk

Magnetic disk storage provides the largest data storage facility in a single unit of equipment (see Figure 13-14). A few million characters can be stored on a number of record or disk surfaces. The technique is similar to that used in recording for the phonograph, except that the recording is on a magnetic surface instead of cut grooves, and data is

Courtesy of IBM

Figure 13-14.   Magnetic disk drive unit.

read back by a magnetic pickup mounted on a movable arm rather than by a needle (also there is no inward spiral of the track). A first apparent difference is that the data is generally contained on a number of disks and there are read heads for every disk. Both upper and lower surfaces are available for read at all times (see Figure 13-15).

The data is stored in tracks (circumferentially on the disk) where each recording surface may contain typically 100 to 250 tracks. Disk diameters may vary from 1 to 3 feet. The disk may be rotated at about 1800 revolutions per minute. Considering the disk alone, the average access time would be about 50 msec. However, there are many possible tracks and usually one head per surface. Adding in the time needed to move the read arm to the desired track brings the overall average access time around

(a)

Courtesy of Burroughs Corp.

Figure 13-15.   Magnetic disk unit details. (*a*) Burroughs Corporation head assembly. (*b*) IBM Corp. head arrangement. (*c*) Typical disk organization.

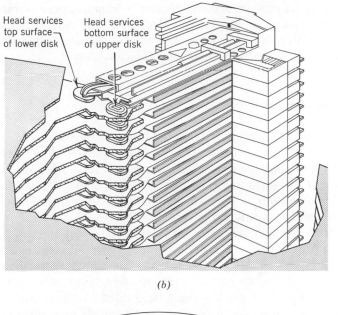

Head services top surface of lower disk

Head services bottom surface of upper disk

(b)

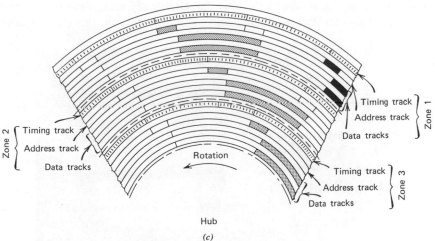

Timing track
Address track
Data tracks
Zone 1

Timing track
Address track
Data tracks
Zone 2

Rotation

Timing track
Address track
Data tracks
Zone 3

Hub

(c)

250 msec. Although this may seem a long time compared to a magnetic drum, it is much shorter than the seconds to minutes with a magnetic tape.

An NRZ recording method may be used to store data. Access is considered random because you need only select the correct head and move it to the desired track. You do not have to read all the data until that desired appears as with magnetic tape. Figure 13-15c shows how data may be organized on the magnetic disk face. It should not, however, be compared to the random access speed of a magnetic core memory. Data may be erased and storage is nonvolatile. In fact, most disk drive units are set up so that a disk pack (containing a fixed number of record disks) may be easily removed and a new one replaced.

13-6. High-Speed Printer

A high-speed printer providing typed data is one of the most popular permanent visual records used with computers (see Figure 13-16). Whereas typewriters generate a character at a time, high-speed printers type a line at a time, thereby adding to its much higher speed. It also gains in speed of operation by sophisticated mechanical design. There are both mechanical and electronic printers available.

One form of printer has separate print wheels or print bars. There are as many print wheels as desired characters per line. Each print wheel contains a complete set of alphanumeric characters and special characters (see Figure 13-17). For the printing of each line, each wheel representing a character of the line must be rotated to the desired character. When all print wheels are in position, mechanically driven hammers (one for each character) are activated and strike the ribbon, thereby printing

Courtesy of Honeywell

Figure 13-16.   High-speed printer units. (*a*) Honeywell. (*b*) Burroughs Corporation.

Courtesy of Burroughs Corp.

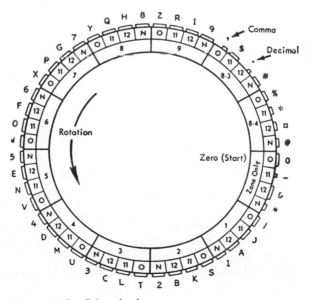

Figure 13-17.   Print wheel.

all characters of the line at once. For each line of print the computer feeds in new data to the printer unit. Since the time to print a line is so slow compared to the computer data transfer rate, the line of information can be transferred either serially or in parallel, depending on how the computer is operated. After each line of print the paper and ribbon are moved slightly, the print wheels rotate to new positions, and the hammers, having moved off, strike again for the next line of print. A printing rate of 200 lines per minute is typical for such a printer unit.

Another form of a printer has a rotating drum with each character on a separate axial line. A drum may contain as many as 120 to 144 characters per line (see Figure 13-18). Commands for all characters of a line are fed

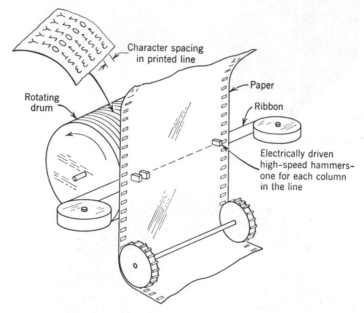

Figure 13-18.   A rotating-drum printer.

to the printer at one time. As each line of the drum passes by the fixed hammers, the individual hammers strike, thereby printing similar characters selectively over the entire line at one time. Within one revolution of drum all characters of a single line are printed. The paper, guided by pin feeds on each side, is provided in a continuous stack. It is perforated at regular intervals so that it may be taken off after a desired recording is complete, without stopping the operation of the machine. Generally, the machine is designed to stop when no more paper is available. The machine also indicates this to the computer so that no new information is fed out at this time. Since the operation is continuous (the drum is always rotating), this type of printer operates much faster than the start-stop operation of the individual wheel printer. Printers of the drum type operate at speeds of a few hundred lines per minute to 1200 lines per minute. They can provide at least 64 different characters for up to 144 characters per line.

A third mechanical printer uses a continuously rotating character belt (Figure 13-19). The individual character hammers strike as the desired

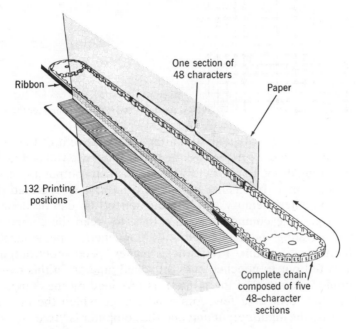

Ribbon

One section of
48 characters

Paper

132 Printing
positions

Complete chain
composed of five
48–character
sections

Figure 13-19.   A belt printer.

character on the belt passes underneath the hammer head. The belt may contain a number of sets of characters to cut down the time until the desired character lines up under a hammer. Printers now available can operate at speeds over 2000 lines per minute (33 lines per second). Synchronizing the operation is important because there is not a single hammer stroke and paper feed operation. Each hammer strikes as the correct character passes under the head. After all hammers have struck once, the paper feed advances one line and the operation repeats. Although these speeds are seemingly very high (and they are), data is being generated hundreds of times faster in the computer.

Electrostatic printers do not require physical contact between paper and hammer surface. Instead, special paper exposed to an electrical discharge from a selected pattern creates the desired character. By using a grid matrix (as in electroluminescent displays), specific grid points are selected for a particular character and are energized to "print" the character (Figure 13-20). Printing speeds of about 5000 lines per minute are possible with this type printer.

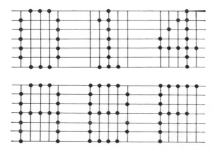

Figure 13-20.   Matrix character formation.

Depending on the particular computer and the extent of the programs being run, one or more printers will be used, and these will be fed directly from the computer memory or via some other input/output unit, such as a magnetic tape unit. In smaller computers the unit is operated directly from the computer memory and no other operation can be done at this time. In larger-size computers the desire is to keep the computer continuously operating and data is fed only to magnetic tape, magnetic disk pack, or magnetic drum. From these higher-speed input/output units the data is fed out to punched card, punched tape or, in this case, high-speed printers. Control of the printout is provided by the computer, but usually in the form of a few commands, after which the operation is taken over by the input/output unit and the computer is "free" to continue processing the program.

13-7.   Teletypewriter Terminals

With the advent of time-shared computer operation the teletype terminal has become a widespread and valuable unit of I/O operation with a computer. The basic teletype unit (TTY) has a keyboard for typing input and a typewriter mechanism for printing output. When a key is pressed an eight-bit ASCII code character, for example, is generated. When a coded character is received it can cause the typewriter print mechanism to operate. When used with a computer the binary coded character is converted into electrical signals for transmission over lines either directly or via telephone to and from the computer.

The use of a telephone line to couple information between TTY and computer usually requires an acoustic coupler to convert between the electrical signals and sound signals. For example, binary data may be transmitted as two different audible sound frequencies for binary 1 and 0.

Figure 13-21 shows a teletype terminal and acoustic coupler. To

Figure 13-21.   Teletype terminal.

operate the unit merely requires the availability of ac power and a telephone — two items found almost anywhere. The computer operating with the TTY can be located anywhere.

The important features of the TTY terminal are its low unit cost and the operation in time-shared mode which provides easy access to a powerful computer and program library at quite low cost.

13-8.   Optical I/O Devices

A device that (although presently quite costly) is gaining importance as an output unit of a computer is the optical display or cathode ray tube (CRT) terminal. A typical I/O CRT terminal (see Figure 13-22) incorporates a typewriter input keyboard and CRT output display. Data is entered on the keyboard as on a computer typewriter and electrical signals are generated for transmission to the computer. The computer-generated binary data is then fed back to the CRT unit as electrical signals to be displayed visually. The fast printing speed of the CRT unit allows for quick display of a file or record of information. Bank transactions and airline reservation systems are examples of CRT display applications. The desired information displayed can be modified via the keyboard and new data stored back in the computer records. When "hard" copy is desired some systems employ microfilm or other reproducing devices to be operated by the computer.

Courtesy of Hazeltine

Courtesy of IBM

Figure 13-22. CRT terminals. (*a*) Hazeltine 2000. (*b*) IBM 2260.

CRT terminals may include storage facility (core or IC storage units) with capacity of, say, 1024 characters. Displayed data is held in the CRT storage section so that the computer need not be involved in the display presentation unless new data is transmitted. The stored data is then repeatedly swept across the CRT screen as the picture on a home TV is scanned. Refresh rates of 60 HZ are common—meaning that the full display is repeatedly written on the CRT, about 60 times per second so that it appears steady. Transmission of data to and from the CRT terminal may be rated in *bauds*. The transmission rate may be 600 bauds, for example.

A CRT terminal may also have magnetic tape cassette input-output capability to provide easy entry or storage of displayed data. Other options may include magnetic card input/output or hard copy from an electrostatic copier, making the CRT terminal a very attractive unit to use.

Some computers used in scientific work have XY ink plotters to obtain hard copy of a graph calculated by the computer. The weather bureau, for one, does an extensive amount of work with graph output on ink plotters. In addition, it is possible to obtain plots on a CRT display in a much shorter time than required by an ink plotter. Hard copy is then easily and quickly obtained from the CRT terminal.

13-9.   Analog-to-Digital (A/D) Conversion

General.   When using a digital computer to operate other devices or processes it may be necessary to include analog-to-digital (A/D) conversion and digital-to-analog (D/A) conversion equipment. In a processing plant, for example, the signals received by the computer system may include direct current voltage, shaft position of some dial or machine part, these signals being analog in form. Since a digital computer only operates on binary numbers it is necessary to convert this analog data into digital data. The conversion from analog to digital is performed by an A/D converter. After the computer has performed its programmed calculations the digital values to be fed as output may have to go through a digital-to-analog conversion to provide the type of analog signal required to operate the output (controlled) devices. In a large system one digital computer is often fast enough to handle a number of inputs and outputs. Depending on the rate of change of the input signal one A/D converter may be used by *multiplexing* (switching between inputs) the inputs to a single A/D converter unit or separate A/D converter units may be required for each input. Various schemes will be considered later.

Accuracy and Resolution. Two important factors of conversion are accuracy and resolution. Whereas accuracy indicates how close the measured value is to the true value, resolution indicates how closely it is possible to discern between two voltages. An accuracy of 1 percent means that 100 volts might really be 99 volts to 101 volts and you cannot distinguish any finer. Resolution of 100 mV means that you cannot distinguish between voltages less than 100 mV (0.1 volt) apart. A voltage of 10.6 volts and 10.65 volts (50 mV apart) would appear the same, since they differ by less than the resolution of a voltage comparator.

It is often not clear that an operation may be done with a greater resolution than the accuracy obtainable. It may be possible to resolve between 10.1 and 10.2 volts, but the real voltage may have been 10.5 volts. The accuracy here was poorer than the resolution. It would seem to make sense to have the resolution only as good as the accuracy makes the value meaningful. On the other hand, a high accuracy and low resolution is also poor, since you may be very close to the real voltage but not able to discriminate in your operation between small differences.

A resolution of 1 volt and accuracy of 1 percent with a 10-volt signal would mean that you cannot distinguish between 9.2 and 9.8, for example, whereas you are accurate to 0.1 volt. Bear in mind this distinction between accuracy and resolution in other areas of work as well, for it sometimes tends to be confusing.

Conversion Time. Conversion time is the time required by the A/D converter circuitry to convert the analog signal into an equivalent digital count. In any system this depends on both the clock rate used and the maximum number of counts (or the number of counter stages). When converting from analog dc voltage to digital count, for example, the usual method (see Figure 13-23) is to compare an input unknown dc voltage to a reference voltage. The reference voltage is then increased in a stepwise manner until it equals or just exceeds the unknown voltage. Increasing a digital count each time the reference voltage is increased one voltage step provides the digital count value desired.

In this example the conversion time depends on the clock rate used — the faster the clock the faster the count advances. The conversion time also depends on the number of counter stages used since it takes longer to achieve a higher count. For example, at a 1.024-MHZ clock rate using ten stages the conversion time would be $(1/1.024 \ \mu\text{sec}) \times 1024$ counts or 1000 μsec (1 msec). Since it takes up to 1 msec to do a conversion there could be as many as 1000 conversions each second. At lower clock rates or for larger counts the number of conversions per second will be less.

The number of counter stages used depends on the desired conversion

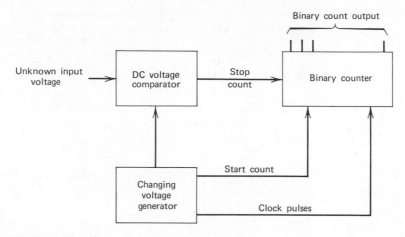

Figure 13-23.   Conversion from dc voltage to binary count.

resolution, since it is possible to have smaller voltage steps in a defined voltage range using more counts or more steps. The clock rate then determines the conversion time. In practice there is an upper clock rate possible dependent on the speed of operation of the counter circuitry. The accuracy of the conversion depends on the dc voltage comparator in the circuit of Figure 13-23.

Other conversion techniques may obtain a digital count without a counting procedure, in which case no conversion time may occur. A gray code shaft encoder, for example, provides an immediate digital value that can be read either serially or in parallel by the digital computer.

One technique for conversion of dc voltage to digital count uses a binary counter driving a *ladder network*, which develops an output dc voltage proportional to the digital count. Figure 13-24 shows the details of this converter circuit. The clock rate and changing voltage are synchronized in this arrangement. The resolution of the circuit depends on the number of counter stages used, which determines the number of steps in voltage developed by the adder network, and the reference voltage, which determines the range of voltage developed by the ladder network. For example, using a reference voltage of ten volts and a counter having 1000 steps (maximum possible count) the resolution would be

$$10 \text{ volts}/1000 \text{ steps per volt} = 0.01 \text{ volt per step}$$

If the counter were increased to 10,000 steps, then each step would then produce a 0.001 volt or 1 mV change. Thus, using more count steps results in less voltage change per step or in higher resolution. On the other

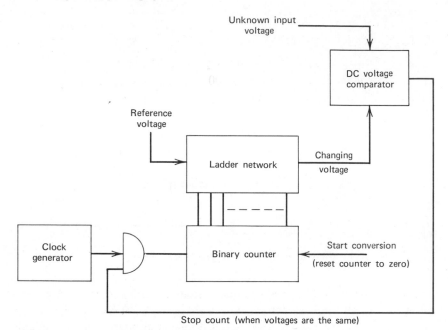

Figure 13-24.   Dc voltage conversion using ladder network.

hand, more count steps results in a longer possible count time and thus slower conversion time.

The conversion accuracy is still dependent on the accuracy of the voltage comparator circuit. A few examples on conversion time and re-solution should help emphasize the main points to consider.

Example 13-1.   What resolution (in percentage) is obtained using an eight-stage counter and ladder network?

Solution: For eight stages $2^8 = 256$. One part in 256 is approximately $(1/250) \times 100\%$ or 0.4% resolution.

Example 13-2.   What resolution (in volts) is obtained using an eight-stage counter and ladder network reference voltage of 10 volts?

Solution: Example 13-1 gave the resolution as 0.4% (approximately).

$$\text{Resolution} = 0.4\% \,(10 \text{ volts})$$

$$= \frac{0.4}{100}(10) = 0.04 \text{ volt}$$

$$= 40 \text{ mV}$$

Example 13-3. For a clock rate of 10 kHz, what is the maximum conversion time using an eight-stage counter?

Solution: Since eight stages require 2^8, or 256, counts in total, and a 10-kHz clock takes $1/(10 \times 10^3) = 100 \, \mu\text{sec}$ per count, the total time elapsed is $100 \, \mu\text{sec} \times 256$, or $25,600 \, \mu\text{sec}$. This is 25.6 msec per conversion (maximum).

Example 13-4. How many conversions are possible using an eight-stage counter driven at a 10-kHz clock rate?

Solution: At 25.6 msec per conversion, there could be about $1/(25.6 \times 10^{-3})$, or $1000/25.6 \cong 40$ conversions per second.

Exercise 13-1. What is the resolution (in percentage) where the following number of counter stages are used?

(a) 12   (b) 6   (c) 9   (d) 11

Exercise 13-2. For each corresponding part of Exercise 13-1 calculate the resolution (in volts) for each of the following reference voltages.

(a) 10 volts   (b) 1.6 volts   (c) 220 mV

Exercise 13-3. For each corresponding part of Exercise 13-1 calculate the conversion time and solutions per second for each of the following clock rates.

(a) 150 kHz   (b) 820 kHz   (c) 1.6 MHz

Exercise 13-4. How many counter stages are needed to get a resolution of about 10 mV using a reference voltage of 25 volts? What clock rate is needed to obtain around 250 solutions per second?

Exercise 13-5. With a clock rate of 100 kHz and resolution of about 0.2%, how many conversions per second are possible?

Operation of Ladder Network. The ladder network is made of resistors of two different values wired as shown in Figure 13-25. The values R and $2R$ might be 1 kΩ and 2 kΩ, for example. As indicated, the TRUE output of each counter stage is connected to a specific resistor in the network. The voltage at these input points could be $+16$ volts and 0 volts (for 1 and 0), and the output voltage depends on where these are applied to the ladder circuit. Let us consider some simple cases first to see how the ladder output voltage is obtained.

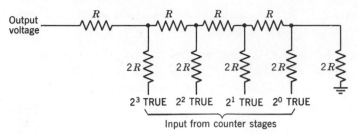

Figure 13-25.   Ladder network.

For all inputs at 0 volts (no input voltage) the output is 0 volts. A count of 0 0 0 0 thus produces an output voltage of 0 volts. Consider + 16 volts as the input voltage representing logical 1 for ease of numerical designation. When the input of the 2^3 stage only is + 16 volts, let us see what the output voltage is. With all inputs at 0 volts except the 2^3 which is at + 16 volts, the circuit for this specific input combination is shown in Figure 13-26a.

Working from right side over, the $2R$ parallel with $2R$ is the same as an R resistor (see Figure 13-26b). This R is in series with another R resistor and can be combined into a single $2R$ resistor (see Figure 13-26c).

Again there are two $2R$ resistors in parallel, giving a single equivalent

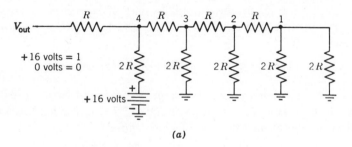

(a)

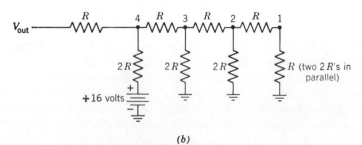

(b)

Figure 13-26.   Ladder network for 1000 input.

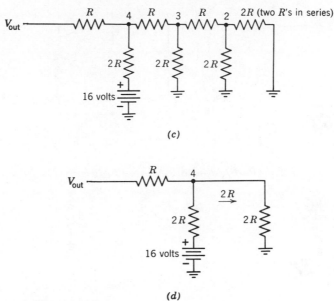

(c)

(d)

R resistor. Adding this *R* to the series *R* resistor connected to it gives 2*R* again looking to the right from point 3. Repeating, we find that there is also 2*R* looking to the right from point 4 (not considering the initial resistor connected vertically at point 4). This reduced circuit is shown in Figure 13-26*d*. As a general rule it can be stated that looking to the right of a node such as 1, 2, 3, 4, the resistance seen is always 2*R*.

Calculating the voltage at node 4 we find that it is the resultant of 16 volts through a voltage divider 2*R* and 2*R* or $V_{out} = 8$ volts. When the count is 8 for a maximum count of $16(2^4)$, the voltage is 8/16, or half the full-scale value. One-half of 16 volts is 8 volts, as obtained. Let us repeat for an input count of 0100. The network for this specific input is shown in Figure 13-27*a*. Since the resistance seen looking to the right is always 2*R*, the circuit can be reduced to that of Figure 13-27*b*.

Calculating the voltage at node 3 using Thevenin's theorem gives + 8 volts in series with *R* as in Figure 13-27*c*. Figure 13-27*d* shows that this can be further simplified adding the two series resistors. The voltage at node 4 can be calculated to be + 4 volts using the voltage divider rule. The resultant output voltage is then 4 volts so that a count of 0100 or 4 out of 16 possible counts (4/16 = 1/4) gives one-fourth the output voltage [1/4(16 volts) = 4 volts]. So far the output voltage developed by the network was the same proportion of the full voltage as the binary count of the full count. Further consideration would show that a count of 0010

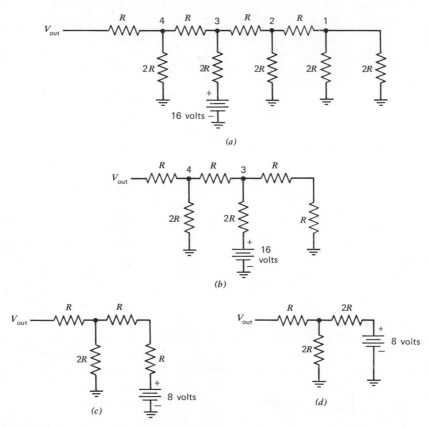

Figure 13-27.   Ladder network for 0100 input.

would result in 2 volts output and a count of 0001 in an output voltage of 1 volt. Since the rule of superposition allows us to calculate the voltage produced by more than one source in a network (more than one 1 in this case), we can find the output voltage for all sixteen combinations of input. These are listed in Table 13-2 for input count and output voltage using a four-stage counter and + 16 volts as logical 1 and 0 volts as logical 0.

Looking at the circuit more generally, we see that the input voltage furthest from the output has the weight of 2^0/total count. This continues in steps of 2 until the closest to the output has the weight of 1/2. For example, using ten stages, the lowest-value stage is $2^0/2^{10}$, or 1/1024. The largest is $2^9/2^{10}$, or $512/1024 = 1/2$.

With logical 1 defined as 10.24 volts, the output voltage for 0000000001 would be $1/1024(10.24) = 10$ mV; for 1000000000 it would be $512/1024$ $(10.24) = 5.12$ volts; and for 1000000001, $5.120 + 0.010$ or 5.13 volts.

Table 13-2. *Count Versus Voltage Output for Four-Stage Ladder Network*
($V_{REF} = 16$ volts)

Input Count	Output Voltage (volts)
0000	0
0001	1
0010	2
0011	3
0100	4
0101	5
0110	6
0111	7
1000	8
1001	9
1010	10
1011	11
1100	12
1101	13
1110	14
1111	15

Example 13-5. What is the output voltage of a five-stage ladder network using $+6.4$ volts $= 1$ and 0 volts $= 0$ for the following binary counts?

(a) $1\,0\,0\,0\,0$ (b) $0\,0\,0\,0\,1$ (c) $0\,1\,0\,0\,0$ (d) $0\,1\,1\,0\,1$
(e) $1\,0\,0\,1\,0$

Solution: (a) $2^5 = 32$; $1\,0\,0\,0\,0$ is 16; thus, $1\,0\,0\,0\,0$ gives $\dfrac{16}{32}$ (6.4 volts) or 3.2 volts.

(b) $0\,0\,0\,0\,1 = 1$, so that $\dfrac{1}{32}$ (6.4 volts) $= 0.2$ volt

(c) $0\,1\,0\,0\,0 = 8$ and $\dfrac{8}{32}$ is $\dfrac{1}{4}$ (6.4 volts) $= 1.6$ volts

(d) Adding, $\left(\dfrac{0}{32} + \dfrac{8}{32} + \dfrac{4}{32} + \dfrac{0}{32} + \dfrac{1}{32}\right) \times 6.4$ volts gives $\dfrac{13}{32} \times$ (6.4 volts) $= 2.6$ volts

(e) $1\,0\,0\,1\,0$ gives $\left(\dfrac{16}{32} + \dfrac{0}{32} + \dfrac{0}{32} + \dfrac{2}{32} + \dfrac{0}{32}\right) \times$ (6.4 volts) $= \dfrac{18}{32} \times$ (6.4 volts) $= 3.6$ volts

Example 13-6. What is the output voltage using an eight-stage ladder network for the following counts? Use a reference voltage of 51.2 volts.

(a) 1 0 1 1 0 1 0 0   (b) 1 0 0 1 1 1 0 1   (c) 0 0 0 1 1 1 0 0

Solution: (a) $V_{out} = \dfrac{2^7 + 2^5 + 2^4 + 2^2}{2^8}$ (51.2 volts)

$$= \frac{128 + 32 + 16 + 4}{256} \text{ (51.2) volts} = 36 \text{ volts}$$

(b) $V_{out} = \dfrac{2^7 + 2^4 + 2^3 + 2^2 + 2^0}{2^8}$ (51.2 volts)

$$= \frac{128 + 16 + 8 + 4 + 1}{256} \text{ (51.2) volts} = 31.4 \text{ volts}$$

(c) $V_{out} = \dfrac{2^4 + 2^3 + 2^2}{2^8}$ (51.2) $= \dfrac{16 + 8 + 4}{256}$ (51.2) $= 5.6$ volts

Exercise 13-6. Calculate the output voltage of a six-stage ladder network with a reference voltage of 12.8 volts for the following binary numbers.

(a) 1 0 1 0 1 0   (b) 1 1 1 1 1 1   (c) 0 1 0 1 0 1

Exercise 13-7. What output voltage is obtained for the conditions shown in the given ladder network (Figure 13-28)?

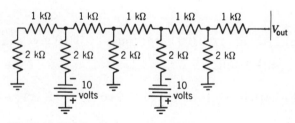

Figure 13-28.   Ladder network of Exercise 13-7.

A drawing of the ladder network output voltage and the clock signal of the counter indicates the stepwise increase of the voltage (see Figure 13-29). The output voltage is often called a staircase waveform for obvious reasons.

Figure 13-30 shows that when the ladder staircase voltage becomes greater than the unknown voltage, a stop count signal is produced by the comparator to end counting. The count now in the counter register is the digital equivalent of the unknown voltage. When the counter is reset to

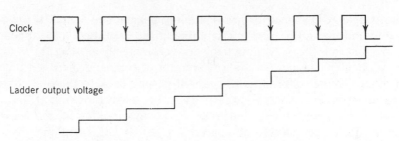

Figure 13-29.   Ladder output voltage (staircase waveform) and counter clock signal.

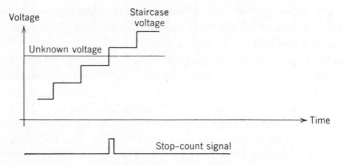

Figure 13-30.   Voltage comparison and stop-count signal.

zero for a new conversion, the staircase voltage returns to zero volts and will cross the unknown voltage at a different time if the unknown voltage has changed.

Multiplexing.   Quite often a single A/D converter unit is used to handle a number of different analog inputs. Then the conversion is completed for one input, the circuit reset, and a new input applied to the converter. The method of switching from one input signal to another to allow one unit to handle many channels of information is called multiplexing. A simple block diagram of this function is shown in Figure 13-31. The figure shows

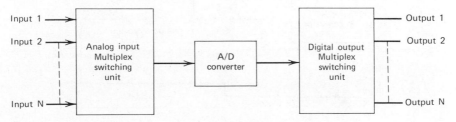

Figure 13-31.   Multiplex switching with A/D converter.

that a single A/D converter handles many channels of signal. If the conversion and multiplex time is fast enough, the operation may appear to be on a *real time* basis. Although the converter is only looking at the signal of a particular channel for a short amount of time and then working on the other channel information, it is still getting back to the one channel often enough per second to appear as if it is always looking at that one signal. The converter will appear to be always looking at one signal if the signal changes slowly compared to the rate of sampling (discrete interval operation on channel). For example, a converter capable of 1000 conversions per second operating with ten channels can appear at each channel 100 times per second. If the signal is changing at a slow rate of 2 cps, the amount of change in 1/1000 of a second is so small as to be negligible and the converter appears to always be looking at the signal. The study of sampled data systems is not necessary in the immediate presentation, but basically it considers the operation of sampling varying signals, as in the example just given, and the relation of the sampled output signal in the system used. Multiplexing itself is the method of switching many inputs into one channel, and the multiplexer is the sampler unit. Since a computer can operate very quickly, this ability to sample many channels with one computer makes it a more useful device in a control setting. One computer per channel would be uneconomical, but one computer for a whole aircraft system or spacecraft system operating many channels becomes a practical reality.

Sawtooth Sweep A/D Conversion.   Another technique of dc voltage to digital number conversion uses a constant varying voltage sweep to compare against the unknown voltage. Figure 13-32 shows a block diagram of this circuit. A linear sawtooth sweep is a constantly increasing dc voltage.

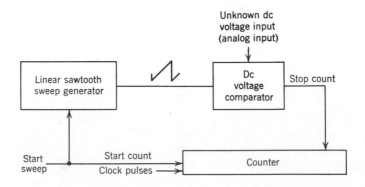

Figure 13-32.   Sawtooth sweep A/D conversion method.

When this voltage becomes equal to or slightly larger than the unknown dc voltage, a stop count signal is produced by the dc voltage comparator. Start of a count and sweep start are synchronized to begin together. An important feature (and a difficult one to implement) is that the full sweep interval and clock rate be properly adjusted so that a full count is obtained in that time. The developed count is then available as the digital equivalent of the analog input voltage. Figure 13-33 shows a few cycles of sawtooth signal superimposed on an unknown dc voltage and the resulting count time interval.

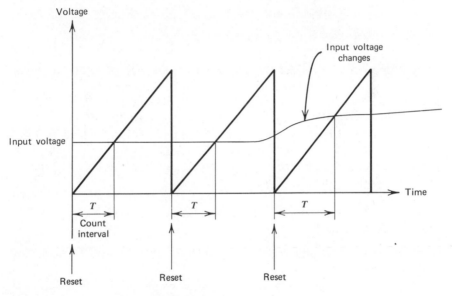

Figure 13-33.   Input and sawtooth voltages.

Shaft Position A/D Conversion.   Another popular conversion develops a digital count equivalent to a shaft rotational position. Consider a single-turn potentiometer whose position can be adjusted 360°. If the amount of rotation is taken as a variable signal, the computer needs the digital equivalent of the amount of rotation or the exact rotational position. On an airplane this might represent the degrees of wing flap rotation or the amount a shaft was rotated to open a control valve. The computer needs this information in its calculations but needs it as a digital number. Where space and design allow its use, an optical encoder is often chosen. The encoder is an optical disk with clear areas and darkened areas and is coded so that each fixed fraction of a degree another binary combination is encoded. Figure 13-34 shows a three-bit encoder using binary code. By

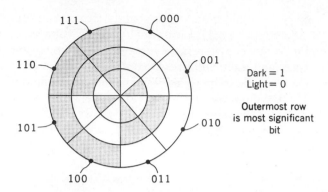

Figure 13-34.   Three-bit optical disk.

using a photocell to detect the presence or absence of light, the eight different sectors around the disk can be distinguished. By using three bits the 360° circumference can be divided into eight parts, so that the nearest 360°/8, or 45°, section can be known. Usually an optical disk containing 10 to 15 bits is employed, allowing resolution as high as 360°/2^{15} or 360°/32,768 ≅ 1 minute of arc. This high degree of resolution requires precise manufacture of the optical disk and a high degree of mechanical precision.

Example 13-7.   What degree of resolution is obtained using a ten-bit optical encoder disk?

Solution: Ten bits allow 360°/2^{10} resolution = 360°/1024 = 0.36° or about 1/3°.

Exercise 13-8.   What resolution (in degrees) is obtained using a twelve-bit optical encoder disk?

Exercise 13-9.   What minimum size (number of bits) optical encoder disk is needed to obtain a resolution of better than 1°.

A major practical problem encountered using an optical disk is that of ambiguity or overlap in reading a code position. For example, 0 0 0 is next to 0 0 1 using the binary code disk. If mechanical tolerance is poor or there is some misalignment, the reading photocells may pick up the bits from both sector, that is, 2^0 bit from the 0 0 0 sector and 2^1 and 2^2 bits from the 0 0 1 sector This does not seem such a problem for a three-bit code, but where the disk is made for sixteen-bit resolution using as small a disk as possible, the mechanical tolerances (for less than 1-minute resolution) become critical. The overlap is a problem when the code word from one sector to an adjacent sector changes by more than one bit. Going from 1 1 1 to 0 0 0 might give erroneous readings if a single-bit detector is misaligned. For example, reading the 2^0 and 2^1 from 111 and 2^2 from 000 would give 011 as the position, which is the position about halfway around the disk. An error in one bit position may indicate a position on the other side of the disk (180° away). In many applications the reading of a position 180° away would cause havoc. One way of correcting this problem is to choose a code that changes by only one bit from one sector to the next. There are many different codes of this type. Of these many codes, one particular code is used almost exclusively. For reading purposes the one-bit change code is desirable. For arithmetic purposes, however, the binary code is still the best. Remember that in the binary code more than one bit changes going from one word to the next so it is not the most desirable code to use on the disk. This means that a conversion from the disk code to the binary code would be necessary, and the particular disk code used is the one of the one-bit change codes that is most easily converted into binary. This particular disk code is called Gray code, and the required conversion is Gray code to binary code. Recalling that the overall operation is conversion of mechanical rotational position into a digital number, the Gray-to-binary conversion is the main part of this A/D conversion. A description of Gray-to-binary conversion follows.

The Gray code is a cyclic code having only one bit change at a time. Cyclic codes are those in which the code words proceed in a set order, and after all possible code words have been used, the next code word is the one used first. In this way the code form can cycle through all words back to the first, completing a cycle. Although all one-bit change codes are not cyclic, the Gray code is. As an example, the Gray and binary code words for decimal 0 to 15 are given in Table 13-3. Look through the table to see that the Gray code only changes by one bit at a time whereas the binary code may change by all four bits (as from 7 to 8).

A description of how to convert Gray Code to binary code and vice versa was given in Chapter 4, which should now be reread. Here we shall discuss the circuit implementation. As mentioned earlier, the Gray code is the most desirable because of the ease of implementing the conversion. Actually, all that is needed is a single flip-flop. However, a shift register is used to handle the data (Figure 13-35).

Data in the form of light and dark areas on the disk are read by picking up the illumination from a source light with the photocells or read heads. When the light passes through a clear area it excites the reader head and when it hits a dark area no light gets through. The read pulses may be

Table 13-3.   *Gray and Binary Code for Decimal 0 to 15*

Decimal	Gray Code	Binary Code
0	0000	0000
1	0001	0001
2	0011	0010
3	0010	0011
4	0110	0100
5	0111	0101
6	0101	0110
7	0100	0111
8	1100	1000
9	1101	1001
10	1111	1010
11	1101	1011
12	1010	1100
13	1011	1101
14	1001	1110
15	1000	1111

developed from a ring counter so that each bit of word is read into the flip-flop serially, most significant bit first. The serial Gray data is fed into the trigger or complementing input of the flip-flop and only complements the flip-flop state on a set direction change, for example, on a 1 to 0 change. If the input then stayed at 0 or if it goes to 1 and stays, the output remains the same. In effect, it does precisely what is required to change the Gray code data into binary code data, and on each shift pulse (or read pulse) the serial binary data out of the flip-flop is read into the shift register. After the proper number of read steps (and shift steps) the number in the shift register is the binary code word (indicating the position of the disk (or rotational position of the shaft). If the shift register is considered a *buffer* register or part of the conversion equipment, the

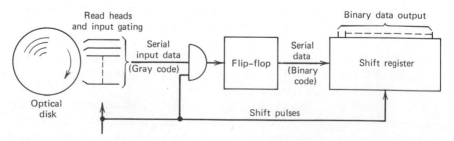

Figure 13-35.   Gray-to-binary code converter.

circuit of Figure 13-35 comprises the entire A/D converter (including the logic gating needed to generate the read pulses). When many optical encoding disks are used, the same converter circuit can handle all inputs if the data is multiplexed. After converting the input from one disk, the multiplexer can switch to the read pulses from another disk so that conversion is done on the word read out of this second disk. After each conversion time the word in the shift register is read into the computer for use in control or calculation.

13-10.   Digital-to-Analog (D/A) Conversion

After a computer has processed its data, which is in digital form, it must use it in the outside system being handled. In general-purpose machines this may be typed data or data stored on punched card, punched tape, or magnetic tape. In the special-purpose machine it is often necessary to use the digital answer to control or move a part of the external system. To obtain such signal form requires converting the digital data into analog form using a D/A converter. Going back to the first type of analog signal discussed, the dc voltage, we find the conversion must take a digital number and develop an equivalent dc voltage. Not surprisingly, the method uses much the same circuitry and technique as for the A/D conversion. Often the same units can be used. Figure 13-36 shows the simplified circuitry needed to accomplish the D/A conversion.

The circuitry is actually the simpler part of the A/D circuits. The digital number when developed by the computer, is fed into the digital buffer register, which feeds the ladder network. For the given number the ladder network, as described in the A/D section provides an output dc voltage equivalent to the digital number. Data can also be multiplexed to handle many channels with a single converter unit. An added circuit is needed

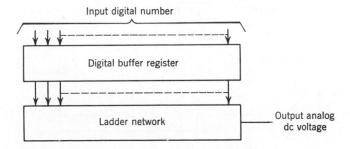

Figure 13-36.   Dc voltage, digital-to-analog converter.

with the output to maintain the dc voltage after the ladder input is removed. The circuit is descriptively called a "hold circuit" and may be simply described as a large capacitor. If the developed ladder voltage is used to charge up a large capacitor, the voltage is held after the signal is removed. Using a capacitor with each channel, we find the ladder output can be employed to develop the many different voltages that are then held for a time period by the capacitor. As long as the voltage for that channel is developed enough times per second (conversions per second), it will appear as a steady dc voltage to the output. Figure 13-37 shows the multiplexing and hold circuitry.

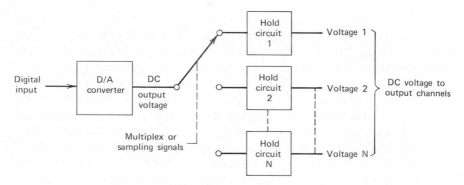

Figure 13-37.   Multiplexed D/A output dc voltage.

To drive an optical encoder to a specific digital position requires more circuitry. First, a drive unit (motor) is needed to move the disk shaft around. Second, a comparison must be made to determine when the disk has reached the desired position. Figure 13-38 shows a typical circuit

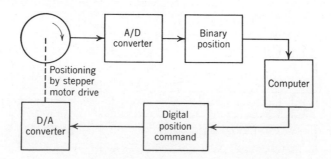

Figure 13-38.   D/A conversion and positioning of shaft encoder.

used for D/A conversion for shaft positioning. The digital number is converted to pulses used to drive a stepper motor. For each pulse the motor moves one position of the disk. By counting down the given digital number, the disk is moved by the desired number of steps. To know where the disk is, a Gray-to-binary conversion is necessary. When the binary position is available, it is compared to the desired binary position (desired by the computer), and the difference is used for count down to drive the stepper motor connected to the disk shaft.

Summary

Input/output equipment plays an important role in the effectiveness of a computer system because it provides the capacity to handle large amounts of data for a large variety of problems. Each type of unit has advantages and disadvantages so that no one type predominates. Punched card is widely used for input. Handling pieces of information about an item on a card is convenient and the most practical method at present. If the card represents a student in a school, the addition of a few more students will require the preparation of only a few separate cards. Putting a computer program first on cards and adding only a few cards or changing others to rework the program have the same advantage. Punched tape, on the other hand, is more troublesome to update or change, since a new tape must be run off. Some advantages of punched tape are low cost and convenience in handling the various lengths of tape.

Magnetic tape and magnetic disk are proving very popular for large data storage. Both allow large programs or amounts of data to be stored and quickly retrieved by the computer. Installations such as banks and insurance companies store all customer accounts on these magnetic units. Although the data is originally put on cards, it is placed on tape or disk before being used by the computer, and the results of computer operations are put back on tape or disk.

Data output may be on punched card, paper tape, magnetic tape, or disk. Where printed output is desired high-speed printers are very popular. Because it operates at rates as high as 4800 lines per minute, the volume of written material from a computer is large. Typewriters are used mostly for running the computer or troubleshooting it.

With special-purpose computers conversion equipment for analog-to-digital or digital-to-analog is important. Conversions of dc voltage or ac voltage and shaft position are very popular and make it possible to use the computer to control operations in such systems as aircraft, rocket, manufacturing plant, and others.

PROBLEMS

§13-2   **1.** Use the punched card code table (Table 13-1) and code in Figure 13-3 to read the card in Figure 13-39.

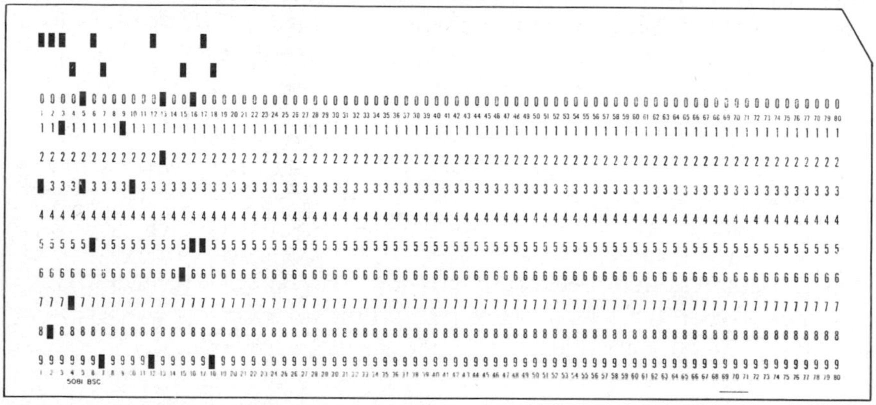

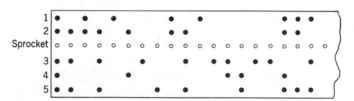

Figure 13-39.   Punched card for Problem 1.

§13-3   **2.** Use the five-level tape code shown in Figure 13-7 to read the punched tape in Figure 13-40.

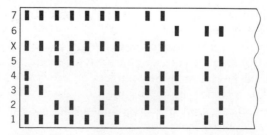

Figure 13-40.   Paper tape for Problem 2.

§13-4   **3.** Use the eight-channel ASCII code shown in Chapter 4 to read the magnetic tape in Figure 13-41.

Figure 13-41.   ASCII code message for Problem 3.

§13-5   **4.** A magnetic disk has 100 tracks of 16,384 bits per track on seven disks. What is the total storage capacity of the disk pack? (Remember that both sides of a disk are used.)

§13-6   **5.** A high-speed printer using a character belt printer has four sets of characters around the belt. If the belt is driven at 100 revolutions per second, what is the approximate number of lines per minute that may be printed?

§13-9   **6.** What is the maximum conversion time of an A/D converter using a clock rate of 512 kHz and a twelve-stage counter.

7. A dc voltage-to-digital converter using a ladder network has a reference voltage of 20 volts. What resolution can be obtained if a twelve-stage binary counter is used?

8. How many counter stages are needed to get a resolution of 1 mV using a reference voltage of 10 volts? What clock rate is needed to obtain around 100 solutions per second?

9. (a) Draw the circuit diagram of a four-stage ladder network using 2 kΩ and 4 kΩ resistors.

(b) Show the same network for an input of 1 0 1 1 (written with least significant digit on right). Use 12 volts to represent the 1 state and 0 volts for the 0 state.

(c) Calculate the output voltage for this condition by circuit analysis.

(d) Compare the answer in (c) with that of the digital count (1 0 1 1 out of 1 0 0 0 0 counts).

10. Repeat Problem 9 for a six-stage ladder network for an input of 1 0 1 0 1 1 and reference voltage of 6.4 volts.

Appendix – Logic Operation of Flip-Flops

A brief nontechnical explanation of the logic operation of a variety of flip-flops is provided below. This will allow those interested to use these devices without detailed technical understanding of the internal circuit operation.

The flip-flop is a most important computer circuit which (with logic gates) comprises the major electronic components of a computer system. A flip-flop can be operated in basically two ways – synchronous and asynchronous. Operated asynchronously, the flip-flop can be made to change state whenever the data input signals change state. Operated synchronously, the flip-flop *only* changes state when a synchronizing or trigger pulse is applied.

TTL Logic

A transistor-transistor logic (TTL) type flip-flop is shown in Figure A-1a. Not all inputs are used at the same time. Figure A-1b shows the inputs used for asynchronous operation. When input S_D goes Lo, for example, it causes the Q output to go Hi (and $\bar{Q}$ Lo) leaving the circuit SET. When input C_D goes Lo it causes the $\bar{Q}$ output to go Hi (and Q Lo) leaving the circuit CLEAR (or RESET). In either case the input signal need not remain Lo for the circuit to hold its present state. It is usual for the SET or CLEAR signal to go Lo only momentarily (to cause the circuit to assume the desired state) and then go back Hi thereafter leaving the circuit "free." The table in Figure A-1b provides a concise description of the asynchronous operation.

Figure A-1c shows the inputs involved in the synchronous operation of the circuit. The data inputs at J and K condition the flip-flop so that the outputs assume the state of the inputs *when* a trigger pulse occurs. This can also be described as the output not changing state *until* the trigger pulse occurs at which time it assumes the state of the input. If the inputs are $J =$ Lo and $K =$ Hi, the output assumes the CLEAR state when the trigger pulse occurs. If the inputs are $J =$ Hi and $K =$ Lo, the output assumes the SET state on the trigger pulse.

566

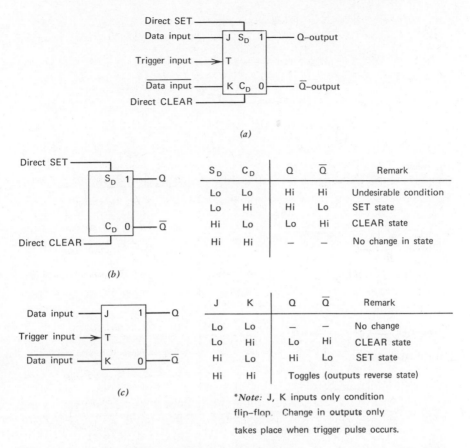

Figure A-1.   TTL (or DTL) Flip-Flop. (*a*) Logic diagram. (*b*) Asynchronous operation. (*c*) Synchronous operation.

If both *J* and *K* inputs are Lo, the occurrence of the trigger pulse results in no change of state for the flip-flop. The condition of both *J* and *K* inputs Hi is most useful as this conditions the circuit to change state (toggle) when a trigger pulse occurs. If the data inputs are left *J* = Hi and *K* = Hi, then each occurrence of a trigger pulse causes the circuit to toggle.

RTL Logic

Figure A-2*a* shows the full RTL flip-flop. Although there are some differences in terminal nomenclature, the unit is still referred to as a JK flip-flop.

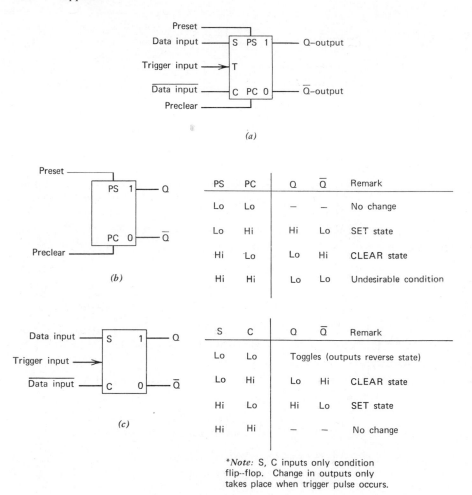

Figure A-2.   RTL Flip-Flop. (*a*) Logic diagram. (*b*) Asynchronous operation. (*c*) Synchronous operation.

Asynchronous operation only is specified in Figure A-2*b*. The direct acting inputs are referred to as preset (PS) and preclear (PC). It should be observed, however, that a Hi input on PC causes the $\bar{Q}$ output to be Lo, although a Hi input on PS causes the Q output to be Lo (not quite what might be expected).

Synchronous operation is specified in Figure A-2*c*. A Lo at the S input (and Hi at C input) results in the $\bar{Q}$ output Hi when a trigger pulse occurs. A Lo at the C input (and Hi at S input) results in the Q output Hi when a trigger pulse occurs.

Answers to selected odd-numbered exercises and problems

CHAPTER 2

Exercises:

2-1. (a) 109   (b) 23   (c) 27

2-3. (a) 0.84375   (b) 0.3125   (c) 0.15625

2-5. (a) 23   (b) 11.625   (c) 27.875

2-7. (a) 254   (b) 174   (c) 99

2-9. (a) 47   (b) 166   (c) 245

2-11. (a) 010 110 011   (b) 011 111 010   (c) 001 011 111 110

2-13. (a) B5   (b) F3A4   (c) 0010 1100 1001
    (d) 1010 0010 0110 1111

2-15. (a) 740   (b) 5003   (c) 1067

2-17. (a) 001011   (b) 1001111   (c) 01001001

2-19. (a) $+000111$ (b) -0000011

2-21. (a) 101   (b) 110   (c) 1001

Problems:

1. (a) 55   (b) 56   (c) 21   (d) 85   (e) 254

3. (a) 0.625   (b) 0.75   (c) 0.125   (d) 0.375   (e) 0.78125

5. (a) 100110.011   (b) 10010000.111   (c) 101000101.101

7. (a) 77   (b) 167   (c) 1161.4   (d) 605.2   (e) 7775

9. (a) 55   (b) 8B   (c) 39F.8

11. (a) 6D   (b) 1010 0010 1100   (c) 0100 1111   (d) 5EA6
    (e) 0010 1001 1101

13. (a) 10011   (b) 10001110   (c) 00110100101

15. (a) 10000100   (b) 01100111

17. (a) 100001   (b) 10100010   (c) 1010   (d) 110

CHAPTER 4

Exercises:

4-1. (a) 0010 0111 0101   (b) 0011 0110 0010
    (c) 1001 0010 0101 0110

4-3. (a) 0011 0111 1010 1001   (b) B6
4-7. (a) 894   (b) 478   (c) 916   (d) 847
4-9. (a) 47   (b) 48   (c) 73
4-11. (a) 110100110110   (b) 11001100110   (c) 01011010010100
    (d) 10101010

Problems:
1. (a) 0010 0100 0111 0011   (b) 1001 0010 1000 0111
3. (a) 647   (b) 251
5. (a) 00100 01011 01110 00111   (b) 10011 00100 10000 01110
9. (a) 0100 1011 1010   (b) 0100 1110 1101
    (c) 0100 1001 1000   (d) 0100 1111 1000
11. (a) 1001000 0101000   (b) 0100000000 0000001000
13. 101101111
15. A1 4B A2 5C A3

CHAPTER 5

Exercises:
5-1. (a) same   (b) not the same   (c) not the same
    (d) not the same
5-3. (a) $AB\overline{C}$ (b) $AB\overline{C}+\overline{B}C$ (c) XY (d) $V+WU$
    (e) $A\overline{B}+\overline{A}B$
5-7. (a) $\overline{ABC+\overline{A}\overline{B}+\overline{C}}$ (b) $(A+C)+[(\overline{A}\overline{B})\cdot(\overline{A}+\overline{C})]$
    (c) $\overline{AB+\overline{A}\overline{B}}$ (d) $\overline{(X+Y)\cdot(\overline{X}\overline{Y})}$ (d) $[XY+(X+\overline{Y})]\cdot(\overline{X}\overline{Y})$

Problems:
1. (a) $\overline{\text{not the same}}$ (b) $\overline{\text{not the same}}$ (c) not the same
7. (a) $(\overline{AB})\cdot(\overline{AC})\cdot(\overline{AC})$ (b) $B\cdot(\overline{A\cdot C})$

CHAPTER 6

Exercises:
6-1. (a) $M=A+B$ (b) $M=\overline{A}+B$
6-7. Output $=\Sigma\ 3,5,6,7,9,10,11,12,13,14=WX\overline{Y}+W\overline{X}Z+WY\overline{Z}+$
    $+XY\overline{Z}+WYZ+WXY$ (one of possible reduced expressions)
6-11. $W=\Sigma\ 5,6,7,8,9$ $X=\Sigma\ 4,6,7,8,9$ $Y=\Sigma\ 2,3,5,8,9$
    $Z=\Sigma\ 1,3,5,7,9;$ one possible solution: $W=A+B\cdot(C+D)$
    $X=A+B\cdot(C+\overline{D})$ $Y=A+\overline{B}\cdot C+\overline{C}\cdot D$ $Z=D$

Problems:
1. (a) $A + C$ (b) $B \cdot (\bar{A} + C) + \bar{B} \cdot \bar{C}$
3. (a) $\bar{A} \cdot \bar{C} + C \cdot D$ (b) $Z \cdot (\bar{W} + \bar{Y}) + X \cdot \bar{Y}$
5. $W = B \cdot C + \bar{A} \cdot C \cdot D$
7. $OP = \Sigma\, 0, 3, 12, 15 = (\bar{A} \cdot \bar{B} + A \cdot B) \cdot (\bar{C}\bar{D} + C \cdot D)$
9. $W = \Sigma\, 5, 6, 7, 8, 9$ $X = \Sigma\, 4, 9$ $Y = \Sigma\, 2, 3, 7, 8$
    $Z = \Sigma\, 1, 3, 6, 8$;   one possible solution: $W = A + B \cdot (C + D)$
    $X = \bar{C} \cdot B \cdot \bar{D} + A \cdot D$ $Y = A \cdot \bar{D} + C \cdot (\bar{B} + D)$
    $Z = \bar{A} \cdot \bar{B} \cdot D + \bar{D} \cdot (A + B)$

CHAPTER 7

Exercises:
7-5. Noise Margin $= 1.7$ volts; transistor in saturation
7-7. Noise Margin $= 2.5$ volts; transistor in saturation

Problems:
3. logic OR gate
9. Noise Margin $= 1.25$ volts; transistor in saturation

CHAPTER 8

Problems:
7. 350 kHz

CHAPTER 11

Problems:
1. 8,192 cores per plane; 16 planes
3. total cores $= 131,092$; 16 sense amplifiers, 16 inhibit drivers
5. 15 register stages (7-X register and 8-Y register); 20 Z-register
    stages
7. (a) 1.65 msec   (b) 30,720 bits/sec   (c) 32.5 μsec/bit
9. (a) 409,600 bits/sec   (b) 409,600 bits/sec

CHAPTER 12

Problems:
1. (a) 0011011   (b) 0100100; 1011011

3. (a) 0 100110 (+ 38)   (b) 0 001010 (+ 10)
5. (a) 0 001010 (+ 10)   (b) 0 101001 (+ 41)
7. 00011011
9. 1010

CHAPTER 13

Exercises:
13-1. (a) 1.56%   (b) 0.2%   (c) 0.05%
13-3. (a) 2.35×10^3 conversions/sec   (b) 1.6×10^3 conversions/sec
    (c) 780 conversions/sec
13-5. 1 MHz
13-7. 3.125 volts

Problems:
1. CHAPTER 13 IS OVER
3. PAPER TAPE NO 26
5. 23 Mbits
7. 5 mV
9. 8.25 volts

Index